District Gazetteers of India Series 200

UNITED PROVINCES OF AGRA AND OUDH DISTRICT

ALMORA

District Gazetteers of India Series 200

UNITED PROVINCES OF AGRA AND OUDH DISTRICT

ALMORA

EDITED AND COMPILED

H. G. WALTON

49 VOLUMES

(VOL. IV)

GYAN

Published by

Gyan Publishing House
5, Ansari Road
Daryaganj, New Delhi-110002
Phone: 011-47034999, 9811692060
E-mail: books@gyanbooks.com

Distribution Network
gyanbooks.com
India, USA, Canada, UK, Australia, France

ISBN: 978-93-6208-218-3 (Set) 49 Volumes
978-93-6208-134-6 (PB)

First Published, 1911

2nd Impression 2024

Printed at: Gyan Press, Delhi.

UNITED PROVINCES OF AGRA AND OUDH DISTRICT GAZETTEERS (VOL. IV)
Edited and Compiled: H. G. WALTON

LIST OF VOLUMES

S. NO.	ISBN NO.	VOLUME	TITLE	AUTHOR	PRICE	PAGES
			ASSAM DISTRICT GAZETTEERS			
1	9788121285926	1st	Cachar	B. C. Allen	600	300
2	9788121285919	2nd	Sylhet	B. C. Allen	750	378
3	9788121285902	3rd	Goalpara	B. C. Allen	400	203
4	9788121285896	4th	Kamrup	B. C. Allen	675	344
5	9788121285889	5th	Darrang	B. C. Allen	725	364
6	9788121285872	6th	Nowgong	B. C. Allen	560	280
7	9788121285865	7th	Sibsagar	B. C. Allen	675	343
8	9788121285858	8th	Lakhimpur	B. C. Allen	690	347
9	9788121285841	9th	Naga Hills and Manipur	B. C. Allen	580	294
10	9788121285834	10th	The Khasi And Jaintia Hills, The Garo Hills And The Lushai Hills	B. C. Allen	675	363
11	9788121285827	11th	The Sadiya and Balipara Frontier Tract	B. C. Allen	375	190
			BENGAL DISTRICT GAZETTEERS			
12	9788121218672	1st	Angul	L. S. S. O'Malley	340	168
13	9788121259637	2nd	Bakarganj	J. C. JACK	970	194
14	9788121218696	3rd	Balasore	L. S. S. O'Malley	450	228
15	9788121259590	4th	Bankura	L. S. S. O'Malley	1000	199
16	9788121218375	5th	Bhagalpur	J. Byrne	390	194
17	9788121218290	6th	Birbhum	L. S. S. O'Malley	300	150
18	9788121259651	7th	Eastern Bengal and Assam - Bogra	J. N. Gupta	940	188
19	9788121218351	8th	Burdwan	J. C. K. Peterson	450	227
20	9788121259538	9th	Calcutta District Gazetteer - Statistics, 1901 - 02		340	68
21	9788121218313	10th	Champaran	L. S. S. O'Malley	410	205
22	9788121259613	11th	Eastern Bengal District Gazetters - Chittagong	L. S. S. O'Malley	1080	216
23	9788121259552	12th	Chota Nagpur Tributary		130	26
24	9788121259415	13th	The Cooch Behar Gazette: Statistics		1460	292
25	9788121218412	14th	Cuttack	L. S. S. O'Malley	490	248
26	9788121261357	15th	Eastern Bengal District Gazetteers Dacca	B. C. Allen	400	207
27	9788121218436	16th	Darbhanga	L. S. S. O'Malley	360	180
28	9789362089335	17th	Darjeeling	L. S. S. O'Malley	500	248
29	9788121259453	18th	Eastern Bengal District Gazetteers - Dinajpur	F. W. Strong	890	178
30	9788121259392	19th	Faridpur	L. S. S. O'Malley	700	140
31	9788121218474	20th	Gaya	L. S. S. O'Malley	540	270
32	9788121214032	21st	Bihar and Orissa District Gazetteer: Hazaribagh	E. Lister	715	234
33	9788121218337	22nd	Hooghly	L. S. S. O'Malley	680	340
34	9788121218191	23rd	Bengal District Gazetteer Howrah	L. S. S. O'Malley	390	199
35	9788121259293	24th	Eastern Bengal and Assam - Jalpaiguri	John F. Gruning	890	178
36	9788121259279	25th	Jessore	L. S. S. O'Malley	960	192
37	9788121259231	26th	Khulna	L. S. S. O'Malley	1100	220
38	9788121259217	27th	Malda	G. E. Lambourn	670	134
39	9788121267854	28th	Manbhum	H. Coupland	600	313
40	9788121218498	29th	Midnapore	L. S. S. O'Malley	500	252
41	9788121218597	30th	Monghyr	L. S. S. O'Malley	560	280
42	9788121259156	31st	Murshidabad	L. S. S. O'Malley	1250	250
43	9788121259576	32nd	Bengal District Gazetteers - Muzaffarpur	L. S. S. O'Malley	940	188
44	9788121259132	33rd	Mymensingh	F. A. Sachse	960	192
45	9788121259118	34th	Nadia	J. H. E. Garrett	1070	214
46	9788121259095	35th	Eastern Bengal and Assam - Noakhali	J. E. Webster	580	115
47	9788121218450	36th	Feudatory States of Orissa	L. E. B. Cobdenramsay	790	395
48	9788121259071	37th	Pabna	L. S. S. O'Malley	710	142
49	9788121218511	38th	Palamau	L. S. S. O'Malley	380	190
50	9788121218634	39th	Patna	L. S. S. O'Malley	500	250
51	9788121218535	40th	Puri	L. S. S. O'Malley	650	328
52	9788121218757	41st	Purnea	L. S. S. O'Malley	440	220
53	9788121258937	42nd	Rajshahi	L. S. S. O'Malley	1080	216
54	9788121256681	43rd	Bihar and Orissa District Gazetteers: Ranchi	M. G. Hallett	1350	278
55	9788121258913	44th	Eastern Bengal and assam - Rangpur	J. A. Vas	890	178
56	9788121218559	45th	Sambalpur	L. S. S. O'Malley	480	242
57	9788121214056	46th	Santal Parganas	L. S. S. O'Malley	940	308
58	9788121218610	47th	Saran	L. S. S. O'Malley	380	190
59	9788121218658	48th	Shahabad	L. S. S. O'Malley	380	190
60	9788121256704	49th	The Gazetteer of Sikhim	H. H. Risley	960	481
61	9788121218573	50th	Singhbhum, Saraikela And Kharsawan	L. S. S. O'Malley	560	280
62	9788121259439	51st	Eastern Bengal District Gazetteers - Tippera	J. E. Webster	730	146
63	9788121259033	52nd	24 Parganas	L. S. S. O'Malley	1420	284

S. NO.	ISBN NO.	VOLUME	TITLE	AUTHOR	PRICE	PAGES
			CENTRAL PROVINCES DISTRICT GAZETTEERS			
64	9789362081728	1st, Vol. A	Akola (Descriptive)	A. E. Nelson, C. Brown	870	436
65	9789362085481	2nd, Vol. A	Amraoti (Descriptive)	S. V. Fitzgerald, A. E. Nelson	1050	524
66	9789362089267	3rd,Vol. A	Balaghat (Descriptive)	R. V. RUSSELL	430	216
67	9789362083494	4th, Vol. A	Betul (Descriptive)	R. V. RUSSELL	610	306
68	9789362085146	5th, Vol. A	Bhandara (Descriptive)	R. V. RUSSELL	580	292
69	9789362088390	6th, Vol. A	Bilaspur (Descriptive)	R. V. RUSSELL	870	434
70	9789362086044	7th, Vol. A	Buldana (Descriptive)	A. E. Nelson	1090	543
71	9789362089014	8th, Vol. B	Chanda (Descriptive)	R. V. RUSSELL	470	234
72	9789362086938	9th	Chhattisgarch Feudatory State	E. A. De Brett	880	440
73	9789362082961	10th	Chhindwara (Descriptive)	R. V. RUSSELL	550	274
74	9789362089342	11th, Vol. A & B	Damoh (Descriptive and Statistical Tables 1891-1901)	R. V. RUSSELL	830	414
75	9789362081230	12th, Vol. A	Durg (Descriptive)	A. E. Nelson	460	232
76	9789362086037	13th, Vol. A	Hoshangabad (Descriptive)	R. V. RUSSELL	860	430
77	9789362086792	14th, Vol. A	Jubbulpore (Descriptive)	A. E. Nelson	950	474
78	9789362089663	15th, Vol. A & B	Mandla (Descriptive and Statistical Tables 1891-1901)	R. V. RUSSELL	370	186
79	9789362086419	16th, Vol. A	Nagpur (Descriptive)	R. V. RUSSELL	790	394
80	9789362080646	17th, Vol. A	Narsinghpur (Descriptive)	R. V. RUSSELL	510	257
81	9789362084835	18th, Vol. A	Nimar (Descriptive)	R. V. RUSSELL	600	299
82	9789362087737	19th, Vol. A	Raipur (Descriptive)	A. E. Nelson	790	396
83	9789362080264	20th, Vol. A	Saugor (Descriptive)	R. V. RUSSELL	570	285
84	9789362081117	21st, Vol. A	Seoni (Descriptive)	R. V. RUSSELL	460	232
85	9789362084965	22nd, Vol. A	Wardha (Descriptive)	R. V. RUSSELL	600	302
86	9789362083401	23rd, Vol. A	Yeotmal (Descriptive)	R. V. RUSSELL	550	277
87	9789362080325	24th, Vol. I, Pt. I	Gwalior (Text and Tables)	R. V. RUSSELL	980	489
88	9789362087133	24th, Vol. I, Pt. II	Gwalior (Maps)	R. V. RUSSELL	400	198
89	9789362086341	24th, Vol. I, Pt. III	Gwalior (Village List)	R. V. RUSSELL	810	406
90	9789362085467	24th, Vol. I, Pt. IV	Gwalior (Photos)	R. V. RUSSELL	1400	698
91	9789362087393	25th, Vol. II	Indore (Text and Tables)	C. E. Luard	1050	524
92	9789362084422	26th, Vol. III	Bhopal (Text and Tables)	C. E. Luard	540	272
93	9789362086815	27th, Vol. IV	Rewah (Text and Tables)	C. E. Luard	500	250
94	9789362087584	28th, Vol. V, Pt. A	Western States - Malwa (Text)	C. E. Luard	1520	762
95	9789362087300	29th, Vol. VI, Pt. A	Eastern States - Bundelkhand (Text)	C. E. Luard	930	463
96	9789362082169	30th, Vol. VI, Pt. B	Eastern States - Bundelkhand (Tables)	C. E. Luard	830	417
			GAZETTEER OF THE BOMBAY PRESIDENCY:			
97	9788121283441	1st, Part I	History of Gujarat	Ed.: James M. Campbell	3220	644
98	9788121285582	1st, Part II	History of the Konkan Dakhan and Southern Maratha Country	Ed.: James M. Campbell	4200	840
99	9788121285568	2nd	Gujarat, Surat and Broach	Ed.: James M. Campbell	2990	598
100	9788121285544	3rd	Kaira and Panch Mahals	Ed.: James M. Campbell	1690	339
101	9788121285520	4th	Ahmedabad	Ed.: James M. Campbell	1860	372
102	9788121285506	5th	Cutch, Palanpur, and Mahi Kantha	Ed.: James M. Campbell	2390	478
103	9788121285483	6th	Rewa Kantha, Narukot, Cambay, and Surat States	Ed.: James M. Campbell	1450	290
104	9788121285469	7th	Baroda	Ed.: James M. Campbell	3260	652
105	9788121285445	8th	Kathiawar	Ed.: James M. Campbell	3790	758
106	9788121285421	9th, Part I	Gujarat Population - Hindus	Ed.: James M. Campbell	3170	636
107	9788121285407	9th, Part II	Gujarat Population - Musalmans and Parsis	Ed.: James M. Campbell	1520	304
108	9788121285384	10th	Ratnagiri and Savantvadi	Ed.: James M. Campbell	2500	501
109	9788121285360	11th	Kolaba and Janjira	Ed.: James M. Campbell	2550	513
110	9788121285346	12th	Khandesh	Ed.: James M. Campbell	3190	638
111	9788121285322	13th Part I	Thana	Ed.: James M. Campbell	2050	413
112	9788121285308	13th Part II	Thana	Ed.: James M. Campbell	1770	357
113	9788121285285	14th	Thana - Places of Interest	Ed.: James M. Campbell	3290	659
114	9788121285261	15th Part I	Kanara	Ed.: James M. Campbell	2340	348
115	9788121285247	15th Part II	Kanara	Ed.: James M. Campbell	1740	348
116	9788121285223	16th	Nasik	Ed.: James M. Campbell	3490	698
117	9788121285209	17th	Ahmadnagar	Ed.: James M. Campbell	3860	772
118	9788121285186	18th Part I	Poona	Ed.: James M. Campbell	2930	586
119	9788121285162	18th Part II	Poona	Ed.: James M. Campbell	2680	537
120	9788121285148	18th Part III	Poona	Ed.: James M. Campbell	2500	503
121	9788121285124	19th	Satara	Ed.: James M. Campbell	3450	692
122	9788121285100	20th	Sholapur	Ed.: James M. Campbell	2730	547
123	9788121285087	21st	Gazetteer of the Bomaby Presidency: Belgaum	Ed.: James M. Campbell	2570	514
124	9788121285063	22nd	Dharwar	Ed.: James M. Campbell	4200	841
125	9788121285049	23rd	Gazetteer of the Bombay Presidency:Bijapur	Ed.: James M. Campbell	3550	712
126	9788121285025	24th	Kolhapur	Ed.: James M. Campbell	2250	450

S. NO.	ISBN NO.	VOLUME	TITLE	AUTHOR	PRICE	PAGES
127	9788121285001	25th	Botany	Ed.: James M. Campbell	2040	408
128	9788121284981	26th, Part I	Materials Towards a Statistical Account of the Town and Island of Bombay - History	Ed.: James M. Campbell	2500	504
129	9788121284967	26th, Part II	Materials Towards a Statistical Account of the Town and Island of Bombay - Trade and Fortifications	Ed.: James M. Campbell	2690	538
130	9788121284943	26th, Part III	Materials Towards a Statistical Account of the Town And Island of Bombay - Administration	Ed.: James M. Campbell	2450	702
131	9788121284929	27th	General Index	Ed.:R. E. Enthoven	2190	428
			MADRAS DISTRICT GAZETTEERS			
132	9788121258814	1st	Anantapur	W. Francis	1140	227
133	9788121258555	2nd	Malabar	C. A Innes & F. B Evans	3010	602
134	9788121258791	3rd	Bellary	W. Francis	1890	377
135	9788121258777	4th	Statistical Appendix For Chingleput		280	56
136	9788121258753	5th	Coimbatore	K. N. Krishnaswami Ayyar	3420	628
137	9788121232814	6th	Madras District Gazetteers District Gazetteer Cuddapah	C. F. Brackenbury	1120	285
138	9788121258715	7th	Statistical Appendix For Ganjam		370	73
139	9788121256766	8th, Vol. 1st	Godavari District Gazetteer	F. R. Hemingway	650	320
140	9788121256803	8th, Vol. 2nd	Godavari District Gazetteer	F. R. Hemingway	160	83
141	9788121258678	9th	Statistical Appendix For Kistna		640	127
142	9788121258654	10th	Statistical Appendix For Kurnool		270	54
143	9788121258616	11th	Madura	W. Francis	1900	379
144	9788121258579	12th	Statistical Appendix For Madura		740	148
145	9788121258630	13th	The Nilgiris	W. Francis	2190	437
146	9788121234276	14th	Madras District Gazetteers Gazetteer Of The Nellore District Brought Upto 1938		1150	386
147	9788121258517	15th	North Arcot		590	118
148	9788121258494	16th, Vol. 1, Part I	Salem	F. J. Richards	1710	343
149	9788121258593	16th, Vol. 1, Part II	Salem	F. J. Richards	1800	360
150	9788121258456	17th	South Arcot	W. Francis	2400	480
151	9788121258470	18th	Statistical Appendix For South Canara		400	80
152	9788121258432	19th, Vol. 1st & 2nd	Tanjore: Main Volume and Statistical Appendix		2070	401
153	9788121258395	20th	Tinnevelly	H. R. Pate	2740	547
154	9788121258418	21st	Statistical Appendix For Tinnevelly		320	64
155	9788121258371	22nd, 1st & 2nd	Trichinopoly: Main Volume and Statistical Appendix	F. R. Hemingway	2440	487
156	9788121241953	23rd	Vizagapatam District Gazetteer	W. Francis	760	385
			PUNJAB DISTRICT GAZETTEERS			
157	9788121255943	1st	Ambala District 1883-84		620	124
158	9788121255967	2nd	Amritsar		1180	236
159	9788121255981	3rd	Delhi		1300	260
160	9788121256001	4th	Ferozepore		950	188
161	9788121256025	5th	Faridkot		350	70
162	9788121256049	6th	Gujranwala 1893-94		1270	254
163	9788121256063	7th	Gujrat	C. E. Luard	1140	228
164	9788121256087	8th	Gurdaspur 1891-92		1260	252
165	9788121256100	9th	Gurgaon 1883-4		1020	203
166	9788121256124	10th	Hazara	H. D. Watson	2290	458
167	9788121256148	11th	Hissar district and Lohar State		1840	367
168	9788121256162	12th	Hoshiarpur		1420	283
169	9788121256186	13th	Jhang		1070	213
170	9788121256209	14th	Jhelam		1010	202
171	9788121256223	15th	Jalandhar District 1883-84		540	108
172	9788121256247	16th, Vol. XIV-A	Jullundur District, with maps and Kapurthala		1990	398
173	9788121256261	17th, Pt. I	Kangra (Proper)		1450	290
174	9788121256285	17th, Pt. II	Kangra (Kulu, Lahual, Spiti)		1800	357
175	9788121256308	18th	Karnal		1930	386
176	9788121256322	19th	Kohat		1540	307
177	9788121256346	20th	The Lahore District 1883-84		1220	244
178	9788121256384	21st	Ludhiana and Maler Kotla		1680	335
179	9788121256407	22nd	Lyallpur		735	147
180	9788121256421	23rd	Mianwali		1170	234
181	9788121256445	24th	Montgomery	P. J. Fagan	1590	318
182	9788121258364	25th	Multan (1901-02)	E. D. Maclagan	2400	480
183	9788121258708	26th	The Rohtak District 1883-84		980	196
184	9788121258746	27th, Vol. III A	Dujana State 1904		500	16
185	9788121256483	28th	Shahpur District		1780	356
186	9788121256506	29th	Simla District		800	159

S. NO.	ISBN NO.	VOLUME	TITLE	AUTHOR	PRICE	PAGES
187	9788121256520	30th	The Chamba State		2040	408
188	9788121256544	31st	The Chenab Colony 1904		1550	310
189	9788121256568	32nd	Kalsia State		270	53
190	9788121256582	33rd	Suket and Mandi		770	154
191	9788121256605	34th	Phulkian States, Patiala Jind And Nabha 1904		2070	414
192	9788121256643	35th	Simla Hill States		2220	443
193	9788121256667	36th	Sirmur		920	183
			RAJPUTANA DISTRICT GAZETTEERS			
194	9789362088994	1st, Vol. I-A & B	Ajmer-merwara (Text and Statistics Tables)	C. C. Watson	1230	246
195	9789362080882	2nd. Vol. II-A & B	Mewar Residency (Text and Statistics Tables)	K.D. Erskine	1700	339
196	9789362088444	3rd, Vol. III-A & B	The Western Rajputana States Residency And The Bikaner Agency	K.D. Erskine	3590	718
			UNITED PROVINCES OF AGRA AND OUDH DISTRICT GAZETTEERS			
197	9789362087560	Vol. I	Agra	H. R. Nevill	2260	452
198	9789362082466	Vol. II	Aligarh	H. R. Nevill	1300	260
199	9789362089779	Vol. III	Allahabad	H. R. Nevill	2050	409
200	9789362081346	Vol. IV	Almora	H. G. Walton	1670	333
201	9789362085658	Vol. V	Azamgarh	D. L. Drake Brockman	1750	349
202	9789362080547	Vol. VI	Bahraich	H. R. Nevill	1410	281
203	9789362085214	Vol. VII	Ballia	H. R. Nevill	1750	350
204	9789362084668	Vol. VIII	Banda	D. L. Drake Brockman	1750	349
205	9789362086518	Vol. IX	Bara Banki	H. R. Nevill	1720	344
206	9789362084101	Vol. X	Bareilly	H. R. Nevill	1640	327
207	9789362086631	Vol. XI	Basti	H. R. Nevill	1610	321
208	9789362083814	Vol. XII	Benares	H. R. Nevill	2290	458
209	9789362086105	Vol. XIII	Bijnor	H. R. Nevill	1820	363
210	9789362081674	Vol. XIV	Budaun	H. R. Nevill	1890	378
211	9789362086891	Vol. XV	Bulandshahr	H. R. Nevill	2100	419
212	9789362081520	Vol. XVI	Cawnpore	H. R. Nevill	2210	442
213	9789362088031	Vol. XVII	Dehra Dun	H. G. Walton	1710	342
214	9789362088710	Vol. XVIII	Etah	E. R. Neave	1600	320
215	9789362082992	Vol. XIX	Etawah	D. L. Drake Brockman	1390	277
216	9789362082220	Vol. XX	Farrukhabad	E. R. Neave	1620	324
217	9789362083869	Vol. XXI	Fatehpur	H. R. Nevill	1890	377
218	9789362085962	Vol. XXII	Fyzabad	H. R. Nevill	1700	339
219	9789362087997	Vol. XXIII	Garhwal	H. G. Walton	1270	254
220	9789362089892	Vol. XXIV	Ghazipur	H. R. Nevill	1600	320
221	9789362085436	Vol. XXV	Gonda	H. R. Nevill	1650	330
222	9789362080271	Vol. XXVI	Gorakhpur	H. R. Nevill	1890	378
223	9789362086129	Vol. XXVII	Hamirpur	D. L. Drake Brockman	1390	277
224	9789362087638	Vol. XXVIII	Hardoi	H. R. Nevill	1680	336
225	9789362081636	Vol. XXIX	Jalaun	D. L. Drake Brockman	1180	236
226	9789362084309	Vol. XXX	Jaunpur	H. R. Nevill	1750	350
227	9789362084187	Vol. XXXI	Jhansi	D. L. Drake Brockman	1960	391
228	9789362089168	Vol. XXXII	Kheri	H. R. Nevill	1650	330
229	9789362086778	Vol. XXXIII	Lucknow	H. R. Nevill	1760	352
230	9789362088635	Vol. XXXIV	Mainpuri	H. R. Nevill	1740	348
231	9789362080424	Vol. XXXV	Meerut	H. R. Nevill	2170	434
232	9789362081087	Vol. XXXVI	Mirzapur	D. L. Drake Brockman	2430	486
233	9789362085443	Vol. XXXVII	Moradabad	H. R. Nevill	1900	380
234	9789362082763	Vol. XXXVIII	Muttra	D. L. Drake Brockman	2140	428
235	9789362089915	Vol. XXXIX	Muzaffarnagar	H. R. Nevill	2260	451
236	9789362086143	Vol. XL	Naini Tal	H. R. Nevill	1890	377
237	9789362086761	Vol. XLI	Partabgarh	H. R. Nevill	1560	312
238	9789362081124	Vol. XLII	Pilibhit	H. R. Nevill	1570	314
239	9789362084453	Vol. XLIII	Rai Bareli	H. R. Nevill	1610	322
240	9789362088284	Vol. XLIV	Rampur	H. R. Nevill	1170	234
241	9789362083654	Vol. XLV	Saharanpur	H. R. Nevill	2190	438
242	9789362083142	Vol. XLVI	Shahjahanpur	H. R. Nevill	1510	302
243	9789362083623	Vol. XLVII	Sitapur	H. R. Nevill	1590	317
244	9789362089939	Vol. XLVIII	Sultanpur	H. R. Nevill	1330	266
245	9789362080851	Vol. XLIX	Unnao	H. R. Nevill	1530	305

ALMORA:

A GAZETTEER,

BEING

VOLUME XXXV

OF THE

DISTRICT GAZETTEERS OF THE UNITED PROVINCES OF AGRA AND OUDH.

EDITED AND COMPILED

BY

H. G. WALTON, I.C.S.

ALLAHABAD:

rinted by W. C. Abel, Offg. Superintendent, Government Press, United Provinces,

1911.

GAZETTEER OF ALMORA.

CONTENTS.

PREFACE.

This Gazetteer is based on Mr. E. T. Atkinson's Himalayan Gazetteer in three volumes. When that book was written the old Kumaon district consisting of the present Almora and Naini Tal districts was still in existence. Details regarding what is now the Almora district are fairly abundant and my task has consisted chiefly in bringing them up to date. For assistance and information I am much indebted to Messrs. E. C. Allen and Stiffe, successive Deputy Commissioners to Messrs. Shaw and Le Maistre, Deputy Collectors, and to the Divisional Forest officers : among non-officials to Mr. Norman Troup of Kausani, Mr. Stevenson of Chaukuri, Major F. Wall, I.M.S., of the 3rd Gurkha Rifles, the Rev. E. S. Oakley, the late Pandit Rai Ganga Dat Upreti Bahadur, and Pandit Rai Dharmanand Joshi Bahadur. But chiefly my acknowledgements are due to Mr. H. R. Nevill who had already compiled a large quantity of material before the duty of producing this book was made over to me.

The Tanakpur Bhabar was transferred to the Naini Tal district while the book was in the press. The Naini Tal Gazetteer previously published naturally contained no description of this region, and it was therefore decided that the references to it should not be removed.

Pilibhit :
December 1910.

H. G. W.

GAZETTEER OF ALMORA.

REFERENCES.

Statistical account of Kumaon.—G. W. Traill.
Reports on Kumaon.—J. H. Batten.
Settlement Reports.—Sir H. Ramsay and J. E. Goudge.
Assessment Reports.—J. E. Goudge and J. C. Smith.
Garhwal Settlement Report.—E. K. Pauw.
Forest working plans by various officers.
Holy Himalaya.—E. S. Oakley.
Martial tribes.—P. Ganga Dat Upreti.
Kumaon Folkloore.—P. Ganga Dat Upreti.

CHAPTER I.

GENERAL.

Almora is one of the three districts of the Kumaon division of the United Provinces. It lies in the north-east of the division between latitudes 28°59′ and 30°49′ north, and longitudes 79°2′ and 81°31′ east. It extends from Tibet on the north to the Naini Tal district on the south and from British Garhwal on the west to the kingdom of Nepal on the east. With the exception of a small submontane tract called the Tanakpur *Bhabar** the entire *district* lies within the Himalayan system, and fully one-third of it lies beyond the outermost great snowy barrier which here exhibits among its more notable summits the peaks Nandakot and the Pancha-chuli group. The country consists of a succession of ridges derived from the snowy range, from which they trend in a general southerly direction. It is not possible to estimate correctly the area of the snow-fields, glaciers and forest-clad mountains and precipitous ravines which characterise the configuration of the district; the survey area of 5,390 square miles is doubtless the area of the projection of the district on a horizontal plane. General.

Almora is separated on the west from Garhwal by a line partly natural and partly artificial. Leaving the Tibetan water-parting at a point west of the Unta-dhura pass the boundary follows the ridge on which the pass is situate to an eastern buttress of Nanda Devi in Garhwal, thence it descends in a direction a little to the west of south, and crossing the Pindar ascends to the top of a range which flanks that river on the south. This it follows to a high point called Badhangarhi from which it strikes across the heads of the western Ramganga and its affluent the Banao to the ridge separating this river from the basin of the Nayar in Garhwal. This ridge forms the boundary for some miles in a southerly Boundaries.

* Transferred to the Naini Tal district by Notification $\frac{1818\text{-I}}{605}$ dated 1st October 1910.

direction; and when the ridge turns off to the west the boundary descends to the Ramganga, which it crosses, and passing over the outer range, drops down to Mohan on the Kosi. From Mohan eastwards Almora marches with the Naini Tal district, from which it is separated partly by the Kosi river and partly by a line following the boundaries of villages composing pattis made over to the Naini Tal district in 1892. On the east the Kali from its source in the Lipu Lekh pass to its issue into the plains near Barmdeo, where it assumes the name of Sarda, separates Almora from Nepal. On the north the water-parting ridge separates Almora from Tibet.

Mountains. In the Almora district the loftiest snowy peaks do not lie along the course of the Tibetan watershed. They are situated at the southern extremity of snow-clad spurs extending south from the water-parting ridge, and at a distance of from 20 to 30 miles from it. They are separated one from another by the deep gorges which carry off the drainage from the southern slopes of that ridge. The chief of these groups both in natural grandeur and in geographical importance is the group of which Nanda Devi is the culminating peak. Its highest summit, which attains an elevation of 25,689 feet above the sea-level, belongs to the Garhwal district, but an eastern buttress 24,379 feet high is situated on the border between that district and Almora. The most easterly peak of Trisul (22,360 feet) also lies on the boundary, and it is connected with Nanda Devi by a ridge exceeding 21,000 feet in height. From this ridge a spur diverges towards the south-west, rising above the Pindari glacier to 20,740 feet and in Nandakot to 22,530 feet. The Nanda Devi group is continued northwards to the Unta-dhura ridge by a chain of peaks 21,772, 22,940 and 20,344 feet high.

Minor groups. The other groups of snowy peaks to which attention has to be drawn, though in themselves of vast proportions, assume a secondary importance when compared with the range just described. East of Nanda Devi and her sisters stands the noble mass of Pancha-chuli, situated between the Gori and the Dhauli. The highest peak has an altitude of 22,661 feet. From the west its aspect is superb; it presents the appearance of a vast white pyramid supported by symmetrical peaks of the same form at each corner. These lower peaks have an altitude of 20,700, 20,783, 21,114 and 19,923 feet. Beyond to the north, between the Dhauli and the Kuthi-Yankti, the range is marked by a number of peaks above 20,000 feet, culminating in the great peak of Yirgnajung above Budhi, in Byans, with an elevation of 20,455 feet. The great clusters of snowy peaks divide the great river basins from each other and the smaller groups separate sections of those basins from each other : thus Nanda-Devi separates the Kali from the Ganges system, and the Yirgnajung and Panchi-chuli minor group separate affluents of the Kali from each other.

Tibetan water-parting.

The principal line of water-parting along the Tibetan frontier is a ridge of great altitude. Its mean elevation exceeds 18,000 feet above the sea. At no point is it possible to enter Tibet from the south without rising to nearly 16,800 feet, and the passes are more commonly above 17,500 feet. The watershed is throughout the greater part of its length a simple longitudinal range, but its structure is a little complicated for a distance of about 30 miles in its western half between the passes of Unta-dhura and Niti; the ridge, which might otherwise have constituted the watershed, is here broken through a little to the south-east of Niti, and the drainage of the Girthi and Tapthal valleys is hence enabled to flow to the south, joining the Dhauli at Malari. The watershed is thus thrown back to the north about 10 miles and follows the range which unites the Balchha, Shalshal, Marhi and Ting-jungla passes with that of Niti.

River basins.

The transverse ridge from the Tibetan water-parting to Nandakot extends southward beyond Nandakot and then sweeps round in a south-westerly direction to the Garhwal border immediately south of the valley by which the Pindar river leaves the district. It thus divides the drainage area of the Kali system, which enters the plains at Barmdeo, from that of the Ganges and its affluents. For a space it forms the boundary between the two districts and then bending to the west, encloses the head waters of the Gumti river and re-enters Almora at the point where the three pattis Palla Giwar and Malla and Bichla Katyur meet. Thence it proceeds in a south-east direction separating the basin of the

Gumti, an affluent of the Sarju, from that of the Ramganga and its tributaries. The range continues to the southern boundary of the district through Binsar and Jageswar, slightly to the east of Lamgarah. The drainage of the whole of the tract to the east of this ridge is carried off by the Kali and its tributaries. The country to the west is drained by the Pindar, the western Ramganga and the Kosi, which ultimately merge their waters with those of the Ganges.

The Kali on the east has its true source in the Kuthi-Yankti which after the infall of the Kalapani river takes the name of Kali. The Kuthi river has a south-easterly course to the junction. After the junction the united stream turns gently towards the south-west and pursues a course nearly at right angles to the water-parting ridge. Next comes the Dhauli or Darma and then the Gori, both with a similar south-easterly direction, meeting the Kali almost at right angles. Last comes the Sarju with a general south-easterly course after taking its great bend at Bageswar. The minor streams which are affluents of these greater tributaries observe the same rule and fall into their principal streams at right angles to their course: such are the Gumti and the eastern Ramganga.

Bhabar. The narrow strip of level country at the foot of the Kali Kumaon hills is known as the Tanakpur Bhabar.* The tract is commonly waterless for nine months in the year except for two or three perennial streams. In former days it was covered with a luxuriant forest; but of recent years a considerable portion of the country has been cleared, though patches of dense forest still remain. The sub-soil of the tract consists of a deposit of gravel and boulders brought down by the torrents from the outer range of hills. It is therefore extremely dry and porous and the water drains off very rapidly. Nearly all the streams too dive into the earth not to emerge again until they have reached the Tarai.

Geology. The southern boundary of Almora begins among the probably very ancient but unfossiliferous slates, schistose slates, quartz-schists and occasional massive limestones, sometimes marmorised, of the lower Himalaya. These become invaded by enormous masses of gneissose-granite in the region of the

* Transferred to the Naini Tal district on 1st October 1910.

central axis of the main chain of snowy peaks. Here their metamorphism is proportionately greater. As this part of the Kumaun division has not been examined in detail but only superficially during rapid marches to the Tibetan watershed further remarks would be out of place here. On the northern side of the central axis the great series of sedimentary marine deposits, extending from lower silurian to cretaceous make this elevated tract exceptionally rich geologically and unsurpassed in any other part of India.*

Mines.

The mineral resources of the Kumaon division early obtained the attention which their traditional value asserted to be due to them, and it was one of the directions to the first Commissioner to procure specimens of the ores to be found in Kumaon and transmit them to the mint for assay. Specimens of copper ore from the mines in Sira and Gangoli were accordingly forwarded to Calcutta in 1815, but the report was not favourable: for, if the specimens sent were fair samples of the ores in general, it was doubted whether the mines could be worked to advantage. The Government however were not satisfied with this report, and in 1817 deputed Mr. A. Laidlaw as mineralogical expert to accompany Lieutenant Wells' party through Kumaon. Mr. Laidlaw's reports have been lost. In 1826 Captain J. D. Herbert submitted his report on the mineralogical survey of the province. Captain Herbert's conclusions may best be summarised in his own words. After alluding to the existence of gold he proceeds: "In the copper, lead and iron however, in which these provinces abound, may be found a more tangible as well as more productive source of wealth. It is certain that the former metals exist in very considerable quantity; and for the iron nothing is wanting but a proper system of management to render it superior to that of England." This was followed in 1838 by a report by Captain H. Drummond on the copper mines at Rai in Gangoli and at Sira in Barabisi. These alone were still working at the time of Captain Drummond's visit, others of ancient fame at Belar, Shor, Gurang and Chinkakoli having all fallen

* See V. Ball, Manual of the Geology of India, pt. v. Economic Geology, pp. 271—273.

in and been abandoned. Captain Drummond was accompanied by Mr. Wilkin, an "intelligent and respectable" Cornish miner. The Rai mine he describes as situated on the eastern side of a hill of moderate elevation. The rock formation is dolomite and talc. The dolomite occurs compact, slaty and crystalline, the talc in beds both indurated and slaty, and it was in these beds that Captain Drummond found his copper ore, which he describes as the yellow sulphuret of copper, or copper pyrites, which in its perfectly pure state yields about 30 per cent. of metallic copper. The Sira mine in patti Barabisi of pargana Sira is situated on the northern side of a hill somewhat higher than Rai, and it is entered by an adit which is driven south in the course of an evidently non-metallic vein. Beds of talc and dolomite rock, as in the case of Rai, constitute the formation wherein the ores of copper are discovered. At the time of Captain Drummond's visit the adit struck a lode about 33 fathoms from the entrance. On this lode a level passage had been driven. The lode itself had been all mined but at the end of the level it seemed to intersect another lode. The ore resembled that found at Rai, but was harder and more contaminated with iron pyrites. The adit was also continued south of the strike of this lode, terminating in a pit half full of water. The lode at the bottom of the pit was said to be very rich, but not easily worked by reason of the necessity of first baling out the water. Captain Drummond also described the native method of working the mines. For excavation a very indifferent kind of pickaxe was employed, the handle being made of a piece of wood with a knob at one end into which a piece of hard iron is thrust and sharpened at the point. This, with a miserable iron hammer wedge and crowbar, constituted all the apparatus that the native miner had to depend upon. Ores and refuse were placed in skins and dragged along the floor to the entrance of the mine. The ores were laid on large hard stones and pulverized by women either with a hammer or with another stone. The cleaning of the ores from slime and other impurities was also left to women, who washed the stuff in baskets against a stream. The drainage also left much to be desired. Captain Drummond advocated the introduction of the most approved Cornish methods, but with the failure of the experiment made in Garhwal by Mr. Wilkin at the instance of the Government the matter appears to have been allowed to drop. At any rate no improvements of any note were introduced. In the year of Mr. Batten's settlement the Rai and Sira mines were yielding only Rs. 101 and Rs. 85 a year respectively. Writing of the former he alludes to "the want of capital and means necessary not only for transforming the present miserable burrows into galleries, but even for reopening the ruined adits and reaching the last worked copper veins." The Sira mine was at that date (1842) being managed directly on behalf of the Government. The dismal state of the mine was by Mr. Batten attributed to dearth of labour. "The Khasyas left all the labour to the Agarias. The latter were found to be rapidly diminishing in numbers from death and desertion, while the survivors were in a truly frightful proportion afflicted with cretinism and goitre." The mines in Kharahi were also in a decayed condition. Mr. Batten noticed thatiron ore was plentiful in various parts of the Chaugarkha pargana, being worked at thirteen different places, at one of which (Jheratoli in Darun) magnetic ore was found. The native industry has now fallen on evil times. Iron and copper can be imported from the plains as cheaply as they can be manufactured within the hills, and the result is that at the present day all the mines have been closed. Khatsari in Palla Giwar, once the best mine in the Province, for a long time held up its head: the cheap rates of grain there prevailing were a great inducement to native prospectors, but as soon as the establishment of the Ranikhet cantonment provided a market for the surplus grain this advantage disappeared. Mr. Beckett's settlement in 1873 completed the ruin of the copper mines. Formerly the villages where the miners resided were included in the mining leases: but Mr. Beckett settled them with the miners, so that the latter were no longer at the mercy of the contractor. The mines nevertheless continued to be worked though on a somewhat insignificant scale. In 1891 they paid a royalty of Rs. 54, in 1892 Rs. 47, in 1893 Rs. 136, in 1894 and in 1895 Rs. 75. The small revenue determined the deputy commissioner to close them down, and this was done in 1895. The lohars however complained at the loss of their livelihood, and in 1900 the mines were reopened. The lohars paid Rs. 5 a furnace and in addition enjoyed the privilege of obtaining charcoal from the district forest department at one-fourth of the ordinary rates. It was found that their demands for fuel and the consequent damage to the forest were in no way proportionate to the revenue they paid, and no leases were granted after 1905. Before that year iron mines at Lobh in patti Kharahi, Raikholi in patti Rithagarh, Mot and Mutkanya in patti Darun had been worked. The output has not been great, reaching 16 maunds in 1903 and 94 in 1904. The methods were crude and only two to two and a half maunds of iron were extracted from 100 maunds of ore.

Of recent years many European prospectors on their own account or on behalf of syndicates have been granted exploring licenses. Curiously enough they appear generally to have confined their attention to mines already worked under native methods and therefore not altogether virgin ground. Colonel Tulloch of Pithoragarh with Mr. Stephens, a mining expert, made a prolonged examination of the Rai mine. They were succeeded by the Himalayan Mining Syndicate, an apparently still-born concern. Later Messrs. Burn and Anderson (the Calcutta Syndicate) explored near Dewaldhar in patti Kharahi and Belar in patti Athgaon of the Gangoli pargana. The metal no doubt exists in remunerative quantities, but fuel is extremely limited and the communications are not adapted either to the carriage of the large machinery and castings which are a preliminary necessity, or to the removal of the metal won.

No records of lead are to be discovered—except that in 1901 certain villagers of Raitoli in patti Baraon petitioned the deputy commissioner for permission to explore within their village. A sample of the ore discovered was found to be iron pyrites and galena in quartz. They received the necessary permission, but nothing seems to have resulted from their operations. Yellow arsenic is found in the northern parts of the district near Munsiari and also close to Almora town. Graphite crops out at the Kalimat hill to the north of Almora and on the spur of Banini Devi facing Almora on the Lohaghat road. Sulphur occurs in Munsiari and in the bed of the Ramganga river, where it is mechanically mixed with carbonate of lime. Silajit, a native sulphate of alumina, is also found exuding from the rocks. It is much prized as a medicine. The limestone quarries are noticed below. Alum is found as an efflorescence on the micaceous schist in the bed of the Kosi below Almora.

Building materials.

Good building stone is found throughout the district, and it is used for the masonry of practically all houses except the lowliest mud hovels. The chir pine affords the staple timber of the district; tun is much appreciated but scarce. Deodar is occasionally used for the timber of bridges. For roofing, slates, stones split thin, or sheet iron are used. Slates are quarried at Baldhoti near Almora, Palari near Dewaldhar and in the Jaurasi forest in Malla Chaukot. Sheet iron is imported from the plains. The best limestone quarries are at Palari, Kharahi near Bageswar, Girdachina (where fuel however is scarce) and Mahakul in Giwar. For dry stone masonry the public works department pay from Rs. 4 to Rs. 9 a hundred cubic feet according to the locality. The dry stone walls made for the district forest department are not quite such polished work: the rate is sometimes as low as Re. 1 or Re. 1-2-0. Stone masonry costs from Rs. 16 to Rs. 20 a hundred cubic feet and masonry in clay Rs. 6 to Rs. 12. Slate roofing ranges between Rs. 10 and Rs. 15 per 100 square feet: plain sheet iron Rs. 24, galvanised sheet iron Rs. 28, corrugated iron Rs. 30. The iron roofs always need a wooden lining.

Forests.

From time immemorial the sole property in all forests has vested in the Sovereign. Mr. Beckett writes of Garhwal, and he has remarked that the conditions throughout the division are identical: "I take this opportunity of asserting that the right of Government to all the forests and waste lands not included in the assessable area of the estates remains utterly unaffected." Owing to the configuration of the country and the absence of communications the forests along the foot of the hills alone possessed any fiscal value in the days before the conquest. They formed an important source of public revenue. The most simple mode of realising this revenue was that actually adopted of subjecting the products of the forest to a small proprietary tax in the shape of duties payable by the exporters. The products consumed within the hills by the people themselves were as a rule too inconsiderable to be taken into account, and, where exceptionally large, as in the case of fuel for smelting ores, were included in the revenue demand. These duties on ordinary forest produce were collected at stations along the foot of the hills, whilst the duty on catechu was fixed at so much per kiln and was paid by the manufacturers. For the first three years of our rule the forest dues were leased with the transit duties on merchandise, and on the abolition of the latter source of revenue Mr. Traill was authorised to farm out the forest dues or *kāth-bans,* and *kāth,* mahals as they were called from their principal items (*kāth*) timber, *bans* (bamboos), and *kāth* (catechu) to the zamindars of the pargana in which they were collected. For the whole of the submontane forests of the Kumaun division the income from these sources amounted in 1817-18 to Rs. 2,481 and in 1818-19 to Rs. 3,200. By 1828-29 it had risen to Rs. 4,025. In the latter year the forest dues were leased to the farmers of the grazing-tax at the same rate, as it was found that the two could not then be usefully separated.

Grazing-tax.

This grazing-tax was one of the many miscellaneous items of revenue that descended to the British from former governments. From the earliest times the landholders in the hills were all subject to a tax on their cattle known as *ghikar,* which with other cesses was abolished at the first settlement. These cesses were called *ghikar*, *gobar* and *puchhiya* in the hills and under the Heris and Mewatis in the Bhabar were called *donia,* from the *dona* or wood bar to which the cattle were tied at night. Each *dona* paid one seer of ghi and four pice a year. The practice of collecting these dues gradually extended from the hills to the Tarai and Bhabar forests, where however only the cattle of plainsmen were taxed. The receipts at first were trifling; but with increased security, due to the efforts of the new police (who had replaced the old chaukidars), cattle-owners began to resort more freely to these pastures. For the year 1822-23 the tax given out in three leases aggregated Rs. 2,077. The boundaries between Kumaon and Rohilkhand had not at this period been settled, and mainy hillmen found themselves called upon to pay dues to the farmers of both provinces. In 1823 the cattle belonging to the *kamins, sayanas* and *thokdars*, or headmen of parganas in the hills, and to *padhans*, or headmen of villages in the Bhabar and those belonging to permanent residents, were exempted from these dues. In 1826 the boundary between the hills and Rohilkhand was finally arranged and separate farms for the grazing dues were established. The principle on which the collections were made was that the farmer within whose jurisdiction the cattle-pens were situate was entitled to collect the tax. The dues were very rarely collected per head, the plan being to count in each *goth* or cattle-pen the *agals* or *donas*, that is, the wooden bars to which the cattle were tied at night. The customary rate was to consider each *agal* as containing eight buffaloes and eight cows liable to a tax of two rupees.

The first attempt at forest reservation appears to have been made in 1826 when on the recommendation of Mr. Traill a proclamation was issued prohibiting the cutting of sal on all the *thaplas* or flats immediately adjoining the lower ranges along the whole extent of the Bhabar. These areas, which may be considered the first reserves in Kumaon, were excluded from the leases of forest produce referred to above. No other steps in the direction of forest conservancy were undertaken. The denudation of trees of all species appears to have continued steadily. It reached a climax between the years 1855 and 1861, when the demands of the railways for sleepers attracted numerous contractors to this region. These men had uncontrolled liberty to cut where and how they pleased, with the result that large numbers of trees were felled and for want of transport were left to rot in the forests. To such an extent was this reckless felling carried on during this period that for several years after the control of the forests was taken in hand by the Commissioner the energy of the officials was occupied in extracting the dead timber thus left by the railway contractors. Fortunately the gravity of the situation was noticed in 1861 by the Commissioner, then Major Ramsay, and he took prompt and energetic steps to stop the further denudation of the forests, and to place the management of this valuable state property on a sounder and more permanent footing. The farming of leases and the indiscriminate felling of trees was stopped. Forest officers were appointed and a system of conservancy was begun under which all trees considered fit for felling were first marked by the forest officials, and fire conservancy was started. The result of the new régime was a greatly increased forest revenue, as we find that the surplus during the decade 1859 to 1868 was nearly seven lakhs of rupees, giving an average annual surplus of Rs. 70,000. In 1868 the forests were first placed under the control of officers of the forest department; Major Pearson was appointed the first conservator, and the forests were gazetted as government forests on the 5th September 1877. During the period 1869-1880 the average annual revenue from these forests was Rs. 2,19,252.

Kumaon Forest division.

The Kumaon forest division originally included some of the forests of the present Garhwal forest division, and extended from the Sarda river on the east to the boundary of the Garhwal district on the west. This tract, which was sub-divided into twelve blocks, was first gazetted as a government forest, under the provisions of section 2 of Act VIII of 1865, by notification no. 407 F.C., dated 5th September 1877. The reserve thus formed consisted of the most important sal forests on the lower hills and the Bhabar (exclusive of the Iron Company's grant) and some tracts containing good khair (*acacia catechu*) and shisham (*dalbergia sissu*) forests. The total area of the blocks which lie in the present Kumaon forest division was, according to the reservation of 1877, 674½ square miles, of which 290·57 square miles were open to the exercise of recorded rights, leaving an unburdened area of 384 square miles of state forests.

On the passing of the Indian Forest Act, VIII of 1878, it was necessary to reclassify and regazette existing state forests into reserved and protected forests. The conservator, in consultation with the commissioner and district officers, gave up 38·67 square miles of the forests gazetted in 1877 and the remaining area of 635·83 square miles was gazetted as reserved forests under section 34 of the Act by notification no. 173F., dated 26th February 1879. At the same time Colonel Garstin demarcated 290·57 square miles of these reserves for the exercise of recorded rights which he tabulated. The reserves open to the exercise of rights were demarcated by means of round numbered pillars, while the boundaries of the reserves are generally well defined by means of square numbered pillars. The villagers living near the forests were given very liberal rights of pasture, timber and forest produce generally.

As the forests of the division increased in area and became too extensive for one charge, the portions to the west of the Dabka river were transferred to the Garhwal forest division, and some of the hill forests west of Kathgodam were made over to the Naini Tal forest division; so that on the 1st July 1901 the area of the Kumaun division was 510 square miles, of which 277 square miles are open to the exercise of recorded rights and 233 square miles are free of rights.

Ranges and Blocks.

The division as now constituted is divided into eight ranges and blocks. Each range is in charge of a ranger or deputy ranger, while forest guards are in charge of two or more blocks. The ranges lying within the Almora district are three in number, the Dogari, Sarra Nadi and Sarda*: their total area amounts to 186·5 miles. The forests are situated on the Bhabar and on the hills overlooking it. The Bhabar forests are divided into two classes, the sal-producing areas and the shisham and khair forests on the old alluvial deposits. The hill forests comprise those situated at altitudes not exceeding 3,000 feet, where sal is the dominant species, with an admixture of sain, haldu and others, and those at a greater elevation containing chiefly the chir pine and oaks. The whole of the Sarra Nadi range consists of hill forest, while the Sarda and Dogari ranges are composed of both hill and plains forests in almost equal proportions.

Working Plans and present system of management.

From 1880 to 1896 the forest revenues were collected by what was known as the chauki system, under which two parallel series of outposts were established; at the upper all dues were realised and passes issued. The passes were checked at the lower line of chaukis. During the first portion of this period (from 1880 to 1885) the felling of trees was regulated by annual

* The portions of these ranges south of the outermost range of hills now belong to the Naini Tal district, since the transfer of the Tanakpur Bhabar in 1910.

plans of operations, in which were detailed the areas to be worked over, the number of trees to be felled and the various works of improvement to be undertaken during the year.

The first regular working plan framed by Mr. Hearle for the Nandhor forests came into operation in the year 1886, and in it fellings were prescribed for the 10-year period 1887 to 1896. This plan, however, only continued in force till 1893, as in 1894 a new working plan was prepared by Mr. Beadon Bryant for all the forests of the division: and this is still in force.

Mr. Bryant's working plan divided the division into ten working circles. His hill circle contains the whole of the Sarra Nadi and the hill portion of the Sarda range already noted. These forests are generally inaccessible and the cost of extracting the produce is therefore prohibitive. It is laid down accordingly that these forests are for the present to be preserved, fellings being permitted only to right holders and to government officials. The greater portion of the Dogari range and a few blocks of the other Almora ranges produce sal. These are treated on what is technically known as the selection method: that is to say, the mature exploitable trees are removed in quantities as nearly as possible equal to the number of immature trees which may be expected to come to perfection within the period of operations. Six feet is taken as the girth at which the sal in these forests may be considered exploitable, and it is calculated that a tree attains this girth at the age of 150 years. One block of the Sarda range—Kakrali—contains mixed forest, chiefly khair and haldu. Khair with a girth of 4 feet and haldu with a girth of 7 feet 6 inches are considered mature. It was prescribed that the fellings should follow a combination of the selection and improvement systems. With regard to bamboos it was considered that to open and close blocks in alternate years and at the same time to prohibit the cutting of the immature shoots of the year would provide sufficient protection and ensure a permanent and healthy growth of bamboos.

Fire protection was introduced in 1876, and by 1901 about 65 per cent. of the entire area of the division was protected. The operations are facilitated by a well devised and complete system of fire-lines 100 feet and 50 feet in width, according to the exigencies of the case. The forest officials state that the people do not resent fire protection, having discovered that the quality of the fodder grass improves thereby while the other numerous forest products by which they make a living in the cold weather months have greatly increased. The benefit to the forest is evident in the dense thickets of poles, saplings and seedlings which have come up in the old ruined forests.

Climber cutting.

The luxuriance of vegetable growth in the semi-tropical forests of the foot-hills is perhaps most noticeable among the larger parasites, chief among which is the gigantic elephant creeper (*bauhinia vahlii*). To such dimensions do these vegetable pests attain that a single elephant creeper with its spreading limbs, like some vegetable octopus, will sometimes cover the tops of the trees over a quarter of an acre of densely grown forest. The suppression and extermination of these natural enemies to tree growth is therefore one of the most important points of forest conservancy and one of the chief factors in the future well-being of a timber-producing area. Regular creeper cutting operations were begun in 1887-88 in the Nandhor and Kalaunia working circles, and these have been systematized and enlarged in the present working plans so as to embrace all the forests which are being worked under the selection or improvement method of treatment.

Present proposals.

Proposals for the revision of Mr. Bryant's working plan are being considered. The forests have undoubtedly improved in condition as a result of past good management and fire protection. It has been observed however that where chir is associated with sal fire protection is beginning unduly to favour the chir. With regard to khair it is probable that trees of 4 feet girth and over are less suitable for the catechu industry than trees of smaller girth. The period allowed by Mr. Bryant in the bamboo blocks for recuperation is probably too short, and it is now proposed to work only one-third of the total area annually. With respect to sal it is proposed to continue the selection system and to bring portions of the hill circle within the sphere of operations, while in the Bhabar sal working circle the introduction of the uniform method is advocated. Before this can be done it will be necessary to divide the forest by a series of conversion-fellings into a number of blocks containing a homogenous forest crop. This will certainly entail loss due to the necessity of felling immature trees, but the initial waste will be more than counterbalanced in the course of time by the improved prices and reduced expenses.

Forest communications, roads and buildings.

The most important cart-road for the forests is the old submontane road known as the *kandi sarak* from Hardwar on the Ganges to Tanakpur on the Sarda. This road runs parallel to the lowest range of hills and communication has been established with the more remote forests by means of feeders running as a rule north and south. The Rohilkhand and Kumaon Railway passing through Lalkua and Haldwani affords additional facilities especially for the export of timber. Tanakpur and the forests of the Kalaunia working circle are connected with Pilibhit by a cart-road, and a railway is now approaching completion. The division is well supplied with rest houses, there being 15 bungalows for the convenience of government officers on tour. The rangers and forest guards are provided with double-storied houses.

Principal products and markets.

Sal is the most valuable and lasting building timber, and supplies also the best sleepers produced in northern India. For general utility this timber is second only to teak. The export of sal consists of logs, beams, sleepers, rafters and smaller scantlings and planks: a considerable quantity of dry poles is also exported for the native marts. Of the indigenous building timber sain is prized next to sal, and there is a fair demand for rafters and planks of this species. Haldu is used largely in Anupshahr in the Bulandshahr district and large quantities of rafters, beams and planks are exported to that town. When not exposed to the weather haldu timber lasts well and it is accordingly used chiefly in the interior of buildings. Dhauri, on account of its close resemblance to sal timber, is styled "white sal" by the local traders, and is not unfrequently passed off in the plains markets as sal. Shisham is used chiefly for the manufacture of furniture at Bareilly. The chief markets are Bareilly, Pilibhit, Moradabad, Rampur, Cawnpur, Meerut and Agra.

Garhwal division.

The jurisdiction of the deputy conservator of the Garhwal division extends over a very small portion of the district. The area amounts to only 11,525 acres, and it lies within the bounds of three blocks of the Chilkia range, known as Era, Jamera, and Kumaria. The forests occupy the outer range of hills and the level land lying between the Ramganga and the Kosi river in the extreme south-east of the district, known administratively as patti Talla Salt. What is now the Garhwal division was formerly included in the old Kumaon division described above. The Garhwal forests are amongst the most valuable, both for timber and bamboos, that exist along the whole line of hills between the Jumna and Sarda. The revenue was in the first place collected from contractors, but in 1854 Captain Read took over the management. He was succeeded in 1858 by Major Ramsay. Ten years later the management of the forest was transferred to the Imperial forest department. The Garhwal forest division originally extended from Koti rao, the territorial boundary between the old Kumaon and Garhwal districts, to the Ganges on the west; but the charge was found too great for a single officer and, after several minor changes, the present boundaries were fixed, and the eastern limit of the Garhwal division is now marked by the Dabka river. The forests of the Chilkia range had been most ruthlessly handled about the middle of the last century, and had been stripped by successive heavy fellings of all their sound timber. The produce is principally sal trees in every stage of growth mixed with sain and miscellaneous species, with fairly large bamboo areas. A working plan was drawn up by Mr. Beadon Bryant in 1896. The Chilkia forests were found to have been so abused that the only possible method of treatment was the improvement system. The object aimed at was to benefit the existing stock by the removal of unpromising stems interfering with others of more importance. The bamboos throughout the division were divided into two series of blocks to be cut over in alternate years. The Chilkia range is traversed by the Ranikhet-Ramnagar cart-road, and by a forest cart-road which branches off from the former near Mohan and, crossing the watershed between the Kosi and Ramganga rivers, comes to an end a mile short of Marchula bridge. The forest is therefore provided with excellent lines of export either by these cart-roads to the new railway station at Ramnagar or by flotation down one of the rivers. The produce of the Chilkia forest thus finds a ready market. Most of the big timber merchants come from Delhi, Agra and Meerut. They buy and saw up a large quantity of first class sal timber, and in some cases a little sain, but will not take any other kind of timber. Smaller purchasers take inferior timber and defective trees which are converted into scantlings and poles. The bamboos are usually exported by river to Cawnpore.

Management.

The Garhwal division is in the charge of a deputy conservator of forests stationed in Naini Tal. In the cold weather, which is also the working season, his headquarters are removed to Ramnagar. A deputy ranger manages the portion of the forest within the Almora district, and under him are foresters in charge of one or more blocks. The headquarters of the range is at Mohan, where there is an inspection house for the use of superior officers and quarters for the ranger and his subordinates. The climate is unhealthy, fever and pneumonia being very prevalent.

Naini Tal division.

The departmental reserved and protected forests within the Almora district other than those situated on the outer range of hills fall within the boundaries of the Ranikhet subdivision of the Naini Tal forest division. These forests may be divided into two geographical areas, those clothing the ridge— traversed by the Almora, Ranikhet and Ramnagar cart-road—which forms the northern boundary of the Kosi basin, together with its spurs to the north and the south known as Airadeo and Siahi Devi respectively, and those situated to the north of Almora in more or less detached blocks. Administratively these forests form three ranges, known as the Almora range to the east, the Ranikhet range in the centre, and the Siuni range to the west. The forests formed a separate division until the beginning of 1886, when they became a subdivision of the Naini Tal division. The Baldhoti and Kalimat plantations on the outskirts of Almora were taken over by the forest department in 1896, free of all rights, and two reserves to the north of Almora, Gananath and Binsar, covering respectively 5,120 and 14,739 acres were notified in 1897 and added to the division. Up to 1887-88 the forests were managed under no regular system; but they were then brought under the provisions of

Mr. Fernandez' working plan, with the exception of Airadeo, Siahi Devi, Bellekh, Bhatraunj and Machor, where management had not been systematized. Trees needed by right holders were marked by the forest ranger and cut and removed by the villagers themselves, and the working plan left it to the discretion of the divisional officer whence to supply these requirements. The forests are now being exploited under a working plan drawn up by Mr. Hearle in 1898. The chief objects aimed at are the supply of timber, fuel and charcoal to Ranikhet, and of the last two commodities to the brewery there. The forest crop is almost entirely chir pine and oak, with an unimportant admixture of rhododendron and ayar. The villagers have rights over various parts of the forests to a supply of fuel, timber and grass, and in some cases they are also entitled to graze their cattle. The grass in the Ranikhet forest is leased to the Supply and Transport department, which require a large supply for its mules and bullocks. Ranikhet is thus the sole market for the produce of the central and western portions of the forest. The forests of the Almora range, with the exception of Airadeo, are not at present being exploited at all except for the benefit of the right holders. For timber there is in fact but little demand, except among the right holders, and there is no cheap method of communication with the plains. Nor is the number of exploitable trees large, so heavily burdened are the forests with rights. In the case of the Siahi Devi block indeed the villagers hold rights to a supply of timber greater than the forest can annually produce. Thus no working plans exist for the Gananath, Binsar and Siahi Devi blocks: but enumerations have been completed in Gananath and are in progress in Binsar. It is proposed to utilise these forests for the supply of fuel to Almora. At present the whole of the fuel supply of that town is obtained illicitly from the district forests. This object will be more easy of attainment now that a forest cart-road has been made from Sitoli on the Ranikhet cart-road to Kaparkhan, a distance of 11 miles.

Baldhoti and Kalimat plantations.

The Baldhoti and Kalimat plantations occupy ridges to the east and north-east of Almora with areas of 493 and 460 acres respectively. Baldhoti was enclosed in 1875 by the district officer and sown with chir pine, successive sowings being made in following years. The plantation was after some time made over to the Forest department, which between 1888 and 1892 continued and extended the sowings. Many experiments were made with different kinds of trees, but chir is the dominant species. Kalimat contained the relics of an old natural forest. Sowings were first started in 1894, and have not yet been extended to cover the whole of the area enclosed. The plantations at present—especially Baldhoti—contain some well-grown young trees, and a small amount of revenue is derived from grass and thinnings: but the main importance of Baldhoti is that it protects one of the sources of the Almora water supply.

Ranikhet cantonment forests.

The Ranikhet cantonment forests cover 2,856 acres within the boundaries of the Ranikhet and Chaubattia cantonments. They are managed by the cantonment magistrate, who refers any professional questions to the forest officer of the division. His control is guided by the working plan laid down by Mr. Hearle in 1897. The chief object of the working plan is the production of fuel for the use of the garrison, and the preservation of fodder for the animals of the Supply and Transport Corps. Chir for timber is becoming scarce, but the requirements of the station can easily be met from the forests outside its limits. The cantonment is exceedingly well wooded.

Turpentine.

The chir pine trees of certain parts of the division are tapped for resin. One-third of each of the Siuni and Ranikhet ranges are the subject of tapping operations but in the Almora range only one-third of the Binsar reserve has been taken in hand, so that there is considerable room for the extension of the industry. In 1908 169,553 trees were tapped, yielding 13,401 maunds of crude resin at a cost of Rs. 18,638, including the cost of carriage to the still at Bhawali in the Naini Tal district. A tree is tapped continuously for five years, after which it is given a rest for ten years. By the end of this period a callus has been formed over the wounds. The durability of the timber of mature trees is improved by tapping, but on the other hand, if young trees are tapped, the grooves cause a certain amount of waste.

District forests.

The district forests stand on a very different footing. The object of their management is to preserve existing forest and to clothe bare ridges. It is not desired to make a profit from them, and all the income realised is allowed to be spent on maintaining and extending them. Before 1893 the forests that had not been taken over by the forest department had been much neglected, and an occasional executive order by the deputy commissioner was deemed sufficient to impose the necessary restraints on the abuse of the forests by the people. In 1893 the principle of state ownership in all unmeasured land so universally accepted in the hills was formally affirmed by a government order declaring all unmeasured land to be protected district forest. The first attempts at forest conservation were however unsuccessful. The small sanctioned staff could not possibly supervise all forest operations and prevent offences against the forest law over an immense tract like the Almora district, containing some thousands of square miles of so-called forest: and in 1903 it was concentrated on certain selected forests. The scheme now adopted divided the existing forests into three classes. Classes I and II comprised respectively forests so remote or of such vast extent as not to require protection and forests which had practically disappeared and were not worth saving. Class III or closed forests included all those areas which required to be closed for protection or reproduction. The classification is now nearly complete. The open forests, i.e. classes I and II, were made over to the padhans (or headmen of villages) and patwaris for management, while the forest staff devoted itself entirely to the closed forests. These blocks are divided into fifty-eight forest guards' beats, each guard living in his beat and patrolling it, supervising the exercise of rights and extraction of produce and preventing or reporting offences: the foresters, four in number, supervise the forest guards and do the more important enquiries of their circles Over the foresters are placed the four deputy rangers, while the technical and professional work of the whole district is supervised and directed by a deputy conservator of forests (lent by the forest department), controlled by the deputy commissioner.

The object of the district forest administration is the maintenance of existing forests, with, where necessary, reboisement Pol of bare tracts so that in the result there may be wood enough for all local needs in the way of fuel, agricultural implements and timber; the protection of pasture land against the encroachments of cultivators; the prevention of soil denudation arising from forest destruction; the protection of the sources of rivers not rising from the snows, and the scientific exploitation of the noble forests in the north of the district which form the chief source of the income necessary for the accomplishment of these objects. Local circumstances vary. In Pali, for instance, Phaldakot and the western portions of Baramandal cultivation has reached its economic limit. The forest area is not sufficient for the needs of the agricultural population. It is necessary therefore to control extensions of cultivation which may damage existing or potential forests and curtail pasture land, already not abundant; and at the same time to provide for the needs of future generations by reafforesting bare ridges. A commencement has already been made on the slopes of the Almora hill and on the Manila ridge in the centre of Pali. In Kali Kumaon on the other hand there is more forest than the people need and moderate extensions of cultivation are encouraged. In the north of the district fringing the great rivers are situated the pine forests whence accrues most of the forest revenue. These forests contain millions of mature pine trees, while the rivers on whose banks they stand provide easy carriage by flotation to the plains. The population is scanty and, provided that provision is made for the maintenance of a forest reserve sufficient to meet all future revenue demands, cultivation may safely be extended. The people are on the whole not ill-disposed towards protection. None of the forests, except the new plantations, are closed to grazing, and the people can get all they want in the way of timber for the trouble of asking for it. Their chief offence from the sylvicultural point of view is their habit of extending cultivation into the forest. They are apt to be extravagant too in their demands for trees, on the principle that nothing is lost by asking, and often cut down a dozen chir poles for timber which might have been extracted from one large tree. In fact the substitution of the saw for the axe would vastly reduce the annual consumption of house-timber. The revenue from the district forests in 1908-09 was Rs. 22,366 and the expenditure Rs. 39,185. The possibility of a more scientific treatment of the district forest is now (August 1910) being considered and great changes in management may shortly be introduced.

The chief tree of the southern forest is the sal (*shorea robusta*). This tree is found up to a height of 4,000 feet and as far north as Malla Askot on the banks of the Kali. In the west of the district, however, it rarely occurs inside the second range of hills. Within the hills it does not reach the size to which it grows in the plains and is chiefly used for house-building. The haldu (*adina cordifolia*) the dhauri (*lagerstraemia paviflora*), the tun (*cedrela toona*), the sain (*terminalia tomentosa*) and the kharik are found up to the same elevation : the tun and the kharik do not often occur in forests. An extremely useful tree—the bhyunl—grows in the valleys and lower hill slopes and is carefully protected by the cultivator, for its leaves afford a very excellent fodder for cattle and rope is made out of the fibre of the young shoots. It is usually grown on the walls between fields. Up to about three thousand feet well-known trees of the plains—the mango, pipal, banyan and shisham—are very common. **Trees.**

Higher, the chir (*pinus longifolia*) is the principal component of the forests up to about 6,000 feet: its limits are between 1,600 feet (where not unduly exposed to the sun) and 7,200 (on a south aspect). It is usually found alone, for it appears to have the power of driving out all other vegetation from the tract it occupies. The chir is the staple building timber in the hills, while vast quantities of trees are exported in the shape of sleepers. Torches are cut out of the living wood. The forest department extract a large quantiy of resin which is sent to the Bhawali factory. The seeds are eaten. In many portions of the district the stems of the chir tree are twisted, the fibre is by consequence spiral and the timber is useless except for fuel. The cause is unknown. **The chir.**

The banj oak (*quercus incana*) though it flourishes from about 4,000 feet upwards, constitutes the bulk of the forest between 6,000 and 8,000 feet, beyond the limit of the chir pine. The tree usually attains no great height. The wood is hard and gnarled and is used for agricultural implements and fuel. The tree is generally common (within its habitat) throughout the district. Associated with it is usually found the tree rhododendron, and in damper situations the ringal bamboo. These flourish up to about 10,000 feet. The ringals are woven into mats and baskets by the Danpur people, and also exported to the plains to be made into pens and pipe-stems. They occur in clumps rising to about 15 or 20 feet at the apex and containing as many as one hundred shoots. Above 8,000 feet the banj gives place to the hardier oaks, the tilonj (*quercus dilitata*) and the karshu (*q. semicarpifolia*). The wood of these oaks resembles that of the banj and is used for the same purposes, but is straighter and less knotted. The timber would no doubt be found very useful if a cheap method of transport to the plains could be devised. Up to 10,000 feet are also found the horse-chestnut (*pangar*) and the sycamore.

Conifers.

The ragha—the Himalayan silver fir—occurs between 7,500 feet and 11,000 feet. It is a tall tree not unlike the cypress at first glance: its branches are short and close. It attains a height of over 150 feet and a girth of 12 feet. The wood is considered to be equal to that of the chir, but owing to its remote situation is seldom used except for roofing shingles. The blue pine (*chil*), the yew (*thaner*) and the cypress (*surain*) are found at the same elevation. They are too well known to require description. The cypress sometimes attains an enormous size. The wood is hard, tough and durable and too heavy for flotation by itself. With these conifers is found the variegated bush rhododendron with flowers of all colours, pink, purple, blue, pure white; and above all is the birch; which grows at a height of as much as 13,000 feet in favourable situations.

Others.

The deodar is not a characteristic forest tree, though in Kali Kumaon deodar forests occur which may be measured in square miles. These are, however, all the result of plantations of former years, for the natural habitat of the deodar is west of the Ganges. These plantations are usually situated around a temple and the deodar is itself, as its name suggests, a sacred tree and is therefore rarely cut. The willow and the alder are common everywhere in damp situations.

Fruit trees of all descriptions are common throughout the district. Up to about 3,000 feet the mango and *jamun* of the plains are often seen, and above that elevation are the wild apple, pear, medlar, cherry, apricot, plum, peach, fig, barbery, *kaphal*, rasp and blackberry, and nearer the snows occur black, red and white currants and the gooseberries. The villagers select for cultivation after a somewhat rude fashion the peach and the apricot, the orange and the plantain. In Almora, Ranikhet, Binsar, Jalna, Dewaldhar and a few other places fruit gardens exist, and here all the finest kinds of grafted English fruit-trees grow to perfection. The walnut is found both cultivated and wild, the kernel of the wild fruit being worthless, and the hazel (called the *Bhotia badam*) is found beyond the snows. **Fruit trees.**

The Chaubattia fruit garden is situated between 6,100 and 6,700 feet on the Ranikhet-Chaubattia hill. It contains an area of 50 acres and its legal position is that of a portion of a reserved forest gazetted free of all rights in 1892.* The garden contains fruit-bearing trees and plants of apple, pear, peach, apricot, plum, cherry, sweet chestnut, quince, currant, gooseberry, fig, mulberry, blackberry and strawberry; grafts for sale and use in the garden, of these species; and seedlings of forest trees for sale and use, such as deodar, walnut, sweet chestnut and horse chestnut. The garden was started in 1869 and placed under the management of Mr. Craw, a trained gardener, controlled by the forest department. The object of management was declared to be "the free distribution of the finer varieties of such fruit trees as would thrive in the climate and soil of the outer ranges of the Himalayas, to show practically the best methods of culture for the various species and to prove what could be done in the outturn of excellent fruit under proper treatment." The Spanish chestnut was introduced in 1880. Mr. (afterwards Sir E.) Buck, then director of land records and agriculture, thought young trees would be taken with avidity by the villagers and the fruit brought into general use as an accessory to their ordinary food staples. The tree does not, however, grow to perfection at so great an elevation as that of Ranikhet, but many thousands of trees were distributed to villagers and public bodies. **Chaubattia fruit garden.**

* Notification no. 736F/347—A-29, dated 16th August 1892.

During the incumbency of Mr. Craw about a lakh and a quarter of fruit trees were given away free to any one who applied: but the results have been disappointing. The villagers took the trees gladly and planted them, but want of protection and general apathy prevented their coming to maturity. After 1890 fruit trees were sold to villagers at half-rates, and were given free to public departments until 1894, from which year full-rates were charged. The garden is now under the control of the Ranikhet range officer and affords employment to nine malis. The income is derived from the sale of fruit and grafts, the former being the more productive item. The fruit is usually sold to a contractor, and brings in between Rs. 2,500 and Rs. 3,000 a year.

Fauna.

This district forms the eastern limit of the western Himalayan tract of naturalists, the river Kali, which becomes the Sarda, demarcating the western from the eastern Himalayan tract. From the plains to the highest mountain peaks—some 25,000 feet—three district zoological zones are included :—(1) the tropical, extending from the plains to about 2,000 feet elevation, is part of the upper Ganges tract of the orièntal region (the North-Western Provinces tract of Blanford) ; (2) the subtropical belt ranges between about 2,000 and 6,000 or 7,000 feet, and constitutes the eastern part of the western Himalayan tract of the oriental region ; (3) above about 6,000 to 7,000 feet the fauna is no longer oriental but holarctic.

Elephant.

The district contains specimens of all the fauna of the provinces. The wild elephant is still found in the Almora Bhabar* but in reduced numbers. The Balrampur kheddah used to operate here. The elephants were usually driven into a *cul de sac* formed by the head of a nullah with precipitous banks, or occasionally wild elephants were run down in the open. The elephant is now protected by legislation and is never shot unless declared a rogue. He does much mischief in the forests to the bamboos, by browsing on the tender shoots and trampling the more mature poles under foot, and also destroys the crops of the Bhabar tenants wholesale at times, particularly in the rains.

* Transferred to the Naini Tal district on 1st October 1910.

Cervidae.

The sambar is the most widely distributed of all the deer tribe, being found in all the forests from the Bhabar up to an altitude of 10,000 feet. The sambar of the hills (where it is called the jarau) is a stouter and more massive beast than his plains congener, and carries very heavy horns. But as his home is in the thickest forest he is hard to drive or stalk. In the plains he can easily be shot from an elephant. The horns are shed during May and the rutting season occurs in October or November. The spotted deer or chital is very common in the Bhabar, where it congregates in large herds, but it is never found in the hills. The stags shed their horns at irregular times from October until July, but chiefly in October or November. The rutting season is equally irregular, since the stags commence to rut as soon as their new horns are perfect. The hog deer is found within the same limits as the spotted deer. It affects grassy swamps or grass jungle along the banks of streams and only retires into forest when much disturbed. The swamp deer is not so common as it was, but it is still found occasionally in the Bhabar. The *kakar* or barking deer, so called from its cry, is common throughout the district up to about 10,000 feet : it is by no means confined to the hills, being frequently seen in the Bhabar. It flourishes apparently between 3,000 and 6,000 feet. It is a pretty little beast, about two feet high, of a bright chestnut colour carrying short forked horns rising from long pedicles. The upper jaw of the male is armed with tusks with which it can inflict severe wounds. The musk-deer (*kastura*) is found in the upper ranges from 8,000 feet to above the limits of the forest, but it so much sought after for its valuable perfume-bearing pod that it is now becoming rare. The pod is an abdominal gland often weighing two tolas and worth about Rs 30. The musk-deer stands about 20 inches high ; it is of a brownish gray colour with harsh and brittle hair. It is generally solitary, very active and sure-footed, and it prefers rocky precipitous ground. Both sexes are destitute of horns, but the males have long slender tusks about three inches long in the upper jaw. The hill men take them in a simple form of snare. A low hedge is built along the ridge of a spur sometimes a mile long and sufficiently high and thick to tempt the game to save themselves the trouble of jumping over. Openings are left in the hedge at intervals of 30 feet in which the snares are set. These are laid flat on the ground, one end being attached to a stout sapling bent over so as to form a strong spring. When the musk-deer approaches the hedge he turns aside until he discovers an opening, through which he walks and puts his foot in the snare. The end of the sapling is released and instantly springs up, suspending the deer by the leg. Many pheasants are taken in the same manner. The flesh of the musk-deer is untainted by his perfume. The nilgai is found occasionally at the foot of the hills and the four-horned antelope in the same localities, and also in the lower sal-clothed hills.

Goats, &c. The gural or Himalayan chamois is found as high as 11,000 feet, but his usual habitat is between 3,000 and 9,000 feet. Both sexes have horns: those of the male average six inches in length, and those of the female about two inches shorter. They generally occur in parties of three or four, but the largest males are usually solitary. They affect moderately steep grassy slopes not too thickly covered with pine. The gural is very tenacious of life and will often carry away a lot of lead. The thar is found in the most precipitous parts of the upper range between 7,000 and 12,000 feet according to the season. Both sexes have horns, but those of the female are much slighter and shorter. An old male is an imposing sight: he stands nearly 3½ feet high, wears a long shaggy coat reaching to his knees, and carries horns 13 or 14 inches long. An animal smaller in size but apparently otherwise identical with the thar is sometimes found at lower altitudes: it is called the khar thar. The sarau though of the same family as the gural is nearly as large as the thar. It is a strange, uncouth beast, very shy and inhabiting precipitous rocks clothed with dense jungle. Its chief accomplishment is the ease with which it can gallop down hill. Its average horn measurement is about 9 or 10 inches. The barhal or wild blue sheep is rarer in Almora than in Garhwal. It frequents high grassy slopes below the snow line between 10,000 and 16,000 feet. A good ram carries horns 25 inches long. The mutton, especially in September, is particularly praised by those who have tasted it.

Tiger. The tiger is found from the Bhabar near Tanakpur up to about 10,000 feet. Those which are found on the outer ranges doubtless migrate to the Bhabar and Tarai, but those found in the interior never leave the hills. They are quite different from the plains tiger, being of a stouter build with longer and more furry hair and shorter and thicker tails. In the earlier years of British rule Katyur and Gangoli were almost deserted on account of man-eating tigers, to such an extent that the circumstance gave rise to the proverb "Khatyari (a village near Almora) for vegetables, Gangoli for tigers." The Bhabar is still famous for its tiger shooting, but the animal is not so common in the hills as formerly. He is however occasionally met with, in the Bageswar valley for instance. No reward is now offered for the destruction of tigers except in unusual circumstances.

Panther. The panther or leopard is extremely common throughout the district. He is a bold and blood thirsty beast. His food consists of the cattle, sheep and goats which he is able to kill. Dogs form an agreeable change of diet, and he occasionally takes to killing man, when his superior audacity and cunning make him a more dangerous pest than even a man-eating tiger. The panther is exceedingly bold, often making descents in search of prey into the heart of a village, and it is said that a few years ago the assistant commissioner of Almora adjourned his court in order to kill a panther which had taken up its quarters in the centre of the town. The natives kill a great number in dead-fall traps (called *jibala*) baited with a dead sheep, goat or dog. The panther in the hills is usually called *bagh* or *baghera*.

Snow-leopard. The snow-leopard is nowhere common to the south of the snowy range, but there are generally one or two on all hills where the barhal or wild sheep is found. It is much execrated by sportsmen as a game destroyer. The fur is of a pale-yellowish ground with dark grey marks all over the body except on the stomach, which is pure white. The skin is valuable.

Three species of jungle cat are found in the district. In the hands of the hill man they are frequently made to personate panther cubs for the sake of the reward. They feed on rats, mice and birds, being particularly addicted to pheasan chicks.

Bears. The sloth bear (*ursus labiatus*) is found in the Bhabar and the lower hills up to an altitude of about 3,000 feet, but he never penetrates into the interior beyond the first range. His principal food is ants, beetles and other insects, fruits, roots and honey, though he does not disdain carrion. The Himalayan black bear (*ursus torquatus*) is very common throughout the district. In the upper ranges he usually hibernates throughout the winter and is in fact seldom seen except during the rains, but those living in the lower hills descend to the Bhabar for the cold weather. He is a good tree climber and feeds on acorns and other wild fruits, but his favourite food is mandua. Much damage is done by black bears in the fruit gardens of Binsar and other places. They occasionally kill cattle, sheep and goats, and like the sloths are not above eating carrion on occasion. The sight and hearing are both keen: and the black bear is a ferocious and courageous beast, not hesitating to attack man if disturbed. Many hillmen are mauled by them every year: the bear invariably attacks the head and face. The red bear (*ursus isabellinus*) is found, though very rarely indeed, in Darma, Johar and Byans, living along or above the upper limit of forest far away from the haunts of man. He feeds on roots, weeds, grasses and even insects, but he will eat the flesh of animals he has killed and has been known to feed on carrion. His scent is keen, but his sight and hearing are dull. He hibernates from December to March, and is a timid, unaggressive animal. The

Others. hyæna is found in the ravines of the Bhabar, but seldom enters the hills. It is a cowardly animal and never shows fight even when wounded. The wolf occurs occasionally in the submontane tract but rarely if ever in the hills. The wild dog is unfortunately by no means uncommon throughout the district, though it is most frequently met with in the Bhabar. The wild dog hunts in packs, the sambhar or chital being its favourite quarry. It is said that a pack hunts in relays, always driving the prey in a circle. The hind quarters and abdomen are the first parts attacked. A pack of wild dogs has been known to bay a bear. Jackals are very common, especially at the foot of the hill, but they are found up to 7,000 feet and they infest the station of Almora itself. Their ordinary food is carrion and vegetable matter, especially maize and pumpkins, but they kill a great many young deer and often catch birds; while they occasionally attack wounded animals. The ordinary plains fox and the mountain fox both occur in the Almora district: the latter is a fine beast with a fine fur. It is a poor runner on level ground, and even on open hillsides an ordinary half-bred greyhound can easily catch it.

The wild pig is found throughout the district from the Bhabar up to 10,000 feet. In the hills it chiefly affects oak forests, living on the mast. The pine marten (*chatraila*) and the otter (*ud*) work considerable destruction among game and fish respectively. The monkeys of the district are the common erubescent rhesus of the plains, and the Himalayan langur, both of which do much damage to the crops, though the latter is often content with acorns and other wild fruits. In the extreme north rare visitors from Tibet are the nyan (*ovis hodgsoni*), the great Tibetan sheep, the kyang or wild ass, the yak, and the Tibetan wolf.

The district of Almora is very rich in bird life. Most of the birds of the plains occur also in the hills, and in addition to these there are many species peculiar to the colder regions. Birds of prey, eagles, hawks, falcons and vultures, are very common, so much so that in former years a tax was imposed upon sporting hawks. The European soon recognizes species allied to those well known to him at home, such as thrushes, water-ouzels, yellow and pied wagtails, swallows, swifts, king-fishers, woodpeckers, cuckoos, tree-creepers, shrikes, orioles, robins, redstarts and warblers. Among game birds the lungi pheasant is found at about 12,000 feet, the brilliant monal pheasant is found from 8,000 to 12,000 feet; the koklas or pokras from 6,000 to 10,000 feet, and the rather uncommon chir pheasant from 5,000 to 10,000 feet. The commonest of all the pheasants is the kalij, which frequents thick forests from the skirts of the Bhabar up to a height of about 6,000 feet. Among partridges the well-known chakor is very common; the hill part-ridge and the black partridge, the last up to about 6,000 feet, are often bagged; the peora (Blyth's hill partridge) is found occasionally in the dense forests. Birds.

The woodcock is not uncommon. It used to be shot fairly frequently in the Baldhoti plantation near Almora before the shooting rules came into force, and sportsmen from Ranikhet still bag a fair number in Dwarsyun. The snow partridge is found on barhal ground, but it is rare. In the extreme north the Himalayan snowcock is found on or near the snow line. Among pigeons the blue rock and the wood-pigeon are common. Vast flocks of snow-pigeons are sometimes seen in the higher ranges. Duck and teal occasionally rest on the rivers. In the Bhabar and lower hills peafowl, spur fowl and jungle fowl are extremely plentiful. The ordinary game birds of the plains —partridge, quail and snipe—are also to be found in the Bhabar.

Fish. Fish abound in all streams and are gratefully eaten by nearly all classes, forming in the riparian villages a very important accessory to the ordinary food stocks. Among the larger species the commonest and most acceptable are the mahseer and the kalabans. The gunch or fresh-water shark is said to inhabit the deeper pools of the Sarju. The Indian trout is rare, but the chilwa swarms wherever there is running water. Fish in the hills have a hard struggle for existence. In the latter part of the hot weather they run up the streams to spawn and to many the initial obstacle of a weir proves insurmountable. Should they conquer it, however, they are liable as they push their way up the most exiguous streams to deposite the ova, to fall victims to the club or spear of the villagers. On the return journey many dangers await them. Conical-shaped baskets are placed at openings three or four feet apart along an irrigation weir, especially where the stream is strongest. An unwary fish coming too close to the weir finds itself hurled into a basket from which there is no escape. Or two men sit on commanding rocks at opposite sides of the river holding each the end of a stout cord which is armed with large hooks every three or four inches: they wait until a fish is seen to pass over the cord when a sharp jerk frequently transfixes it. This contrivance is called the *raksha*. Many fish escape maimed. A third method is the diversion of the stream: the fish left in the larger pools of the old stream are taken out as required or, more often, allowed to perish, and those that attempt to run down the new stream find their escape barred by a net. Heavily weighted casting nets are also successfully used, the chief victims being kalabans under a pound in weight. The most important spawning grounds in the district are found along the course of the Sarju and Ramganga, which are not snow-fed, and it is therefore along the course of these rivers that these poaching operations are most frequently pursued. They are however legal, and the right to take fish according to these methods is usually conveyed by the settlement agreements, all rivers being, like waste land and forest, the property of the Government. The rights are very valuable, and the villagers of Masi on the Ramganga point with pride to a fine pool below the bridge still harbouring some immense fish, which was the subject of prolonged litigation ultimately settled by the High Court. Poisoning and the use of explosives are frequently used, but these are illegal. The erection of weirs not expressly recognized by the settlement agreements is also prohibited. The rivers of the district still afford excellent sport to the angler, the most favourable seasons being in March and April before the snow water comes down.

Major F. Wall, I.M.S., has kindly furnished a note on the snakes of the district. In all 36 species have been identified in the Western Himalayas, but two are of somewhat doubtful occurrence in this district. Of the thirty-four that remain twenty-six are harmless in the sense that they are non-poisonous, while eight are venomous. The cobra is very common in the hills, where it may be found up to 6,000 feet; beyond that altitude it rarely occurs. *Bungarus coeruleus* is the karait of the plains and is very uncommon outside the submontane tract or the low hills overlooking it. This snake grows to a length of 54 inches. Its colour above is deep lustrous blue-black uniform, or streaked and reticulated with white: below it is white. *Bungarus Walli* (Wall's karait) has much the same general appearance as the common karait. It is of a glistening black colour on the back marked with milky white cross lines formed of smallish oval or round spots. Below it is white, mottled with slate towards the tail. It grows to a larger size than the common karait, the largest on record being 5 feet 4½ inches. *Naia bungarus* (formerly *n. elaps* or *ophiophagus elaps*) the king cobra grows up to 200 inches. It is difficult to distinguish between young specimens and the cobra; they are however of a pure jet black The

Snakes.

adult female is olive brown with pale cross bands deeply edged with black, the underside being mottled white with black about the tail: the throat is yellow. *Callophis MacClellandi* grows to about 30 inches and is rare in Kumaon. The body and the tail are reddish brown with generally a black vertebral line from the nape to the tip of the tail, and the head and the neck are black with a yellow bar behind the eyes: the belly is yellowish with black cross bands or quadrangular spots. A variety, *nigriventer*, has been found in the western Himalayas. This snake though venomous is not fatal to a man. It occurs in the sub-tropical belt of the Himalayas. *Vipera Russelli*—Russell's viper—grows to 54 inches and is common up to about 6,000 feet. The colour above is greyish or reddish brown with three rows of blackish brown annular ocelli, each surrounded by an inner white and an outer black ring, down the back and sides. It has a broad arrow mark on the head formed by two pale lines from the snout over the eyes to the temporal region. *Ancistrodon himalayanus* is the only hill snake found above 8,000 feet. In colour it is dark brown, indistinctly marked with darker spots edged with black. The belly is black marbled with yellow. A blackish band extends from the eyes to the gape. It attains a length of 25 inches and is venomous though not fatal to man. *Lachesis gramineus* (formerly *trimeresurus monticola*), the green-pitted viper, grows to a length of 37 inches. It is one of the handsomest of the tree snakes and is common in the Bhabar. Its bite too is not necessarily fatal to man.

Of the non-venomous snakes the python is most notable. It grows to about 30 feet, but specimens over 20 feet are rare. It is common in the Bhabar, but its rarity in the upper hills has invested the few specimens seen with almost supernatural terrors. There it is called the *charao* and it is said to be of enormous size with a flowing mane of red hair, and to make use of a large pine tree as a walking stick when descending the mountains. The rat snake or *dhaman* of the plains is also extremely common. It grows to 91 inches.

The other reptiles call for little remark. The blood-sucker lizard grows to a length of 14 or 16 inches. In summer the males have the body red and the head and neck yellowish picked out with red. In spite of its name it is perfectly harmless.

The leech is of sufficiently common occurrence to deserve a short note. It is particularly active during the rains, and its favourite habitat is an oak forest. After a smart shower it appears in myriads, and any barefooted wayfarer is soon made uncomfortably aware of its presence. Another pest to travellers is the small stinging fly called the *mora*. Its bite causes small painful sores and intense irritation.

The hill cattle are usually small in size, active and sure-footed. The cows are wretched milkers, producing usually not more than a seer of milk a day. The cattle are usually kept at night in the *goth* under the dwelling house or in separate cow-sheds. They are littered with oak leaves and at the end of the year or possibly more often the shed is cleared out and its contents taken to the fields. Fodder consists chiefly of grass carried in from the more precipitous hillsides by the women, bhyunl, mulberry or oak leaves, or straw. Grain and salt are rarely given. The cattle graze among the stubble of harvested fields, and in the forests and village pastures. Fodder is seldom preserved except in the north, where meadow land is divided among the hissedars, each cutting and storing his own, or, if he prefers, grazing it. But hillsides that are too steep for safe grazing act as a natural reserve. Surplus straw is stacked upon trees near the homestead and consumed as required. In the summer the villagers of the neighbourhood drive their cattle up to the great oak forests on the higher hills; there they make a more or less permanent cattle station, not leaving it until the rains have well set in. Dudatoli in the Garhwal district and Dunagiri near Dwarahat are famous grazing resorts for cattle. In the extreme north the grassy expanses between the upper limit of the forest and the region of perpetual snow are the summer grazing grounds of the whole body of cattle belonging to the villages in the vicinity. From the southern and middle parganas cattle are driven down to the Bhabar in October and kept there until the break of the monsoon, or, in the case of cattle owners who have no Bhabar cultivation, till March. Sales of cattle are rare. The cultivators usually breed their own plough animals.

Cattle.

Buffalos do well, but the male is never used in the plough. Cattle are often visited by the rinderpest, called *man-rog*, which in almost all cases is imported from the Bhabar by animals returning from their winter grazing grounds. The disease is very deadly, and is, as would be expected, commonest in the centre and south centre of the district. Dysentery (*chhera*) usually appears in the same tract. Haemorrhagic septicaemia (*bamka*) causes considerable loss in the northern parganas. The people are well awake to their own interests and usually take effective measures for the segregation of infected animals.

Very few bullocks have been broken into the cart, even by people living near the cart-roads, and it is a common sight to see a family pursuing its way down a cart-road to its Bhabar cultivation, driving the plough cattle in front, empty or but lightly laden, while the men, women and even the little children bear their household property on their heads. In 1898-99 there were only 315 carts in the district and probably some of those belonged to plains carriers. Little cattle-breeding is conducted in the district, and the only trade that exists is the sale of some rather poor young bulls to the Muktesar Bacteriological Laboratory. Mr. Stevenson of Chaukuri introduced some plains breeds upon his estate, but he found that though the calves produced were good the cows lost condition through seeking their food on the hill pastures, and a further disadvantage lay in the fact that the pure plains breed wintered badly. He therefore crossed the indigenous breed with plains bulls and has produced an animal that meets his double object of milk and manure ; an animal that can graze from morning to night in all weathers, does not require blanketing in the winter and gives a fair amount of rich butter-producing milk. Mr. Stevenson has thus proved that if necessary the hill cattle can be materially improved ; but at the same time the Kumaoni prefers a small active bullock for field work, and his buffaloes give him all the milk he needs.

The yak.

The yak is occasionally in the extreme north tamed and reduced to domestic servitude. But it cannot safely be brought much lower than ten thousand feet, and hybrids are more commonly used. When the sire is a yak and the dam is a hill cow the product is called *jubu*; when the parentage is reversed, *garjo.*

The yak will carry two or three maunds, is docile and sure-footed and is often ridden. The wild yak is very rarely found in British territory. It is a much finer beast than its domesticated cousin, and, in the expressive words of the peasant, the liver of a wild yak is a load for a tame one.

Sheep and goats. The sheep found in the lower hills differ from those of the plains in some minor respects, the chief characteristic being the shortness of the tail. The hillmen refuse in fact to eat the flesh of the plains sheep, its long tail according to Mr. Traill constituting it in the eyes of the highlanders a species of dog. The sheep is bred chiefly for the sale of the meat, and in a very minor degree for its wool. The indigenous goat of the middle and southern parganas is exactly the same as the goat of the plains. It is no good for milking; and is chiefly esteemed for its flesh and for its manure. Goats are sacrificed to the gods—sheep are not.

The pack animals of the Bhotia are of a very different class. The sheep they use for carrying loads are of a strong, long-legged Tibetan stock bearing no resemblance to the diminutive animal of the lower hills. The Bhotias themselves rarely breed their animals, though some keep a few ewes. They buy a great many Chamba sheep from the Kangra people, who bring them down to Ramnagar for sale. Sheep are also bred in the Badhan pargana of the Garhwal district and in Danpur, Talla Johar and Malla Askot: these regions also breed goats. The Bhotia goats are stout, shaggy animals, natives either of Bhot or of the Western Himalayas. The loads are carried in saddle-bags made of hempen sack-cloth, or worsted, backed with leather. These are secured on the animal by means of girth, breast-band and crupper. A goat's load is about 12 seers, and a sheep's 10 seers. At the cattle census of 1898-99 101,373 sheep and 84,715 goats were enumerated.

Ponies. The trade in Bhotia ponies (which are really raised in Tibet and imported by the Bhotias) is nearly dead. They are seldom used for carrying loads, for which purpose, indeed, they are much too valuable. A good saddle animal commands a high price. The pony most commonly seen in the hill-villages is not to be differentiated from the plains *tat*: there are also some which appear to be of impure Bhotia descent. They are used in the saddle chiefly, but also occasionally for the transport of goods. Most of the small hill shopkeepers possess one or two animals of this description. The carrying trade between the Bhabar markets and the hills is in the hands of plains Muhammadans or Kumhars, who drive herds of ponies or mules. The horses and ponies numbered in all only 3,653 in 1898-99 and mules 491.

Climate.

It has already been pointed out that the great snow-clad peaks lie not on the northernmost ridge that forms the boundary between the district and Tibet, but on the extremities of the lateral ranges extending southwards of the main range and situated generally at a distance of twenty or thirty miles from it. The tract between the snowy range and the plains is in its main physical characteristics Indian. The country which lies between the snowy range and the water-parting is on the other hand entirely Tibetan in its characteristics. To the south the climate is thoroughly Indian. The order of the three seasons is the same as in the plains of Upper India; a well-marked winter, almost entirely without snow, is followed by a summer of nearly tropical heat which is again succeeded by a season of periodical rain. After the close of the rains at the middle or end of September the sky is serene and the atmosphere transparent. The months of October and November are characterized not only by clear skies and calms, but by a great temperature range and heavy dews at night. These conditions prevail through the greater part of December, and during that month and those which precede and follow it the exposed thermometer usually records several degrees of frost at night. In midwinter however clouds often interfere with the free radiation of heat at night and some rain usually falls at this season, which above an altitude of about 5,000 feet appears in the form of snow. These conditions, with intervals of bright fine weather, ought to continue through January, February and March. Meanwhile the thermometer rises gradually and by the middle of April the heat increases rapidly, while the air becomes exceedingly dry. During May and the first half of June, while the nights remain cool, the temperature continues to increase, though less rapidly than in April, and as the rainy season approaches the range of temperature diminishes and the nights become hot and close. Rain rarely falls in the hot weather, but hailstorms of considerable violence accompained by thunder and lightning are not uncommon. They are practically confined however to the vicinity of high mountains and are exceedingly local in their effects. The crops in half a field may be cut to pieces, while in the other half they are left untouched. During the latter half of June the sea-winds increase in strength and gradually advance along the foot of the Himalayas until by the beginning of July the rains have usually set in all over northern India. Breaks are frequent and, if long maintained, are fatal to the crops, for owing to the rapid slope of the hills the water soon drains off and in a few days the ground is dry and hard, while a fortnight's fine weather renders it almost as dry and dusty as in the middle of the hot weather. General Strachey writes of the seasons in the mountain zone. "The same general sequence of the seasons takes place in the mountains as in the plains. Here however every altitude has its own special temperature, from the lower valleys where the heat is still overpoweringly great to the regions of eternal frost; but at all elevations in summer the force of the sun's rays is excessive. The summer rains too gradually diminish in strength as we move along the chain from east to west . . . The heaviest falls invariably take place on those portions of the chain most exposed to the south, increasing in amount up to a certain height (not very exactly determined, but probably about 4,000 feet); at the same time every high and continuous ridge most sensibly diminishes the supply of rain that falls on the country to the north of it, and we find as we approach the Indian watershed that the quantity is very small and that the monsoon only just drops a few partial showers on the southern border of Tibet. The winter as may be supposed is extremely rigorous on the summit of the tableland; and at this season or in spring the only important precipitation takes place in the form of snow, but it is exceedingly small in quantity." The mean annual temperature diminishes as the height increases. But conclusions drawn from the altitude alone are apt to be misleading. Places which lie behind the outermost high ridge are subject to a much smaller rainfall than stations situated on the ridge or in valleys opening to the south end exposed to the full force of the rainy winds. The Bhabar* or strip of level land at the foot of the hills adjoining Tanakpur, has a climate almost identical with that of the submontane districts of the plains except that it enjoys about double the rainfall.

In the river valleys from April to October, except during or shortly after heavy rain, the heat is always excessive, a result due partly to the intensity of the sun's rays through the comparatively thin hill air but chiefly to reflection from the two steep hillsides which usually enclose the valley on either side. In the cold weather the climate is more pleasant, but cold fogs often follow the winter showers. Hoar frost may be found on the grass in the valley while the hillside a thousand feet or so above is quite free from it. In open situations 500 or 1,000 feet above the valley the climate is more equable, though in all places below 5,000 feet the heat is excessive during the months of May and June. Above 5,000 feet the shade heat in the summer is sufficiently tempered by the altitude to make it agreeable to the European consitution; while the winter, if too cold for comfort except during the middle of the day, is still far from approaching the low temperature of the same season in England. Snow in the south of the district rarely falls below 5,000 feet, though in the north it occasionally falls as low as 4,000.

In the valleys beyond the snowy range, the Bhot of the inhabitants of the lower hills, entirely different conditions prevail. The heavy falls of snow in the winter give to the climate at that season an even more than Tibetan rigour. From the middle of November to the middle of April everything above 10,000 feet is buried beneath a covering of snow. The summer is always temperate, and during its continuance the snow-line retreats to an altitude of 18,000 feet. The periodical rains fall only as moderate showers.

Rainfall. The observed annual rainfall in the district varies from 40 inches at Almora and Ranikhet to 98 at Tanakpur. The actual mean of the whole district is 60 inches; but this figure is of little value, because the rainfall in any given place appears to depend so entirely upon its surroundings. The maximum falls occur at the two points where a general rise in elevation

* Transferred to the Naini Tal district from the 1st October 1910.

takes place; that is to say at the foot of the outermost range of hills and at the foot of the snows. There is unfortunately no rain-gauge in the district situated near the snowy range. The most northerly station is Dharchula. At the foot of the lowest range is the Tanakpur station, where the average annual rainfall is about 98 inches. The principle in the central belt of the district appears to be that, so far as the monsoon rains at any rate are concerned, in the vicinity of high hills the rainfall is heavy while at a distance from them it is light. At Almora for instance, which stands at an elevation of about 5,600 feet but is surrounded by higher hills such as the Gagar range with Muktesar on the south, the Siahi Devi hill on the west and Kalimat on the east, the rainfall is about 40 inches in the year; and, as Mr. Goudge observes, "it is a familiar experience to those who have lived on the Almora spur that they should be in bright sunshine, while watching the rain and mist sweep over and be intercepted by the high ridges surrounding it. Naini Tal for instance, which lies on the high outer intercepting ridge, has an average rainfall double that enjoyed by Almora." Ranikhet occupies a ridge higher by about 500 feet than that on which Almora stands: it too, to a certain extent, is dominated by the Chaubattia peak, and its rainfall for the 10 years ending with 1907 was the same as that recorded at Almora. The other rain-gauges, Champawat, Pithoragarh, Lohaghat (recently abolished) and Kausani (maintained by Mr. Troup of the Kausani Tea Company) are all situated on hills of between 5,000 and 6,000 feet in elevation: they record an average rainfall of between 50 and 60 inches, which may therefore be taken as the standard for the hilly portion of the district. This standard is exceeded in a remarkable way by Mr. Stevenson's rain-gauges at Berenag and Chaukuri, both situated in patti Baraun and at a distance of about four miles from each other as the crow flies. The average precipitation for these two places is 72 and 92 inches. Some explanation of these figures is afforded by the topography of the neighbourhood. The two stations lie near a mountain knot where many lateral ridges meet, and it would appear that the rain clouds are deflected from their northerly course to converge and burst near Berenag and Chaukuri. Dharchula, again, lies in the

Kali valley overlooked by many massive ranges, and they intercept the rain clouds to such an extent that the recorded rainfall during the ten months the station has remained open amounts to only some 44 inches. The rains usually break earlier than in the plains, heavy showers apparently of local origin, accompanied by northerly and westerly winds, frequently occurring about the same time that the monsoon approaches Bombay.

CHAPTER II.

Agriculture and Commerce.

The district contains very little level ground. The best cultivation is on terraced fields, kept continuously under the plough except for the periodical seasons of fallow. These terraces cost a vast amount of labour and capital to make and maintain, and one cannot be made in a single working season. Stones at the lower half of the field are built into a wall, and at the same time an excavation is made in the upper part until the whole becomes approximately level. As however the soil is very thin on most hillsides and lies over a stony sub-soil the effect of carrying out the whole of this operation at once would be to bury the soil under the stones. Usually a small wall is built up and a small excavation made during the first year, the operation being completed in the course of time by weather, tilth, and diluvion from higher fields. Mr. Goudge writes: "The most distinguishing characteristic of hill cultivation is the continued improvement in existing terraces. Every year's ploughing removes more stones, improves and strengthens the retaining walls, levels the slopes and makes the crop more remunerative. The labour involved is of course very great and the least neglect results in an overgrowth of the thorn bushes, wild raspberry, barberry, *ghingaru* and other scrub jungle which grows so quickly and profusely in the hills." Unterraced cultivation is called *khil* or *katil*: this consists in burning scrub jungle on steep hills and sowing the land so cleared. *Khil* cultivation is more properly described as intermittent than as occasional. The land is generally speaking regularly cultivated but the period of fallow allowed between crops is so long that to the casual observer the land appears to have been abandoned altogether. This long period for recuperation is necessitated by the fact that the land being in no way terraced suffers much from the scouring of the rain, while the only

Cultivation.

manure allowed is the ashes of the burnt scrub. A third class of land intermediate between the continuously cultivated terraced land and the intermittently cultivated *katil* is known as *ijran.* This is the poorest kind of terraced land, often not very carefully built, carelessly cultivated, sparsely manured and never watered. It generally lies fallow for two or three years at a time.

Soils.

Cultivation in the hills depends very much less upon the composition of the soil than upon the more important factors of height and aspect, and irrigational facilities. Broadly speaking, the worst land if capable of being irrigated is of more value than the best land unirrigated. The northern slopes of the hill are usually less abrupt and less denuded by the action of the rain than the southern slopes. Fields with a north aspect therefore are more cheaply excavated and when made contain thicker and richer soil, and, not being exposed so much to the solar heat, they retain moisture for a longer period. Again, for no obvious reason, some hills are naturally damper than others. Irrigation is however the most important factor of all in determining the system of agriculture and the crop rotation to be pursued. Irrigation benefits the crop in the obvious way of providing it with the moisture so necessary to its existence and development, and as irrigation is in the hills entirely by flow the channels deposit upon the field a very valuable top dressing of virgin silt carried down from their upper courses. The classification adopted by settlement officers has therefore been *talaon* (irrigated), 1st class *upraon* (dry), 2nd class *upraon, ijran* and *katil*. The *talaon* lands again are of two kinds. In the first the water-supply is perennial, and the fields are carefully levelled and can be flooded with an inch or two of water when required. Fields of this description are called *sera ;* they are usually sown with the finest rice and they occur generally low down near the irrigating stream. The soil is alluvial, the position hot, the water supply constant : these fields are therefore the richest and most productive in the village. Where the water is apt to be scanty except during and immediately after the rains the rice is sown in seed beds at the proper season (usually April) and transplanted into other fields with the advent of the rains, when the stream has increased in volume sufficiently to flood the whole of the *sera.* The other class of *talaon* land is called *panchar* and the term means capable of being irrigated, rather than irrigated. These fields are usually situated in the uplands, and they are frequently not well levelled, but water can be led to them in a canal and they can thus be sprinkled occasionally. The importance of this somewhat intermittent irrigation is not great. The fields are not suitable for the best kind of rice, and in ordinary seasons irrigation is not necessary, as the rain if normal does all that is necessary. In dry years on the other hand when artificial watering is necessary the canals are naturally lower than usual and in practice prove barely sufficient for the *seras.* At the same time in such years every effort is made to give the fields a sprinkling sufficient to germinate the wheat: and if canals are not available for the purpose, the women carry up water from the nearest spring or stream in *gharas.* The *panchar* land therefore hardly differs in value from the *upraon.* The dry land or *ukhar* is according to its situation of very diverse capacity. *Khil* for instance is always sparsely sown and the crop poor and thin. The Kaklasaun pattis on the other hand own a class of soil locally known as *talliya,* "which is a level alluvial unirrigated block above the river bed, but low down, free from stones and growing crops which are scarcely inferior to those produced with irrigation."*

Canals.

Water is brought into the fields from rivers or rivulets by means of channels called *guls* cut along the contour line of the hill. The length of the *gul* varies according to the height of the land to be irrigated above the bottom of the valley and the fall of the stream. The head works consist of a small temporary dam laid across the stream, by which the water is directed into the *gul.* As the channel of the stream is scoured deeper and deeper by the annual rains it becomes necessary to raise the dam, and finally to abandon it and make new head works higher up. These *guls* are often more than a mile long and are made at considerable expense, which the zamindars pay out of their own pocket.

* Settlement Report : J. E. Goudge.

There are rocks to be carved with wedges or if this is impossible circumvented by means of wooden troughs, and the same method is employed for carrying the *gul* across a ravine. Small streams are usually tapped, for in small streams the fall is great and the length of the canal proportionately short. Nor do the people commonly possess either the capital or the engineering skill necessary for handling the largest rivers. An exception to this general rule is furnished by the *seras* that line the Ramganga river in its course through Giwar. Here however the irrigated land lies very low in or near the present or old beds of the river. A favourite stream for irrigation is one about ten miles in length issuing if possible from high hills. This will contain a perennial supply of water sufficient for the land commanded and at the same time the fall will be rapid enough to admit of a short canal. The people are however daily becoming more ambitious in their ideas on the subject of irrigation, and during the famine of 1908 many big schemes were examined. Few however came to fruition, the chief reason being that a long canal must of necessity pass through the lands of more than one village. Mutual jealousy and distrust prevented the people from co-operating.

Most of the *guls* turn one or more water-mills (called *garat*) during their course, and the amount of water in a stream or canal is estimated according to the number of water mills it is capable of turning. Thus *do nal* or *do garat ka pani* means a stream of two mill-power. Some of the ancient settlement mills offer the greatest possible obstruction to irrigation. The millers claim the sole right in the water used by their mills, which in some cases means the whole of the stream, while in others the mills have been so constructed at commanding points as to render tapping the stream an impossibility without the demolition of the mill. Each of these mills pays a small annual fee to the Government.

Methods of cultivation. To prepare the ground for seed it is first of all ploughed once in the case of coarse kharif crops such as the millets *jhangora* and *mandua* and twice in the case of all others. It is noticeable that in the double cropped area the land is less carefully prepared for wheat or barley than for the kharif crops. The seed is often sown among the half-ploughed-in stalks of the preceding crop. On the other hand the fields are scrupulously cleaned after the rabi harvest before they are deemed fit for the reception of the kharif seed. In the case of rice and sometimes wheat the clods are broken up after each ploughing with a long-handled mallet, and the ground is smoothed over with a toothless harrow. The seed is then sown and ploughed in with the manure. When the kharif crops have reached the height of a few inches above the ground the toothed harrow called *dandyala* is applied. Then until they begin to come into ear they are regularly weeded. The crop is cut with a sickle, rice being cut off close to the root, while in the case of *jhangora* or *mandua* the ears only are first cut, and after the stalks have dried they are cut and stored as fodder. Wheat and barley are cut about the middle. On the arrival of the sheaves at the threshing floor the ears are chopped off for threshing while the stalk is given to the cattle. In ordinary years what remains on the field is grazed off by cattle or even burnt. When grass is scarce it is however carefully cut and preserved for fodder.

In irrigated land rice, instead of being dealt with as above, is usually sown in a seed bed, from which the young plants are transplanted into the remaining irrigated land. All the finer kinds of rice are produced by this method, which has the advantage of rendering land for which no water is available during the hot weather as valuable as perennially irrigated land. Pepper is similarly dealt with. "The agricultural features of the district" writes Mr. Goudge "vary of course with altitude and situation. The best class of cultivation and crop is found in villages of moderate altitude between 3,000 and 5,000 feet having access on the one hand to good forest and grazing ground and on the other to riparian fields in the depths of a river valley. Here all crops that can be raised in the Himalayas grow to perfection; a healthy elevated site is available for the dwelling-houses, and herds of cattle can be comfortably maintained. Generally it may be said that most of the villages in the district approximate more or less to this ideal; some have everything necessary, some have no forest, some are entirely upland with ample forest but no rich soil, some have the rich riparian cultivation but no grazing. These advantages and disadvantages compensate one another in a surprising manner and there is really far less diversity in the value of villages than one would at first suppose."

Crop-rotation.

The standard rotation observed throughout the *upraon* lands occupies a period of two years. Rice is sown in April and reaped in September. It is followed by wheat sown in October and reaped in April. Then *mandua* is sown in May and reaped in October after which the land remains fallow till next April. *Jhangora* is sometimes substituted for rice, and barley for wheat. Villages are divided into two portions, known locally as *sar*. One of these is apportioned to *mandua* and one to rice, so that the whole of the village lands are cultivated during the kharif. The *sar* in which the *mandua* happens to be, will remain fallow during the succeeding rabi season. In the following year the *mandua sar* will be sown with rice and the rice *sar* will be under *mandua*. Beans and vetches, such as *urd, mung, bhat* and *gahat* are sown in the kharif, chiefly only as subsidiary to *mandua* and with the object of preventing the exhaustion of the soil. The system of leaving fallow a whole block of land instead of scattered fields here and there, has its advantages when the cattle returned loose to graze on the remnants of the straw, and the grass that can be found on the terrace walls. For this reason half or nearly half the village will always be found apparently lying waste in the winter.

The above rotation is, however, practically confined to unirrigated land or land in which the irrigation is very poor. The irrigated land, lying as it usually does at the bottom of a valley, is as a rule the warmest in the village. Moreover, there is no risk if the rice is somewhat late. It is protected by the irrigation against any damage which might be done to late rice on dry land by an early cessation of the rains. The rice harvest begins at the top of the hills and goes down to the bottom, whereas the spring harvest proceeds in the opposite order. For these reasons in irrigated land it is always possible to grow two crops, one of rice and one of wheat, in the year; and as the rice is a deep-rooted crop and the wheat a short-rooted crop, while the process of irrigation in itself constitutes a dressing of the land, this rotation leaves little to be desired. However, the wheat crop in the cold weather, besides being poorer than in the corresponding unirrigated land (the native explanation of this is that the soil is too damp and cold), has a prejudicial effect on the quality and yield of rice, and is therefore not infrequently omitted altogether.

Manure. The cattle are kept in cow-sheds (called *goth* or *gaushala*) often the lower story of the house but now more commonly a separate building. They are bedded on oak leaves, and the litter mixed with the droppings of the cattle is taken out once or twice a year and spread on the fields immediately before the seed is sown. Leaf mould from the forests is also largely used. In *katil* and *ijran* the shrubs and grass are burnt and their ashes ploughed into the soil. After the crops have been cut, the straw is usually left standing in the fields. The cattle are then turned in to eat it down, or penned on the fields and fed with grass. In either case the operation of manuring is greatly simplified by keeping the cattle on the fields they are intended to enrich.

Crops. Throughout the greater part of the district there are as in the plains two harvests. But owing to the cooler climate the crops demand a longer period for their full development and are therefore sown somewhat earlier and reaped somewhat later than in the plains. The kharif is sown between April and June and reaped between September and November. Most of the crops are already well above the ground before the onset of the monsoon ; if this is delayed second sowings are often necessary. Dry rice for instance is sown as early as the beginning of April and sometimes by the end of March : it depends for its existence upon the rather uncertain storms that sweep across the hills from the north-west during April and May. These storms often go astray or fail altogether, so that dry rice is a most precarious crop and the cultivator is not unhappy if he gets only an eight-anna harvest. *Kauni* is the *kakwan* or *kagni* of the plains. It with *china* and maize comes to hand rather earlier than the main kharif crops. *China* and *kauni* are nominally 60 days' crops and are not infrequently reaped by the middle or end of July. Then follows *jhangora* about the middle of August: next *mandua* and rice in late September and October. Other important crops are the pulses *gahat, urd* and *bhat*, buck-wheat (*ugal*) and sugarcane. In Almora the latter is always

Kharif.

the giant *ganna* or *paunda*, and it is eaten as a fruit. *Chuwa* (amaranth) in the north is a crop of common occurrence and above about 6,000 feet it is the only kharif crop grown except in Bhot. In the lower hills *tur* takes the place of the *arhar* of the plains which it closely resembles except that it is sown in March and reaped with the main kharif crops.

Rabi.

The rabi crops are wheat, barley and mustard. The last mentioned flourishes best at low elevations and is commonly reaped some time before the main rabi crops. Ordinarily the rabi harvest lasts from the end of April to the middle of May : but it becomes later as greater altitudes are reached. Thus at 7,000 feet the spring crop does not ripen until June, and at 8,000 feet it comes to hand in July. In the snows Himalayan barley (*ua jao*), a beardless variety, is grown at 6,000 feet and upwards being followed in the kharif by *phapar* or *chuwa*. In the higher snow-valleys close to the glaciers a fine species of wheat known as *napal* is grown as a *kharif* crop. That is to say the seed is sown when the snow melts in May or early June (it would not benefit by being sown in the autumn and allowed to lie under the snow during the winter) and reaped in November, unless as sometimes happens heavy snow falls unusually early in the autumn and prevents the crop from being reaped at all. In the lower villages *masur* also is occasionally grown but gram is quite unknown.

Other crops.

The western portion of the Pali pargana, especially the Salts—Malla, Talla, Walla and Palla—produce much turmeric and pepper, very valuable crops which command a ready sale at Ramnagar. *Ugal*, a superior kind of buck-wheat which is used by Hindus on fast days, is also grown in the same region. In south-east Danpur besides turmeric and pepper, ginger is grown. These three valuable crops are also cultivated in less or greater degree throughout the district at suitable elevations and it is on one or more of these that many a cultivator depends for his revenue. The villages near Ranikhet and Almora make a considerable income out of the produce of their market gardens; potatoes and onions are the chief products, but all English vegetables are grown. The climate appears to be particularly suited to peas and cauliflowers. Among indigenous vegetables may be mentioned *pinalu,* yams, *baigans,* various scandent beans and pumpkins, both wild and cultivated. Wild asparagus, yams, onions, rhubarb and mint abound, the three latter in the higher ranges. Excellent water-cress is to be found by the sides of the smaller and less precipitous streams.

Hemp. Hemp is cultivated in the Gangoli and Chaugarkha parganas chiefly, and to a lesser extent in parts of Kali Kumaon. The ostensible objects of hemp cultivation are the fibre and the seeds. The former is used for the manufacture of ropes or of *bhangela* or sack-cloth, made into bags or clothing; from the latter oil is expressed, or they are used as a condiment, or eaten, fried with wheat. *Charas* is made from a resinous exudation from the ripe leaves, stems and seeds of the female plant. The manufacture of *charas* is now illegal but it is by no means extinct. The best fibre is produced from the male plant, and it is to be noted that the wild hemp is of little use for this purpose. The stalks are cut green, and dried for several days in the sun until they become quite brown. When they are sufficiently dry they are tied up into bundles and steeped for 15 or 16 days in pools or running streams, being kept under water by stones laid upon them. They are then taken out, beaten with wooden mallets, and again dried in the sun. The fibre is then peeled off from the thick end of the stalk to the top and after being cleaned is tied up into hanks for sale, or for the manufacture of sack-cloth. There is a certain prejudice against growing the plant. In Garhwal, the Khasiyas who grow and spin hemp do not wear the sacred thread, and similarly in the Almora district its cultivation is usually conducted by the Doms. The Khasiyas may however manufacture rope, and traffic in the seeds and fibre is not considered degrading to any caste, but the weaving of sack-cloth is left to the Kolis, a sub-division of the Doms.

Tea. In 1827 Dr. Royle drew attention to the prospects of a successful cultivation of tea in the mountains of Kumaon; in 1834 a committee which was appointed to investigate reported favourably and in 1835 tea seeds were procured from China and from them plants were raised in Calcutta and sent to Assam, Kumaon and Garhwal. Tea nurseries were established, and in the two latter districts they were placed under the superintendence of Dr. Falconer of the Botanical Gardens at Saharanpur. In the Almora district the selected site was Lachhmeswar near Almora town. In 1841 this garden contained 3,840 plants and in this year Dr. Falconer was able to report in very sanguine terms of the prospects of tea cultivation. He had contented himself with watching the growth of the plants and reproducing them, abstaining from any attempt to manufacture tea for which he had no skilled workers, and being unwilling to prejudice the industry by producing an inferior kind of tea. He applied for establishments of Chinese tea manufacturers for the nurseries in Garhwal and Kumaon. They arrived in April 1842. In December of the same year Dr. Falconer was compelled by bad health to leave India. He arrived in England in June 1843 taking with him the first specimen of Kumaon tea, which was very favourably received. Dr. Falconer was succeeded by Dr. Jameson, and under his management the tea plantations were greatly enlarged. It appeared however that the tea plants introduced into India in 1835 were not of the variety most approved in China, and to remedy this Mr. R. Fortune was in 1848 deputed by the Court of Directors to visit China. Mr. Fortune was most successful. "As the result of this mission" he says "nearly twenty thousand plants from the best black and green tea countries of Central China have been introduced to the Himalayas. Six first-rate manufacturers, two leadmen, and a large supply of implements from the celebrated Hwuy Chow districts, were also brought round, and safely located on the government plantations in the hills." Although Mr. Fortune took exception to some of the practices that had been followed, he reported in 1851 on the condition of the industry in sanguine terms mentioning in addition to the Lachhmeswar garden that at Hawalbagh acquired in 1841 by the Government from Major Corbett. He also seems to have visited a private plantation, called the Katyur garden, near Baijnath, an expansion of a four-acre garden planted by Captain (after Sir Henry) Ramsay in 1850. He described the soil and climate as admirably suited to the tea plant. Mr. Batten, the Commissioner, then formulated his proposals. He suggested that the Government should grant liberal loans to cultivators for the improvement of existing cultivation and prizes to those whose produce was of the best class. To this the Government agreed, but was unable to accept his third proposal, that for the remainder of the current settlement all leaf should be taken over by government factories at a uniform rate of Rs. 8 a maund. In 1864 and 1865 as opportunity offered the government tea estates (which were held to have accomplished their object of proving the possibility of profitable tea culture) were disposed of to private speculators. The hill cultivator has not been persuaded to grow tea as anticipated by Mr. Batten and what tea is now grown is the produce of the manufacturer's own estate.

The prospects of the industry in Kumaon are now dismal in the extreme. The Almora planters—in spite of the cart road built for their benefit in 1892 from Hawalbagh to Baijnath—cannot compete with Assam tea which is not handicapped by the same difficulty and expense in the matter of transport. The central Asian market has not been captured and with heavy Russian import duties on Indian tea and the monopoly of the Chinese trade in the hands of Tibetan officials who do their best to prevent the importation of Indian tea into Tibet, it cannot be expected that Kumaon tea will ever reach the heights of prosperity so confidently prophesied for it 50 years ago.

The manager of the Berenag tea company by a lucky chance discovered the secret of the manufacture of Chinese brick tea. His tea has been admitted by unprejudiced Bhotia traders to be far superior to the Chinese article imported into Western Tibet *via* Lhassa, and he is able to place it on the market at a price which is 50 per cent. below that demanded by the Tibetan official monopolists. In 1907 he disposed of about 12,000 pounds, but it is probable nevertheless that the conservative prejudices of the Tibetan and Bhotia consumers and the opposition offered by the Tibetan officials will before long close the market against Berenag brick tea altogether. There are now in the district 20 tea estates, some containing more than one plantation, with a total area under tea of 2,102 acres. The total produce in 1908 was 258,522 pounds of black tea and 18,057 pounds of green tea. The largest estate in the district is Malla Katyur with 506 acres and an output of 88,976 pounds ; next comes Kausani with 396 acres and 56,792 pounds. 1908 was a bad year, and the output in 1907 was 10 per cent. better. Lachhmeswar has now ceased to be cultivated as a tea garden, and Hawalbagh, now belonging to Lala Udai Nath Sah of Naini Tal, is much dilapidated. It produced in 1908 only 7,317 pounds of black and 1,195 pounds of green tea from an area of 187 acres.

Land tenures.

The system of land tenures in the hill differs radically from that which obtains in the plains. The Almora district like the rest of Kumaon is a land of small proprietary holdings, each man owning and tilling his own land. There are very few large zamindars, and those that exist in the Pali pargana approximate more to the type of superior proprietors with few legitimate rights beyond the collection from the real owners of the soil of an allowance for malikana. The other exception is that of grantees, tea planters and the like, but these are not indigenous. The term zamindar in the hills has not therefore the honorific significance which attaches to it in the plains: in fact it is frequently used self-deprecatingly in very much the same way as *ganwar* in the plains. It will be sufficient here to describe broadly the Kumaon land system, leaving the student of details to examine Mr. Stowell's "Manual of the land tenures of the Kumaon division." There are at present three classes of interest in land, held respectively by the *hissedar*, the *khaikar*, and the *sirtan*. The *hissedars* form the proprietary body. Usually each *hissedar* possesses an ascertained area of land. The village common or *gaon sanjait* is treated in various ways: it is made over to the village servants in part payment of their dues, or cultivated by the headman (*padhan*) on behalf of the village community, or leased to ordinary tenants. Each *hissedar* is responsible for the payment of the revenue of the whole village. The *hissedar* is free to sell or otherwise dispose of his holding but he can only transfer his interest in undivided *gaon sanjait* not specified fields in it. The other co-sharers of the village within the third degree can claim pre-emption against an outsider, and those related to him can claim against other village co-sharers less closely connected.

The *khaikar* is peculiar to the hills and deserves some notice. To understand his status it is necessary to remember that under the native kings the proprietary right in the land was vested in the Sovereign and inalienable. Grants were made by the Sovereign from time to time for the maintenance of deserving officers. These grants were however often made at the expenses of existing grants, which were thereby resumed : but the occupants were permitted to remain on the estate sinking into the position of cultivators called *khaikars* in distinction from *thatwan,* grantee. Mr. Batten derives the word *khaikar* from *khana* to eat and *kar* the royal revenue, that is, he may enjoy the land so long as he pays the revenue. The *khaikar* also paid certain dues in addition to the revenue. This class of *khaikar* partakes therefore of the nature of the under-proprietor of the plains. A second class (called formerly the *khurni* or *kaini*) consisted of new tenants settled on the estate by the grantee and never moved. The old name is now unfortunately obsolete and the term *khaikar* therefore connotes in one sense " under-proprietor " and in another " occupancy tenant " : and then is naturally the cause of much confusion, not always accidental. The *thatwan* is now replaced by the *hissedar,* often a *thokdar* or *sayana,* who does all he can to depress the *khaikar* of the first class to the status of the *khaikar* of the second class. Villages held by under-proprietors are usually purely *khaikari* villages : in these the *hissedar* has not been able to secure cultivating possession. He cannot in any way interfere with the *khaikars,* their lands or their cultivation : all he does is to collect the government revenue plus a *malikana.* If a *khaikar* dies without heirs his holding reverts to the village community. His interest is heritable but for some rather obscure reason not transferable. This limitation is probably the result of the confusion of terms. The *khaikar* of the second class is merely a permanent tenant paying the revenue plus *malikana.* Khaikars

The *sirtan* is literally a tenant who pays the *sirti* or government revenue. Formerly he used to pay nothing else. There are also two kinds of *sirtan.* The first consists of the descendants of old cultivators whose interest was subject to that of the *khaikars,* or *hissedars* ; these are probably in many Sirtans.

cases old *khurnis* or *kainis* who failed to get their rights properly recorded. They often claim a right of occupancy. The second class is the modern tenant at will with no claims to permanency, who cultivates by virtue of a lease. No mere length of tenure will save a *sirtan* from ejectment unless he happens to have broken up and reclaimed at his own expense the land which he holds.

Waste-land and forest.

In the Almora district rural phraseology has divided all land into two classes—measured and unmeasured, *nap* and *benap*. Measured land is land which has been measured at the settlement and recorded as the property of individuals. In Almora all areas once shewn as cultivated in the settlement maps and records are the property of individuals whether they have relapsed into forest or not : in Garhwal relapsed plots are numbered and recorded as the property of the State. Unmeasured land, whether forest, waste, or broken up for cultivation, is the property of the State by an indefeasible title which the present Government inherited from the Rajas and the Gurkhas, and which the people themselves have always admitted. But in 1880 Sambat, 1823 A.D. Mr. Traill made a great measurement of all land of every description in the district, fixing nominal boundaries for all villages and including inside the boundaries cultivated land, forest, and waste : though he affirmed the principle of the State's sole right in uncultivated land. These are called the *assi sal* boundaries but they are supposed to have existed from time immemorial. They represent approximately the area over which the village with the acquiescence of the State exercises rights of pasture and wood cutting. Waste land is brought under cultivation in two ways; if the land the cultivator wishes to break is of comparatively small extent and adjoins existing fields, he (with or without the permission of the Deputy Commissioner) extends his cultivation into it. Where the land is remote and large in area he makes formal application for a *nayabad* grant. Such a grant confers on the grantee the fullest proprietary rights. The *nayabad* question is an extremely difficult one: the adjustment of cultivation to population on the one hand and of cultivation to its necessary adjuncts,—pasture and forest—on the other, needs particularly delicate treatment.

Prices. The chief markets in the district are those of Almora, Ranikhet, Champawat, Pithoragarh and Dwarahat. The prices fixed at these markets for the vend and purchase of food grains have but little interest for the great majority of the people. They exist almost entirely for the convenience of the extremely small foreign and non-agricultural community. The people, as Sir H. Ramsay remarked so long ago as 1874, rarely export their grain. And the Board of Revenue, reviewing Mr. Goudge's settlement report, remarks: "It is hardly an exaggeration to say that the main object of cultivation in the hills is to provide food for people whose livelihood is derived from other occupations and who reside in a tract where the cost of importing grain is almost prohibitive." It must further be premised that a cultivator short of food will not repair to the nearest market, but to a friendly neighbour who will purvey him the necessary grain on much easier terms. The advance of prices in Almora is a most striking index of the progress of the district. Some 50 years ago wheat sold at 40 to 50 seers to the rupee : fine rice at 24 to 30 seers : coarse rice at 40 to 50. In 1908 (a famine year) wheat was selling at 5¼ seers. Excluding famine years modern prices would work out at about 10½ to 12 seers for wheat, 7½ to 10 seers for coarse rice, and 4½ to 7 seers for fine rice. At the same time, it is in the famine years alone, when prices are highest, that the hill-man is compelled to buy food grain.

Wages. The records of wages are, like those of prices, not a true criterion of the value labour is able to put upon its services. Much of the farm work is done by the Doms who are paid in grain in addition to certain annual gifts from their masters. An ordinary labourer in the district will content himself with 2½ or 3 annas a day, but in or near Almora or Ranikhet he will usually insist on four annas a day, though if paid by the month he will accept Rs. 5 or Rs. 6. The latter is the wage usually paid to the class of men who perform the duties of syce, messenger, water-carrier, *jhampani*, or garden-cooly—these services are performed by Khasiya Rajputs or Brahmans, generally of respectable land-owning families. Masons, carpenters or blacksmiths of ordinary intelligence get Rs. 10 or Rs. 12 a month;

a good man will easily command double that wage. The high wages demanded by labourers and artisans have rarely any connection with the prices. They merely indicate that the workmen are well off, sometimes own land of their own, and do not feel it worth their while to work for less. On the other hand it often happens that the spare man of a family of good standing will accept work for a wage that can hardly be remunerative, though it is always gladly accepted and treasured in the family coffers, the food necessary for the maintenance of the adventurer being sent from his home.

Weights and measures.

The *nali* sometimes identified with the *passeri* is the standard of capacity most commonly used. The *nali* of wheat weighs almost exactly two seers; most other grains weigh rather less, a *nali* of rice for instance weighing 1¾ seers. Twenty *muthis* (handfuls) make one *nali* and sixteeen *nalis* make one *pirai,* and twenty *nalis* one *rini.* In the hills the 80-tola seer and in the Bhabar the 100 seer maund are current. The *nali* again is the unit of superficial measure. A *nali* of land is the area in which one *nali* of wheat can be sown. Used as a measure of land the *nali* is sub-divided into sixteenths called annas. The superficial *nali* was standardised by Mr. Traill at 12 yards by 20 yards, or 240 square yards. Twenty *nalis* make a *bisi,* or 4,800 square yards, that is to say 40 square yards short of an acre. The long side of the superficial *nali* is Mr. Traill's 20-yard *jarib* or chain. In the Bhabar,* the land measures follow the use of the plains and there 20 *kachwansis* make one *biswansi* and 20 *biswansis* make one *biswa* and 20 *biswas* make one *bigha.*

The *timasha* is often mentioned. It was originally one-fifth of a rupee and is now considered the same as three annas. It figures occasionally in lists of feudal dues exacted by *thokdars* and represents a now extinct currency. The Gurkha rupee is obsolete; it was worth 12 annas of British coinage, and it occasionally survives in certain semi-religious or ceremonial payments. Thus the price of a bride is usually reckoned in Gurkha rupees.

Food of the people.

Mandua is the staple food of the ordinary rural classes, either boiled into a porridge or ground into flour and made into

* Now transferred to the Naini Tal district.

bread. Wheat and rice are however much more generally eaten than they used to be. Formerly the cultivators used to live on the kharif crop and pay their revenue out of the produce of their *rabi*, but now that the pressure of the population upon the land is so great in many parganas the people eat all that their field brings forth at both harvests. Fish and vegetables and the meat of goats and short-tailed hill sheep are gratefully accepted by all. Even the Brahman with rare exceptions freely indulges in a flesh diet. Fruits and vegetables wild and cultivated greatly supplement the more generally recognized food staples. Mention should be made of the amaranth or *chuwa*. Its leaves are boiled with a little grain and eaten gladly by the cultivators whose stock has run down; in extreme cases in years of scarcity the people have been known to live on nothing but the leaves until the advent of their first crop, but food of this kind is liable to cause diarrhoea. Wild nettles too are used as a spinach. The hill man is indeed specially blessed by the presence in almost every jungle of fruit, vegetables or roots to help him over a period of moderate scarcity.

Famines.

The heavy rainfall of the hills insures them to a great measure against the periodical crop failures which so devastate the plains, and on the rare occasions when both the monsoon and the storms of local origin fail the strong financial position of the people generally carries them over the failure of a single crop. Famines of some importance however occurred in 1868 and 1878, of which the records have been lost. In 1889 the monsoon, though copious, was untimely and the *mandua*, *mandira*, *kangni* and *bhat*, which form the staple food of the agricultural population, were very short. The rice crop was also deficient. The scanty autumn harvest was followed by a complete failure of the usual cold weather storms, except in the *pattis* immediately below the snowy range. Those inhabitants of the southern parganas who had no Bhabar cultivation found themselves without food, though by no means without money. Whenever the district is visited by scarcity, Pali will always be found in the greatest distress, and in this instance it provided no exception to the general rule. It was decided to import grain at the Government's expense and to sell it to purchasers at depôts established at Bhikia Sen, Dwarahat,

Almora and Champawat. Operations began in March 1890. A capital of Rs. 18,000 was employed, and so brisk was the business and so large the turnover that in all 12,102 maunds of grain were bought at the sub-montane marts, imported, and sold for cash or credit. In 1892 a deficient rabi following a bad kharif again reduced the food stores of the people to a very narrow margin. The measures which had proved so successful in 1890 were again adopted. Pali as usual was in worst case, and depôts were opened at Gujarghati, at Ranikhet, and at Mohan at the foot of the hills, thirteen miles east of Ramnagar. Later in June a similar depôt was opened at Devi Dhura for the advantage of the eastern parganas. It was thought the people had probably not entirely recovered from the scarcity of 1890 and preparations were therefore made for the issue of grain on credit. To prevent confusion at the depôts a system of grain credit orders was devised. Practically every man in the hills is a landed proprietor *(hissedar)*, an under proprietor or occupancy tenant *(khaikar)* and therefore possesses good credit, measured by the amount of the land he holds. The remainder of the population are the village menials who were once the chattels of the proprietary body and whose claims to support are now always most generously admitted. The district officers issued to villagers orders for grain bearing a value proportionate to that of their holdings, and the villagers themselves proceeded to the depôts and thence received grain to that value. But in order to render credit unattractive, grain was also sold for cash at rates 12½ per cent. lower than the credit rates ; and in order to induce the people who had acquired grain on credit to pay up promptly, borrowers repaying before the end of November receive a discount of one anna in the rupee. In all 3,589 maunds of grain worth Rs. 10,968 were sold for cash, and 5,505 maunds worth Rs. 22,921 were advanced on credit, and it was calculated that no less than 11,665 persons had been relieved. For the benefit of the destitute and creditless a road work between Danpau and Siuni was opened, but no gratuitous relief was given. In 1894 local distress in the Malla Danpur *patti* was met by cash advances.

1907-1908. The rains of 1907 began late and closed very early throughout the centre and south of the district. The kharif therefore was generally an extremely poor crop. The rabi, where sown, failed to germinate, and though the sky was often overcast rain held off and the people began to lose heart. In December the existence of scarcity was officially recognized and test works were opened at Bhikia Sen in the centre of Pali, and near Hawalbagh. The people did not however take readily to the labour thus offered, chiefly no doubt because those who were really hard up in Pali could get more remunerative work in the forests while those living near Hawalbagh could earn a day's pay whenever they liked by carrying a load of wood or a bundle of grass into Almora. Good rain or snow fell throughout the district during the second week of January; the seed which had lain dormant in the earth for two months or more now began to germinate, while tracts which had been too hard and dry to be worked at the proper season were ploughed and sown, wherever the warmth of the locality promised a speedy development of the crop. Heavier rain fell at the end of the month and hope everywhere revived. Relief works were abandoned and the ordinary rural occupations were resumed. February and March however remained dry, and the tender young growth of the crops sown in January withered. In the middle of March it was recognized that the produce of the spring harvests could not go far towards replenishing the food stocks so diminished by the failure of the rice and millet crops in the autumn. The people began to clamour for the import of grain and recourse was had to the grain order system. It was decided that orders should be met at the foot of the hills and that no grain should be imported into the interior; it was thought that this condition placed on the supply of grain on credit would act as an automatic test to separate the really needy from those not yet at the end of their resources. No man who was not hungry, it was argued, would undertake the wearisome journey to the foot of the hills in the hot weather. Depôts were therefore opened at Ramnagar, for the Pali pargana and the west of Barahmandal, the most seriously affected tract in the whole of the district; at Haldwani for the south and south centre of the district, and at Tanakpur for the south-east of the district. Officers were continually moving round the district and meeting the villagers to whom they issued grain orders, and the villagers themselves proceeded to the sub-montane markets with them. These were met by subsidised traders who took advances of money from the Government. In all Rs. 2,30,000 worth of grain was thus advanced, the cash value being recoverable in four instalments extending over a period of two years. The system worked excellently and was without doubt the most effective means that could have been employed to meet the grain scarcity within the hills. The only point at which criticism may assail it is that it failed to make any provision for those who had money to spend. Probably, if grain had been made available for cash sales at a somewhat cheaper rate than that accepted in converting the cash values of the orders into grain, the hill people would have produced their money instead of falling into debt. As it was cash rates were as high as credit rates, and most people, even if they had money, succumbed to the temptation to acquire grain on credit.

The grain order system was supplemented by the opening of a number of works in various portions of the district. Two extremely useful cart roads, that from Gujarghati on the Ramnagar-Ranikhet cart road to Bhikia Sen and a forest road intended to facilitate the import of fuel into the town and station of Almora, were taken in hand; the former was not finished when famine operations were closed. Other useful works were a number of bridle paths, forest walls to enclose and protect plantations, and tree guards on the road sides. These cost in all Rs. 32,939. Five aided works at a cost of Rs. 3,450 were also completed, consisting of irrigation channels, *guls*, and *bandhs* to protect village land, in or near stream beds, from erosion. For the very young and the very old, infirm, maimed or blind, gratuitous relief to the extent of Rs 21,489 was administered. As in former years no large departmental works were undertaken; the obstacles in the way of such work are difficulties in the matter of sanitation and the supply of drinking water, and the Kumaon custom that women shall not work except in their own fields. Moreover field operations in the hills must be conducted throughout the hot weather, and it was not thought advisable to remove the people from their homes. For these reasons also the wages were raised above the rates sanctioned by the Famine Code in order to leave a margin sufficient for the support of women and children left in the villages. Only in the case of aided works, which were in all cases small and did not attract labour from beyond their immediate vicinity, were the wages kept at a lower standard.

The scarcity was by no means universal. The people owning the rich *seras* of Giwar and the Danpuris generally made great profit by the sale of their surplus stock, and the latter are said to have brought out grain hoarded against such an opportunity for many years.

Besides tea-making, the only industries of importance in the district are the manufacture of baskets and matting from the ringal bamboo, and hemp and wool weaving. The first is almost entirely restricted to certain *pattis* of pargana Danpur, especially Malla Danpur. The ringal must be cut when it is leafless, and most of the people are occupied in this work through the winter. Excellent matting for floors is turned out, and baskets of all sorts are made especially the box-basket termed *kandi*, which is sometimes furnished with hinges and a lock and strengthened by being covered with an untanned skin. These are all sold at the annual Bageswar fair. Industries.

The fibre of the hemp having been extracted in the manner already described on page 51 is spun on a wheel into yarn and then woven into narrow strips of cloth. This cloth is extremely durable and makes very stout bags; and in the form of wearing apparel it is much appreciated by the people of the middle hills. The hemp weavers are invariably Kolis, a sub-division of the Doms.

The people of most of the northern *pattis* spin and weave the wool of their indigenous sheep. The staple is short and the texture of the wool coarse and only the roughest of blankets can be woven. These are rarely sold being required in almost all cases entirely for the use of the weaver and his family. The Bhotias are the great weavers of the district. For the finer work they use the wool of the Tibetan sheep; this they weave either into a kind of rough serge from which they make their clothes, or into wraps. The coarser wool, often the shearings of their own pack animals, is woven into blankets. The spinning is all done by hand and no Bhotia driving his pack animals along the roads, or northern shepherd tending his flock, is ever seen without his constantly revolving spindle. As soon as he has finished his march for the day, usually about 9 a.m., and tended his animals, the Bhotia sets up his loom and spends the rest of the day weaving. Weaving is also the constant occupation of the women and children left behind in the sub-alpine camps. The Bhotias in addition to the manufacture of woollen cloth and blankets can also produce a very creditable imitation of the Tibetan rugs. In 1909 a weaving school was opened at Almora, chiefly with the object of introducing an industry which might in some sort relieve the great pressure on the land. Pupils to the number of 30 are attracted by the offer of a stipend of Rs. 6 a month, and though the school is still in the experimental stage, the Bhotias are beginning to attend in small numbers, and they note with keen interest the demonstrations given at the annual Bageswar fair. It is hoped that each of the pupils will in course of time become an expert in all the processes of weaving, and act in his own village as a centre for the diffusion of the art; and that ultimately small factories will be established in various parts of the district where the excess population may find in the industry a subsistence which they now extract with difficulty from the over-burdened land. At present some 12,000 maunds of wool are exported annually to Cawnpore, whence some of it is again imported into the hills in the form of rugs and broad-cloth. The factory will do good if it only meets the local demand for woollen goods.

A few people living by the banks of the Sarju and Kali rivers in Kali Kumaon make catechu out of the *khair* tree, and derive a very fair profit from the industry. They pay a license fee of Rs. 30 a still to the Government, and the average annual receipts from each still may be taken at Rs. 70.

Tibetan trade.

The Bhotias, a race of Mongolian extraction, enjoy the monopoly of the trade with Tibet, and they are quite the most prosperous class in the whole of the district. The traffic is burdened with many complicated taxes imposed by the Tibetans and still, notwithstanding the Treaty of Lhassa, paid by the Bhotias without demur.

The Johari Bhotias use the Untadhura pass which is open only in June, July and August. This pass surmounted, the trader has the choice of two routes, the eastern and most direct over the Jauti and Kungri Bigri passes (the latter marking the frontier) and the northern, across the Girthi river over the Ungi pass and thence by a low and easy pass into Tibet. The draw-back to the first route is that all three passes, though very severe, must be crossed in one day between sunrise and sunset, for there are no camping grounds or grazing facilities in between. **Joharis.**

First however a Tibetan envoy called *satu* comes to enquire if there is any disease of man or beast in the Bhotia villages; being assured that there is none he opens the passes but not before the preliminary due of 90 *bhelis* of gur or Rs. 45 in cash, called *la-thal* and considered by the Bhotias a grazing tax, has been paid at Milam to the *sarji*, a messenger deputed, like the *satu*, by the Jongpen of Daba. The *sarji* also exacts a poll tax of three annas a head on every man, woman or child other than the Bhotias, that is to say on Ladakhis, Bashahris, Khampas and down-country Kumaonis. The Johari Bhotias pay nothing but the *la-thal*. No further taxes are levied on persons going from Milam to Tibet by the Untadhura pass. The *la-thal* is collected by the headman of Milam who in consideration of his services is allowed one riding pony and one pack pony, and free supplies of food and fodder during his trading sojourn in Tibet. Originally all Tibetans used to pay *choo-thal* or one-tenth part of all goods brought in from Tibet to Milam. This was paid at Milam to the Milamwal *kamin* or headman. The Tibetans never raised any objection to the tax, but some forty years ago the British Government ordered that *choo-thal* should not be levied. The marts to which the Johari Bhotias resort in Tibet are Gyanema, Chakara, Shib Chilam, Khiungling, Darchan, and Gartok; of these the first and the last are the biggest.

The route used by the Darma Bhotias crosses the Himalayan water-shed at the Darma pass, which remains open during June, July and August, but is now, owing to cracks in the glaciers, rather dangerous. Formerly the inhabitants of Malla and Talla Darma and Askot used to trade with Tibet, but of recent years **Darma.**

only the Malla Darma people are allowed to enter the country. The taxes they pay are *sa-thal* or land revenue at the rate of 51 *bhelis* of *gur* for each of the four quarters of Darma, that is to say 204 *bhelis*, worth Rs. 102, and some food, drink and cloth. This is collected by the Political Peshkar and by him handed over to the servant of the Barkha Tarjum in Tibet, whither the Darma people themselves carry it. Further the Barkha Tarjum sends 200 goats laden with salt which the Darma people have to take; they give in exchange three loads of grain for one of salt.

Byans. The Bhotias of Byans have two passes. The Lankpya Lekh open for four months—June, July, August and September—is used by the people of Kuthi Gyanema and Darchan. The Lipu Lekh, open all the year round but not much used in January and December, is the best and easiest pass of all; the trader following this route must take his wares to Taklakot or Darchan. The Chaudansis also use the Lipu Lekh Pass. Very heavy taxes are levied by the Tibetans. *Sa-thal* is taken both in cash and grain; Kuthi for instance pays 350 seers of grain. Every village also pays Rs. 3 or Rs. 4 under the head *sa-thal*. A goat tax called *loog-thal* is exacted from every village without reference to the actual number of goats; it amounts to about Re. 1-8-0 on each village. The Tibetans also take cloth, fuel, timber, liquor, vegetables and food (*sattu* and *puris*). All these taxes are collected by the Political Peshkar and are paid by him to the Nirbah (or clerk) of the Taklakot Jongpen at Gunji for Malla Byans and at Garbyang for Talla Byans. Further *la-thal* is paid to the Thiti Makpen in the form of grain, cash, and food from each village in Malla and Talla Byans. After entering Tibet the Bhotia traders pay *chung-thal* or trade tax.

Besides these dues Byans and Chaudans trader have to pay to the Jongpen 45 boxes of grain (each box containing about 30 seers) when they reach Taklakot. This tax is called *naika* in Tibet. The traders of Kuthi in Byans and some other Byansis, though they pay their dues to the Jongpen of Taklakot, pursue their trade at Gyanema. There the Barkha Tarjum takes a money payment, except from the Kuthi people who pay nothing but the *la-thal*.

The existence of, and the necessity for, these various imposts is explained by the administrative system of Tibet. The minor officials buy their appointments at Lhassa and live on what they can wrest from the people under their care. They hold their offices for a brief period only and they are anxious to make their fortunes as soon as possible. To this day they claim a species of sovereignty over the country inhabited by the Bhotias, and their claim is always admitted by the Bhotias themselves. Until quite recently the latter used to lay their quarrels before the Tibetan tribunals for settlement; and when a few years ago the British Government decreed that no taxes were to be paid to the Tibetans, the latter promptly replied by closing the trade routes. Their action reduced the Bhotias to the verge of ruin, and at their earnest request they were permitted to pay the Tibetans their demands and to engage once more in trade. The taxes levied on the various clans of Bhotias appear capricious, and so indeed they are; for they are imposed not by the central authority but by local officers commanding different passes, who know best how much they can afford to ask.

Exports and imports.

The chief exports are food grains, such as wheat, and barley, rice, *mandua,* and *jhangora,* brass, copper and iron, sugar, tobacco, and silver treasure; and the imports are borax, salt, wool, raw and manufactured, yaks' tails, ponies, sheep and goats. Tibet produces very little grain and depends for its food almost entirely on imports from India, which are very considerable. The most important of the imports from Tibet are salt, wool and borax. The trade in the first is fast declining. Formerly on their return to India the Bhotias used to get three measures of grain for one of salt. When borax was booming, they neglected salt, and their former customers were compelled to use salt from the plains for which they acquired a taste. The Tibetan salt does not compare favourably with salt from the plains; and it is is now in small demand among the people of the upper *pattis.* The Bhotia therefore never brings down salt if he can get anything else, but he will not of course return empty handed. The borax trade also has of recent years yielded to the competition of Italian borax. These disadvantages however are more than compensated by the great advance in the wool trade. In 1907, the total imports of wool reached the enormous figure of 11,925 maunds: in 1840, there was practically no demand and only 22 maunds of wool were brought down by the Bhotias. The Cawnpore Woollen Mills now keep an agent at Tanakpur who enters into contracts with the Bhotias and gives them advances for the purchase of wool in Tibet.

The Bhotias enter Tibet at the beginning of June, carrying their goods on pack animals, goats, sheep, yaks and their mules with domestic cattle called jabbu and garjo, ponies, and occasionally bullocks; but the larger animals rarely descend below the upper depôts. The richer traders take money with them also, but the poorer are compelled to do business by barter chiefly: a less profitable system, for it means that as a smaller weight of salt, borax or wool is given in exchange for grain, some of their animals must return without a load. Certain marts are apportioned to the various passes, and within these marts the Bhotia trader can do business only with his established correspondent. The pressure of trade is now, it is said, breaking down this old custom, particularly at Taklakot. In the season, which lasts for a short period only, the Bhotias will make two or three journeys from their base depôts. They dispose of the salt they import from Tibet to the inhabitants of the upper *pattis*, and as the winter advances they begin to export the remainder of their Tibetan merchandise to the south. The villages in the upper valleys are deserted early in November, snow rendering them uninhabitable, and the Bhotias establish camps for their women and children, and depôts for their stock in trade, at various points along their road through the upper midland parganas. On their way to these depôts and on the further journey to the south, excursions are usually made into the villages on either side of the route which purchase such salt and wool as they require. Finally the merchandise which has not been disposed of on the way reaches the plains at Haldwani, Tanakpur, or Ramnagar where it is sold for cash, or exchanged for grain at advantageous rates. Two or three journeys are sometimes necessary before the goods left in the depôts are finally disposed of: and on the return journeys the Bhotias often carry up grain or salt for up-country *banias*. The Bhotia never gives his animals any grain, and the result of this practice is that they require the greater part of the day for grazing. The day's journey is by consequence extremely short, seldom exceeding six or seven miles, and is always over by 9 or 10 a. m. in all weathers.

Formerly few Bhotias ventured farther south than Bageswar or Almora; there they disposed of their imports and thence they took back the grain desired by the Tibetans. The system has now changed. The Bhotias prefer to deal directly with the *banias* of the sub-montane markets and thus they avoid the middleman's profits; while the central portions of the pargana have no longer spare grain sufficient to feed the Tibetans. Bageswar and Thal are however still fairs of some importance, but the former is no longer the rich market it once was, while at the latter the Bhotias do little more than dispose of their unsold wool, settle their accounts with the *banias,* and meet the Government officers to whom they pay their land revenue.

Present position of the trade.

Traffic registration posts have been established at Milam for the Johar Passes, and at Dharchula for those of Byans and Chaudans. The figures for exports and imports furnished by the clerks in charge of these posts are not perhaps strictly accurate; if anything they under-estimate the extent of the trade. The value of the imported wool alone for 1907 was over two lakhs of rupees; and the borax was worth about the same. In addition to the principal imports already mentioned, a large number of Tibetan sheep and goats are brought into the district, not for pack purposes, for they cannot stand the heat of the Bhabar, but for food; they are sold chiefly to butchers in Almora and Ranikhet. The exports are undoubtedly understated; silver treasure is an instance. The Bhotias do not in all cases spontaneously declare the amount of money they take with them, and it cannot be guessed. Pearls and precious stones to the value of Rs. 25,000 are returned; but these also are small commodities liable to escape notice. The best proof of the present prosperity of the trade lies in its enormous advance since 1840, and more particularly in the last three or four years due, in the latter case, to the good effect produced by the Treaty of Lhasa and the visit to Tibet of Mr. Sherring, the Deputy Commissioner. Many down-country traders would gladly pay any dues to be allowed to trade, and a small number now venture over the Johar pass; but they do not know the language or possess the necessary transport animals, nor have they acquired business connections in Tibet; and many more are deterred by the report, sedulously spread by the Bhotias, that the Tibetans will not trade with people who cannot eat with them.*

Internal Trade.

Grain beyond requirements for home consumption is either disposed of by the hill cultivators to the Bhotias from whom they take a cash price or, more frequently, salt or wool from Tibet, or else it is sent to one of the small markets, or perhaps to Almora itself. Few parganas however have any surplus grain for sale. The Salams grow considerable quantities of the fine *bansmatti* rice which they sell to the *banias* of the Almora bazar. Sira and Shor, the granary of Kumaon, find a market for their surplus wheat and rice at Pithoragarh, where the Mission creates a considerable demand, or at Almora itself. The small bazars of Champawat and Lohaghat are now somewhat decayed, the former with the decline of the borax trade and the latter with the removal of the garrison; they still however do a little business in cloth and grain, the latter bought from the neighbouring villages and sold chiefly to the official population of Champawat, the head quarters of the Tahsildar. Potatoes are grown on a large scale by a European planter in Kali Kumaon, and also in Dwarsyun, Riuni, Mahruri, Uchyur and Bisaud, for the benefit of the people of Ranikhet and Almora. Pali, with the exception of the Giwars, consumes all and more than it can produce; many of the *pattis* however specialise in valuable crops such as turmeric and chillies, and *ugal*, a superior kind of buck-wheat much appreciated by Hindus on fast-days. These the cultivators carry down to the Ramnagar bazar and either sell for cash or barter for other commodities of which they stand in need. In Pali all the chief roads are dotted with shops, the owners of which, in addition to retailing ordinary articles of food to wayfarers, often buy up the more valuable produce of their neighbourhood and convey it to Ramnagar on their ponies, thus acting as middlemen between the cultivators and the traders. Shor also produces a fair amount of *ugal* and

* V page 99.

Kali Kumaon turmeric and ginger; these are all either sold to the Bhotias or carried down to Tanakpur bazar.

The pastoral regions of the district are the parganas of Danpur, Shor, Sira, and *pattis* Dolphat and the two Tikhuns in pargana Barahmandal. The people keep large herds of cattle, from the milk of which they prepare *ghi*. This is sold in Almora or Ranikhet, or in the Bhabar marts. Among jungle products which command a ready sale may be mentioned honey, ringal bamboo stems, used according to size for fishing rods, walking-sticks, pipe-stems and pens, *phulel*, a saponaceous fat expressed from the seeds of the *churi* or butter tree (*bassia butyracea*), mosses and lichens, medicinal plants such as chiretta, horns, skin and a little musk. Most of the articles are sold at the periodical fairs or brought in to the Almora bazar.

Many of the villages dispose of a certain quantity of their valuable crops, such as chillies, turmeric, and ginger to their less-favoured neighbours for food grains. Villages which contentrate their efforts on these special crops are often hard-pressed in time of scarcity and only obtain their food after rather complicated transactions, which involve their bartering their chillies for *gur* in the Bhabar marts and then again exchanging the *gur* for *mandua* or some other food grain from their neighbours in the hills.

The Bhabar trade.

The chief commodities for the supply of which Almora is dependent on outside markets are cloth, sugar, and salt. The northerners get salt through the agency of the Bhotias, but there is an increasing tendency to reject the somewhat contemned Tibetan article for salt imported from the plains. Villages therefore which have a superabundance of food grain usually bargain with the Bhotias on their return from the Bhabar markets, and acquire salt and sugar in return for wheat and rice, which the Bhotias again export to Tibet. If their wealth consists of chillies, turmeric, or the like, they will usually carry it down themselves for sale or exchange, and carry up their year's supply of salt, sugar and iron themselves, or they will dispose of it to roadside shopkeepers. Most ordinary householders however make at least one journey to the Bhabar. Imports are nearly always for personal and home consumption. In times of scarcity the purchases also include grain, and the journeys then become greatly multiplied, for a family cannot generally carry up more grain than will suffice for the food of a single month. It is during such seasons of semi-famine that the owners of pack animals reap a golden harvest. They are generally plains Muhammadans or Kumhars and they drive ponies or mules which, though in poor condition, are capable carriers.

Communications. Railway.

The Rohilkhand and Kumaon Railway approaches the district at three points but possesses no station within it. Kathgodam is the terminus of a metre gauge line from Bareilly, which was opened for traffic in 1884. More important to the Almora district than the terminus is the thriving mart of Haldwani which gives its name to a station some four miles south of Kathgodam. In 1907 a branch from Moradabad with its terminus at Ramnagar was completed. A cross line connects Ramnagar with Lalkua on the Bareilly-Kathgodam line. Kathgodam and Ramnagar are both in the Naini Tal district and they tap the south-centre and west of the district, respectively. The east of the district depends chiefly upon Pilibhit, a station on the main Lucknow, Bhojipura and Bareilly section of the Rohilkhand and Kumaon railway. An extension of the line as far as Tanakpur, an important mart in the Bhabar, is under construction.

Roads.

A list of the roads in the district will be found in the appendix, arranged in accordance with an official classification, devised to describe cart roads metalled and bridged throughout at one end of the scale, and the roughest, steepest and narrowest hill tracks at the other. The best bridle paths are usually about ten feet wide, carefully graded and aligned and carried by bridges over all considerable streams. All such paths however have a tendency towards narrowness when carved out of solid rock, and as the rock is frequently part of a precipice overhanging a formidable gulf the practice of economy in this respect is not to be commended. The roads of the district will here be considered in two classes: those connecting portions of the district with the plains and those which are merely internal communications or connect the district with its neighbours to the east and west.

From Ramnagar.

Ramnagar lies thirteen miles west of the small bazar of Mohan, the nearest place in the Almora district. A good partly metalled cart road runs from Ramnagar along the right bank of the Kosi river as far as Kumaria. Thence it slowly ascends the ridge which forms the northern watershed of the Kosi. The ascent comes to an end a short way above Tuta Am, and thence the road continues almost level as far as Ranikhet. Inspection bungalows of the public works department have been built at Kumaria, Tuta Am (" the broken mango "), Machor and Ranikhet, and there are camping grounds for carts at various points, such as Tuta Am, Gujarghati, Danpao, Siuni where there is also a forest bungalow, and Tarkhet. The road was originally made for the convenience of the cantonment at Ranikhet; but with the extension of the railway to Kathgodam and the opening of the cart road from the Naini Tal brewery to Ranikhet, a cheaper and more speedy connection was established. For years the road carried very little traffic. The opening of the Ramnagar station has however invested it with new importance, and much of the grain imported into Ranikhet from the west of the United Provinces or the Punjab is now carried along this road. Two branch cart roads are worthy of remark: the first is a forest road which leaves the military cart road at Mohan and thence surmounting by a low pass the dividing range between the Kosi and the western Ramganga rivers terminates at Chaknakal, a distance of seven miles from Mohan. It is continued by a bridle path which crosses the Ramganga at Marchula and then following the Deogadh torrent skirts the eastern boundary of the Garhwal district. The Ramganga is rarely fordable and wayfarers from all parts of the Salt *pattis* meet by converging paths at the Marchula bridge whence they follow the bridle path and the cart road. The second road diverges from the military cart road at Gujarghati and runs down a ridge bounding the Naurargadh on the west, almost due north nearly as far as Bhikia Sen, a small but busy bazar, situated some eleven miles from Gujarghati. Up to 1908 merely a bridle path existed, but this was widened and where necessary realigned by famine labour, and it is now feasible for light cart traffic. From Mohan again a fair bridle path crosses the southern ridge in a north-eastern direction. It then drops gently down in the valley of the Ramganga. This road traverses the Salt *pattis*, and skirts the northern edge of the Kaklasauns near Bhikia Sen where it meets the light cart road from Gujarghati. As far as Masi it runs between the two Nayas and thence passes through the middle of Talla Giwar as far as Ganai always following the valley of the Ramganga.

This in the reverse direction was the old pilgrim route followed by the pious returning via Pandwakhal from the great shrines at Kedarnath and Badrinath in Garhwal. When the railway was opened from Bareilly, Kathgodam station became their objective, most of the pilgrims being anxious to reach the railway as soon as possible, and they used to leave the district via Dwarahat, Majkhali and Khairna. Now however that the Moradabad branch of the Oudh and Rohilkhand Railway has been extended to Ramnagar, the pilgrims have reverted to the original road, and when the last two miles of the Bhikia Sen Gujarghati road are completed it will be thronged with carts carrying in comfort over the last stages the aged, the sick and the weary. Pilgrim dharamsalas and hospital have been projected at suitable points.

The roads described chiefly benefit the pargana of Pali Pachaon, the most densely populated and cultivated sub-division of the district. Its thus finds an easy outlet for the pepper crops for which it is famous.

From Haldwani.

Access to the centre of the district is made possible for heavy goods by the cart road through Bhawali and Khairna up to Ranikhet. Only the last section of about 15 miles is within the boundaries of Almora. The road enters the district by a fine iron girder bridge across the Kosi and steadily ascends the Sher Danda ridge through the Chaugaon and Malli Doti *pattis*. It is metalled and bridged throughout but in the lower portion owing to the absence of shade and the sandy nature of the soil is usually inches deep in dust. The district forest department once proposed to plant or sow trees in broad belts on each side of the road, but the project was not received with favour by the public works department. There are large camping grounds at Bhujan near Khairna, and at

Bamsyun six miles higher up; and an inspection house at the last place. From Khairna to Ranikhet the hillmen and loaded coolies usually follow a rough path along the Kuchgadh stream. Beyond the Ranikhet dâk bungalow the road bifurcates. Heavy goods taking the branch to the left strike the Ramnagar cart road at Ganiadeo, and thence turning to the right make their way round tho foot of the hill into the bazar. Travellers and their property, the regiments and their kit, keep to the main road. From Ranikhet the road follows the ridge to the north of the Kosi through Majkhali gradually descending to the river near Hawalbagh. From Hawalbagh a road made in 1892 for the benefit of the tea gardens runs up the right bank of the Kosi through Someswar to Baijnath, while the main road winds gently up the Sitoli ridge and terminates in Almora. The foot traveller can materially shorten his journey to Almora by leaving the cart road at Majkhali and following a path which meets the Almora-Garhwal road at Daulat-ghat.

Fifteen miles to the north-east of Ranikhet lies the large village of Dwarahat which supports a market of some local importance. This is connected with Ranikhet by a good bridle path which descends the slope to the north at a gentle gradient, crosses the Gagas river at Darmad, and after winding among a maze of low bare hills meets the old pilgrim road about a mile east of Dwarahat. From Dwarahat, Ganai lies ten miles to the north on that road, while a good bridle path runs due east as far as Someswar 12 miles away. The pilgrim route, till lately, followed the road to Almora for about five miles and then turned south through Majkhali, skirting the western slopes of Siahi Devi and descending to the Kosi valley at Kakarighat where it left the district.

Another path leaves Ranikhet near the rifle range and descends through the forest to the Gagas river near Silor Mahadeo: there it bifurcates. A rough tract follows the Gagas river to Bhikia Sen, while a rather better path to the right terminates at Pali village. There it meets the lower road to Garhwal, which passes through Masi in the Ramganga valley three miles to the west.

To Almora.

People travelling afoot or riding ponies and pack animals follow the bridle path to Almora. It leaves the Naini Tal cart road at Ranibagh and passing Bhim Tal, Ramgarh and Peora, all in Naini Tal, enters the Almora district by a bridge over the Sual river at Gurari. Thence a toilsome ascent has to be faced before the station is reached. The distance from Ranibagh to Almora is 35 miles; of the total length only five miles are in the Almora district.

Almora to the north.

From Almora two main roads afford communication with Bhot. The first is the well-known Pindari glacier route which leaves Almora by the Kalimat hill, and descends gradually to the bungalow at Takula which marks the first stage of 15 miles. The journey is however sometimes broken at the Dinapani forest bungalow seven miles from Almora. From Kaparkhan beyond Dinapani a loop diverges to the right and proceeds to Binsar, rejoining the main road at Takula. From Takula the traveller crossing the high ridge of Dewaldhar descends steeply to the valley of the Sarju, and following the right bank of the stream reaches Bageswar, a distance of eleven miles from Takula. From Bageswar, a branch roads run to Someswar on the south-west, 15 miles, and to Baijnath on the north-west following the Gumti river, 13 miles. Two roads with a general easterly direction ascend the water-parting ridge between the Sarju and the Eastern Ramganga descending into the valley of the latter stream at Nachni and Thal, respectively; crossing the river, the former continues eastwards to Mawani in the Gori valley, down which runs a road from Munsiari to Askot, while the latter proceeds direct to Askot. The main road pursues its course along the Sarju river to Kapkot, a distance of 13½ miles. Here there is a dâk bungalow. The next stage is Loharkhet. From Loharkhet onwards, bungalows have for the convenience of travellers been placed at half stages: at Dhakuri 6 miles; Khati 5 miles; Dwali 7 miles; Phurkiya 3 miles. Thence to the foot of the glacier is a distance of four miles. The second route is that followed by the Bhotias to and from Milam in Johar. It leaves the first at Kharbagar near Kapkot 40 miles from Almora. From this point the road turns to the north-east crossing the Sarju river by a suspension bridge. Shama is 8 miles and Tejam on the eastern Ramganga 16 miles further on. From

Tejam the road follows the valley of the Jankuli, one of the main feeders of the Ramganga, and ascends the watershed between the Ramganga and the Gori river at a height of about 8,500 feet. It descends through a fine stretch of forest to Munsiari whence begins the difficult and costly road up the valley to Milam, a distance of some 30 miles and a rise of over 5,000 feet. From Munsiari a road runs down the Gori valley to Askot. The stages between Munsiari and Milam are Bagodyar and Rilkot. The last village below Milam is Laspa, and the final stage is 12 or 13 miles and a very stiff journey either way on account of the difficult nature of the narrow road which is maintained along or just above the river bank. From Milam onwards the track into Tibet follows the Shillang stream, a tributary of the Gori over the Untadhura Pass. Ralam is six miles to the east of Laspa but separated from it by a high ridge passable only in the height of summer. It lies in a side valley two days journey from Bin on the main road. From Ralam a track crosses over to Sobala in Darma but owing to its height (about 18,000 feet) and extreme it difficulty is seldom used. During the winter the whole of the valley is blocked with snow and when the Bhotias return at the end of May or the beginning of June, the first of them usually go up on the snow overlying the river-bed. By July the road is clear and it remains so till the middle of October.

Almora to Garhwal.

Four roads connect Almora with Garhwal. The first stages are identical in all. The path leaves the Almora-Ranikhet cart road at Sitoli and descends gently to the Kosi river. A dry weather track crosses it by a ford below Hawalbagh, but in the rains the traveller must have recourse either to the girder bridge which carries the cart road across the river or else to the Hawalbagh suspension bridge. From beyond the Kosi the path follows the Nanakosi stream to Bhainskhet 13 miles from Almora. A short branch to the left connects Bhainskhet with Majkhali, and another to the right arrives via Airadeo at Someswar. The main road drops down into the moderately level plateau watered by the Gagas river and its tributaries and proceeds over a series of undulating hills to Dwarahat, a distance of 12 miles. Dák bungalows have been established at both these stages. From Dwarahat the path descends into the valley of the Kharrogadh which it follows as far as Ganai, ten miles away where there is a good dâk bungalow. Here it crosses the Ramganga by a suspension bridge and running up the Khetsari valley leaves the district at Pandwakhal about 6,000 feet high. The first stage in the Garhwal district is Lohba.

For the second route the traveller leaves Almora by the bridle path to Hawalbagh and thence proceeds along the cart road past Someswar to Baijnath, already described. Thence a march up the Gomti valley brings him to Gwaldam, the first stage in the Garhwal district. These two routes are followed by those whose objective is upper Garhwal.

The third route leaves the first at Dwarahat and following the ridge which divides the basins of the western Ramganga and Gagas rivers reaches Pali, a distance of 13 miles. Pali can also be reached from Ranikhet by the path already described. From Pali the road drops rapidly down Masi on the Ramganga which it crosses yb a suspension bridge. Thence the ridge between the Ramganga and Banao river must be ascended, and a pleasant walk through pine forests brings the traveller to the fertile plain of Tamadhaund. Here the Banao river is forded, and a sharp climb follows to Agaspur and thence to Saraikhet on the borders of Garhwal. The road proceeds by Baijrao and Pokhri to Pauri.

The fourth route leaves the first at Ganai, ascends the ridge between the Banao and the Ramganga on which stands the dâk bungalow of Kelani, nine miles from Ganai. Thence is a gentle descent to the Banao river at Deighat where it is crossed by a suspension bridge. Thence by a gradual ascent the road passes the watershed between the Banao and the Nayar river, leaving the district some six miles from Kelani. The road proceeds by Bungidhar, Kainyur, Saknyana and Musagali to Pauri. This is the line generally followed by travellers between Almora and Pauri. The total distance is 98 miles.

Eastern Kumaon.

The great market of Eastern Kumaon is Tanakpur on the Sarda or Kali river. It is 37 miles from the railway station of Pilibhit by a cart road which becomes impassable during the rains; thence it is continued by a bridle path which, after ascending the first range of hills, is met by another obstacle, the Ladhiya river, here unbridged. Beyond the Ladhiya it reaches Champawat (30 miles from Tanakpur) by a steep ascent and thence Lohaghat (six miles further). The next stage is Chira whence the road drops down to the Sarju river and after an ascent of about equal distance Gurna is reached, and thence Pithoragarh. There is a dâk bungalow at each stage. From Pithoragarh the road bifurcates, a respectable bridle path running east to Jhulaghat 13 miles away on the Kali river, here crossed by a suspension bridge, the only permanent means of communication between Nepal and the district. Hence some of the Bhotias follow a rough path up the bed of the Kali as far as its junction with the Gori, thus escaping the heavy hills between Pithoragarh and Askot. It is hoped eventually to make this, after some slight re-alignments, the main route, superseding the present main route which proceeds to Askot via Kanari China. The roads to the passes in Darma will be found described in the notice of that pargana. From Askot a branch proceeds up the Gori river joining the Johar route already mentioned at Munsiari.

The second branch drops down from beyond Pithoragarh to the eastern Ramganga valley and follows it through Thal to Tejam where it joins the Johar route. This is the line taken by the Johari Bhotias who trade with Tanakpur.

The Champawat road from Almora runs south-east by Jalna and Dol to Devidhura, one line following the high Mornaula ridge and the other dropping into the Panar valley and joining the first again at Devidhura. At Kheti Khan, between the *pattis* of Gangol and Pharka, they again divide—one branch going to Lohaghat and one to Champawat. There are dâk bungalows at Lamgara, Mornaula, Devidhura, and Dhunaghat on this line.

The eastern road leaves Almora by Baldhoti and bifurcates at Barechina. The less important tract takes the left hand and reaches the first stage Dhaulchina 13½ miles from Almora where there is a dâk bungalow. Here the path crosses the Binsar-Jageswar range beyond which it descends to the Sarju. The next stage is Kanari China, then Ganai and beyond that again Berenag. From Berenag the road drops down to the Ramganga near Thal and finally joins the Tanakpur-Garbyang road at Askot. At Berenag it meets the road from Bageswar to Thal.

The second path keeping to the left and proceeding almost due east arrives at Panwanaula, a camping ground and dâk bungalow 14 miles from Almora, and following the Jageswar range passes Naini, 10½ miles, and thence descends to the Sarju river here spanned at Harara by a fine suspension bridge. The remaining stages are Gangolihat, 10½ miles, Bans, 10 miles, and Pithoragarh, 7½ miles. From Pithoragarh the road continues due east to Jhulaghat on the Kali, and thence, by the sole suspension bridge that crosses the Kali, into Nepal.

Fairs and markets. There are no periodical markets in the district. The only fairs of any numerical or commercial importance are those held at Thal and Bageswar. They are described in the notices of these places. In addition to the sale of petty goods and the worship of the gods in whose honour the fairs are held, the Kumaoni takes the opportunity afforded by a large concourse to indulge freely in his favourite pastime of gambling. A list of all the fairs will be found in the appendix.

Bungalows. The district is exceedingly well provided with bungalows. There are in all 32 dâk bungalows, seven of which—those at Almora, Takula, Bageswar, Someswar, Ranikhet, Majkhali, and Dwarahat—are in the charge of *khansamans*; six inspection houses of the public works department, ten rest houses belonging to the district forest department, besides a number belonging to the Kumaon, Naini Tal and Garhwal forest divisions. The stages of the main roads are all marked by dâk bungalows or inspection houses, and their position has been roughly indicated in the description of the roads. The district forest department has laid out a line of bungalows from Almora to Askot at Barechina, Kanari China, Ganai, Berenag, Thal, Dindihat, and Askot.

CHAPTER III.

THE PEOPLE.

Population.

An estimate of the population of the old district of Kumaon which included the present Almora and Naini Tal districts was made by the first Commissioner of Kumaon, Mr. Traill, in 1821. The inhabited houses had been enumerated for the purposes of his survey of the economic condition of the people, upon which was founded his settlement of 1823; and he allowed an average population of 6·5 persons for each house. The houses had been enumerated separately by parganas, and it is thus possible by leaving on one side those parganas now included within the boundaries of the Naini Tal district and applying to the remainder the figure of 6·5 persons per house to arrive at a rough estimate of the population of the tract which afterwards became the Almora district. These calculations give a population of 135,533 souls. Estimates of the population of the Kumaon district were made by Mr. Batten in 1848 and Mr. Beckett between 1863 and 1868, while a census was taken in 1852. It is not possible to extract from those results without an incommensurate amount of labour any information regarding the state of what is now the Almora district. Calculations are vitiated by the fact that about this time the exploitation of the Bhabar and Tarai began in earnest and that the portions afterwards allotted to Almora and Naini Tal respectively were not then administratively demarcated. The Almora district was not constituted until 1891, but it is possible to deduct from the totals for Kumaon the population which must be assigned to the area now included in the Naini Tal district. In 1872 the population of the district amounted to 354,579 souls, which gives a density of 66 to the square mile. In 1881 it had risen to 360,967, of whom 185,641 were males and 175,326 females. Ten years later the figures were 211,068 males and 205,800 females, giving a total of 416,868, and at the census of 1901 the population was found to have increased to 465,893. Thus since 1872 the population has advanced steadily, though it is still scanty considering the great area of the district. The density is only 86 to the square mile. Mr. D. C. Baillie, the Census Superintendent of 1891, doubts the accuracy of the returns of 1881. Mr. Partridge proved the truth of the allegation as regards Garhwal and commenting on his remarks Mr. Baillie writes: "For Kumaon, with a lower increase and a considerable amount of immigration, the omissions are not proved to have been so large. The population estimated from that of 1881 by adding births and deducting deaths is much lower than the present census figures shows it to be, but there can be no doubt that these figures over-estimate the deficit in 1881 and that in Kumaon deaths are better reported than births. With an average death-rate at least 10,000, possibly 15,000 persons must have been omitted in Kumaon at last census."

Movements of population. A preliminary census was taken in all hill districts during the autumn of 1900. The final figures adopted were those of March 1st, 1901. The difference between the two totals for the Almora district are most interesting. In the autumn of 1900 the total population was returned at 501,938; and on March 1st, 1901 at 465,893. Two well-defined but quite independent general movements of large numbers of the populace are known. As the winter advances the upper parts of Bhot—the region lying chiefly behind the snows and inhabited by the Bhotias—become deserted. By the middle of November the higher villages are buried in snow and the inhabitants, having completed their commerce with Tibet, begin to move southwards. Camps are established at convenient points and here the women and children remain with their flocks and herds, other than pack-animals, and the bulk of the Tibetan merchandise. The men begin to make their journey to the submontane marts—a journey to be repeated several times before the whole of the goods have been transported. These traffickings continue until about the middle of May, when near all the traders with their wives and children return to their homes near the great passes for the summer, during which period they conduct their trade with Tibet. Thus at the preliminary census the population of Malla Darma was 5,995; on the 1st March it was 325: in Byans the figures were 3,225 and 68.

Again, as the rains dry up and fever abates very many of the inhabitants of the lower pattis descend to till their rich holdings in the Tarai and Bhabar, and do not return until after the rabi harvest has been reaped, about the middle of March. Their ancestral fields in the hills are roughly sown before they depart and but little tended in the meanwhile, the crop being reaped on their return. Whole villages are emptied of all their able-bodied inhabitants, and in Riuni, for instance, the total cold weather population consists of one or two decrepit old men left to guard the property of the absentees. Thus in patti Assi the autumn population was 4,029, the spring population 598. In Sipti the figures were 3,199 and 956: in Malli Seti 1,037 and 515: in the two Charals 4,763 and 1,745: in the two Tikhuns 11,413 and 9,460. The Phaldakot pattis, too, offer contrasting figures for the two seasons. The destination of many of these emigrant cultivators is the Naini Tal Tarai, but numbers visit the Tanakpur Bhabar. Thus the autumn figures for that police circle were 5,515; by March 1st the population was found to be 12,812. Not all the emigrants are however cultivators; many of them spend the winter in the forests with their cattle, earning good wages by felling trees or sawing wood. The two Silors, for instance, are famous for the large numbers of skilled sawyers living in those somewhat congested pattis. The Salts at the south-western extremity of the district also send their superfluous population to earn a living in the Garhwal and Kumaon forest divisions by cutting grass and bamboos. The figures need not be repeated, but they show that a considerable proportion of the inhabitants spend their cold weather away from home. And it must also be remembered that the winter is the period when the hillman pays his visits to the Bhabar markets for his year's supply of salt, sugar, iron and cloth.

Religions. Hinduism.

The vast majority of the people are Hindus. The actual figure is 460,013 or 98 per cent. The orthodox Hinduism of the hills does not differ in any essential from that of the plains. Mr. Oakley writes, "Popular religion in the Himalayas may be conveniently divided into two main types—the worship of the greater gods of modern Hinduism and that of the local deities. In this respect there is a general likeness to the whole of north

India, with the exception that the local godlings are perhaps more in evidence here than in other parts of the country". The orthodox or *smartas* worship the five great gods Vishnu, Siva, the Sun, Ganesh, and Devi. In the hills they are chiefly Brahmans of undisputed plains extraction. One or other of these deities is selected for special worship as the Ishta Devata or chosen god. Devi is the Sakti or female energy of a god, assuming the names of Uma, Kali, Durga, Parvati, Bhawani, or Nanda. Under the latter name she is the female energy of Siva and a favourite deity in Almora having a local habitation in the great peak on the north-west borders of the district which bears her name. An interesting tale is related by Mr. Oakley. The goddess had a temple in the Almora fort which Mr. Traill removed. Some time later Mr. Traill happened to be struck with snow-blindness on the lower slopes of Nanda Devi : this was accepted as a sign of the displeasure of the goddess, and Mr. Traill is said to have vowed to build her a temple. This vow he fulfilled on his return to Almora and was delivered from the curse.* The worship of Siva or Mahadeo is in the hills much commoner than that of his great rival Vishnu. Siva has many connections with the hills. His consort is called Parvati (the mountain-born), daughter of Himanchal, a personification of the snowy range. The triple peak of Trisul is his trident, and his most famous temple lies below the Kedarnath mountain in Garhwal. Stevenson remarks :—"If it may be asked what local deity Siva represents and what was his ancient name, I would state as a probable conjecture that Kedar was the original Hindu name of Siva. Though adopted into Sanskrit there is no real derivation of Kedar." The symbol of the linga too, writes Mr. Atkinson, may have arisen from the pointed peaks around his original home. Siva finds no place in the Vedas though he is identified by the Brahmans of later times with Rudra, who has his home among the Garhwal hills. Rudra, again, is a form of Agni, the god of fire and lightning, and later he became the howling god of thunder and storms, the personification of nature in her most terrible aspect. Siva himself assumes the form of a mountaineer and he is described as roaming about "in dreadful

* *Holy Himalaya*, page 162.

cemeteries, attended by hosts of goblins and spirits, like a madman, naked, with dishevelled hair, laughing, weeping, bathed in the ashes of funeral piles, wearing a garland of skulls and ornaments of human bones, insane, beloved by the insane, the lord of beings whose nature is essentially darkness." This description is put into the mouth of an enemy of the god—Daksha, his father-in-law—and suitable deductions must be made on account of the personal bias of the narrator, but Siva's characteristics appear to be those of a god of barbarian highlanders. Atkinson concludes "Weber regards Siva as doubly derived from Agni and Rudra, the howling storm and crackling flame—both striking and terrible objects. Flame the cause of wind and wind the cause of flame, unitedly formed the great and terrible being. Hence the epithets assigned to him are separable into two classes. Those which make him 'dweller on the mountains' 'having dishevelled hair,' cruel, fierce, healer, auspicious are derived from his character as lord of storms: and those such as 'blue-necked' (nilakantha) like wreathed smoke, 'golden-armed' (hiranya-bahu), and 'thousand-eyed' like sparks, belonged to him as lord of fire. In the older writings there is no trace of his names Isa or Mahadeva, or of his form as the linga or phallus."

Buddhism in an effort to enclose all classes within its pale began gradually to assimilate first the Tantric ritual and afterwards the aboriginal cults. In this process it absorbed Saivism and other worships and about 700 A. D. there was little to choose between the Brahmanical and Buddhist cults. It was this corrupt Buddhism which the great reformer Sankara Acharya expelled from Kumaon: or rather it would be more correct to say that he purged the germs of Hinduism from the contamination of the degraded Buddhism, and re-established the famous temples at Kedarnath, Badrinath and Joshimath.

Kumaon or as it was anciently called Kurmanchal is famous as the scene of the god Vishnu's second or tortoise (Kurma) incarnation. Vaishnavism appears originally to have been antagonistic to Saivism; it supported caste and the Brahmanical supremacy and generally refused to admit aboriginal cults into its system, while it rejected animal sacrifices. "The Vaishnava temples are called Thakurdwara, or 'gate of the lord.' There are four of these in the town of Almora, and they are common throughout the province. They are separately named after either Vishnu, the sun, Badrinath, Krishna or Nara Singha. Not only is there the usual worship and offering as described above, but a kind of popular service takes place at times in these temples called Katha, when the smritis or shastras ... are read and expounded."* Unlike Siva, Vishnu is mentioned in the Vedas where he is apparently identified with the sun, but he is not the chief god. His worship was re-established in the hills by Sankara Acharya, who founded a temple at Joshimath to Vishnu under the name of Basdeo or Vasudeo, and another at Badrinath. Basdeo was according to Mr. Atkinson an heroic ancestor worshipped by the Kirata aborigines. His name and attributes appear to have been transferred to Vishnu. The district does not support many temples to Vishnu nor do the tenets of the sect—forbidding as they do the use of meat—find much sympathy with the average hillman.

Demonism.

Mr. Oakley in his book, *Holy Himalaya,* has a most interesting chapter on the part played by ghosts and godlings in the spiritual life of the hillman. "The people of Kumaon," he writes, "reckon two classes of gods—those of royal descent and those of demoniacal origin. The former are supposed to be possessed of more reasoning power than the latter, to be indeed almost omniscient; while the demons are often of only half-human intelligence and may easily be deceived by false show or promises. The royal deities are generally well disposed, or may be made so by employing proper means of persuasion, and are asked for boons. The demons, on the other hand, are spiteful and evil-minded."

Mr. Traill in his *Statistical Sketch* has described most of the members of the ghost tribe, which he says is divided into numerous varieties. The *bhut* is the ghost of one who has died a violent death and whose remains have not been honoured with funeral rites. *Masan* is the ghost of a child. The *tola* is the ghost of a bachelor—that is to say of a male of full age who has died unmarried. *Airi* is the ghost of a person killed in hunting. The *Acheris* are fairies who bewitch young people of either sex. The

* E. S. Oakley: *Holy Himalaya.*

deos are the village gods or demons. Although constant communication with the plains through the pilgrims has had a marked influence on the religion of the inhabitants of this portion of the Himalaya, still the belief in demons and sprites, malignant and beneficent, is implicit, and their worship as general and sincere as that of Siva and Vishnu. Of these minor gods one of the most interesting is Bholanath. Udai Chand, Raja of Kumaon, had two sons. The elder arrived at man's estate, took to evil, courses and was disinherited, and the younger, Gyan Chand succeeded his father. Later the elder brother returned and in the guise of a religious mendicant took up his quarters near the Nail tank. His disguise was penetrated and Gyan Chand, alarmed for his kingdom, had his brother assassinated. After his death the elder brother became a *bhut* under the name of Bholanath, and his mistress (the wife of a Brahman) became a *bhutini*. Another legend makes Bholanath a mendicant killed in a passion by a former Raja. The interest of the tale lies in the deification of a mortal, and the fact that now among the better classes Bholanath is identified with Mahadeo and his mistress with a form of his Sakti, thus exemplifying the process, adumbrated above, by which the orthodox Saivites have absorbed local cults. Bholanath has eight temples in Almora. Ganganath is one of the favourite deities of the Doms; like Bholanath he was an exiled prince (of the royal house of Doti in Nepal) and like Ganganath he pursued an intrigue with a Brahman woman. He and his paramour were murdered by the aggrieved husband; and with their unborn child became ghosts, and are propitiated with gifts. Goril is, to judge from his general repute and the number of temples to his name, the most popular of all the deities worshipped by the lower classes in the district. He has formal temples at Chaur, Garura, and Bhanari in Bordrau, at Tarkhet in Malli Doti, Manila in Naya, Gol Chaur in Kali Kumaon, Kumaur in Mahar, and Gagan Gol in Katyur. He was the son of one of the Katyuri rajas of Champawat, who suffered many vicissitudes of fortune at the hands of the raja's wives, whom he ultimately discomfited. His name he owes to the fact that he floated in an iron cage down the Gori Ganga. Airi is, according to Mr. Atkinson, a sylvan god, but he may well have originated as Mr. Traill writes. He is represented as hideous and repellent with eyes on the crown of his head and four arms filled with various weapons. He wanders abroad at night accompanied by crowds of fairies, borne in a litter, and followed by a pack of hounds. Khsetrpal or Bhumiya is a tutelary god of fields and boundaries, with a rude temple in every village. Kalbisht or Kaluwa was a neatherd living near Binsar two hundred years ago. He was murdered by his brother-in-law Himmat and became a benevolent spirit. Chaimu is like Kaluwa a tutelary god of cattle. He has a temple on the boundary between Riuni and Dwarsyun, where he is worshipped under the form of a ling. Harua was in his mundane existence Haris Chand, a raja of Champawat, who in his latter years exchanged the burdens of kingship for austere meditation. Many of the Katyur rajas are worshipped in Katyur and Pali. Runia is a demon who "haunts the north parganas of Kumaon, removing occasionally from one place to another; in his migrations he makes use of a large rock for a steed, on which also he nightly perambulates the villages in the vicinity of his residence. Though invisible to the eye his approach is indicated by the clattering of his massive courser: he molests only females: should he in his excursions fall in with and take a fancy to a woman her fate is assured: from that moment she is haunted by him incessantly in her dreams, and gradually wasting away she falls eventually a victim of his passion".* The offerings to such minor gods consist of he-buffaloes, goats, pigs, lizards and pumpkins. The rites accompanying the sacrifices are fervently believed in by women of all castes, by the rustics generally, and especially the Doms, and to those who accept the anthropomorphic theory of the origin of deities, the food provided—objectionable in most cases to the orthodox—will seem of a nature not unsuited to the objects worshipped by low caste aborigines.

Islam. Four thousand and forty-one persons profess Islam, 2,482 being males and 1,559 females. Under the Hindu rajas and the Gurkha governors the Muhammadans enjoyed little religious indulgence. The position they held is obvious from the prohibition of cow-

* Traill, *Statiscal Sketch*, page 67.

killing ordained by these rulers, and continued for some years by the British. Mr. Traill writes, " Either from the absence of any intimate connection with Mahomedan powers or from an abhorrence of the excess committed by Mahomedan invaders against the Brahminical worship, in this and other countries, strong prejudices were ever entertained against that sect. The profession of the Mahomedan religion was rather tacitly permitted than openly tolerated in both Kumaon and Garhwal and no public processions, tazias, &c., were ever suffered to take place either at Almora or Srinagar, at which places only Mahomedans are to be found in any number." A large proportion of the Musalmans is to be found in the two large towns of Almora and Ranikhet. In the former place 972 were enumerated in the municipality and cantonments, while the Muhammadans of Ranikhet amounted to 732. This latter figure does not include the hot weather Muhammadan population of Ranikhet, which amounted to 1,471 : the difference is accounted for by the fact that many of these persons belonged to the Supply and Transport Corps, or were domestic servants or camp followers. They descended to the plains with the troops in the autumn and had not returned by the 1st March, the day appointed for the final census. Most of the town or cantonment Muhammadans are merchants, shop-keepers or servants. Large numbers also work as carriers, driving from the plains their ponies laden with cloth, salt, and other commodities not produced in the hills. Muhammadans of this class are usually recent immigrants. The only Musalmans formerly known within the hills were certain families of shikaris and cooks, who received favour at the hands of the rajas, the former for killing game and ridding the country of wild beasts, the latter for preparing suitable food for any Muhammadan guest of rank.

There are also, however, the descendants of Muhammadan servants of the Hindu period who were workers in horn and are now Manihars and cultivators. Sir H. Ramsay writes, " They call themselves Mahomedans : but with the exception of acknowledging Mahommed they are not much different from Hindus, and I should say consult Brahmans oftener than their prophet." The Musalmans have now for many years enjoyed a fair measure of religious and civil liberty. They possess mosques at Ranikhet and Almora, and an ancient cemetery at the latter place.

Christians.

The Christian population numbers in all 1,427, of whom 677 are males and 750 females. In 1891 the Christians numbered 706, so that the Christian population has more than doubled in the ten years that have elapsed since 1891. Considered racially 354 are Europeans and 44 Eurasians. The Indian Christian community thus amounts to 1,029. Of these 133 belong to the Congregationalist community, 523 are Methodists, 40 Presbyterians, 36 Church of England, while 142 did not specify their denomination.

London Mission.

Most of the Congregationalist Indian Christians are the results of the efforts of the London Missionary Society, which started work in Kumaon in 1850 under the direction of the Revd. J. H. Budden. A high school was established in Almora which for a long period was the only place of secondary education in Kumaon or Garhwal, and which has at the present time (1909) 395 scholars, of whom 40 are studying for the Intermediate B. A. examination of the Allahabad University. The name of "Ramsay Collegiate School" was given to this institution in memory of Sir Henry Ramsay, who from the beginning took a warm interest in the work of the mission, especially on its educational and philanthropic sides. The Leper Asylum, originally started by him, and the mother of similar institutions in India, was handed over to the care of the mission, and has now 110 inmates, of whom a large proportion have become Christians.

The operations of the mission, which has at present seven European agents (three men and four ladies) at work, extend to the northward from Almora, centreing around ten small stations. These include some of the villages of the Bhotias, in the Milam valley. In some of these outstations elementary vernacular schools are maintained, and, in two or three, small dispensaries with qualified medical attendants. In Almora, in addition to the collegiate school, there is a girls' high school under the care of Miss M. Budden, with 117 scholars, orphanages for boys and girls, a refuge for homeless women, and a women's hospital and dispensary under a European lady doctor. The Indian Christian community in Almora has organised itself into a church, with a pastor of its own, and carries on indigenous mission work by voluntary effort in the town of Ranikhet, having agents there and a large school. The total number of Christians connected with the mission is 455, of whom 157 are church communicants. These numbers are far in excess of those recorded at the census, of 1901 but the mission has been making great progress of late, and in the last three years 200 baptisms have occurred. The total is made up of 25 boys and 80 girls in the orphanages, 33 women in the Women's Home, 101 Christian lepers, 130 members of families domiciled in Almora, and 85 in outstations.

M. E. Mission.

The work of the American Methodist Episcopalian Mission in the Almora district began with the opening of a dispensary in Dwarahat in April 1871. In 1873 a medical missionary was appointed to Lohaghat and a dispensary opened there. On the withdrawal of the London Mission from Pithoragarh the head quarters of the M. E. Mission were changed from Lohaghat to that station. Here a hospital was built and an extensive medical work began, which has continued ever since. A house for a missionary was built in Dwarahat in 1876 but no missionary was appointed to that station till 1881. In both eastern Kumaon and the Dwarahat district schools for boys and girls were opened. The mission purchased land for farming purposes in Pithoragarh and the work was done by the widows in the home at that place. In 1885 at the request of the missionary stationed at Pithoragarh the Mission to Lepers purchased property and started the asylum, which has gradually grown to its present proportions ; it now contains seventy inmates. From Pithoragarh the work of the mission extended to Bhot and buildings were erected in Dharchula, Chaudans, and other centres. Here too the greatest attention was paid to medical relief. There are at present according to returns furnished by an officer of the mission 622 native Christians in Pithoragarh, 102 in Dwarahat, and 47 in Bhot. These numbers greatly exceed the census figures for 1901. It will be seen that the work of the Mission has been largely on medical lines, and though schools have not been neglected the medical feature has been the prominent one, there being at present four medical missionaries working in the Almora district.

Minor religions.

The Buddhists numbered 217. They are trading Tibetans who happened to be in the district on the night of the 1901 census. The Bhotias, it may be observed in passing, profess Hinduism. One hundred and seventy-four Aryas were recorded: of the total 103 were Brahmans and 69 Rajputs. The remaining two were Bania women. The failure of the Arya movement among the Almora Banias is rather curious. The majority of the Aryas are to be found in the Champawat tahsil. There remain four Parsis—the family of a Ranikhet shopkeeper—two Brahmos, two Jains, and a single Sikh.

Hindus. Biths.

The rural Hindu population consists of Biths and Doms. The former are sub-divided into Brahmans and Khas-Brahmans and Rajputs and Khas-Rajputs. The Khas-Rajputs are the Khasiyas whose claim to be Aryan immigrants is generally allowed. They are somewhat looked down upon by other Aryans who have settled in the hills by way of the plains. It is supposed that the Khasiyas formed one of the earlier waves of invasion from the North-West. Some conjecture as to their origin will be found in the historical chapter. The Khasiyas are contumeliously described as knowing no Brahmans and they would appear in the first place not to have professed the Vedantic religion until the arrival of Sankara Acharya. After the religious cataclysm which resulted in the extermination of the Buddhists the Khasiyas adopted Brahman priests from plains settlers, or their tribal priests from performing the functions of Brahmans arrogated also their title. The immigrant Rajputs and Brahmans from the plains profess to have accompanied adventurers or pilgrims or to have been themselves invited by ruling chiefs. The Khasiya is distinguished from the pure Rajput by his not wearing the *janeo*: but now that there is no danger of punishment for the unjustified assumption, most Khasiyas have adopted the thread. Beyond being somewhat looked down upon the Khasiyas suffer no particular disability. If they can afford the luxury they can marry into the best Rajput families, while in the hills where caste prejudices are much relaxed, both Brahmans and Rajputs will eat bread cooked by a Khasiya. The minor sub-divisions of Bith castes are usually known from their *thats* or lands on which they were originally settled, such as Nainwal from Nainoli, Bargali from Bargal, Padholia from Padholi, Palial from Pali, and so forth. These are all the names of Khas-Rajput clans, but Brahmans are also designated by similar local names and such Brahmans are distinguished from their higher caste-fellows as *halbanewale*—cultivators—or Pitaliya Brahman from the custom they had of wearing a bracelet of brass instead of the triple thread.

Brahmans.

The Brahmans in all numbered at the census of 1901 111,810, of whom 56,772 were males and 55,038 females. The census returns do not distinguish between the various sub-divisions of Brahmans. The more respected sub-castes are generally admitted to have immigrated into Kumaon in comparatively recent times from the plains. The Pants state that some twenty-one generations ago their ancestor Jaideo came to Kumaon and obtained from the raja of the time a grant of Uprara in Gangoli. One sub-division eats meat, and generally resembles the indigenous hill Brahmans. A famous member of the clan was Purukhottum or Purkhu the general of Rudra Chand who fell in battle with the Garhwalis. The Pandes are said to have come from Kot Kangra and from the plains: those from the hills became the rajas' family priests and those from the plains became their cooks. Some eat animal food and some abstain. The Joshis of the hills occupy a much more important position than their brethren in the plains. The name is variously derived from Jyotishi, an astrologer, or Jhusi an ancient village near Allahabad, the legendary home of the ancestor of the Chand dynasty. The Joshis are and have been for many years a very important clan in the hills. For the last two centuries they have been the master-movers in all intrigues and at the present moment they hold a large number of Government appointments. It is here sufficient to mention Shib Deo Joshi, the king-maker of the latter days of the Kumaon raj, and Harak Deo, the regent of the Gurkha conquerors. Tiwaris are for the greater part cultivators, priests, teachers, and Government officials. Other Brahman septs are the Upretis, Upadhyas, Pathaks, Dugals and Bhats. These high caste Brahmans are divided into various families according to local distinctions such as the Pants of Gangoli and of Syunarakot, the Joshis of Selakhola, Galli, China Khan, Jhijar and Dania, and the Pandes of Patiya, according to the villages where they originally settled. The high caste Brahman families have been for generations in the service of the Kumaon rajas or the British Government and have representatives settled in Almora. Those who remain in the villages live by the practice of medicine, astrology and priestcraft in addition to agriculture. Most of the hill Brahmans however belong to the Khasiya nation: they are almost to a man engaged in agriculture or personal service, though a few also subsist on what they can make by ministering at the shrines of the less respectable village gods.

Rajputs. Two-hundred and twenty-four thousand three hundred and seventy Rajputs were enumerated. The census classifies them all as "others"—that is to say, none of the famous sub-divisions of the plains are represented within the district. Less than ten per cent. can be distinguished as immigrants from the plains. By far the most illustrious in descent and the most respected at the present day are the Rajwars and Manrals or Manurals. Both families are descended from the Surajbansi Katyuri rajas who once ruled in the north of Kumaon. The Rajwars now live in Jaspur of Bichla Chaukot, and Askot to the extreme east of the district, where they hold an impartible raj. The Manrals represent the branch which on the deposition of Birdeo, the last Katyuri king, and the annexation of his kingdom by the Chands, settled in Pali. Their name is connected with the Manila peak in Palla Naya above Bhikia Sen, and the village of Sain Manur on the same ridge in Walla Salt. The families are said to hold sanads granted by various members of the Chand dynasty, and by the Gurkha governors of later days. The head of the Jaspur Rajwars was the feudal lord of the wild Lakhaura tract on the Garhwal borders, now included in Bichla Chaukot, and still in the possession of the family. The Manrals are a still stronger body, holding many thokdaris, chiefly in Bichla Chaukot, but also in Walla Salt and Giwar. The heads of the Tamadhaund Manrals and of the Jaspur Rajwars are still among their own people saluted by the title Sayana, which connotes a more honorific office than a mere thokdari. The account they give of themselves is that they were assigned grants of land, to which were attached the duties of wardens of the marches. Their fiefs are situated to the west of Pali in the centre of the debatable land, and one of their most important posts was the Jhuniyagarh fort. With the disappearance of the border warfare in which they played such important parts and the consequent decline of their emoluments, the Manrals and the Rajwars are now much reduced in circumstances. They still however remember their royal descent and as already mentioned the titles they once held are always popularly accorded, and they consequently assume an independent attitude in their dealings with petty officials. They are also, it must be said, on bad terms with each other. The Raotelas are the descendants of the junior members of the Chand family, whether legitimate or illegitimate. As their number increased it became necessary to give them employment or means of subsistence at a distance from Champawat and Almora. They are therefore to be found planted all over the district. Various villages in Barahmandal, Chaugarkha and Pali were given as fiefs to dispose of the superfluous members of the Chand families and now, owing to the increase in their numbers and to intermarriages, little but the name remains. Other Rajput septs of plains origin are the Padiyars, the Bangari Rawats and the Dosadh Bishts. The remainder are for the greater part Khasiyas. Their main sub-divisions are named Rawat, Bisht and Negi, unqualified by any local prefix such as distinguishes two of the higher castes just mentioned. These names have reference originally to the occupation of their owners; *neg* means a perquisite, *negi* one who receives perquisites, and hence *par excellence* an official of the Government. The Negis are those Khasiyas of Garhwal and Kumaon who took to military service and gradually owing to the vicissitudes of such a life separated into a caste. They are much less numerous in Kumaon than in Garhwal. Bisht, the appellation of another Khasiya sub-caste, is more correctly *vasisht,* meaning "excellent, respectable" and its origin is a title rather than a caste name. Rawat means a ruler, and the members of the caste who call themselves by that name appear to be the descendants of petty civil officers employed under the Hindu kings. Other Khas-Rajput clans of some interest are the Boras of Borarau and the Kairas of Kairarao, the Mahars or Maharas, and the Hits. Pandit Ganga Datt Upreti mentions in all 889 clans, the members of whom he considers sufficiently martial to be enlisted, and if to these are added those whom he admits to be unwarlike it will be seen how extremely minute is the caste and clan sub-division that prevails in the district. He accepts 26 castes or sub-castes "as near and real kinsmen of Kshatriyas or reigning rajas," and hence called Jankari or real Rajputs.

Doms.

The Doms, who number 98,870, are as far as can be ascertained the aborigines of the country. They are found wherever the Khasiyas are found, living with them in a state which is even now in some of the more remote villages not far removed from serfdom. The Doms are the village menials. They rarely cultivate, and practically never hold land as zamindars. They do rarely use the term Dom in speaking of themselves but call themselves Tallijati (low caste), or Baharjati (outcaste), or more frequently describe themselves by their occupational sub-divisions. The chief of these are the Lohars or Agaris, iron miners and blacksmiths; the Kolis, weavers; the Tamtas, brass-workers; the Orhs, carpenters; the Bhuls, oilmen; the Mochis or Baisuwas, leather-workers; the Aujis, also called Das, tailors who also make music, and the Hurkiyas, wandering musicians who prostitute their women.

Banias.

Banias number 3,111, and belong chiefly to the Agarwala sub-division. They are found in the various small bazars throughout the district, but principally in the two main markets of Almora and Ranikhet. They are descended from immigrants from the plains. Some number six or seven generations spent in the district. The traders and bankers included in the caste are a wealthy and important body, and many of them have established branches of their business at Ranikhet and Naini Tal. The Sahs or Sahus of Almora and Dwarahat belong to the Vaishya clan. One of them was in former times appointed Chaudhri of the Almora bazar. The office remained in the family for some generations, and the title—though no longer the office—has now become hereditary. The Almora treasury has been in the hands of the same Vaishya family ever since Kumaon came under British rule. Jai Sab, a former treasurer, was rewarded with a *jagir* for Mutiny services. He left a will hypothecating the whole of his property to the Government as security for the treasurership. The Government accepted the hypothecation, and on his death his eldest son became treasurer. The office is now practically hereditary in the family, which claims to have come from the plains with the first Chand Raja.

It is fair to the Vaishyas to remark that they indignantly repudiate the allegation of the census report of 1901 to the effect that certain classes of them intermarry with Doms. It is prima facie improbable, for the Dom is held in the utmost contempt in the hills, where the Vaishyas are much respected, and as far as can be discovered the only actual case in point is that of an Almora Bania who abandoned caste and family for the love of a Dom woman.

Almora contains far more Bhotias than any other district in the United Provinces. At the census of 1901 9,099 were recorded. Their country is called by the middle hill people Bhot, and it lies in the main to the north of the great snowy peaks, and between them and the Tibetan boundary. Bhot or more correctly Bod is really the same word as Tibet. In the records of the Tartar Liaos in the eleventh century the name Tibet is written T'u-Pot'e, in which the latter syllable represents 'Bod.' The Chinese character for '*po*' has also the sound '*fan*' and with the addition of '*si*' or 'western' the portion of Tibet to the north of Kumaon is called 'si-fan' and the people 'Ta-poti'. The name Tibet is seldom applied by Kumaonis to their northern neighbour: they call the people Hunias and the land Hundes. The Bhotias of the Almora district inhabit three valleys flanked on either side by the eternal snows. Inter-communication between subdivisions so isolated is therefore difficult, if not impossible, and—as would be expected—they exhibit many differences in habits, customs and language. Some have so far become Hinduised that they have forgotten their original dialect and now speak the ordinary hill dialect common to their Khasiya neighbours, yet there are five living dialects still in daily use. They all belong to the Tibetan branch of the Himalayan group **Bhotias.**

of the Tibeto-Burman family. These are Rankas or Shankiya Khun, current in Goriphat, Johar and four villages of Malla Danpur; Mr. Sherring records 614 people who speak it: Byansi spoken by 1,585 people of patti Byans: Chaudansi spoken by 1,485 people in patti Chaudans: Darmiya spoken by 1,761 people in patti Darma, and Bhotia or Hunia spoken by 820 Hunias, Khampas and Bhotias scattered in different places. Bhotias who speak one of these dialects often cannot understand another. All Bhotias have two castes, Rajputs and Doms. The latter differ in their functions in no respect from the Doms of the lower hills already described. There are no Bhotia Brahmans, although there are many Brahmans domiciled in Bhot, who have entered it from the south and are in every way the same as their fellow castemen in the rest of Kumaon. The chief subdivisions of the Bhotias classified according to their language are the Jethoras, who speak Rankas or Shankiya Khun and live in Goriphat, Malla Danpur and Johar: the Tolchas and Marchas of Johar who have forgotten the old dialect and employ the ordinary hill language of their southern neighbours: the Rawats or Shankas or Shokas (a corruption of Shokpa) of Johar who also no longer use their original language: the Byansis; the Chaudansis and the Darmiyas, who live in the pattis from which they derive their name and who speak their own language.

Jethoras. The Jethoras derive their name from *jeth*—elder—and claim to be the descendants of the first Bhotia settlers. Their subdivisions are named after the villages in which they live. The Jethoras are, unlike all other Bhotias, not traders but cultivators, not itinerant or migratory, but stationary. They affect superiority, apparently relying on the alleged derivation of their name, but their claims are not recognized by their neighbours, who will not marry or eat with them. They are now almost entirely Hinduised as to their worship and customs, except that they do not strip to eat rice and have not yet generally assumed the sacred thread.

Tolchas. The real home of the Tolchas is in Garhwal. A few are settled in Johar, but they do not intermarry with the Johari Shokas.

Shokas or Rawats.

The Shokas or Rawats are divided into a number of groups called after the village in which each lives. The Rawats are traders. Their way into Tibet is by Untadhura, above Milam. The ancestor of the Milamwal Rawats obtained permission from the Gartok Garphan to establish himself in trade, and built Milam and Burphu, and received the grant of Chumpal from the Huniyas. Marriage within the village group is not permitted, and though the Shokas are earnestly striving to follow all the ordinances of Hindu religion, orthodox Hindus do not consider them within the pale and will not eat with them.

It is noteworthy that among these partially Hinduised Bhotias of Johar every man and every woman is married, the reason being that marriage depends upon the will of the parents of the contracting parties, whereas in Darma marriage is not solemnised until the parties have reached maturity, and many men and women remain unmarried because they do not feel attracted towards the married state or because their efforts in the direction of matrimony have been unsuccessful. In Johar polygamy is not uncommon. The dead are cremated, but a head-bone is kept to be thrown into the holy lake of Mansarowar or into the Ganges. In addition to the gods of the Hindu pantheon Tibetan deities are still worshipped by the semi-Hinduised Bhotias. The Nikhurpas propitiate Dhurma: at Burphu and Tola Lhamsal is adored. Acheri is worshipped everywhere, and in Darma, Nungtang. The Jethoras worship Balchan and Runiya and the Milamwals resort to Sain for guidance when a sheep or goat is lost. When bears are raiding the sheep-folds, or when an animal is sick, shepherds in Darma and Johar make supplication to the brothers Sidhwa Bidhwa. On the other hand the deities Bir Singh and Jammnu-Danu have lost their vogue. It is to be understood that all partially Hinduisod Bhotias also perform their orisons to the gods of the Hindus. The question of taking food with certain persons and not with others, which is of absorbing importance to the ordinary Hindu, is treated in some respects very seriously, for the Rajputs do not eat with Doms, and in other respects very lightly, in that they are quite willing to eat with cow-killing Tibetans. Bhotias do not care as a rule to partake of the Tibetans' food, solely because the latter are abominably filthy in their habits, and generally eat rice and meat which is only half cooked, while Bhotias, who are of much better social condition and enjoy greater material prosperity, look with contempt on such poor food: but supposing that the food is properly treated and clearly cooked, all Bhotias will willingly join Tibetans at a meal. The Johari Rawats profess not to eat with Tibetans but only to drink tea with them. As a matter of fact the beverage called tea contains in it besides tea, large quantities of butter, salt, *sattu* and frequently flesh, so that these professions of the Rawats are not of much value. All Bhotias, whether of Niti, Johar, or pargana Darma, eat wild pig and fish of every kind, but not snakes, lizards, jackals, beef, fowls, or the long-tailed goat. In Johar the men eat first and then the women, and leavings are always for women and juniors. In pargana Darma there is no such custom: men, women and children all sit down and eat together. It is impossible for the Bhotias to worship any of their deities without plentiful supplies of the liquor called *jan*. This is a fermented liquor and differs from *daru*, which is distilled. Both are made from rice, wheat and grain of all kinds.

Darma Bhotias.

The Darma pargana is divided into three pattis, Byans, Chaudans, and Darma, and the residents in these three pattis have customs which distinguish them by a sharp line from all other Bhotias, and further the customs of the three pattis are not all exactly alike.

The Rajput Bhotias of pattis Darma, Byans, and Chaudans freely intermarry and it is a recognized rule that marriages must take place with some person of a different village, and if the contracting parties both belong to the same village it is absolutely necessary that they should be the descendants of different stocks. The best marriage for a man is with his father's sister's daughter or his mother's brother's daughter, but a man may not marry his father's brother's daughter, or his mother's sister's daughter. Similarly a girl should marry her father's sister's son, or mother's brother's son, but not her father's brother's son, or mother's sister's son.

Practically the universal custom of the three pattis Darma, Byans, and Chaudans is to arrange marriages at the Rambang, which is the village club and generally a very disreputable place. The Bhotias of Johar and Niti look down upon the Rambang and will have nothing to do with it in their own country, having given it up many years ago, though they are quite willing to avail themselves of the Rambang when they visit Darma. In every village is set apart a house, or some spot, called Rambangkuri, or place of the Rambang, at which men and women meet and spend the night singing lewd love songs and drinking and smoking. Married and unmarried men go there, also single women, and married women up to the time that their first child is born. Girls start to go to the Rambang from the age of ten years and practically never sleep at home after that age, the result being that a virtuous girl is unknown in the Darma pargana. The dead are cremated, but the corpse is placed on the bier in a sitting position, and the accompanying rites differ greatly from those approved by Hinduism, and the ceremony is followed by a feast. A pathetic custom still prevails in Byans and Darma. Should a man die far from home a clue of wool is laid along the ground to guide the soul home.

The eastern Bhotias erect shrines called Saithan for their gods in some quiet place outside the village. Frequently this is represented by a simple stone and by it is fixed a tree trunk with a few branches left on the top, with floating strips of cloth tied to it. Before the annual exodus to the lower hills auguries are taken from the entrails of animals sacrificed before the shrine. Each village has a deity of its own and each patti has its favourites. Gobla is universally worshipped. The god of Kuthi village is Gulach; of Nabi, Thappung; of Gunji, Namti; of Chhangru, Maden; of Garbyang, Kungr, the god of rain. But the most potent deity of all in the estimation of the people of Garbyang, Budhi, and Chhangru is Namjung, the name being taken from a mountain on which can be distinctly seen two stone figures from a great distance. The figures are said to be those of a Shoka and a girl he abducted, who were frozen to death on the top of the mountain. The men of patti Chaudans place their faith in Shyangse and hold an annual festival in his honour. In patti Darma the noble group of the Pancha Chuli peaks dominates the minds of the inhabitants. They are locally known as Majula, and the goddess on the summit bears the same name. Here the god Chan is worshipped for mountain sickness, and here too is the home of the dual deity Kibang Rangchim, who is both male and female. The Darma Bhotias also worship at all Tibetan monasteries, and while in Tibet they pay their vows to all the devil gods of that country.[1]

The Bhotias are shrewd traders and are taking kindly to education and its consequences. Their most famous men in the Almora district are Rai Kishan Singh Bahadur and Rai Pandit Gobaria, names with that of Pandit Nain Singh Milamwal, C.I.E., deceased, familiar to those versed in the annals of Tibetan exploration. The former is the well-known Pandit A. K. of the Survey, whose labours, in the cause of Tibetan cartography, earned him the distinction of a price upon his head. Mention may also be made of Babu Dalip Singh, formerly tahsildar of Almora, to correct the popular impression that the Bhotia is an utter barbarian.

Others. Religious mendicants are not rare in the district. Fifteen different orders are known, but the Dasnami and the Barapanthi alone are numerically important The former are an order of the Gosains. Many members of the religious fraternities have now adopted agriculture and marriage and except in certain peculiarities of their dress are not distinguished from ordinary hillmen. The Naiks (766) originated in Kumaon during the reign of Raja Bharati Chand, whose aggressive expeditions kept his soldiers so long in the field that they contracted temporary alliances with the women of the country. Their offspring gave rise to the caste of Naiks. The girls are early apprenticed to the trade of prostitution, the males acting as pimps. The caste is not considered disreputable and the males are able, by paying for the luxury, to acquire wives from Rajput families. The Naiks own some rich valleys in the Giwar valley and the caste has even secured a thokdari for one of its members. The Rajis or Rawats, who must not be identified with the Khasiya Rawats already mentioned, are an aboriginal tribe in a low state of civilisation. They are now found only in Askot. They have been identified with the Kiratas or Rajya Kiratas by Mr. Atkinson and they themselves profess royal descent. To such an

[1] From a note by C. A. Sherring, C.S.

extent are they obsessed with this idea that they refuse to salute any one, while they speak of the Rajwar of Askot as their younger brother. They are a wandering forest tribe known to their more settled neighbours as *ban-manus*, or men of the woods. They support themselves chiefly by *katil* cultivation with the produce of which they eke out the subsistence they derive from the beasts and fish they are able to capture. They speak a separate language of their own which is described by one observer as being like the twittering of birds and is said to belong to the Tibeto-Burman family. A cognate tribe inhabits the adjacent tract of Nepalese territory. They have been brought within the pale of Hinduism, but their chief gods are Bagh Nath, the tiger lord, Khudai and Malikar Jan; and on one day in the year they worship Nanda Devi. They have been on somewhat slender grounds connected by Mr. Traill with the Doms, a connection which they indignantly repudiate, and if their huts should happen to be defiled by the entrance of any member of the servile race they deem it necessary to purify it with water brought from 22 different sources. Mr. Sherring suspects them of polyandry. The census report records 22 Rajis but it is probable that this is far below the mark, as the shy men of the woods appear to have deprecated enumeration. There are probably at least 50 of them.

Occupations.

The figures of the 1901 census show how greatly the people of Almora are dependent upon the land for their living. Four hundred and twenty-eight thousand and fifty-three persons were recorded as agriculturists, or over 91 per cent. of the total. The vast majority of these people possess a proprietary interest in the land they till, though individual estates are often extremely small, and it must be remembered that a man holding the most exiguous plot of land in full ownership, and therefore compelled to resort to other occupations for his living, will always declare himself a zamindar, suppressing the fact that he also does cooly labour. Thus the field labourers are extremely few, amounting to only 3,337, and it is symptomatic of the Kumaon social system which leaves most of the field work to women, that two-thirds of these should be females. General labour supports 3,869 persons : these are coolies who carry loads and work in tea gardens, roads, or forests. The total bears no relation to the numbers who in reality derive the greater part of their income from work in the forests, but, as in the case of the field labourers, many small zamindars contented themselves with declaring only their more honourable if less important calling. Blanket weavers number 2,870; of these 2,412 are females, often the wives of Bhotia carriers who are otherwise employed, leaving their wives at home. Numerically those classified as engaged in "defence" are important, for they number 1856, but in reality most of them belong to the Gurkha regiment stationed at Almora and their connection with the district is adventitious. Personal service accounts for 3,529: these are domestic servants, male and female, cooks, sweepers, water-men, syces, messengers and the like. The only remaining occupation of importance is iron-working, which provides for 1,987 persons. The mines in the district have ceased working, and most of these people are lohars who work with the imported iron of the plains. The Bhotias combine the operations of transport and general dealing, and they appear to have been classified in the census report under the latter head. Very few mule or pack-pony drivers appear to have been enumerated; the majority of them ply their trade between Haldwani and Almora, and it appears probable that they were enumerated in the Naini Tal district, in which lies the greater portion of the road they use. The trade is known to be important.

Marriage. Some of the customs peculiar to Almora have their origin in the status of the women. Polygamy is not general, but it is said that every man who can afford to keep two wives does so. The correctness of this view is obvious from a consideration of the census figures, which show 111,865 married males and 123,940 married females. The figures are even more convincing if it be remembered that a considerable portion of the population of the towns of Almora and Ranikhet consists of men who are married but have left their wives behind them in the plains. Marriage among the Khasiyas nearly always partakes of the nature of a sale. The bride's father receives a sum for his daughter, which may be as low as Rs. 25 or as high as Rs. 1,000. The bride-price is now said to be merely a compensation to her family on account of the wedding expenses incurred, and this may be to a slight extent the case. But the value of women among a semi-migratory population is evident. They stay at home, tend the fields, and guard the household during the periodical excursions of the men to the plains for food or work. The women do all the field work except the actual ploughing. They sow, weed and reap and between harvests are fully employed in carrying in fuel and fodder from the neighbouring hills. Complete *pardah* does not exist and is indeed impossible among a rural population where no scavenging caste exists, but the men, though they exact a full tale of work from their wives and daughters in their own villages, do not approve of their appearing too openly before men of another village. Thus female labourers are rarely seen working on a public road. The bride-price is paid to the bride's father or nearest male relative by the bridegroom. Formerly the transaction was held to create a transferable right in the person of the woman acquired and she could be freely sold as could children. Marriage by sale is almost invariably between castes who are able according to Hindu law to intermarry, and any divergence from this rule is deprecated by all right-minded hill people. The ceremony is brief and consists almost entirely of the Ganesh puja.

Levirate.

As women are pecuniarily valuable, a wife is not allowed to go out of the family on the death of her husband, but is made over to the younger brother.[1] No rites are celebrated. The widow merely takes up her abode in her brother-in-law's house. The connection is considered respectable and any children who may result from it are legitimate, provided that the couple live in the same house. Should there be no surviving brother a cousin or other near relative will protect the widow and when there is no relative at all the property of the deceased husband is occasionally transferred to an outsider on condition that he maintains the widow. The practice is regarded as somewhat immoral. The protector is called the *tekua* or lover.

Tekua.

Ghar-jawain.

A man with a daughter and no son often marries her to a son-in-law who remains in the house and ultimately inherits through his wife the property of the father-in-law.

[1] Never to an elder brother. The proverb justifying this custom is "The upper wall (of a field) rests on the lower wall."

Sautia bant.

A consequence of polygamy is to be found in the *sautia bant*, whereby on a man's death his property is divided among his sons according to the number of his wives. The offspring of each wife is considered a separate entity for the purpose of inheritance. This custom is not universal and the courts require the strictest proof.

Language.

The language current in Almora is technically known as the Kumaoni form of Central Pahari. Many dialects are current and it may almost be said that the dialect varies with the pargana. Samples are given by Pandit Ganga Datt Upreti in his book *The Hill Dialects of the Kumaon Division*. He mentions the dialects of Almora, Champawat, Shor, Pali, Danpur, Johar, Bhot and the Almora Doms. At the same time it may be observed that colloquially the language is not framed altogether according to the Pandit's pattern. Elisions are the rule and mispronunciations, according to the plains canon, very common. The few words of Persian origin are nearly all misapplied technical terms. Most Kumaonis are bilingual and while all, even the most highly educated, use their own language in conversation with other Kumaonis, they can speak the ordinary Hindustani of the plains to Europeans and plainsmen. The script in common use throughout the district is Nagri in which all official records are maintained. In all 94·67 *per cent.* of the population were recorded at the census of 1901 as speaking Kumaoni. The languages of lesser importance are Gurkhali spoken by the men of the Gurkha regiment at Almora and by pensioners settled in the district, Dotiali spoken by Dotialis from the western border of Nepal who have immigrated into the eastern pargana, and Bhotia spoken by the Bhotias of the Darma and Johar parganas.

Condition of the people.

Mr. Traill, in concluding a report on Kumaon and its inhabitants wrote, "From the sub-divided state of landed property which here exists few individual land holders have the power of acquiring wealth; but though all connected with the soil are confined to a state of equality, their condition as a body is no doubt superior to that of any similar class of tenants in any part of the Company's territories." Commenting on these remarks Sir H. Ramsay (then Commissioner) wrote in 1874, "If this was really the state of the Kumaonis upwards of 40 years ago it is much more applicable to them now. I entirely agree with Mr. Traill and consider that Kumaonis are better off than any peasantry in the whole of India. With the increasing prosperity of Ranikhet and Naini Tal, the price of grain or labour will not fall, while the prospects of tea cultivation are so hopeful that, as far as I can judge, there is every reason to look forward to still greater prosperity among the people." Sir H. Ramsay's prophecy has proved true. The population has now increased to such an extent that it can no longer be fed on the products of the country, and while the birth-rate has greatly advanced in the last ten or fifteen years, the death-rate has remained stationary or has slightly declined. Cultivation too has been extended to almost its fullest limits, and the increased demands for the food of an expanding population are now met by an improvement and intensification of existing cultivation. Mr. Goudge, the last settlement officer, has commented on this phenomenon. The result of the experiments made in a few villages of Shor was to show that the land had improved 30 per cent., and in Kali Kumaon it was found that the ijran cultivation had improved 60 per cent., while there is also a distinct tendency to adopt the cultivation of better crops. Prices have risen to an extraordinary degree, and are now five or six times what they were 50 years ago. The chief cause is undoubtedly the advent of the railway to Kathgodam. With the greater pressure on the land and the presence of a large consuming population in Almora, Ranikhet and Naini Tal the demand for commodities of all kinds has greatly increased, with the result that producers raise their prices. During the last 30 years the tea gardens, with their very large consumption of grain by the coolies and other hands employed, have contributed to raise prices in the outlying districts. At the same time, except in these backward regions, the people have not greatly benefited by the advance in prices. The grain produced by the district is in fact seldom sufficient to feed the indigenous population—rarely if ever is there any surplus. There are therefore no big grain dealers and no marts of any local importance with the exception of Almora and Ranikhet, which exist solely for the benefit of a non-agricultural population. Thus the prices quoted in the bazars are not real in that they do not reflect the rates at which food grains change hands among the great mass of the population, and therefore the enormous risė of prices in recent years is not a criterion of the prosperity of the district. It must be observed that generally speaking these marts are stocked by imports from the plains and the prices charged are those of the submontane markets *plus* carriage and the dealers' profits, which go near to doubling them. The fortunate, but rare, cultivator who can grow more than his family eats can get nearly the same price. The main effect indeed of the great demand for food grains has been to increase enormously the value of land, and as a result the credit of the agricultural population has much expanded. Nevertheless the standard of comfort has risen greatly. Mr. Goudge writes, "Huts have been replaced by masonry houses, each of which costs Rs. 300 or Rs. 400. In some of the more prosperous villages, such as Riuni on the Ranikhet cart road there are houses which must have cost as much as Rs. 5,000 or more. Only in the remote pattis of Danpur or Talla Darma do the people still live in straw thatched huts, and in these parts they are yearly replacing them with substantial stone structures." He quotes also the testimony of Mr. Stevenson of Berenag. "When I first came to these parts in 1867 there was no road nearer than Bageswar and Gangolihat" (each about 20 miles from the locality meant) "and unless one had the bump of locality very strongly marked, one could not rely on reaching one's destination without a guide. Not one man in a hundred had ever been 12 miles from his village; the bulk of the land was under jungle, and it was quite a common occurrence to meet, as one went about, sambar, bear, pig and wild dogs. In a few of the old Brahman villages there were stone-walled, stone-roofed houses, but the bulk were simply grass hovels; the vessels were of earth, wood or iron, and if a man had a locally made copper vessel he was considered quite a wonder: brass vessels one never saw. A wretched cotton, the plant of which was about six inches high, giving a fibre about one or two inches in length, was grown, and from this a very coarse cloth was woven, and this cloth was used for women's skirts and men's loin cloths and caps. Men and women could not have dressed worse. The poor Dom at present dresses better than the wealthiest Brahman of those days. Every villlage used to have stocks of grain buried, for no one came to them, and the villagers went nowhere, and I used to buy at 2 maunds per rupee. Ghi and oil in those days were sold at 4 seers per rupee. To most folks in Almora these parts were unknown. Grain is now rarely over 25 seers per rupee, ghi about 1¼ seers, oil 2 seers."

The greatest advantage which the hill man has over the plainsman is the small revenue he pays, and the general regularity of his rainfall, and the consequent rarity of famines. The incidence of the land revenue is only Rs. 3 per family—a sum which could easily be earned by a few days' cooly work between Almora and the plains. The people on the whole feed better. It used to be said that the kharif sufficed for food and the rabi for profit—it was sold to pay the revenue, and buy cloth and other necessaries or luxuries—but now, though the staple is still mandua, the wheat is eaten instead of being sold. It is found to be cheaper to earn the extra few rupees in one of the many easy ways now open to the Kumaoni. One of these sources of income is labour in the forests, where thousands of Kumoni coolies resort at the beginning of the cold weather and work until March. The work is of many grades, but the unskilled wood-cutter can get four or six annas a day working either for a contractor, in which case they fell and 'convert' trees, or for the department, when they clear firelines or remove climbers. Others again take service in the stations of Naini Tal, Almora, or Ranikhet, performing the office of jhampanis, water-carriers, syces and so forth. The pilgrimage has not such an important effect upon the finances of Almora as it has upon those of Garhwal, for the portion of the road that lies within the district is not long and the pilgrims usually engage Garhwali coolies for the complete circuit at the beginning of their journey. Nor is it probable that the inhabitants of the rich corn-lands of Giwar which borders the portion of the pilgrim way in the Almora district would accept service as coolies. Still the passing of some 60,000 pilgrims in the year implies a demand for food which is profitably met by the cultivators near the route. A few of the inhabitants of the upper pattis of Danpur and Johar are recruited for the Garhwal Rifle regiment at Lansdowne and much of the pay they earn finds its way into the family coffers. The Kumaoni having once made the acquaintance of the plains will wander far in search of a living. He is to be found enlisted in the Burma Police and other semi-military forces, as well as in the United Provinces Police. Others of slightly superior education have taken service in the Survey department and are to be found anywhere between Baluchistan and Darjeeling. Ghi in the upper pattis is an important industry, and in the lower pattis valuable crops of ginger, pepper, turmeric and vegetables are grown. The Doms have as a class advanced more than any others. Under the paternal rule of Sir Henry Ramsay roads were maintained and materials for bridges and building collected largely by *utar*, that is to say statutory labour engaged for by the landholders at the settlement. This labour was by the hissedars thrust upon the Doms, the village drudges, who got no pay and much ill-treatment. With the advent of the Public Works department the system came to an end except in respect of the small village paths which the hissedars are bound by their settlement engagements to maintain. The Doms as skilled smiths, masons or carpenters at once began to command what was by comparison a colossal rate of pay, and many of them have now become respectable artizans or even contractors for whom their former masters are often glad to carry stone or earth on their heads for a cooly's wage. The conclusion is that the increase in the population though it has contracted the indigenous resources of the people has not depressed them, but on the contrary has driven them to find wealth beyond the boundaries of their own congested district; and at the present day the proposition affirmed by Mr. Traill and Sir H. Ramsay—that the Kumaonis are the most prosperous body in India—is more than ever true.

Character.

It has long been the custom to insist on the sloth of the Kumaoni. The charge apparently rests upon his objection to carrying cooly loads. He carries his own load cheerfully enough, and if on an errand for food, will think nothing of an extra ten or fifteen miles to secure a slightly more favourable price, and he is a laborious cultivator. Mr. Goudge, the Settlement Officer, may again be quoted, "When the great toil of merely keeping his field walls in repair, which are continually falling from the pressure of the soil above or from the force of water in a heavy rainfall, is considered, as well as the expenditure of labour and money necessary to reclaim new land from the natural hillsides, I think he will not be found deficient in the qualities which distinguish the Indian peasant elsewhere." The zamindars of Kumaon are—as has already been remarked—probably the most prosperous rural body in all India. They are for the greater part outside the necessity of earning an occasional four or six annas by carrying a load. The element of compulsion also without doubt makes the work still more distasteful. And there are in all classes of life plenty of people who will willingly carry their own baggage but object to carrying that of others. Idle the Kumaoni may be, but he is seldom indolent. He cannot be acquitted of falsehood. Few Kumaonis in any rank of life affect strict verbal accuracy, and the newcomer is often hard put to it to square report with fact. There is however usually a germ of truth in the statements made and in almost all cases when not strictly true they tend to exaggerate or depreciate the actual circumstance rather than to misrepresent it entirely. The Kumaonis' truths in brief are not whole truths, nor are his lies entirely false. He is conservative to the last degree and therefore childishly suspicious of anything new or unfamiliar; to any change he objects on principle. He is jealous of his neighbour's goods and litigious to the last degree. He is possessed of a certain amount of independence; and displays no great reverence for authority, spiritual or temporal. At the same time he is intensely superstitious and has peopled every grove, peak or rill with devils or gods. His honesty is above question. A verbal bargain is seldom repudiated, and theft is almost unknown. In the lower pattis the Kumaoni has the reputation of being a shrewd man of business; he no longer feels unable to hold his own against the reputed rogues of the plains. Further north he is a simple creature, hospitable and charitable: good natured on the whole, but more easily led than driven. All classes are inclined to neglect their ablutions and all smoke to excess. Gambling is the sole vice of Kumaon. The women are represented as somewhat frail, and it is a fact that accusations of adultery or abduction are frequent. Honour however is easily satisfied and few cases are prosecuted to a finish.

The hillmen of lower and central Almora resemble in general appearance the people of the submontane districts. The complexion is perhaps rather fairer, the face lanker and the body more wiry. A fat Kumaoni, unless he be a retired official, is a rarity. The cloths worn are of cotton, and the people are not sartorially distinguished from the plains men. The small cap is however universal, the *pagri* being rarely seen. The women wear usually a tight-fitting bodice, preferably of velvet, and a loose chintz skirt the foot of which is usually tucked into the waist in a peculiarly unbecoming fashion. Elsewhere they wear a robe which covers the breast in front, where it is supported by a corner brought over the right shoulder and attached in such a manner as to leave both shoulders and arms bare. Further north in the Danpurs, Talla Johar, Talla Darma, and Malla Askot physique improves, the complexion is darker and the people are dressed in blankets secured by brass pins on either shoulder. The men seldom exceed 5 feet 4 inches in height but they are extremely sturdy with the best of thighs and legs. The hair is worn long, curling picturesquely over the ears and neck. The women usually affect no head covering, though they sometimes wear cloth folded like a *pagri*, when working in the snow carrying loads. The hair is allowed to hang down the back in pigtails. Still further north are the Bhotias, a Mongolian race of itinerant merchants, wearing trousers and frock coat of hemp. They are usually taller than the Hindus on their southern border, well proportioned, active, energetic, always busy spinning wool as they drive their sheep along the road.

Villages and houses.

The villages in the Almora district are usually small, the average population being about 92. The ideal site for a village is about half way up an airy spur, with the cultivation above and below, and if possible a two-fold water supply, for the Doms are not allowed to use and befoul the springs meant for their betters; and from a distance the prospect of a hill village is generally very pleasing. The houses are solidly built of stone (the mud-huts of the plains are almost unknown) and roofed with slate, or, in the wilder parts, with shingles of pine wood. There is no overcrowding, the houses being generally arranged in neat rows, and occasionally a man lives apart in the middle of his holding. Except in the case of the Doms, houses of two stories are the rule, and of three not uncommon. The ground floor is called the *goth* and is usually tenanted by the cattle though there is, with the growth of more luxurious ideas, a general tendency to build separate sheds for the cattle. The houses of the better classes are usually surrounded with a paved courtyard or compound protected on the *khad* side by a low parapet wall and bordered with fruit trees. The less adjacent trees are lopped and used as receptacles for straw and grass. Two separate residential quarters are recognized, for the Biths (or Rajputs and Brahmans) and for the Doms. Filth is the characteristic of both. Great heaps of manure and sweepings, removed to the fields once or twice a year, lie in front of each house and engender the hordes of flies for which Kumaon is famous, besides emitting a suffocating stench.

The thokdars now represent the sole remaining rural aristocracy of the district. Their origin is thus described by Mr. Traill, "The country was allotted in separate divisions for the payment of troops to the commander of which was entrusted the civil administration of the lands assigned." "The collection of rents from the assigned lands was . . . left to the commanders, and as these from their military duties could seldom be present for any length of time in their respective assignments" they employed deputies called kamins. The kamin was therefore merely an official revenue collector. The sayana and the thokdar on the other hand appear to have been originally farmers of revenue, who afterwards acquired proprietary rights. And the sayanas were the more important of the two. Mr. Pauw in his Garhwal Settlement Report remarks that the terms kamin, thokdar and sayana describe the same office. This is probably not the case in Almora. Sir H. Ramsay writes, "Tej Singh, sayana of Kahargaon, Narain Singh of Tamadhaund, Kalyan Singh of **Thokdars.**

Jaspur, Malk Singh of Danpur were quite different from ordinary thokdars . . . When I came to the province Malk Singh was a king; his word was law in Upper Danpur. He did what he liked: he took what he wanted and the people did not grumble." Kahargaon, Tamadhaund and Jaspur are all in Chaukot, where sayanas and thokdars exist side by side; the former are of royal blood and had in the time of the Chands the privilege of being inducted with beat of drum and flying colours, and to the present day represent a much higher stratum of rural society than the thokdars. The sayanas are only found in Chaukot, that is to say, near the Garhwal borders, and if there is any meaning in the military pomp of their induction it is that they were in command of the local levies so often engaged in border warfare.

At the present day the offices of sayana and kamin are extinct and many of the ancient holders have had to content themselves with the official title and emoluments of thokdar, though the people ordinarily address the former by their ancient style. These revenue collectors it should be noted were not universal throughout the district even under the rajas, who administered the crown lands through the agency of wazirs and bhandaris, and they have gradually decreased in number since the earlier settlements by British officers. Mr. Traill found them oppressive and reduced their dues to three per cent on the revenue, but this order was never really carried into effect. In 1856 the Senior Assistant Commissioners of Kumaon and Garhwal (afterwards Sir H. Ramsay and Sir J. Strachey) drew up a joint memorandum recommending that they should be relieved of their police duties at once and gradually extinguished. Sir H. Ramsay later altered his opinions, deeming the maintenance of the better class, at least, of thokdars a necessity to ensure the due performance of police duties by the village headman, and he increased the emoluments of some of the more important to ten per cent and six per cent. After Mr. Goudge's settlement the sums hitherto received under the previous settlement were confirmed to the thokdars: that is to say, only in the case of the three per cent thokdars was there any increase corresponding to the enhanced revenue. These dues are in the nature of a commutation of the old feudal dues exacted by the thokdars under native rule. These comprised a leg of each goat killed by the subordinate padhans, half a seer of ghi in the rainy season, and a basket of maize in Sawan. They also received two rupees on the occasion of the wedding of a padhan's daughter. Although these dues were commuted by Mr. Traill for a three per cent allowance on the revenue they continued to be exacted, and at the present day the more powerful and respected thokdars are still able to collect them. The Chaukot sayanas used to collect from their khaikars one rupee a family every third year, one pice a family every Dasehra, the breast and one leg of every goat killed, one seer of ghi, besides curds and gabah (the tender shoots of the pinalu) in Sawan, and as *bhent* took two ploughings at each seed-time for their sir land from every tenant.

The present position of the thokdar is chiefly ornamental. Every thokdar has one or more villages in his thok from which he exacts his dues; but not every village is included in a thokdari. They are supposed to supervise the padhans in their work as police, but their chief usefulness depends upon their influence with the people in their jurisdiction. The office is strictly hereditary and descends by the rules of primogeniture, but appointments are made by the Commissioner. Thokdars are exempted from the provisions of the Indian Arms Act in respect of a gun and a sword. But the thokdars have of late years been declining in power and influence. The village, not the thok, is now the social unit, and with the affairs of any village—except one in which they own land—few thokdars of the present day can effectually interfere. The families which furnish the more important thokdars have already been noticed. The old sayanachari families are now represented by Mohan Singh Manral of Tamadhaund, Daulat Singh Manral of Kahargaon, Madhan Singh and Daljit Singh Bishts of Timli and Gulab Singh of Bharsoli of Malla Chaukot, who have now become thokdars. A fourth important thokdar, also of Bichla Chaukot, is Hira Singh Rajwar. The Manrals and the Rajwars are of royal Katyuri descent. Other Manral thokdars are Partab Singh of Chaukana, Raja Singh and Rup Singh of Sain Manur, both villages in Walla Salt: and Bhagat

Singh of Nagarh, Palla Giwar, Gulab Singh Dungwal of Binoli, Malla Kaklasaun, Parbin Singh of Barkina, Palla Naya, Lacham Singh and Ratan Singh of Chamiari, Malla Chaukot and Deb Singh Bisht of Ira, Bichla Dora may be named among the more important thokdars. All are men of much local influence. All these thokdars exercise their powers over villages in Pali pargana. In Baramandal are Chanar Singh Dhamswal of Dhamas, Talla Tikhun, Bhawan Singh of Ana, Bichla Katyur, and Har Chand Takuli of Supi, Malla Danpur. In the rest of the district there are numbers of thokdars but few are of more than purely parochial importance.

Padhans. The padhan cannot be better described than in Mr. Traill's words: "The padhan is the village ministerial officer entrusted with the collection of the Government demand and with the supervision of the police of his village. He is commonly one of the village appointed with the approbation or the other joint sharers and is removeable for malversation or at the requisition of the majority of sharers. He collects the Government revenue agreeable to their several quotas. He pays also the rent of his own immediate share of the estate. He is remunerated by fees on marriages and a small portion of land set apart for the purpose. There is no hereditary claim or right to the situation of padhan, but generally the son succeeds without opposition unless incapable from youth and want of talent, in which case the sharers are called upon to choose another padhan from among themselves. Uncultivated lands which may not have been subjected to division among the proprietors are managed by the padhan and the rents yielded from their cultivation are accounted for by him to the body of proprietors, who take credit for the same in the quota of the Government cess to which they are respectively liable." In his revenue aspects the padhan answers to the lambardar of the plains. He is also the headman and is required to perform all the duties assigned to him in the Chaukidari Act and the Code of Criminal Procedure. As a police officer he is supposed to be supervised by the thokdar. He also represents the village in all its dealings with the Government in which is included the duty of providing for transport and supplies for officials and travellers. There is usually one padhan for each village, but occasionally when a village is held by two or more clans there is a separate padhan for each clan ; and often a large land-holder or thokdar is padhan of more than one village. In these cases he is required to appoint a mukhtar-padhan to act as his agent in villages other than those in which he resides. Mukhtar-padhans are also occasionally nominated by a padhan who is a minor.

The ghar-padhan is the padhan of a purely khaikari village nominated by his fellow-khaikars to act as their agent in all communal matters. He pays the revenue he collects to the proprietor, but he is in no way his agent, and is to be differentiated from the mukhtar-padhan. His remuneration is usually the padhanchari land. His nomination requires the Deputy Commissioner's assent before he can take office.

In a district like Almora where there are no regular police, no village watchmen, and no patwaris (as the office is understood in the plains) the maintenance of the dignity of the padhan is an administrative object of the greatest importance. In a way the padhan is merely *primus inter pares* in the village but a padhan of any character can make his influence felt in innumerable ways. His exemption from the obligation of statutory labour is the envy of his fellows, and the responsibility of reporting breaches of the forest laws and failure to furnish supplies naturally adds to his prestige. The padhan has of recent years advanced in importance as the thokdar has declined. The office is now recognized as hereditary subject to the proviso that the heir succeeds to at least a portion of the family lands and that he is not unfitted for the post by physical or mental incapacity. He is no longer removable at the requisition of the majority of the *hissedars* unless some definite charge of wrong-doing or unfitness can be established against him.

Leading families.

The titular Raja of Almora represents the ancient Chand line. The present holder of the title is Raja Anand Singh. Partab Chand, the grandson of the usurper Mohan Singh and son of Mahendra Singh the last reigning raja, who lost Kumaon to the Gurkhas, was granted by the British Government a political pension of Rs. 250 a month. This pension was at first continued in full to his son, Nanda Singh, but later it was reduced to Rs. 125. On the death of Nanda Singh, his son Bhim Singh during his minority got no allowance, but when he arrived at man's estate he was given government posts and under Mr. Beckett he served as a Settlement Tahsildar. The Katyur rajas are represented by the Pali thokdars mentioned above and the Askot family, of which a more detailed description will be found in the directory. Mention may be made also of the late Rai Bahadur Badri Datt Joshi, the head of the Dania Joshis. This family traces its origin to the small town of Jhusi near Allahabad, whence they say they were originally invited to Kumaon by Raja Som Chand, the legendary founder of the Chand dynasty which from its humble beginnings in Champawat in time overran all Kumaon. They claim to have been originally Pandes. The Joshis of Galli say they are the descendants of Nathu Raj and Bije Raj who came from Kanauj to worship at the shrines of Kedarnath and Badrinath, and being well versed in the sciences of astrology and astronomy obtained the protection of the Katyur rajas and later of the Chands. From these rajas they obtained grants of land and subsequently attained the position of large landholders. The Jhijar Joshis claim descent from Sadhanidhi, a learned pandit who is said to have discerned by means of his science the promise of future greatness in Som Chand, whom he found wandering about the ruins of the Jhusi fort in a deplorable condition. He accompanied Som Chand to Kumaon and became his adviser. The Jhijar Joshis still enjoy a jagir near Champawat, the capital of Som Chand. To this family belonged the generals and statesmen who played so important a part in the troublous times that preceded the fall of the Chands, Harak Deb, Shib Deb, and Jayanand. Pandit Badri Datt of this family still draws a pension of Rs. 50 a month on account of the services of the family at the expulsion of the Gurkhas.

The family now known as the China Khan Joshis repudiate any connection with any other Almora Joshis. They trace their descent from three Brahmans of Kanauj who settled in the hills at the invitation of one of the Chand Rajas. Later the family was granted the village of Dhura near Almora in jagir, but towards the end of the 18th century Chandramani, the head of the family and faujdar of the Bhot Mahals, removed to Almora town and settled himself in the quarter known as China Khan. Pandit Ganga Datt, a well-known enquirer into local folk-lore, was until his death in 1910 the head of the Upretis. His grandfather Suba Jai Kishen Upreti brought in a large body of local levies to assist the British invaders against the Gurkhas and was rewarded with a pension of Rs. 200 a month for his lifetime; a reduced pension of Rs. 40 a month was granted to the second generation.

A large number of estates in the Almora district are held in fee simple grant, under Lord Canning's rule of 1861. These rules provided for the redemption of the land revenue at 20 years' purchase in the case of estates already settled, and for the acquisition of waste land at fixed rates per acre. Many very large estates were acquired in this way in the middle of the last century and planted with tea. The Dunagiri estate near Dwarahat was purchased in 1866 by Mr. J. W. B. Money for Rs. 5,128. One-tenth share was sold to Mr. Larpent in 1867 and the whole was sold to Mr. Craw in execution of a decree in 1874. On Mr. Craw's death in the early nineties the estate passed to his wife, and she devised it a few years later to her nephew Mr. Earle and her husband's nephew Mr. Henderson, of Lodh. The estate now owned by the Kausani Tea Company was purchased from the indigenous proprietors in 1856 by Mr. McLeod of Tirhut, from whom the company acquired it. The company purchased the fee simple about 1862. It possesses also other lands held in ordinary revenue-paying tenure. The Malla Katyur Tea Estate is the property of Captain Colin Troup and Mr. Norman Troup. It comprises lands situated in Wajula, Ayar Toli, Arkhali and Chattia, all held in fee simple together with the *khalsa* villages of Bunga and Kotura. Wajula and Megri were bought from the hill owners by Captain Troup in 1860, and by him formed into the Kumaon and Katyur Tea Company. Subsequently Jauna was acquired as a government grant and included in the company's properties, and afterwards the fee simple was acquired under the Board of Revenue's rules. When the Troups separated from the company Wajula

Fee simple estates.

fell to their share, and Megri and Jauna were taken by the company and sold to the Messrs. Nash in 1892. Chattia was in like manner originally acquired by General Story from the zamindars and the fee simple having been bought, was sold by him to Mr. N. Troup. Ayar Toli and Arkhali were sold in fee simple by auction by the Government and knocked down to the Troups in 1876. In addition to Megri and Jauna, Messrs. Nash also hold Damlot, which was taken up as a grant about 1861 by Messrs. McIver and Murray and made freehold in 1869. Mr. Dalzell acquired the property in 1873, and from him it passed to the Rohilkhand and Kumaon Bank in 1888. They in their turn sold it to Mr. H. M. Hewett and Lala Krishna Sah, Rai Bahadur, from whom it was bought by the Messrs. Nash in 1895. The Berenag fee simple estate was bought by Mr. Dennis Hely on behalf of a company about 1866, and next year, Mr. Hey having been killed by lightning in the Berenag bungalow the management was taken over by Mr. J. G. Stevenson, who gradually acquired the full proprietary rights. Chaukuri was bought by Mr. Ebenezer Meakin and by him sold to the Kumaon and Oudh Plantation Co., Ltd., a short-lived concern which went into liquidation in 1868. From the company Mr. Stevenson acquired this estate also. Another estate belonging to the company, Jaltola was also held in fee simple and it passed into the hands of Munshi Itman Ali. Major Hennessy's property at Lohaghat was originally purchased from the Government by General Danzey. The Bhaisora estate was originally acquired in fee simple in 1869 by Lala Jai Sah Thalgharia, and purchased later at public auction by Lala Chiranji Lal Sah, son of Lala Jai Sah. It was sold again to Lala Durga Sah, who is still in possession. The Shiali estate was another of General Story's acquisitions. He acquired the fee simple in 1872 and sold it with Chattia to Mr. Troup as already related, who gave it, in recognition of his long services to the father of the present proprietors Gobind Singh, Kishan Singh, Narain Singh and Mohan Singh. The estate known as Hawalbagh (the site of the earliest British military station in the district) was purchased by the late Lala Amar Nath Sah of Naini Tal in 1879 direct from Government for Rs. 37,500. The estate consists of two blocks, Hawalbagh garden and Halwalbagh forest. The adjacent estate known as "The Lines" was originally purchased by Mr. Oldham of the Geological Survey in 1866, from whom it passed into the hands of the Rohilkhand and Kumaon Bank, and from them to Mr. J. G. Bellairs (who afterwards changed his name to Stevenson and is alluded to above) in 1886, the price paid being Rs. 14,000. It was sold a month later to Lala Amar Nath Sah for Rs. 22,500. Lala Amar Nath Sah died in 1909 and was succeeded by his son Lala Udai Nath Sah. Last of all is the Pati estate sold in fee simple direct to P. Badri Dat Joshi, Rai Bahadur, and held by his descendants.

CHAPTER IV.

REVENUE AND ADMINISTRATION.

The district.

Up to 1891 the Kumaon division consisted of the three districts of Kumaon, Garhwal and the Tarai. The hill *pattis* surrounding the summer sanitarium of Naini Tal and the Naini Tal Bhabar then formed an integral portion of the Kumaon district and were administered subject to the control of the district officer by an assistant commissioner stationed at Naini Tal. On the 13th October 1891 an important readjustment of the boundaries of the districts was made under a resolution* of the Government in the Revenue department. The objects in view were to place in charge of a single officer the large State properties in the Tarai and Kumaon Bhabar; to retain in one district and bring under the direct supervision of the district officer the Kumaon-Bhabar and those hill *pattis* which furnished the Bhabar with its cultivators; by making Naini Tal the head quarters of a district, to bring it under the immediate control of the magistrate there stationed, and, by reducing the size of the Kumaon district, to make its administration more amenable to the personal control and supervision of the district officer.

It was further decided that the head quarters of the new districts should be at Almora and Naini Tal, respectively, and that as the Tarai was no longer applicable as the name of a district of which only a third of the area was *tarai* country, and as Kumaon had ceased to be a suitable name for the northern district, which no longer contained the whole of ancient Kumaon, the new districts should be renamed Almora and Naini Tal, respectively. At the same time, the chief officers of the districts

* No. $\frac{2533}{\text{I.—725A.}}$ of 13th October 1891.

were styled deputy commissioners instead of senior assistant commissioners or superintendents.

The area severed from the old Kumaon district was comprised in six parganas—Chhakhata, Kota, Dhaniyakot, Ramgarh, Kotauli and Dhyanirao. These however were not handed over in their entirety. The *patti* of Mahruri Dolphat in Mahruri, as well as eleven villages of Malli Mahruri and the *patti* of Talli Rao in Dhyanirao were retained in Almora. At the same time two *pattis* of pargana Phaldakot known as Malla and Talla Kosian were added to the pargana of Dhaniyakot while Talla and Bichla Bisaud were given to Kotauli from Barahmandal. In 1893 a joint enquiry by officers on the staff of each district resulted in certain minor transfers. Three villages, were taken from *patti* Malli Mahruri of Naini Tal and included in Malla Bisaud of Almora, while Nayeli was taken from Malla Bisaud and added to Bichli Mahruri: Lakni was taken from Talla Salam and included in Chaubhainsi, and Wara taken from *patti* Chalsi of Almora was added to the same *patti*. The effect of these exchanges was a shorter and better defined boundary, and incidentally a loss to Naini Tal of eighteen square miles of territory, and an addition of five persons to the population and sixteen rupees to the revenue.

In 1896 the portion of the Bhabar known as the Talla Des or Tanakpur Bhabar which had been transferred to the new Naini Tal district in 1891 was again made over to Almora.* The Tanakpur Bhabar is situated to the extreme south-east of the Almora district, on the banks of the Sarda river: it is severed from the rest of the Bhabar by thirty miles of uninhabited forest, and is therefore more accessible to the deputy collector of the Almora district stationed at Champawat than to the deputy collector in charge of the Naini Tal Bhabar. Another reason was that the Tanakpur region adjoins the Kali Kumaon pargana of Almora, the cultivators of which alone hold land in the Tanakpur Bhabar. In making the transfer of the tract it was agreed that the Jagbura river should be the southern boundary, and in consequence a small portion of the Bilheri pargana

* Notification no. $\frac{4090}{1-723A}$, dated the 28th October 1896.

in the Tarai was also transferred to the Almora district. The reason for adopting this boundary was that the whole of the arable land to the north of the Jagbura could be irrigated from the Barmdeo canal in the Tanakpur Bhabar. The result of this exchange was that Naini Tal lost 4,313 acres in area, 5,367 persons in population and Rs. 354 in land revenue.* In 1910 the Tanakpur Bhabar was again transferred to the Naini Tal district. It was considered uneconomical to keep up a separate establishment under the control of the Deputy Commissioner of Almora for a small tract of land which could easily be managed by the Khatema peshkar of the Naini Tal district. The area of the tract transferred is 16,318 acres with a winter population of 7,429 persons.

Sub division.

For the purposes of revenue administration the district of Almora is divided into 12 parganas and 101 *pattis*. Of the former, Johar, Danpur, Barahmandal, Pali Pachhaon, Phaldakot, Chaugarkha and Gangoli form the Almora tahsil, while the remainder, Darma, Askot, Sira, Shor, and Kali Kumaon belong to the Champawat subdivision. A table showing the *pattis* belonging to the several parganas is given in the appendix.

There are two tahsildars with head quarters at Almora and Champawat respectively. The jurisdiction of the Almora tahsildar extends over all the parganas which compose the Almora tahsil, and he has two deputies called peshkars, one stationed at Ranikhet and the other at Almora. The Champawat tahsildar is only concerned with the affairs of the Kali Kumaon pargana of the eastern tahsil. Up to 1910 a peshkar was stationed at Pithoragarh in charge of Shor, Sira, and Askot, while a political peshkar with head quarters at Garbiyang in the hot weather and at Dharchula in the cold weather exercised jurisdiction over the Darma pargana. A political deputy collector was also maintained in the northern portions of the district; his chief duties were to facilitate trade with Tibet in every possible way and especially to watch over the interests of British traders sojourning in that country. In 1910 however important changes took place. The political deputy collector was transferred to Pithoragarh and the political peshkar was made more directly his

* Naini Tal Gazetteer.

subordinate and was brought to the same place and given charge of all Bhot. The deputy collector in charge of Kali Kumaon was stationed in Lohaghat, whither the Champawat tahsil will shortly be removed. A joint magistrate in charge of Pali was posted to Ranikhet.

Below the tahsildars and peshkars are the kanungos, each in charge of one or two parganas, and below them again the patwaris, 86 in number, in charge of the *pattis*. Kanungos.

There are six officers within the district charged with the duty of supervising the work of the patwaris. They all draw Rs. 25 a month each in pay: three, whose office is hereditary, are styled kanungos and the other three superintendents of patwaris. The former are the official descendants of the *daftaris* who, under the Hindu rajas and the Gurkhas, performed duties corresponding closely to those of the tahsildar of the plains. On the British occupation the office of kanungo in Kumaon was found divided amongst two families, one of Chaudhris and one of Joshis. The parganas had not hitherto been distributed amongst them, and the duties were performed jointly, each being aided by deputies known as *likhwars* or writers. Practically however the Dwarahat Chaudhris furnished kanungos for Pali and Barahmandal; the Daniya Joshis, one for Shor and one for Chaugarkha, and the Jhijhar Joshis, one for Kali Kumaon; and all acted generally as collectors of the land revenue, writers and record-keepers. They were formerly remunerated by lands held in service tenure and they also received half an anna in the rupee on the revenue, from which they paid their deputies in each pargana to look after the collections and the cultivation. These lands were frequently resumed and again restored by the former governments. The *nankar* lands were assessed at Rs. 1,979 in 1819 and brought on the revenue roll and a monthly allowance of twenty-five rupees was granted instead to each of the kanungos. The first patwaris were entertained and paid from the surplus revenues of these resumed lands, and as the revenue increased, other patwaris were appointed who performed duties somewhat similar to those formerly entrusted to the kanungos and their deputies. The latter however appear merely to have kept up lists of villages and the names of headmen or *padhans*, whilst the patwari has gradually become a sort of local sub-tahsildar. The office of kanungo was considered hereditary so far that the succession remained in one family, but both the former Governments and the British authorities have always exercised their discretion of selecting the most capable member of a family for the office without reference to claims of seniority. In 1829 the kanungos were invested with powers to try civil suits, but these powers were withdrawn in 1839, and for a time apparently but little use was made of their services beyond such miscellaneous duties as the district authorities could assign them. Now however they have plenty of work to do, and that of a varied character. In addition to their prime duty of supervising the work of the patwaris they are often employed in making enquiries into the more important cases, either civil, revenue or criminal, for kanungos have within their circles the powers of an officer in charge of a police station. In addition to these six officers there is a *sadur* or registrar kanungo attached to the land records office, making in all seven posts. Four of these are held by the families mentioned above, but special parganas are not now as formerly assigned to each family. The fifth hereditary kanungoship, one of the two belonging to the Chaudhri family was included in the establishment of the Naini Tal district when it was separated in 1891. The field of selection for the more recent post of superintendent of patwaris is unlimited and the Deputy Commissioner makes the appointments as he thinks fit.

Patwaris.

The patwari of the hills has nothing in common with his brother of the plains. The hill patwari is in fact almost everything except a village accountant. He is a British institution and was unknown under the indigenous form of government though some of the *daftaris* or kanungos in the larger *pattis* enjoyed the assistance of writers called *likhwars*. They were remunerated from the half-anna cess collected by the *daftaris*, and, after the conquest, disappeared with the abolition of that cess. On settling the resumed kanungo lands in 1819 Mr. Traill found a surplus of nearly Rs. 500, which he recommended should be devoted to the establishment of patwaris at a salary of Rs. 5 a month in nine of the principal parganas. The advantage of the work done by these patwaris in recording lands reclaimed from waste were recognized at the second settlement, and patwaris were therefore placed in three other parganas.

The records of the kanungos were imperfect and incomplete as those officers had always remained at head quarters, and for the local knowledge of the assets and capabilities of each village they trusted to the reports of their deputies who resided in the parganas. By the absorption of the smaller parganas in the larger ones to which they formerly belonged, the number was reduced to fourteen and the arrangement now made provided one patwari for each of the larger parganas. In 1825 a further addition was made, the cost of which was met by a reduction of the tahsil establishment, and in 1830 the measure was extended to the whole province of Kumaon. At this time, there were over seven thousand estates on the revenue roll in the two districts. In many of them the land revenue was less than five rupees a year and the proprietor was the only cultivator. To ensure the collection of such a detailed assessment peons had hitherto been stationed in each pargana to look after the cultivation and collect the revenue. Thirty patwaris were added to the establishment and the expense was met by a corresponding reduction in the number of peons, so that the new measure was little more than the substitution of what may be called a better class of peons, without the official title; for many educated and respectable persons were found ready to undertake the duties of a patwari who would have considered it a degradation to wear the badge of a peon. The establishment thus consisted of sixty-three patwaris, giving on an average one to every 120 villages and to every Rs. 3,300 of revenue, and costing at Rs. 5 a month each Rs. 315 a month.

At the present moment there are 86 patwaris in the district. Each is usually in charge of a *patti*; in a few cases two or even three small *pattis* are placed in the charge of a single patwari. A patwari's salary is Rs. 10 a month, but he also receives from the zamindars within his charge a number of well-recognized perquisites, such as the *bhent* or *pitai*—a *nazrana* on first appointment, usually one rupee a family,—and a *nali* of grain at each *harvest*; food for himself, his servant and a pony is provided by the villages which he visits when on tour. The patwari is the general factotum of the district officer. He may be called upon to apprehend a murderer or report on indigenous fruits and roots used by the poorer classes in famine time; to hold an inquest or provide coolies and supplies for the camp of an officer or traveller. He has the powers of a sub-inspector of police, and is entrusted with the collection of the revenue from the *padhans* and its prompt payment into the treasury. He may have to execute the decrees of a civil court or serve summonses and execute warrants from a criminal court, and he is also required to report at regular intervals to the district officer all matters of interest occurring in his circle. His appointment and his transfer from one *patti* to another are entirely in the hands of the Deputy Commissioner and the village proprietary body has no say in these matters.

Civil administration.

On the expulsion of the Gurkhas Mr. E. Gardner was appointed to the charge of the province of Kumaon in 1815. His political duties compelled him to accompany the expedition to Nepal and the general administration of the province devolved upon Mr. Traill. As Mr. Traill did not relinquish the charge of the province until 1835, the whole of the arrangements made for the administration of both civil and criminal justice originated with him or received his sanction. In 1821 Mr. Traill in one of his letters made several proposals for the improvement of the administration, and in it occurs this remarkable passage:—"It is probable that many of the suggestions have already formed the subject of legislative enactments; if so, I have only to offer in excuse that, as the regulations do not extend to this province, I have not been furnished with or seen a single regulation for the last six years." Mr. Traill was not only administrator but also legislator for his province. For many years his was the only civil court in the district. He required plaints to be presented on an eight-anna stamp. If the plaint was not rejected in the first instance the plaintiff was furnished with notice to serve on the defendant. This process proved sufficient in three-fourths of the cases instituted to produce a compromise. If the plaintiff failed to get satisfaction in this way, the defendant was summoned and the case regularly adjudicated. The parties first and then, if necessary, their witnesses were called and examined. Oaths were seldom administered. No law agents were permitted to practice. Suits seldom lasted more than twelve days. Copies of the decree were granted to the parties on an eight-anna stamp : and the price of this together with that of the paper on which the original plaint was presented together with process servers' fees constituted the whole costs of a suit in the Commissioner's court.

The first munsif was appointed in 1829, and later the seven kanungos in the province were invested with the title and powers of munsif, while the title of *sadar amin* was conferred on the court *pandit* when he was invested with civil jurisdiction. These officers continued to exercise the functions of civil judges in petty cases until 1838, when their offices were abolished. Act X of 1838 provided that there should be two districts, Kumaon and Garhwal, in each of which were to be stationed one senior assistant, one sadar amin and one munsif.

In 1838 the province of Kumaon was placed under the control of the Sadar Board of Revenue in fiscal matters. The Commissioner was declared to have the same powers as a Commissioner in the plains. A senior assistant commissioner was to exercise the same powers as a collector and a junior assistant the same powers as a deputy collector. In the same year the province was made subject to the jurisdiction of the Sadar Dewani Adalat in civil matters. In 1839 the Assam rules for the administration of civil and criminal justice with certain limitations applicable to Kumaon were put into force. Between 1836 and 1838 great changes were made in the administration. In the former year the traffic in slaves was prohibited and the courts were forbidden to receive suits for the recovery of slaves. In 1837 the importation of slaves into the plains was declared to be illegal and criminal, and in the same year magistrates were forbidden to order the restoration of wives to their husbands.

All these orders promoted regularity. In 1855 revised rules for the guidance of the revenue courts in summary and regular suits were introduced which with modifications continue in force to the present day. The Assam rules were superseded by the Jhansi rules in 1863 and extended to Kumaon by section 2 of Act XXIV of 1864. This act further provided for the extension of the law of limitation to Kumaon and declared that the Indian Penal Code was in force.

The present Kumaon Rules came into force in 1894 and in 1906 various portions of the Land Revenue Act of 1901 were extended to the Kumaon division.

Criminal administration.

The criminal administration during the earlier year of British rule gave little trouble in Kumaon. In 1816 Mr. Traill writes :—"The small number of offences committed in this province has rendered the criminal police an object of secondary consideration ; accordingly no separate report has hitherto been submitted to Government on the subject. Murder is a crime almost unknown throughout this province, and theft and robbery are of very rare occurrence—a remark which applies equally to all offences the ultimate cognizance of which would, by the regulations, rest with the Court of Circuit. From the period of the introduction of the British Government into this province the persons confined for criminal offences here have never exceeded twelve—the greater part of whom have always been natives of the plains. The number of prisoners at present in jail amounts to seven, of which four are natives of the plains. Under the late government the punishment of offences of a petty nature formed a source of revenue, all cases of infringement of caste, assault, fornication, adultery, abuse, &c., were made subject to fines and the cognizance of such offences and levy of the fines were farmed out in separate divisions or districts to the best bidder. Crimes of a serious nature, including murder, theft to a large amount, killing of cows, &c., were reserved for the decision of the principal *bharadars* present in the province."

In July 1817, however, Regulation X of 1817 was enacted to provide for the trial of persons charged with the commission of certain heinous offences in the Kumaon district and other tracts of country ceded to the East India Company by the Raja of Nepal. It applied to Dehra Dun, Kumaon and Garhwal, Jaunsar Bawar, Pundar, and Sandokh and other small tracts of country between the Jumna and the Sutlej. By it a Commissioner was appointed for the trial of heinous offences subject to a report to the Court of Nizamat Adalat, who passed the final sentence, which was then carried into effect by the local officer. The question regarding the extradition of criminals with Nepal also arose and was settled on the basis that only those charged with heinous offences and for whose arrest the warrant afforded *prima facie* evidence that they were guilty of the offence imputed, should be delivered to the Nepalese authorities; otherwise, general usage did not recognize the principle of apprehending or surrendering to a foreign power petty delinquents seeking an asylum within our dominions.

British administration.

Writing in 1822, Mr. Traill remarks that during the previous year there were 65 criminals confined in the jail, of whom only six were charged with heinous offences, and only in three cases were the offenders able to escape detection. Affrays of a serious nature were unknown and even petty assaults were infrequent. Many robberies occurred in the tract along the foot of the hills but they were perpetrated by people from the plains, who retired there with their booty. The offence of adultery was very common, but it seldom formed a subject of complaint in court unless accompanied by the abduction of the adulteress. The suicide of females was common. Applications to the court on the subject of caste were numerous, due doubtless to the fact that under former governments the cognizance of cases involving deprivation of caste was confined to the government court. This description of the people during the earlier years of our rule is confirmed by the testimony of an officer who visited Kumaon charged with the special duty of inquiry into the administration of justice.

Reforms.

Mr. Glyn was deputed to Kumaon in 1822 to hold a sessions of jail delivery and to report on the police and criminal administration. His report is full and interesting and confirms the account already given by Traill. There was a general absence of heinous crime of every description, and the few gang robberies that were reported took place in the strip of country lying along the southern frontier, and more particularly within the jurisdiction of the authorities of the plains districts. Disputes regarding women were the most fruitful cause of complaint, and the ready attention given to these cases by the authorities without doubt prevented the occurrence of more serious crime. In consequence of suggestions made in this report it was ordered that forced labour for the carriage of goods should cease, and that inquests should be held in all cases of sudden deaths, a precaution rendered necessary by the number of deaths reported as due to the attacks of wild animals, snake-bites, suicides and accident. In 1824 the number of deaths attributed to these causes was 237. Attention was also drawn to several other matters requiring reform. In the resolution on the report made by Mr. Glyn the Government of India also bear testimony to the success of Mr. Traill's administration and the entire fulfilment of the sanguine anticipations of his peculiar fitness for the important duties he then fulfilled; and in 1825, in consideration of the judgment and zeal with which he discharged the duties of Commissioner, he was authorised to draw the full pay of a Judge and Magistrate.

Adultery. Slavery.

Amongst the customs of the country which were now abolished two deserve special mention : the right to slay an adulterer and the sale of human beings, children and grown-up persons, as slaves. The former was prohibited by a resolution in 1819 which demonstrates the prevalence of complaints of this nature in the local courts and the necessity there was for paying full attention to them to prevent graver crimes. The sale of children and grown-up persons which had arisen during a long period of misrule and oppression had formally received the sanction of the previous governments, who levied a duty on the export of slaves. This duty was abolished at the conquest, but the practice itself was too deep-rooted to be at once eradicated. In 1822 Mr. Glyn wrote to the Commissioner:—"The practice of selling children and grown-up persons by inhabitants of this province amongst one another or into the hands of strangers is still in a mitigated degree continued, though I am aware of your anxious endeavours to abolish this barbarous practice." The Bhotias on the north and the Pathans on the south were the principal customers. The Government considered that the natural affections of the parents might safely be relied upon as a remedy against a resort to the sale of children, except as a relief to both parents and children in times of extreme distress. As the prosperity of the province and the comfort of the people increased, this practice would diminish and eventually cease; at the samo time the sales of wives by their husbands, of widows by the heirs and relations of the deceased and of children to be taken out of the country chiefly for the purpose of being made household slaves, were forbidden and made penal. But slavery in the form in which it existed continued and flourished, and as late as 1837 the Commissioner reported thus:—

"Slavery in Kumaon appears to be hereditary. The classes of slaves are distinguishable into household slaves and slaves kept for the cultivation of the land, the former, Khasiya Rajputs, the latter Doms. This state of bondage would seem to have existed from a very remote period. The slaves are dependent upon their owners for food, lodging and clothing, and for the discharge of marriage expenses. The purchase or temporary engagement of such persons for carrying on cultivation as well as the purchase of females for prostitution are still common and have never been prohibited. Such transactions are accompanied by a deed of sale. The recognition of slavery by the courts is confined to the sale of individuals by their parents. Claims for freedom or servitude are heard like other suits."

Slavery was extinguished merely by refusing to permit suits for the restoration of slaves or for the enforcement of slavery to be brought in our courts. The prohibition of slavery in its first form was followed by the abolition of *sati* in 1829. In 1837 Colonel Gowan, the Commissioner, reported that murder and theft are yet rare amongst the people, and although crime had increased since 1821, yet the total number of criminals confined in jail on the 1st of January, 1837, numbered only 142, of whom 28 were convicted of gang robbery in the tract along the foot of the hills and were natives of the plains. Complaints on account of injuries received by sorcery and applications in caste matters were however still very numerous.

Courts and powers.

The Deputy Commissioner of Almora as District Magistrate possesses, in addition to the jurisdiction common to all District Magistrates, the power conveyed by section 30 of the Code of Criminal Procedure, to inflict enhanced penalties in certain cases. His civil powers are those of a District Judge, except so far as the Indian Succession Act is concerned; in cases under that Act the

Commissioner of the division discharges the functions of the District Judge. The Deputy Commissioner is also Collector and Registrar. The Assistant Commissioners of the first class in addition to their ordinary revenue and criminal powers are empowered to take cognizance of civil suits whose valuation does not exceed Rs. 5,000. The limit of the civil jurisdiction of Assistant Commissioners of the second class and of Tahsildars is Rs. 500 and Rs. 100 respectively. In civil matters the High Court for Kumaon is that of the Commissioner. The Government can however refer matters decided by the Commissioner's Court to the High Court at Allahabad for its opinion, and it may alter or reverse the the decisions of the Commissioner, in accordance with the answer given by the High Court to the reference. In succession cases however the Commissioner is the Judge and the High Court is the High Court of the North-West Provinces at Allahabad. On the criminal side the Commissioner is also the Sessions Judge and hears appeals from, and cases committed by, the Deputy Commissioner as District Magistrate, and his subordinates; the High Court is that of Allahabad.

Police. There is no regular police in the district except at Almora and Ranikhet. During the pilgrim season wayside guard-houses with accommodation for two or three constables are occupied by police sent by the Superintendent of police for Kumaon. The roads traversed by the pilgrims are patrolled daily. Such guard-houses exist at Ganai and Bhikia Sen.

The few peons attached to the courts and tahsils perform, with the assistance of the patwaris, *thokdars* and *padhans,* the duty of apprehending offenders and escorting prisoners. The *padhans* arrest offenders and report crime to the patwaris and provide for the despatch of persons charged with heinous offences for trial. The *thokdars* are bound to report crime overlooked by the *padhans* and few offences are concealed for the village officials in their duty have to make so many enemies that any concealment on their part can hardly escape detection. Sir H. Ramsay writes :—

"I believe our rural police system works better than in any other part of India, and it would be most unwise to interfere with it. It has the great merit of being cheap, i.e. costs the State nothing (except the Bhabar police) and the absence of annoyance and worry inseparable from a paid police is not its smallest recommendation."

Fiscal history—The Rajas.

The old fiscal principle that the property in the soil is vested in the State has never been lost sight of and has been reiterated by both Gurkha and British settlement officers. This is still the case in Nepal and in Tehri Garhwal. The revenue of the Rajas of both Kumaon and Garhwal was not wholly confined to a land-tax, but included dues of various kinds and in addition taxes on commerce, mines, the administration of justice, law proceedings and forest produce. An impost was laid on *ghi* or clarified butter payable by the owners of the cattle at a rate fixed for each animal, and amounting to four annas on each female buffalo.

"The weavers throughout the province," writes Mr. Traill, "were also subject to a separate tax. The assessment of land was, generally speaking, light, the Government demand on agriculture being rated at only one-third of the gross produce in ordinary lands, and at one-half in the very fertile. In mines, the royal share amounted to one-half. The collection was made in two forms, being imposed one year on the land, and a second year levied by a capitation tax on the inhabitants. As these, however, consisted solely of persons connected with agriculture, the source from which the payments were made was necessarily the same, though the mode and detail of cess varied." The *gaicharai* or grazing tax had from time immemorial formed a portion of the public assets in the assessments made in the tract immediately below the hills. In one of Mr. Traill's many valuable reports he writes:—"The agricultural assessment or *sirti* (cash payment), as originally fixed, was extremely light, and its rate and amount would appear to have been very rarely revised. To supply the increasing expenditure of the State numerous other taxes were successively imposed on the landholder. Of these the principal were a capitation tax and a house tax, and the whole were summed up under the designation of *chhatis rakam* and *batis kalam* or the thirty-six items of revenue and the thirty-two items of ministerial fees. These numbers appear to have been used arbitrarily as including the regular and contingent cesses, the total to which the landholder was liable never actually amounted to sixty-eight; but they were sufficiently onerous to leave him little beyond the means of subsistence. As the public demand was not regulated on any consideration of the produce, the relative proportions which they bore to each other can only be estimated by the analogy of the rates paid to the free holders by the *khaikars* and *kainis*.* These varied in different parganas from one-third to two-fifths of the gross produce. Rents were commonly paid in kind (*kut*) at an invariable rate fixed on the land and payable in some specified description of grain without reference to the annual fluctuations in the amount and nature of the produce."

Under the Gurkhas the system was changed. The cess on agriculture was augmented while most of the 68 extra taxes were abolished. *Nankar* (capitation tax), *tandkar* (loom tax), *mijhari* (tax on Doms), *ghikar* (tax on *ghi*), *salami* (presents to officials) and *soniya phagun* (offerings on festivals) alone were retained, and the only ministerial fees that remained in force were those payable to the kanungo, the *kamin* and the *padhan*. The gross demand was equivalent to a tax on every kind of income. It was by no means excessive had the central Government been strong enough to restrain the exactions of the military commanders to whom had been assigned various portions of the district. Mr. Traill has left on record the Gurkhas' revenue roll for 1812. It amounted to 1,64,426 Gurkha rupees for the whole of Kumaon proper, and was derived from various sources. On the British occupation the only duties retained were those on forest produce, which partook more of the nature of a land tax on uncultivated land. These formed the nucleus of what subsequently became the revenue of the Forest Department of which an account has been given elsewhere.

It must be premised before proceeding to a sketch of the fiscal history of the district as it now exists, that the figures for the earlier settlements are approximate only. Statistics for each separate pargana of the old Kumaon district are extant, and the figures for what is now the Almora district have been arrived at by deducting from the total for Kumaon the figures referrible

* An occupancy tenant of lower rank than the *khaikar*. The term is now obsolete.

to the parganas transferred to the Naini Tal district. But whole parganas were not always handed over in their entirety. *Pattis* and even individual villages have been separately transferred, and for these it has not been possible to deduce the separate figures.

First settlement.

The land-tax of the first settlement of the district yielded Rs. 70,699. This was effected by the Hon'ble Mr. Gardner in 1872 *samvat* (1815-16 A. D.). The assessment was based on the actual receipts of the Gurkhas during the preceding year, as owing to the destruction of records and the ravages caused by the war, it was impossible to obtain any more reliable data on which a calculation could be made. In Kali Kumaon and Barahmandal it was necessary to make some reductions as many villages had been destroyed by the enemy. One-fourth, too, was deducted to enable the people to pay in the coin current in the plains instead of the Gurkha *timashas* and rupees which were hitherto current. The settlement of Bhot also was fixed in the Government currency instead of partly in Gurkha currency and partly in kind, as had hitherto been the practice, and with a light assessment and the introduction of security to life and property it was believed that the revenues would be realised without difficulty, and a progressive increase might be hoped for in future years. So far had matters progressed that it was resolved to place the administration of the province under the general superintendence of the Board of Commissioners, the predecessor of the present Board of Revenue. At the same time, the authorities did not contemplate the introduction into Kumaon of the regulations generally as a part of the proposed arrangement, but " it appeared expedient that the Commissioner should, in his capacity of Collector of the revenue, be placed under the control of the Board of Commissioners, and that their relative powers and duties should be defined by the general principles established throughout the provinces." In practice there was little interference with the work of a man so peculiarly fitted for the charge which he undertook as Mr. Traill. The second settlement was formed by him in 1817 at a total of Rs. 73,359 with the *padhans* or headmen for their respective villages.* This

* The records of the Gurkha regular settlement in 1864 Samvat which was fixed generally on actual observation of each village, were also referred to.

Second settlement.

mode of collection was new to the people and as the power and responsibilities of the *padhans* remained to be ascertained, the arrangement was only partially introduced and the leases were restricted to one year. Mr. Traill thus describes the principles on which this settlement was formed:—"The rights of no individual have been compromised, as the *kamins* continue to receive their established dues from the villages included in their subdivisions and are the channels of communication in matters of police between the Government and those villages. In a few villages, owing to their smallness or the difficulty of communication, the *kamins* were still admitted to engagements. The first settlement was formed in whole parganas or in *pattis;* hence, on the formation of a village settlement, it became necessary to fix the land revenue according to the actual produce, and as this, from the nature of the country, could not be ascertained by actual measurement or survey, and as the estimates of the kanungos exhibited only the gross estimated assets of each *patti,* recourse was in consequence had to the village landholders themselves. The gross demand on account of each *patti* being communicated to the whole body they were directed to fix the detailed assessment themselves—a task which they executed with much equity and fairness as no complaints were received."

Third settlement.

The third settlement was effected in 1818, and was for three years. It gave a land revenue of Rs. 79,930, which Mr. Traill still considered extremely light and short of what the Government was entitled to demand. The settlement except in Bhot was everywhere made with the village proprietors and the number of individual engagements was considerably increased. The methods followed were those of the previous settlements; both worked well and the full demand was realised with ease.

Fourth settlement.

The fourth settlement was also for a term of three years. The tenantry under the stress of Gurkha oppression had acquired a wandering habit, continually changing from one village to another, so that the smaller landholders were not prepared to contract for a long term of years. By the settlement of 1821 the revenue of the district was fixed at Rs. 87,320.

Writing in 1821, Mr. Traill was able to call attention to the improvement visible in the condition and prospects of the Kumaon peasantry. The value of land had largely increased, the quantity of waste land newly brought under the plough had never been equalled, the people were beginning to build substantial houses for themselves, and great numbers of the smaller landholders themselves now carried on the trade in the produce of the hills which was formerly monopolised by a few wealthy families of Sahus. The causes of this prosperity are not far to seek, and may be briefly summarised thus ; firstly, the lightness of the general assessment; secondly, the high price of grain which had risen some four hundred per cent., since the introduction of the British rule ; thirdly, the large sum, amounting to four lakhs of rupees, expended on public works, private holdings and the carriage of stores, nearly all of which fell to the labouring classes ; and fourthly, the reduced price of merchandise from the plains owing to the abolition of all transit duties.

The difficulties caused by the habit of migrating from one village to another common to most of the cultivators had not ceased on the expiration of the second triennial settlement in 1823, so that a settlement for five years was agreed to as most acceptable to the people. Strange to say, this habit of migrating was seldom due to any objection to the individual assessment and occurred most rarely in the parganas which were most heavily taxed and which had a numerous population. The report on this settlement gives no details and merely states that the general result of the revision was a revenue of Rs. 96,425. It was suggested also that in all the parganas where the cultivation was advanced and where the landholders did not object, the present settlement should be extended for a second period of five years from 1828 A. D. By this arrangement leisure would be afforded hereafter in the resettlement of the remainder of the district for the ascertainment of the existing resources of villages. In Kumaon there were over six thousand estates separately leased, and in consequence the proceedings in each case were very summary and the adjustment of the new demand was made rather on a previous knowledge of the state of each village obtained by a lengthened

Fifth settlement.

residence in the interior of the district than on any new investigation of the assets. Sanction was accordingly given to a settlement for ten years in parganas Pali, Barahmandal, Chaugarkha, Phaldakot and Danpur, and in the rest of the province a revision and re-settlement for four years at the expiry of the existing quinquennial leases. This revision took place in 1829, giving a net result of Rs. 1,04,980. The greatest improvement took place in the parganas bordering on the Bhabar owing to the nnmber of new villages established there. Taking the whole tract along the foot of the hills from the Ganges to the Sarda, the revenue, exclusive of forest dues, in 1815 yielded only Rs. 1,450, whilst in 1829 it gave a land revenue of Rs. 14,800.

Sixth settlement.

Of his fiscal system and the rural economy of the district at this time, Mr. Traill writes :—" On the introduction of the British Government in 1815, the most fostering attention was found necessary to enable the cultivators to recover from their destitution. The public assessment was imposed under a single head and was founded on the acknowledged collections of the preceding year. All extra cesses were struck out of the demand, and though the remission from this measure was for the most part nominal, the simplification of the system of collection proved no small boon to the landholders. At the five succeeding settlements the State demand has progressed with the improvement of the country though still in the aggregate below the Gurkhali settlement of 1812. In its detail, the settlement is formed separately for each village, the engagement for which is taken from some one of the sharers under the designation of *padhan*. This officer is remunerated by a small parcel of rent-free land set apart for the purpose, and can demand from the other sharers no more than the exact quota of the public assessment which may attach to their individual shares. These sharers hold in severalty : consequently in the greater part of the province, that is in the villages cultivated by the actual proprietors, the settlement has all the advantages of a *ryotwari* assessment without its uncertainty ; the cultivator is thus secure of enjoying the whole profit of his farm after payment of the public dues, and before he puts his hand to the plough, he knows the exact sum which he will have to pay. But though the revenue of the Government and the individual income of the landholder be circumscribed by the existing state of landed property, it is by no means certain that the interests either of the public or the individual would be benefited by a more unequal division of land. Large farms require for their support either a local consumption or a foreign market. Now the population of the interior is wholly agricultural and the sole unproductive consumers are the few government servants stationed here. From the nature of the country and consequent difficulties of transport few articles of agricultural produce can bear the expense of carriage in exportation. The Bhotias, it is true, take off a large portion of the surplus produce of the northern districts for the Tibetan market, but only in the way of barter, in which salt or borax is exchanged for grain. The only certain demands on which the interior agriculturist can here depend are the markets at the military stations."

Seventh settlement.

The settlement in those parganas in which agreements for four years only were taken expired at the end of August 1832, and just at the moment the new assessment was being made, flights of locusts settled down all over the country and so injured the growing spring crops that a bad harvest was the result. In the following year, when the remainder of the leases fell in, a deficiency in the rainfall caused some injury to the rain crops. These untoward circumstances alarmed the landholders and they generally objected to entering into new engagements. Abatements were in some cases found necessary, and an attempt was made, so far as the wishes and interests of the landholders would allow, to reduce the number of persons allowed to engage for the revenue. Mr. Traill proposed a settlement for five years only, which resulted in a revenue of Rs. 1,07,044.

The Board of Revenue recommended that the settlement of 1832-33 should be extended for a period of twenty years; but the Government refused to sanction this arrangement without having the opinion of Mr. Traill, who wrote as follows:—

"The extension of the new settlement for a term of 20 years would doubtless be attended with advantage in those parganas of which the villages are fully populated and cultivated; but in other districts where population and cultivation are at a low ebb, and where waste lands abound, such a measure would shortly be followed by a loss of revenue from the facilities with which new locations are there obtainable. The habits of the cultivators are extremely unstable and migratory; vacancies arising from desertion are not readily filled by new tenants, while the general poverty of the landholders and tenantry render them incapable of meeting from their own funds the additional burthen entailed by such desertions. In these cases leases would be thrown up and remissions in the demand indispensable to save the village from total desertion: at the same time no advantage could be taken of the growing improvement in other villages. It may be doubted whether the landholders in these districts would willingly engage for so long a period unless the tenants of their respective villages should be considered as parties in the engagements and remain bound for the same term. Under the Gurkhali Government, when a fixed village settlement was promulgated, the above principle was fully recognized and the claim of the landholder followed his tenant wheresoever he might migrate." Colonel Gowan, who succeeded Mr. Traill as Commissioner, was however directed to report in what parganas the extension of the term of settlement as proposed by the Board of Revenue would be acceptable to the body of the landholders. Colonel Gowan was not successful in his persuasions and he was therefore directed to continue the existing settlement for one year and in the meantime to do all in his power to induce the landholders to agree to a settlement for twenty years.

Ninth settlement.

The ninth settlement was made by Mr. Batten during the years 1842—46, and was for 20 years. He was guided by his experience in Garhwal and made no attempt at a survey, though he relied to a small extent on Mr. Traill's estimates of area. His assessments were based upon those of the expiring settlement. The result of his revision was a revenue of Rs. 1,12,264. He drew up rules for the leasing and management of estates and the appointment of *padhans*, the boundaries of villages and settlement of disputes concerning them, the right to waste land, the pasture grounds and forests, the assessable area of estates and measurement of land.

It was further arranged that no attempt at the actual demarcation of waste lands included nominally within a village boundary should be made where there was no dispute, disputes being rare owing to the existence of the rule whereby newly broken up lands were offered to the landholders of the nearest villages first rather than to strangers. It was not through any fault of Mr. Batten that the detailed survey and record effected by Mr. Beckett at the settlement of 1863 was not taken in hand twenty years earlier. He pointed out that a regular survey of the mountain parganas would be costly, and not remunerative in its effect on the revenue and therefore not likely to be undertaken by the Government. Its result would be to exclude from the assessable wealth of the people everything except the produce of the land. He considered that as the result of his operations the district was over assessed rather than under assessed.

" Though no actual hardship is experienced, though pauperism is unknown, though a hill labourer is always better lodged, and often better paid and clothed than his fellow in the plains, and though a general feeling of content and loyalty exists, still one can perceive in the present state of affairs (1846) no elements of increasing wealth of which revenue will be the future sign and expression. In the ill-inhabited tracts, the low assessment is owing to causes which, except in the most insalubrious valleys, may give way before the march of population. But in the well-inhabited tracts the revenue is paid by the people themselves more as a capitation tax than anything else ; in the same degree that the fisc improves in Katyur and Gangoli will it in all probability decline in Pali and Barahmandal."

Character of the settlement.

The characteristic feature of Mr. Batten's settlement was the record-of-rights that was framed for each village. This contained a complete description of the rights of every occupant ; the past history of the assessments ; the boundary arrangement ; the engagement paper *(ikrarnama)* of the inhabitants in regard to the remuneration of the *padhan* and the collections of all sorts to be made under the heads of *thokdari, sayanachari* and *hissedari* dues and to certain regulations in regard to the public service and good administration, and the *fard-phant* which showed the names of the *padhans,* the distribution of the revenue payers amongst the several *padhans* where more than one were elected; the quotas of revenue payable by the several share holders or occupants; the division of the non-proprietary tenantry amongst those recorded as proprietors and the names and liabilities of the *pahikasht* and other cultivators whenever discoverable. In addition to these documents there was a memorandum *(rubakari)* summarising the whole; and the numerous petitions presented, depositions taken, and orders passed during the course of the settlement on miscellaneous matters formed separate files in the proceedings.

Three hundred and forty-four villages with a total area of 11,225 *bisis,** exclusive of unmeasured waste, were held free of revenue as endowments of temples, and 93 villages with an area of 2,382 *bisis* were held free of revenue by individuals.

Tenth settlement.

The tenth settlement of the Kumaon district (excluding the Bhabar) was effected by Mr. Beckett during 1863—73 and was for thirty years. Unfortunately Mr. Beckett was obliged by ill health to take leave before writing a report, so that we have nothing but two ponderous volumes of statistics and a short introduction by Sir H. Ramsay to give us an account of this, the most important for its procedure and results, of all the settlements of Kumaon. Mr. Beckett's operations were preceded by the first actual measurement of the cultivated area that had ever been made. The measurements were made on the same system that had been usual in the verification of land in civil and revenue suits up to that time, and which had been applied by Sir H. Ramsay himself as district officer in Kumaon in 1852 to the measurement of the *sadabart pattis* of Kotauli and Mahruri. The estimate made by Mr. Traill in 1823 was of little use except for boundaries. It was prepared by native officials who sat on some commanding position and summoned the *padhans* of the villages within sight, and from them noted down the boundaries and estimated the areas and

* A *bisi* is nearly an acre.

thus afforded some very rough idea of the size of each village. The *fard-phant* of Mr. Batton gave information only of the number of sharers and cultivators and the revenue demandable from each. Being prepared by the villagers themselves, whose object was to conceal their numbers and make their village appear as poor as possible, the revenue was distributed amongst a very few of the share holders, and except where the *khaikars* were on bad terms with the proprietors, a very large proportion of them was omitted. It was of use, however, in accustoming the people to think that they had rights worth recording and during the currency of the past settlement many villages were properly surveyed, and the people became accustomed to the idea that an accurate record of the capabilities of the land formed the best basis for the contract between them and those from whom they held and between their village and the Government. Consequently when measurement operations actually commenced, the staff found the people ready to receive them and willing to co-operate in the objects of the survey. The measurement was carried out on these principles :—(1) all terraced land was to be measured unless it had relapsed into forest, but forest clearings and intermittent cultivation known as *khil*, were not to be measured and each enclosure or field was to be measured separately; (2) the whole of the terraced land was to be shown under four qualities, *(a)* irrigated ; *(b)* first class dry ; *(c)* second-class dry and *(d)* casual cultivation or *ijran*. The surveyors however did not adhere to these instructions and it was found necessary to classify all the culturable area under *(a)* permanent cultivation ; *(b)* casual cultivation and *(c)* waste. By 'waste' all through the records is meant terraced land thrown out of cultivation. The term does not include the grassy slopes or forests within the nominal area of a village.

The instrument used was a hempen rope, sixty feet long, divided into ten lengths of six feet each. The area of each field was computed separately. The longest length was first measured and then one or more measurements for breadth were taken according to whether the shape was regular or irregular. Most of the fields however were irregular and the labour of measurement was immense. Many of the villages contained as many as 6,000 fields, some not more than ten yards in extent and yet each can be readily identified on the map. As a check on the surveyors each cultivator was given a *parcha* or extract from the survey record relating to his own holding and he had thus the means of bringing before the settlement officer any omissions before the final record in the books, on which the assessment was made. By an ingenious procedure all the land in the village was then brought to one common standard of quality. Second class dry land known in the hills as *duwam upraon* was selected as the standard and each of the other three classes was brought to this standard by trebling the irrigated, by adding one-half to first class dry and by reducing casual cultivation by one half. Thus, if a village comprised areas of 10 *bisis* irrigated, 12 first class dry, and 12 *ijran*, these were taken for assessment purposes as equivalent respectively to 30, 18 and 6 *bisis* of second class dry land, or a total of 54 *basis*. The next point was to ascertain the rates to be applied to the areas thus found and in the absence of *jamabandis* or rent rolls, it was necessary to estimate the produce of each class of soil. In irrigated land it was very common for the proprietor to take one half the produce ; in first-class dry, one-third, and in second-class dry one-fourth to one-fifth. Then came the question of the produce per *bisi* which varied with the position, cultivation and soil. In some places, irrigated land yields as much as 60 maunds of unhusked rice per acre while 40 maunds is a common yield, and good first-class dry land gives 40 maunds of wheat or *mandua*.

Taking everything into consideration an average rate of one rupee per *bisi* of second-class dry land was held to be fair and it is noticeable that this rate was less than one-twentieth of the average annual value in money of the produce, as calculated by Sir H. Ramsay. The incidence of this revenue standard when applied to the whole assessable area in the district worked out at Re. 0-13-10 per *bisi*.

Other considerations were taken into account in applying these rates to the particular villages such as the vast changes due to the great amount of money brought into the district by the tea-planters and the public works at Ranikhet, the great advance in the price of grain, which had almost doubled, and the increase in population. The last has always been an important factor in hill assessments and is well recognised by the people themselves. In many places, owing to the paucity of inhabitants, the able-bodied cultivators are of equal importance with the land in estimating the assets of a village. Another of Mr. Beckett's processes was applied to bringing out the value of this factor in the assessment. He ascertained (*a*) the average population per each hundred measured acres for the whole district; (*b*) the average population per each hundred acres of the cultivated area; (*c*) the average population per each hundred acres for the cultivated area with half the *ijran;* and (*d*) the average on three-fourths of the total area. For example, the average population per each hundred acres on the whole district being 141, a village with a population of 70 to the hundred acres would give a rate of eight annas, the land rate being one rupee, the mean of the two or twelve annas gives the average rate according to population. Were the population of the village 280 in the same circumstances the average rate would be Re. 1-8-0. Under the second form of calculation the average population for one hundred acres of cultivation being 195 and the revenue rate only Re 0-14-6 per acre, a population of 98 would give a rate of Re. 0-7-3, or taking the mean of the two, eleven annas per acre. Under the third calculation the population average being 185 for one hundred acres and the revenue rate Re. 0-13-6 per acre, if the population were 92, the population rate would be Re. 0-6-9 and the mean, ten annas. The average of the resultants was considered the population rate of the village.

The statistics of area compiled for each village also aided in the assessment. These comprised (1) the total area measured by the villagers; (2) cultivated land with additions for quality (i. e. the application of the process already described for reducing all to the standard of second-class dry land); (3) cultivation with half *ijran;* (4) three-fourths of the total measured area with additions for quality. Any excess in (1) over (3) showed that there was too much waste land: excess in (2) over (3) showed a large predominance of permanent cultivation, and if (2) exceeded (1) it showed that the land was exceptionally good or well-irrigated. Excess of (3) over (2) showed too much *ijran:* in (4) over (3) too much waste, and in (4) over (1) that the land was good. Mr. Beckett did not however rely solely upon his manipulation of statistics; he personally inspected every village, and it was a consideration of its circumstances so discovered that led to the modification of his statistical rate.

The total revenue imposed by Mr. Beckett on those portions of Kumaon which now constitute the Almora district amounted to Rs. 2,26,700, an increase of 101 per cent. This substantial enhancement was never felt as a burden and coercive processes were never found necessary. Arrears where they existed were usually due more to a lack of energy on the part of the patwari than to difficulty in the matter of payment, and Mr. Goudge, who revised the settlement, testifies that he has never heard that the demand was beyond the powers of any village.

Current settlement.

Mr. Beckett's settlement expired in 1902. The work of revision was begun by Mr. Goudge in 1899. No attempt was made to alter Mr. Beckett's work, but new cultivation, which in several parganas at least was of great extent, was measured and assessed, and valued at Mr. Beckett's rates. The most important part of the Settlement Officer's duties was however the imposition of an all-round enhancement on each patti proportionate to its progress since the last settlement. The rules directed him to consider the "improvement in the material prosperity of the village and in the productive powers of the land as indicated by the improvement in soils, population statistics, rise in the prices of produce and value of land, with any other circumstances which indicate progress in the economical condition of the people." The causes which have produced an improvement in the economical condition of the people have already been noticed in a previous chapter and require no repetition here. The net income of each *patti* from all sources was prepared by the patwaris and afterwards checked by the tahsildars, and, though admittedly rough, was accepted as, on the whole, a reliable measure of the prosperity of the people. In the hills the soils and the value of individual fields must tend to improvement. Every year the wall which supports the field-terrace is improved, the field is made more level, stones are removed and there is a constant tendency to change intermittent into permanent cultivation. Thus fields classified by Mr. Beckett as *ijran* were frequently found by Mr. Goudge to have been transferred by care and tilth into first or second-class *upraon*, with the result that the total number of soil units had increased 17 per cent. The result of Mr. Goudge's operations was the imposition of a revenue of Rs. 2,67,559, an increase of 22·47 per cent. over the expiring demand.

Fiscal history: Bhot.

The fiscal history of Bhot differs to some extent from that of the rest of the district. The origin of the Bhotias has not yet been decided; it is enough here to say that they differ alike in physiognomy, religion, and customs from the Tibetans on the north and from the hill Hindus on the south. Bhot was for a long time ruled by the semi-independent Rajwars of Askot on behalf of the Chand Rajas, but the Bhotias have always admitted the claims of Tibet to suzerainty—"an anomalous state of subjection which their paramount interests in continuing to be the medium of commercial intercourse between Hindustan and Tibet will tend to perpetuate." So wrote Mr. Traill in 1825, and his prophecy has been amply fulfilled. In that year the revenue demands of the Tibetans consisted of *sinh thal* (land revenue), *ya thal* (tax on sunshine), and *kyun thal* (tax on the profits of trade). The revenues exacted by their Hindu conquerors, to quote again from Mr. Traill, have ever been more costly and more extensive. On their final subjugation the Bhot mahals were subjected to a tribute in gold dust. The assets made available to the government demand were profits of trade, *tandkar* or loom tax, produce of agriculture, produce of jungles (roots and drugs), musk, hawks, and wild bees' nests The tribute was for mutual convenience commuted into silver and goods. The government revenue was imposed on each pass in one sum and the detailed assessments left to be settled by the *burhas* or village headmen among themselves. The tribute was levied alternately on land and on property. When the Gurkhas conquered Kumaon the resistance on the part of the Bhotias joined to an exaggerated reputation for wealth, marked them out for peculiar exactions: thus the demand for Johar was Rs. 12,500, for Darma Rs. 10,000, and for Byans Rs. 5,000, and the irregular demands of the military commanders amounted to probably at least as much more. The result was that the Bhotias were reduced to the verge of ruin, and a Gurkha officer of reputation, Bhakti Thapa, was sent to revise the settlement. He reduced the demand to Rs. 8,000 for Johar, Rs. 7,000 for Darma, and Rs. 2,700 for Byans, besides ordering the restoration of the illegal exactions. At the first British settlement in 1815 the collections of the previous years were assumed as the standard of assessment, but a more favourable rate of cash commutation in respect of the dues hitherto paid in kind was permitted and the change of the currency from Gurkha to Farrukhabadi rupees resulted in a reduction of the nominal assessment by 25 per cent. In 1818 the taxes on trade, musk, bees wax and hawks were all abolished, and the revenue demand was thus reduced to a total of Rs. 4,130 on Johar, Darma, Byans and Chaudans.

The settlement in 1840-41 was made by Mr. Batten, who considered that Mr. Traill had made an excessive sacrifice of revenue by taxing only the produce of the fields and the forests: but his assessment on the general capabilities of the district were moderated by the political consideration of keeping the borderers contented and amounted to only Rs. 4,791. Mr. Beckett in 1872 and Mr. Goudge in 1902 followed the principles of Mr. Batten and taxed the Bhotias on their general prosperity derived from whatever source—trade or agriculture—and assessed them at Rs. 7,883 and Rs. 10,255 respectively.

Gunth. The term *gunth* signifies assignments of land revenue made for the maintenance of the great temples of Garhwal. Such assignments were under the Hindu rajas very large and nearly all were upheld by the Gurkhas and the British. The value of the assigned revenue is now Rs. 9,849. The more powerful temples have from time to time arrogated to themselves the most extensive rights in *gunth* villages, but the present position is, according to Mr. Traill, that the grants are merely assignments of revenue and convey no proprietary right in the soil; and this opinion was confirmed by a government order in 1895, which declared that the temples had no right over waste land in *gunth* villages.

Sadabart. *Sadabart* is the term applied to an endowment provided by the land revenue of assigned villages, originally for the purpose of providing food for indigent pilgrims visiting the shrines of Kedarnath and Badrinath but now expended mainly over the upkeep of dispensaries on the pilgrim way. The fund is managed by the Deputy Commissioner of Garhwal, and its history will be found more fully described in the Gazetteer of that district. The annual value of the endowment derived from the revenue of assigned villages in this district amounts to Rs. 1,427.

The only *sadabart* dispensaries in the district are at Ganai, and Bhikia Sen in Pali.

Excise.

The duty on spirits locally manufactured and on hemp drugs has formed a portion of the revenue ever since the British occupation of Kumaon. Owing to the frequent changes in the administrative divisions of the province it is not easy to trace the excise history from the earliest times. Up to the formation of the present district of Naini Tal in 1891 the Tarai was entirely separate from the rest of Kumaon in this respect, being at first under the control of the Collectors of Bareilly and Moradabad, and later under the Superintendent. Up to 1821 there was no separate excise administration for Garhwal, but that district and the whole of Kumaon were included in a single farm. From 1822 the district of Kumaon was farmed separately. In 1822 the total excise revenue of Kumaon was only Rs. 534, and up to 1837 it never rose above Rs. 1,300 in any year. In 1872, however, it had risen to Rs. 18,663, and in 1882 to Rs. 29,013. This increase seems to point to a very great spread of drinking habits amongst the people; but we are assured on the authority of the then Commissioner that this was not the case. "There is no consumption among the rural population of the hills—and I sincerely hope there never may be." There certainly were very few shops, and it is still true that the hill people do not, as a rule, indulge in liquor. The increase was due to the presence of troops and the large influx of lowlanders from the plains. Nevertheless, the income from Kumaon rose to Rs. 46,548 in 1891, and the importance of the hill *pattis* of the Naini Tal district and the Bhabar, for the Tarai was still excluded, is shown by the fact that in the following year the revenue for the Almora district fell to Rs. 16,409. In 1896 there was a further transfer of the Tanakpur-Bhabar to Almora;

but the total income from that pargana does not amount to more than Rs. 500 annually. In 1894 an excise inspector on preventive duty was appointed for the whole Kumaon division—a step that has been attended with the most beneficial results.*

Liquor.

There are now in the district eight liquor shops, producing a revenue of Rs. 22,757. The shops were until recently put up to auction separately, and what is known as the outstill system prevailed: that is to say, each vendor has attached to his shop a still in which he manufactures the liquor he proposes to sell. The greater part of the district was in 1910 brought under the contract system in vogue in the plains.

Until 1899 the farming system was in vogue. Ordinarily the right to sell liquor throughout the district would have been farmed to a single contractor; but the vast area was beyond the power of any individual, with the result that the farm was subdivided. In the result there was no great difference between the systems and the change made was not reflected in the revenue. A coarse spirit is manufactured from the millet known as *mandua*, but in the more civilised parts *gur* and *shira* are used. The Kalwar caste is unknown in the hills: the manufacture of liquor is in the hands of hill Rajputs.

The Bhotias have always possessed the right to brew liquor for their own consumption. They make beer called *jan* or *chhang* from rice, wheat or barley, and manufacture their own yeast called *balma*. They also distill spirit from the residue left after the beer has been taken off. The Bhotias have the reputation of being excellent distillers. They use a simple pot still (*khoni*) in most parts, but in Darma a more complicated retort (*jama*) with a receiver inside it is used.

The hillmen are generally speaking temperate: on the average one shop exists for every 50,000 of the population.

Ranikhet Brewery.

The Ranikhet Brewery, the property of Messrs. Meakin and Co., is situated on the south-west side of Kumpur hill at Ranikhet. It was built and started in the year 1878 by the late Mr. H. G. Meakin. The buildings, comprising all those requisite for the carrying on of brewing and malting, stand in the form of a square, and there are in addition large storage

* Naini Tal Gazetteer, page 175.

godowns, workshops and the like. The grain used is all imported from the Punjab districts. The average annual output amounts to 2,500 hhds. The whole of the working is under European supervision.

Drugs.

Bhang, charas and ganja are manufactured in various ways from the hemp plant, which is indigenous to the country. Its cultivation is not prohibited, but it is understood that only the fibre and the seeds are to be used, the production of drugs being now illegal. This latter prohibition does not however carry much force, for it is impossible to prevent the extraction of charas. Charas is the resinous exudation from the ripe leaves, stems and seeds of the female plant, and it can be made by the simple process of rubbing these parts of the plant in the hand. Bhang and ganja, except among sojourners from the plains, command no sale. The drugs shops in the district are those at Almora, Ranikhet, Pithoragarh, Bageswar, Lohaghat, Ganai, and Champawat. They are sold separately on a three years' lease. Only Yarkand charas is allowed to be sold. The price has greatly risen with the prohibition of the manufacture of hill charas in 1906 and the raising of the duty to Rs. 6 a seer. As much as 5 annas to 8 annas a tola is now paid, and when the drug is sold in pice packets, the rate per tola works out at 12 annas.

Opium.

The cultivation of the poppy is not permitted in the district. The chief consumers of opium are the Muhammadan settlers from the plains, but the practice of taking it is to some extent spreading among the hill people. They however prize it chiefly for its medicinal properties. There are opium shops at Almora, Ranikhet, Ganai, Pithoragarh, Bageswar, and Lohaghat.

Educational.

In 1823 Mr. Traill wrote :—"There are no public institutions of the nature of schools, and private tuition is almost entirely confined to the upper classes. The teachers are commonly Brahmans who impart to their scholars the mere knowledge of reading, writing, and accounts. The children of respectable Brahmans are also taught Sanskrit and are occasionally sent to Benares to complete their studies, where they pass through the usual course of Hindu education." In 1841 a Sanskrit school was opened by Mr. Lushington, the Commissioner, but it closed after a brief existence of eight years. In 1842 schools costing Rs. 20 a month were started. In 1844 the Missionaries opened a private English school in Almora. This is now the Ramsay College. Still there must have been a considerable amount of private instruction, for Mr. Thornton's report in 1850 based on returns furnished by Messrs. Batten and Ramsay shows for Kumaon and Garhwal 121 Hindi and Sanskrit schools held in private dwellings or the houses of teachers. Of the 121 teachers 54 taught gratuitously and 67 had fixed incomes averaging Rs. 9-8-0 a month. There were 522 pupils, over four-fifths of whom were Brahmans. In addition there was one school with ten pupils in which Urdu was taught. In 1857 the present educational system was inaugurated by the formation of the Kumaon circle under the department of Public Instruction. In September of the next year tahsili schools were established at Someswar, Dhamar, Satrali, Dwarahat, and Nirai; these five schools were attended by 225 pupils. In March 1859 seven more schools were added, at Champawat, Pithoragarh, Gangolihat, Syalde, Ganai, Bhikia Sen, Deighat, and in that year the total enrolment amounted to 900. By 1867 there were twenty-two schools, and in 1872 the total number of scholars was 1,815. In that year 16 of the schools were reduced to the *halkabandi* or village standard, and in 1869 Mr. Beckett opened 15 *halkabandi* schools. In 1871 these schools had an enrolment of 1,091. Schools were maintained at the tahsili standard in Someswar, Dwarahat, Berenag, Darma, Dewalthal, and Chaupakhiya. Those at Berenag, Darma, and Dwarahat were subsequently removed to Syalde, Khetikhan, and Bagwalipokhar. Sir Henry Ramsay writing in 1874 describes his educational policy :—" It is considered more beneficial to impart to many the useful knowledge of reading and writing sufficient for their everyday use than to give to a smaller number a better education by employing qualified but more expensive teachers;" and he expresses the opinion that Kumaon could show a higher percentage of literate persons than any other district in the province. The teachers in the *halkabandi* schools were at that time getting only Rs. 5 a month. In July 1887 all the tahsili schools became *halkabandi* schools, and one tahsili school was opened at Almora. The tahsili schools are now denominated middle schools, and they are five in number—Almora, Pali, Pithoragarh, Kanda and Khetikhan.

Aided schools appear to have been started about 1872. In that year there were 24 such schools with a total of 1,262 scholars. The first girls' school was opened at Milam in Bhot in 1867, and in 1871 there were 18 girls attending it. There are at present 10 girls' schools in the district. All are aided schools. The total enrolment is 244. The normal school, opened in 1906, is a resuscitation of the old normal school which closed in 1887. This school takes a certain number of teachers from the schools of the division and instructs them in modern methods of pedagogy.

A list of the schools of the district at present in existence will be found in the appendix. Many of the village schools are housed in miserable hovels, but the buildings are being improved year by year as funds permit. Education is nevertheless extremely popular in the district. The census recorded 26,428 persons as literate, that is to say, able to read and write. The proportion—567 in 10,000—is very high and is exceeded only in the districts of Garhwal and Dehra Dun. If the figures for males alone be taken the proportion rises to 1,088 per 10,000, and in this calculation Almora occupies the third place behind Garhwal and Benares—the latter, it is to be remarked, a famous centre of Hindu education. The taste for education is largely due to the pressure of the population on the land. Agriculture alone can no longer support the Kumaoni, and he therefore has recourse to service through education. The present condition of education, considering the great physical difficulties of the country, affords cause for some satisfaction, though there are points in which improvement appears possible. Inspection is necessarily intermittent. Some of the teachers look on school-mastering as a mere means of livelihood till something better presents itself—a patwariship for instance. Female education can hardly be said to be popular; as the hillman says, girls are too valuable to be allowed to waste their time over book-learning: they have plenty of work to do in the way of carrying in wood and grass and tilling the fields.

The education of the district is under the care of the district board advised by the inspector and assistant inspector of schools for the Kumaon division. The board employs within the district one deputy inspector and three sub-deputy inspectors. Their chief duty is the inspection of the village schools, and the co-ordination of their curricula. The middle schools are in the care of the assistant inspector and the high schools in that of the inspector, but these officers also occasionally visit schools of lower standards.

Medical. The charges in Almora incurred over the price of medicines, and the maintenance of dispensaries and hospitals are met by the district board fund, the *sadabart* fund and private bodies. Medicines are dispensed free and a limited number of in-patients are fed also at the public expense, but in most cases they are expected to provide for themselves. The district board has a hospital in Almora and it contributes towards the cantonment general hospital at Ranikhet, where the R. A. M. C. officer in charge of the hospital at present performs also the duties of a Civil Surgeon. The only *sadabart* hospitals in the district are at Ganai and Bhikia Sen and exist for the benefit of pilgrims returing from the Garhwal shrines. The London Mission Society maintains a dispensary at Bageswar, and the tea-planters of Katyur one at Baijnath. The American Methodist Episcopalian Mission have a male and female hospital at Pithoragarh, and a dispensary at Dwarahat, and in Almora itself are the Zanana Hospital and the Mission Consumptive Hospital. All these institutions are aided by the district board. There is also a dispensary at Tanakpur in the Bhabar* formerly maintained by the Government Estate now taken over by the district board.

Diseases. Among the diseases, either endemic or epidemic, in the hills may be mentioned plague, cholera, small-pox, malarial and other fevers, diarrhoea, dysentery, goitre and leprosy. The identity of hill plague locally termed *mahamari* with the ordinary Indian or Hong Kong plague has been the subject of some discussion. According to tradition the Rawal of Kedarnath in Garhwal about 1823 once deviated from the orthodox rites in the performance of *hom* and perished with all his assistants from the disease, then

* Transferred to the Naini Tal district in 1910.

recognized for the first time. The investigations of the Plague Commission led them to reject Dr. Koch's theory that the epidemic in Bombay had its origin in the plague of these hills and that it was not imported from Hong Kong—a theory which did not attempt to explain how it had travelled so far without leaving any tracks by the way. And in the past hill plague has rarely shown any tendency to spread into the plains. At the instance of the Plague Commission, Captain H. J. Walton and Lieutenant Douglas Stuart, both of the I. M. S., were deputed to the hills to investigate the circumstances of hill plague. These officers convinced themselves by personal enquiries that the disease must be recognized as plague. They were assured by the Tibetan envoys who, according to custom, visit the Bhotia villages to satisfy themselves, before the opening of the trade routes, of the absence of epidemic diseases in Britith territory, that no disease of the kind was known in Tibet; and they therefore came to the conclusion that hill plague was endemic in Kumaon. They failed however to find any cases of *mahamari* in the district and they were therefore unable to make any bacteriological comparisons. It was not until 1902 that the identity of hill plague, not with India or Hong Kong plague, but with the Egyptian or Levantine plague, was bacteriologically demonstrated by Major Chaytor White, who had been sent to investigate an outbreak in Choprakot of the Garhwal district. In hill plague the non-bubonic form of the disease is more common than the bubonic form, whereas in true Indian plague the reverse is the case; the mortality is greater, amounting to 95 per cent. of all cases; pneumonic plague is unknown. The bubonic form of hill plague is usually termed *phutkia*, or *gola rog*, these words signifying in the hill language a swelling. The symptoms of the disease and its epidemiological circumstances however all point to the fact that *mahamari* is a form of plague. No epidemic has occurred in the district since 1876 though outbreaks have occurred more recently in Garhwal; isolated cases however have been reported from the tracts towards the snows.

Sanjar is the name applied by the hill people of Kumaon to designate a disease with continued fever without the accompaniment of swellings. *Sanjar*, in one of its forms, corresponds **Sanjar.**

to famine or relapsing fever and the *spirillum* (*s. obermeirii*) has been found in the blood of those suffering. The word is often loosely applied to a contagious fever of any kind unaccompanied by swellings. It might therefore be applied erroneously to cases of septicaemic plague in which there is no external bubo. It is not so fatal as hill plague, only about 20 per cent. dying, and not so much feared. An outbreak is not preceded by a mortality among rats, though this is also true of some outbreaks of hill plague. Properly speaking, then, *sanjar* is relapsing fever and it is only through a faulty diagnosis that the term is otherwise employed. The disease is due to privation and want of cleanliness and is prevalent in years of scarcity and famine. Epidemics of it occur from time to time. When this disease breaks out the entire village is at once isolated and, if possible, the people leave their houses and live in the jungle until the disease has abated, and all the dwellings are cleaned and plastered or whitewashed before being used again. An epidemic occurred among the prisoners in the district jail in 1881; they were removed to Binsar and placed in tents and huts and nine of them died of the fever. Relapsing fever is caused by a micro-organism belonging to the genus *spirillum.*

Small-pox. Small-pox in Almora is rare. Something in the nature of an epidemic occurred in the years 1907 and 1908, when 706 died, chiefly in the central *pattis* of the district—Kairarau, Borarau and Katyur. As a consequence the Bageswar fair was by the order of the Deputy Commissioner intermitted for the year 1908. Vaccination is however extremely popular in both Garhwal aud Almora; its wonderful success appears to be due to the fact that a similar remedy against small-pox had been known to the people in inoculation, and they therefore were prepared to accept vaccination as a substitute when they found it to be free from the dangers of inoculation and also more efficacious as a prophylactic.

Fever. A reference to Table IV of the appendix will show that here as elsewhere in the provinces fever is responsible for the greater portion of the annual mortality. Malignant or pernicious malarial fever prevails in the densely wooded villages of the

Bhabar. The sufferer becomes of a turmeric yellow colour and frequently vomits blood, and, becoming insensible, rapidly sinks. This fever is not periodic and does not yield to quinine. Periodic fever is common throughout the hills, though more prevalent in the hot valleys than in more temperate regions. Bowel complaints are, after fevers, the most deadly enemies of the Kumaoni. For the last ten or twelve years Garhwal and Almora have shown the highest mortality from dysentery and diarrhoea. The Dotiali and Garhwali coolies who come for work to the neighbourhood of Almora or who pass through it on their way to the sub-montane forests suffer considerably from intestinal worms of all kinds, and from the chronic rheumatism called *bat*.

Visitations of cholera are unhappily not rare. In 1892, 5,103 persons died of the disease, in 1903, 1,395, in 1907, 1,143, and in 1908, 602. Outbreaks of cholera are generally attributed to infection imported from the plains, either by the pilgrims on their way back from the Garhwal shrines or by the Kumaonis themselves returning from one of their periodic visits to the plains. When once the disease has appeared it spreads with terrible speed. Stricken villages are deserted incontinently; in many cases the sick are allowed to die uncared for. Corpses are left to rot in houses, or thrown unburied by the banks of a stream which carries the infection to villages drinking its water in lower reaches. A cholera corpse is according to the superstition of the hill people too foul to be brought into contact with the pure element, fire, and the smoke from a burning corpse is also believed to spread the infection. Cholera corpses are therefore buried, to be exhumed and duly cremated many months later. To this custom is often due a recrudescence of the disease when it had apparently died out. **Cholera.**

Leprosy is very common in parts of the hills. Colonel Hamilton writes:—"There is only one leprosy which assumes two forms, one tubercular and the other anaesthetic; in the latter there are parts of the body absolutely devoid of sensation so that if the patient is blindfolded he is quite unconscious when these parts are pricked with a pin. The so-called white leprosy as a rule has nothing to do with leprosy and although unpleasant to look at is quite harmless." **Leprosy.**

At the last census the district was found to contain 927 lepers. Many of these come from Doti in the west of Nepal. A leper suffering from the disease in its ulcerated stage is always ostracised by his fellow villagers and is compelled to take up his residence outside the village and to use for his water supply a spring or runnel not required by the rest of the village. The Leprosy Act has been extended to the district and lepers can now in certain circumstances be forcibly detained. They are also prohibited from following some specified occupations.

Leper Asylums.

In 1836 Ensign Ramsay (afterwards Sir H. Ramsay) of the regiment stationed at Almora began giving periodical alms to the lepers who frequented the town. On his return to Almora in 1840 as a civil officer, he put up a few rough stone huts for the accommodation of about 20 lepers at Ganesh ki gair on the eastern slope of Almora. In 1848 a house was taken in the Almora bazar near the site of the present hospital. In 1851 the institution was placed under the charge of Mr. Budden of the London Missionary Society, the number of lepers supported at that time being 31. The accommodation proving insufficient, the Mission Committee in 1854 made an appeal to the public, to which generous response was made, and the present site of the asylum was acquired, about a mile to the south of Almora. The premises have been from time to time enlarged and improved, and now consist of hospital, dispensary, school, church, store-room, washing houses, nine barracks of five rooms each, and a caretaker's house, all standing in a compact area of over six acres, beautifully wooded, and enclosing fields and gardens cultivated by those of the lepers who are fit for such occupation. The sexes are segregated in the asylum, and if any young children are brought by new-comers they are placed in the Mission Orphanage.

From the beginning the asylum has been largely supported by gifts and contributions from English people living in the district, and also from Indian gentlemen, especially Pandit Badri Datt Joshi, Rai Bahadur, and the late Lala Moti Ram Sah, who helped at times of scarcity by raising large subscriptions. In 1864 Sir Henry Ramsay secured the transfer of a government tea-garden at Hawalbagh to the asylum as an endowment fund. Sanction for this was given in appreciative terms by the Lieutenant-Governor in a government paper dated May 24th, 1864. The garden was afterwards sold, and the proceeds, amounting to Rs. 48,000, were invested in government securities. Lala Moti Ram Sah of Naini Tal gave a sum of Rs. 5,000 in 1877. In 1879 the Mission to Lepers in India began to help the asylum, and at present it gives an annual grant of Rs. 2,400. From time to time much attention has been given to the curative treatment of the disease. The Leprosy Commission spent a considerable part of their time at Almora, and many of their conclusions were based on observations in the asylum.

The number of inmates at present (1909) is 110. It would be impossible, with the income available, to support such a large number and give them necessary aid, were it not for the system adopted, of getting the stronger inmates to help the weaker ones in cooking food and bringing water. Thus a large staff of servants and attendants is not required.

Since 1864 over 500 lepers have professed Christianity. The majority of the inmates attend the daily and Sunday services in the chapel attached to the asylum, though such attendance is, of course, entirely voluntary. The fact of the lepers being outcastes from their Hindu society removes the usual obstacles in the way of adopting the Christian faith. Mr. Oakley writes:—"An interesting fact is that in the course of some thirty-five years about fifty children of lepers brought to the asylum at different times have been removed from their leprous parents and brought up in the Mission Orphanage, and of the total number only two or three have become lepers, which would seem to prove that the disease is not hereditary, though there may be predisposition, as in some other maladies, and that it is got by actual contagion rather than self-developed."*

The American Methodist Episcopalian Mission has a leper asylum on the heights of Chandagh above Pithoragarh.

* Holy Himalaya.

CHAPTER V

History.

Introductory.

The following brief account of Kumaon is derived almost entirely from Mr. Atkinson's history contained in Chapters III to VII of his Gazetteer. The history he has compiled is the result of wide research, patient observation, and brilliant conjecture ; and it would have been reprinted here almost in its entirety but for considerations of space.

Ethnography.

The Sanskrit classics contain some materials towards the reconstruction of the state of Kumaon before the period covered by well-authenticated history, and in so far as they are corroborated by admitted facts they are not unworthy of examination. The Vishnu Purana, the Mahabharata, and the Varita-Sanhita mention a number of tribes dwelling on the borders of Bharat, and of these the Sakas, the Nagas, the Kiratas, the Khasas and the Hunas may with a certain amount of confidence be referred to the portion of the Himalayas now known as Kumaon. The Sakas are pointed out by local tradition as one of the earliest ruling races in the Kumaon hills, and the royal houses of Garhwal, Doti and Askot claim to be descended from the famous Salivahana. The claim will not perhaps bear careful scrutiny, but it is safe to assert that it would never have been advanced if the Sakas had been unknown in the regions once subject to these dynasties. Of the mysterious serpent race called Nagas once so widely spread there are many traces. There are serpent temples at Bastir in Mahar, at Kedar Kalinag in Pungaon, Beni Nag (Berenag) in Baraun, Vasuki Nag in Danpur, Nagdeo Padamgir in Salam, all in the Almora district; besides an even greater number in Garhwal and the Dun. The Kiratas or Rajya Kiratas were a tribe of foresters, and they are doubtfully identified with the Rajis, an almost extinct race found in Askot. These represent themselves as descendants of one of the aboriginal princes of Kumaon who fled with his family to escape the destruction threatened by an usurper; and in virtue of their regal descent they never salute any one. The Hunas may be a pastoral tribe occupying parts of the Punjab, or they may be the Bhotias dwelling along the northern border of Kumaon, or again they may be the Tibetans, still called by the lowlanders Huniyas. The name Khasa is of very wide significance. The name is by a rather bold speculation traced from Mount Caucasus in the west as far as the Khasia hills in the east; and though there is no reason to acquiesce entirely in this theory the names of Kashmir and Khasdes (an ancient synonym for Kumaon) may with tolerable certainty be accepted as evidence of the importance of the Khasiyas before they yielded place to the more agile genius of the Brahman and Rajput immigrants from the plains. Mr. Atkinson's conclusion is that the Khasas were like the Nagas a very powerful race who came at a very early period from that *officina gentium* Central Asia. The account that the modern Khasiyas give of themselves tallies in all respects with the indications from other sources. They always profess to be Rajputs who have fallen from their once honourable position by the necessity of living in a country and in a climate where the strict observance of the ceremonial usages of their religion is impossible. The Khasiyas are to this day the most important people numerically in the hills, though the line of division between them and the immigrants from the plains is daily becoming fainter.

It is safe to assume that during the dark ages the country now known as Kumaon consisted of a multitude of petty principalities, consolidated after centuries of warfare into one state under the Chand Rajas. Whether these local chiefs ever owned any nominal allegiance to the kings in the plains is doubtful, but it is of interest to note that, according to Ferishta, the Porus who opposed Alexander at the passage of the Hydaspes is identified by the Brahmanical historians with a Raja Phur of Kumaon. In another passage Ferishta relates that Ramdeo Rathor between the years 440 and 470 A. D. was opposed in his conquest by the Raja of Kumaon who inherited his country and his crown from a line time of ancestors that had ruled upward of 2,000 years. The Kumaon Raja was defeated with the loss of all his elephants and treasure and fled to the hills, and was compelled to give his daughter in marriage to the conqueror. The Katyuris were according to local tradition for many centuries the ruling family in Kumaon. Their capital was originally at Joshimath in Garhwal, whence, probably as the result of religious quarrels, they found themselves forced to retire to the Katyur valley where they built a city called Karttikeyapura. The only extant records of the Katyuris consist of six ancient inscriptions five of which are grants engraved on copper while one is inscribed on stone. The last belongs to the temple of Bageswar, at the confluence of the Gumti and Sarju. It records the names of eight kings of the Katyuri line. Four of the copper-plate grants are preserved in the temple of Pandukeswar near Badrinath; and of these two are dated from Karttikeyapura and contain three royal names found also in the Bageswar stone inscription. A third copper-plate is addressed to the officers of Tanganapura, and purports to grant villages in that district to the temple of Badrinath. Tanganapura is to be identified with the Bhagirathi-Alaknanda Doab. One of the plates further extols a Katyur victory over an enemy employing war elephants. From these inscriptions it is safe to conclude that the realm of the Katyuris extended as far north as Tapoban above Joshimath, conveyed by a copper-plate grant to the Pandukeswar temple; as far south as the plains, and westward beyond the Ganges. The last king of the Katyur line was Bir Deo, who exasperated his people by his incompetence and oppression and was murdered. After his death, dissensions broke out amongst his family and every man of royal blood seized a portion of the kingdom for himself, whilst the countries beyond Kumaon and Garhwal that had always paid tribute to the Katyuris threw off their allegiance. Thus in the early days of the Chand family there was a Domkot Rawat reigning in Kali Kumaon in subordination to a branch of the Katyuri family which had established itself in a fort on the Giri range. Another branch was settled in Doti, a third in Askot, a fourth in Barahmandal, a fifth still occupied Katyur and Danpur and a sixth had several settlements in Pali, chief of which were Dwarahat and Lakhanpur.

Besides these dynasties sprung from the original stock we find others who had no connection with the Katyuris established at this time in Kumaon. Phaldakot and Dhaniyakot fell into the hands of a tribe of Kathi Rajputs who claimed to be of Surajbansi origin. Chaugarkha was held by Padyar Rajputs with a capital at Padyarkot. A family calling themselves Chandrabansi Rajputs came from Pyuthana in Doti and established themselves at Mankot in Gangoli. The southern country became subject to the leading Khasiya families, whilst Shor, Sira, Darma, Askot and Johar were annexed to the Doti kingdom.

Rise of th Chands.

Whilst Kumaon was thus broken up into a number of petty kingdoms under rulers of different tribes, Katyuris, Khasiyas and others, a family established itself in the eastern pargana near the Kali river which was destined to rise to the height of power and finally, though after the lapse of many centuries, to reunite the whole province under one ruler. The founder of this family was Som Chand, a Chandrabansi Rajput. He may or may not be a mythical personage, for there are one or two stories as to how he originally gained a footing in Kumaon, but taking him to be historical it may be assumed that he came from the plains as an adventurer, married the Raja of Sira's daughter and later supplanted his father-in-law. There is also more than one theory put forward as to the date of his accession, but the one selected by Mr. Atkinson in his account of Kumaon history may be accepted, namely 953 A. D. He gives three lists of Chand princes obtained either from leading Brahmans or from official records, and having regard to the probabilities and the degree of reliability that can be placed on each list, sets forth the history of the Chand rulers with dates which will be followed throughout this sketch of Kumaon annals.

It must be remembered that in its earliest significance Kumaon denotes the tract of country lying along the left bank of the Kali river and that it is not till after the Chands had established their capital at Almora (1563) that the name Kumaon covered the present limits of the Almora and Naini Tal districts and Kali Kumaon was restricted to its original signification. Som Chand built his first home on the fifteen-acre plot given him by his father-in-law, calling it Rajbunga, a name which gave place subsequently to Champawat. The whole country was subdivided into *pattis,* in each of which was a semi-independent ruler. These again took part in the quarrels of the two great factions, the Maras and the Phartyals. To their internecine strife may be attributed both the intrusion of the Chands in the 10th century and their final ruin in the 18th. The chief village of the Maras was Kot with the fort of Katolgarh and the chief village of the Phartyals was Dunjan near Sui. Som Chand was a sagacious administrator. To the head of the first clan he granted the rank of chief civil adviser, while the head of the Phartyals was made commander-in-chief. He restored to their ancient dignities the headmen of villages, called *burhas* or *sayanas,* and entrusted them with minor police and fiscal duties. The immediate courtiers of Som Chand were Joshis, Bishts, and Pandes of the Kanaujya subdivision in the plains; the general civil and military administration was entrusted to the Joshis, while the Bisht and Pandes held the offices of *guru, purohit, baid* and *rasoya.* At his death [975 A. D.] he possessed the southern part of the present pargana in right of his wife and the remainder by right of conquest. But all this tract he held as feudatory of the Maharaja of Doti, even as many of his successors did, so that at this period the Chand family was little better off than the majority of the more important landholders in the region.

Atma Chand and his successors 975–1055 A. D.

Som Chand was succeeded by his son Atma Chand. No events of outstanding importance occurred during this reign, but from the court paid by the neighbouring rulers to Atma Chand at Champawat it may be inferred that the work of consolidating the power and influence of the little state progressed none the less surely. Atma Chand was succeeded by Purana Chand, a noted hunter, and he by Indra Chand, who is credited with the introduction of the silk worm into Kumaon, and he by Sousar, Sudha and Hammira in turn, of whom nothing is known but their names. After Hammira came Bina, a weak and irresolute monarch who entrusted all state affairs to unscrupulous and irresponsible servants. He died childless, and his death was the signal for a general revolt of the Khasiyas. The Chands were ejected by a Khasiya dynasty of which little except the names of some of the rulers is known. It must however be assumed that the Chand chronology as given in Mr. Atkinson's lists (p. 165) ought not to be disturbed by this revolution and that the Khasiya dynasty was contemporary with that of the Chands and only came into collision with the latter when Sonpal Khasiya and Bira Chand, a relative of Sonsar Chand, finally decided the question of the pretensions of their respective families to the tract along the Kali. The Khasiya revolt was a national rather than a dynastic commotion, and similar disturbances extended eastwards as far as Nepal. All the Brahmans and Rajput immigrants from the plains who had conciliated the favour of the Chands found themselves the object of a fierce persecution. They rallied round the standard of Bira Chand and the restoration was completely successful. Sonpal was slain and Bira established himself at Champawat, and recalled the Joshis to office as a reward for the aid they had given him in his restoration. From Bira Chand to Garur Gyan Chand there is nothing but a bare list of names with no account of any reign save that of Trilok Chand who annexed Chhakhata to Kumaon, and fortified Bhim Tal to protect the frontiers towards Pali and Barahmandal where the Kathis and Katyuris still held independent sway. A branch of the latter dynasty was at this period still reigning in its ancient capital at Karttikeyapura, near the modern Baijnath in the Katyur pargana.

Garur Gyan Chand. 1374—1419 A. D.

The Musalman historians furnish the suggestion that the Chand rule over the tract of country at the foot of the hills was inefficient or non-existent. The Hindus of Katehir, the country below it, appear to have been pushed further and further north by the Muhammadans and to have encroached upon the possessions of the hillmen. Consequently Gyan Chand on his succession thought it his first duty to proceed to Delhi and petition the Emperor for the grant of the strip of country at the foot of the hills which had of old belonged to the Katyuri rajas. He did so and was favourably received by the Emperor, who not only granted his petition but also bestowed upon him the name Garur owing to his having cleverly shot a vulture which was carrying away a large snake. Later the Musalman governor of Sambhal seized the Tallades Bhabar but was driven out by Gyan Chand's favourite officer Nalu. The latter was handsomely rewarded but became an object of envy at court, so much so that his enemies led by one Jassa of Kamlekh contrived to poison the Raja's mind and induced him to blind two of Nalu's sons. This so incensed Nalu that he attacked the Raja, and captured him and Jassa, whom he slew. The Raja's life was spared but that prince ill requited his captor's generosity by causing his death some time afterwards. Garur Gyan Chand died in 1419 after a reign of 45 years and was succeeded for a few months only by his son Harihar Chand.

Udyan Chand. 1420—1421 A. D.

Udyan Chand succeeded his father Harihar Chand in 1420 and, impressed with the heinousness of his grandfather's crime, he spent the first part of his short reign in appeasing the wrath of the gods by restoring the great temple of Baleswar and inviting a Gujerati Brahman to consecrate it. He then proceeded to seize the posts held by the Padyar Raja of Chaugarkha, the Rajas of Mahryuri and of Bisaud. At the time of his death his possessions extended from the Sarju on the north to the Tarai on the south and from the Kali westwards to the Kosi and Sual rivers. To the north of the Sarju lay the estates of the Mankoti Raja of Gangoli. The Maharaja of Doti held Sira, Shor, and Askot and the Bhotia villages of Johar and Darma. The Raja of Jumla ruled over Byans and Chaudans, and Katyuri Rajas were established in Katyur, Syunara, and Lakhanpur of Pali. A Kathi Rajput still held Phaldakot and a Khasiya family reigned in Ramgarh and Kota. Udyan Chand reigned only one year and was succeeded by his son Atma and grandson Hari, each of whom reigned but one year.

Vikrama Chand. 1423—1437 A. D.

Vikrama Chand succeeded his father Hari in 1423 A. D. and carried out the restoration of the Baleswar temple commenced by the pious Udyan Chand. Vikrama Chand was dispossessed by his nephew Bharati Chand with the assistance of one Shor, a Khasiya.

Bharati Chand. 1437—1450 A. D.

During his comparatively short reign, Bharati Chand extended the encroachments begun by Gyan Chand which ended in the consolidation of the whole of Kumaon under Chand rule. He proceeded against the Raja of Doti who had for generations been acknowledged as suzerain of the Kali Kumaon district and fixing his camp at a place called Bali Chaukur, plundered the neighbouring country. After twelve years of this desultory warfare Ratan Chand, the son of Bharati Chand, with the aid of the Raja of Katehir, entirely defeated the

Doti prince so that the latter was forced to relinquish all claim to the suzerainty he had previously enjoyed. Bharati Chand was so pleased with his son's prowess that he abdicated in his favour in 1450 A. D. He himself died in 1461 A. D. Ratan Chand (1450—1488 A.D.), on taking the reins of government, found conditions exceedingly favourable. Believing therefore that such good fortune was sent by the gods, he lost no time in endowing the temple of Jageswar with several villages. He was the first raja to make any fixed administrative arrangements, for he formed a settlement with the resident cultivators and in other ways managed the affairs of government in orderly fashion. Meanwhile the Raja of Doti had again risen and Ratan Chand was compelled to interfere and restore the country to the Sahi raja who had been ejected. He made further conquests including that of Shor which was for a time annexed to Kali Kumaon. He was succeeded in 1488 by his son Kirati Chand.

Kirati Chand, 1488—1503 A. D.

This prince bore as warlike a reputation as his father and made several conquests. Shortly after he came to the throne the Dotiyals invaded Kumaon in force before the scattered outposts could be called in. When his main body could be set in motion, he was dissuaded by a holy man from taking the field himself. He accordingly sent his general, who thoroughly discomfited the Doti forces, so that they did not for a long time dare to attack Kali Kumaon again. The holy man, whose name was Nagnath, naturally acquired great influence in the Raja's counsels and advised him to extend his conquests westwards. There he said the raja would find a *guru* called Satyanath who would instruct him in what he should do.

Acting on this advice Kirati Chand marched westward and after slight opposition occupied both Barahmandal and Pali. This was the first conflict between the Katyuris and the Chands. The latter were however too strong and the remaining Katyuris retired to Salt and built a fort at Manil, where they were for a long time allowed to live in peace. The conquest of Phaldakot was next undertaken and proved a more difficult task. After much stubborn fighting reinforcements had to be sent for and at last the Chands prevailed. The total destruction of the Kathis was ordered, and so effectually was this carried out that Kirati

Chand was able to parcel out the land among his followers. He next took possession of Kota and Kotauli and then returned to Champawat, consolidating his conquests by the appointment of administrative officers as he went along. Finally he established a post in the lower country at Jaspur. Kirati Chand must be regarded as one of the most active and successful princes of his family, for at the time of his death he ruled the whole country occupied by the present Almora and Naini Tal districts with the exception of Katyur held by a Katyuri Raja, Danpur, Bhot, Askot, Sira, Shor and the Mankoti raj of Gangoli. The period between 1503, the date of the death of Kirati Chand and 1555 is occupied by the uneventful reigns of Partab Chand (1503—1517), Tara Chand (1517—1533), Manik Chand (1533—1542) celebrated for the hospitality which he showed to the refugee Khawas Khan, Kalyan Chand (1542—1551) and Puran Chand (1551—1555), none of whom extended their sway, but contented themselves with consolidating and maintaining intact the heritage derived from Kirati Chand.

Bhikam or Bhishma Chand. 1555—1560.

Bhikam ascended the throne in 1555. He had no son and therefore adopted a son of Tara Chand, called Kalyan or Balo Kalyan Chand. Disturbances again arose in Doti and Balo Kalyan was sent to quell them; but during his absence the Raja was troubled by news of a rising in Pali and Syunara and himself proceeded to pacify that portion of his dominions. These risings convinced the Raja that his kingdom required a more central capital than Champawat. He therefore decided to settle near the old fort of Khagmara and make it his seat of government. A plot was formed to frustrate this design and a semi-independent Khasiya chief of Ramgarh in the Gagas hills named Gajawa with his men entered the Khagmara fort and slew the Raja and his followers while they were asleep. Gajawa's triumph was short lived. Balo Kalyan Chand on hearing the news hastily came to terms with Doti and hastening to the spot took exemplary vengeance on all the Khasiyas of the neighbourhood. This event occurred in 1560 A. D.

Balo Kalyan Chand. 1560—1565 A. D.

Balo Kalyan Chand on his accession made the Khagmara hill his capital, calling it Almora. Soon after his accession his troops found occupation by invading Gangoli to the north-east of Almora, where rajas of the Chandrabansi line still held an independent kingdom. A struggle had occurred there between the Pants and the Upretis in which the former had won the day, but Narayan Chand, a descendant of Sital Chand, the nominee of the Pants, had given offence to Balo Kalyan Chand whereupon the latter quickly overran Gangoli and annexed it to his possessions. His great desire however was to acquire the country between Gangoli and the Kali river. He urged his wife to beg from her brother, the Raja of Doti, the pargana of Sira as dowry. The Doti raja refused though he consented to let Balo Kalyan have Shor. This the Kumaonis took, but failed in an attempt to take possession of Sira also. Danpur was next taken, internal dissensions rendering it an easy prey. In these newly acquired tracts it was the custom for cadets of the Chand house to be entrusted with the management. These junior members of the Chand house were called Raotelas and were given considerable grants of land for their own support. This busy reign lasted only five years and on Balo Kalyan's death Rudra Chand his son [1565—1597 A. D.] reigned in his stead.

Rudra Chand. 1556—1597 A. D.

One of the earliest acts of the new raja was to re-establish the worship of Mahadeo at Baleswar. Not long after his accession the Tarai and Bhabar were occupied by Husain Khan Tukryah. This man was governor of Lucknow in 1569 A. D., but was deprived of his charge. He then resolved to lead a crescentade against the hills with a view partly to destroying the idols of the infidels but chiefly to plundering the treasury of the Kumaon Rajas who were believed to possess immense sums hidden away. He ravaged the lower country, penetrating also into the interior as far as Doti, but heavy rains coming on, his followers refused to remain longer and he retreated to the plains, suffering severe losses on the way. On his return Husain Khan was granted the governorship of Shahjahanpur. A few years later in 1575 he made his second expedition, this time towards the eastern Dun, which he ravaged and plundered. On representations being made to Akbar, Husain Khan was recalled to Delhi, where he died. The hill tradition is that shortly after the death of Husain Khan, Rudra Chand, having attained his majority, drove the Mussalman officials from the Tarai.

Complaints were made to Delhi and reinforcements were sent to aid the governor of Katehir. Rudra Chand, feeling that he could not defeat the enemy in the open field, proposed that the claim to the Tarai should be decided by single combat. Rudra Chand represented the Hindus, and after a long struggle defeated the Moghal champion. Later Rudra Chand visited the Emperor at Delhi and was allowed an audience. The story of the combat is probably pure fiction, but the boast is pardonable when we have the acknowledgment that the Moghals were never able to penetrate into the hills. It is further recorded that Akbar was so pleased with the conduct of the Kumaon prince that he invited him to Lahore, where he sent him with his troops to assist in the siege of Nagor. There the hillmen so distinguished themselves that Akbar conferred on their leader the formal grant of Chaurasi Mal and excused him for life from the duty of personal attendance. Rudra Chand moreover made Birbal, the celebrated minister of Akbar, his *purohit*, and up to the close of the Chand rule the descendants of Birbal used to visit Almora to collect the customary dues. The visit of Rudra Chand is not so highly spoken of by the Mussalman historians. Budaoni * relates that "in 1588 A. D. the Raja of Kumaon arrived at Lahore from the Siwalik hills for the purpose of paying his respects. Neither he nor his ancestors (the curse of God on them!) could ever have expected to speak face to face with an Emperor," and goes on to describe the outlandish presents brought by the visitor. At the same time the negative testimony of the Ain-i-Akbari proves conclusively that no portion of the hills ever paid tribute to Akbar. Rudra Chand is famous for being the first Chand ruler to occupy in earnest the Bhabar and Tarai and to settle it thoroughly. We gather from tradition and the Muhammadan historians that this tract in the 11th century was covered with dense forests interspersed with patches of grazing land and cultivation. The huts were of a very temporary nature, but there were forts here and there for a refuge in times of trouble. It was not till the 12th century that the Kshattrya clans entered Katehir and gave it their name. They were gradually, by Muhammadan pressure from the south, forced to cross the

* Elliot V., 541. *Ibid*, VI, 352.

Ramganga and bring the forest country under the plough. In the 13th century these Hindu tribes suffered severely at the hands of Nasir-ud-din, Ghyas-ud-din, and Firoz Shah. The claim advanced by the earlier Chand rulers to this tract, has but little foundation on fact; and actually the lower *pattis* in the hills did not come into the possession of the Chands until the conquests of Kirati Chand and Ratan Chand and the transfer of the seat of government to Almora in the 16th century. The southern portion of the lowland tract or the Tarai proper was first taken permanent possession of by Rudra Chand, who was also the first to take measures to ensure the obedience of the nomad and semi-barbarous inhabitants to the central authority. The name of this tract was Chaurasi Mal or Naulakhya : it was supposed to be eighty-four *kos* in length—whence the former name—and to yield a revenue of 9 lakhs assessed on it, whence the latter name. Rudra Chand established governors in the different parganas and founded towns. On his return to Almora ably assisted by his blind son Sakti Gosain he introduced many sensible reforms and instituted measures for the land settlement.

Conquest of Sira.

The Raja's mother, who had formerly failed to obtain Sira as a dowry, refused to become *sati* on the death of her husband and until her son should take Siragarh. Rudra Chand made one attempt, but was defeated with heavy losses. He then sent for Parkhu the nephew of a Sira Brahmin in order to discover the strength of the enemy and the character of the defences of Siragarh, as Parkhu was supposed to have great influence as well as much treasure. Three times however were the forces of Rudra Chand defeated. Parkhu fled and while fleeing stayed to rest under a tree. The story goes that he saw a dung beetle trying to move a large piece of cowdung into its hole. Four times it failed, but the fifth time it succeeded. Parkhu called for food and rice boiled in milk was brought to him on a plantain leaf : he lost much of it while eating, and an old woman who was looking on said "you are as great a fool as Parkhu; he cannot take Sira and you cannot eat *khira*. Begin from the edge and work into the middle of the platter and you will lose no rice, and if Parkhu had begun from the outside and stopped the supplies from Johar and the undergrourd way to the river the garrison of Sira would soon yield." Parkhu without revealing his identity went off and acted on this advice, with the result that in a short time Hari Malla abandoned the fort and fled to Doti. Henceforth Sira belonged to Kumaon. Parkhu was rewarded with several villages, and there is a grant in his favour dated 1581 A. D. Rudra Chand also took Askot, Darma and Johar, but allowed the Raja of Askot to retain his patrimony as zamindar, and to the present day this is the only estate in Kumaon held in pure zamindari to which the rule of primogeniture is attached. Rudra Chand now (1581) called upon Parkhu to carry out a promise made by him to capture Badhangarhi in the Pindar valley, a part of the Raja of Garhwal's territory. The route to that fort lay through Someswar and the Katyur valley, held at that time by Sukpal Deo, the last reigning Raja of the ancient Katyura family. Dularam Shah, Raja of Garhwal, offered to help Sukpal, and sent two forces, one towards Gwaldam and the other towards Ganai. Parkhu and his army were checked and cut off and he himself killed by a Padyar Rajput near Gwaldam. The Kumaonis fled to Almora and Rudra Chand determined before invading Garhwal a second time to punish the Katyur Raja. He overran the valley, and captured the Raja and all his family. As he was about to punish him, one Ratu, a headman of a village, offered to stand security for the good behaviour of Sukpal Deo and to produce him after six months to be dealt with. Ratu obtained his wish, but later refused to give Sukpal Deo up to Rudra Chand, whereupon the latter invaded the valley, slew Ratu as well as Sukpal Deo, and banished the family, laying waste the whole country. Rudra Chand died in 1597 before he could make a second expedition to Garhwal.

Lakshmi Chand. 1597—1621 A. D.

Though not the eldest son, Lakshmi Chand took up the reins of government as Sakti Gosain was blind. The latter however was a most able administrator and carried out a complete settlement record of the land, making the *bisi* * the standard of measure. He also put the civil and military establishments on a stable footing, dividing the officers into three classes, *sirdars*, *faujdars*, and *negis*. The long-continued wars had given rise to a body of professional soldiers who sought as a reward grants of

* 20 *nalis* or 4,800 square yards.

land in the conquered districts. These were now administered for the first time on a fixed system, and regular assignments of land were made for the support of troops in camp and garrison under the name of *bisi banduk.* Lakshmi Chand was less fortunate in his department of the administration. He seven times invaded Garhwal, to be repulsed each time with heavy loss. So hard pressed was he in his last expedition that he escaped with his life only by concealing himself in a litter under a heap of soiled clothes and in this ignominous position made his entry into his capital. Being conscience-stricken and fearing that a lax observance of religious duties was accountable for his reverses, he built the Lachmeswar temples at Bageswar and Almora, and made grants to other great temples. He also completely restored the old Bageswar temple and, encamping at the confluence of the Gumti and Sarju rivers near Bageswar, paid his devotions to the gods before commencing his eighth expedition. This time he was so far successful that he was able to plunder the frontier parganas of Garhwal and to return in safety and dignity to Almora, but he failed to make any permanent impression in the country. He, like Gyan Chand and Rudra Chand, paid a visit to the Imperial court which is mentioned by Jahangir in his memoirs. He died in 1621 and was succeeded by his son, Dalip Chand, of whom little worth recording is known.

Bijaya Chand.

Bijaya Chand (1625 A. D.) came next, but as he was a minor all state duties fell into the hands of three men of Shor, Sukhram Kharku, Piru Gosain, and Binayak Bhat. He married a daughter of the Badgujar house of Anupshahr in the Bulandshahr district, and the three counsellors bent on keeping the power in their own hands confined the young Raja to his women's apartments, which they took care to fill with attractions which rendered him oblivious of his duties and the outer world. One member of the royal family, Nil Gosain, a son of Lakshmi Chand, protested against this treatment of the head of the state. He was seized and blinded, and the triumvirate then proceeded to get rid of all Bijaya Chand's near relations. Trimal Chand, another son of Lakshmi Chand, fled to Garhwal, while Narayan Chand, a third son, escaped to the Doti lowlands, and a son of Nil Gosain, afterwards known as Baz Bahadur Chand, was taken care of by a Tiwari woman, the wife of his *purohit.* The Raja of Garhwal promised to aid Trimal Chand if he would agree to consider the western Ramganga as the permanent boundary of the two kingdoms. His official astrologers, the Joshis, however predicted from his horoscope that he would eventually be Raja of Kumaon in any case, and he refused the offer. The only act of Bijaya Chand's reign worthy of mention here was the building of the entrance gate to the fort of Almora, but the three men of Shor resenting even this display of initiative slew the Raja while he slept, intoxicated with *bhang,* in the inner apartments. Sukhram then gave out that the Raja had died suddenly and that he would continue as chief of the administration until a fitting successor should be found. This was however more than the people could bear and both Maras and Phartyals resolved to act. The Maras with Trimal Chand were the first to reach Almora and the installation was proceeded with at once though according to certain dissident Joshis the constellations were not propitious. The Phartyals with Narain Chand at their head arrived immediately afterwards at the ford of the Sual below China Khan, but dispersed on hearing of the Maras' success.

Trimal Chand. 1625—1638.

Trimal Chand though possibly not guiltless of the murder of Bijaya Chand resolved to gain some popularity by the punishment of the actual assassins. Sukhram Kharku was put to death; Binayak Bhat was blinded and his property confiscated; but Piru Gosain was allowed to proceed to Allahabad on condition that he would commit suicide under the sacred fig tree. Trimal Chand while an exile in Garhwal had written to Piru and promised him protection and advancement if he caused the death of Bijaya Chand; and for this reason Piru was treated with greater indulgence than his companions in crime. Not much is known of this reign. Trimal Chand had no son and, unwilling to permit his rival of the Phartyal faction to succeed him, he searched everywhere for other members of the Chand family. He finally selected Baz Chand, supposed to be a son of Nil Gosain, though there are other accounts of his origin. Baz Chand was duly adopted and given the title of Kunwar, and in course of time succeeded to the throne.

Baz Bahadur Chand. 1638—1678.

During part of the reign of Baz Chand the Tarai seems to have been very prosperous and to have therefore excited the envy of the Katehir Hindus who with the connivance of their Moghal rulers gradually occupied the lower villages. In this design they were much aided by the weakness of the Almora government during the previous thirty years. Baz Chand accurately realized the situation and determined to invoke the aid of the Emperor Shahjahan. On his arival at Delhi in 1654 he was directed to join the force then proceeding against Garhwal. The Raja obeyed and so distinguished himself there that he received the title of Bahadur and full recognition of his right to the Chaurasi Mal, with an order to the Muhammadan governor to aid him in checking the Katehir chiefs. He regained full possession of the Tarai, founded the town of Bazpur, and appointed governors and a regular establishment to carry on the administration. Rudrpur and Bazpur were the head quarters of the Tarai officers during the cold season and Barakheri and Kota, on the spurs of the outer range of hills, during the hot weather. Nearly the whole of the Tarai was cultivated, and Mr. Batten * notices that at Kota, Barakheri and elsewhere in the lower hills are remains of forts and residences and mango groves which go far to show that the climate at those sites was not in former time so insalubrios as at present. The Raja, after perfecting his arrangements in the plains, returned to Almora and initiated some of the fashions of the Moghal court, amongst others a poll-tax (1672), the proceeds of which were regularly remitted as tribute to the Emperor.

Baz Bahadur next proceeded to wipe out the disgrace that had previously attended Kumaon arms in the contest with Garhwal and was successful, by an invasion at two points, in seizing the border fort of Juniyagarh and carrying away an image of the goddess Nanda, which he installed in a temple at Almora. Complaints having reached his ears of the hardships inflicted by the Huniyas on pilgrims journeying through Tibet to Kailas and the lake of Mansarowar, he next equipped in 1670 A.D. an expedition to Bhot and, crossing by the Johar pass, attacked and captured the fort of Tuklakhar. He wrested the

* Report on Kumaon, p. 168.

control of the passes from the Huniyas and made them promise to allow pilgrims to the lake to pass free. He further set apart in sadabart the revenue of five villages near the passes for the purpose of providing pilgrims with food, clothing, and lodging.

On his return to Almora Baz Bahadur found that his enemies had been at work poisoning the mind of his son, Udyot Chand, who was suspected of having designs on the throne. Udyot was accordingly sent to take charge of Gangoli and the tracts beyond the Sarju. The Garhwal Raja too had taken advantage of Baz Bahadur's absence in Bhot to regain the territory he had lost. Reprisals followed and the Garhwalis were driven back as far as Srinagar itself. Here a hasty peace was patched up and Baz Bahadur returned to Almora, taking with him several Bisht families from Sabli and Rawats from Bangarsyun, to whom he gave the post of headmen of certain villages. The Katyuris were next dealt with and the last remnant was ejected from Manila, where they had taken refuge, on suspicion of having aided the Garhwalis against the Kumaonis (1672). The Raja then made a tour through the eastern parganas, inflicting summary punishment on the Raja of Chitona who had assumed a certain amount of independence. He then invaded and annexed Byans. The last years of Baz Bahadur Chand's reign were unfortunately clouded by his cruelties to men whom he suspected of unfriendly intentions towards himself. He had several blinded, through the machinations of an unscrupulous Brahmin priest, and although he afterwards punished the latter for his deception, he died miserably alone and uncared for in Almora in 1678 A. D.

Udyot Chand 1678—1698 A. D.

Udyot Chand ascended the throne amid general rejoicings and was soon on the move to invade Garhwal. The first attempt was unsuccessful, but in 1681 he was more fortunate, penetrating by the Lohba route as far as Chandpur, which he captured and plundered. The next move on the part of the Garhwal Raja was an alliance offensive and defensive between himself and the Raja of Doti by virtue of which in 1681 Kumaon was attacked on two sides. For two years the war raged, but in the end the Kumaonis were successful. In 1688 Udyot Chand captured Khairagarh, putting an end to the power of the Doti Raja, who yielded and agreed to pay in future tribute to the Kumaon

Raja. These victories were celebrated with great pomp at Almora and temples were erected at various places to commemorate them. Eight years later (1696) the Doti Raja repudiated his agreement and Udyot Chand was forced to take the field in person against him, but with such ill-success that he had to return to Almora for reinforcements, leaving the troops under the command of Manorath and Siromani. The latter was murdered by Dotyals and the troops dispersed and the Raja was obliged to recall the remainder. Udyot Chand, like his predecessor, is famous for the encouragement that he gave to wise men to settle in Kumaon and for his patronage of learning. He devoted the last few months of his life to religious meditation and prayer and died in 1698 A. D., leaving his kingdom to his son Gyan Chand. Gyan Chand immediately proceeded to invade Garhwal. He laid waste the Pindar valley as far as Tharali and in the following year overran Sabli, Khatli and Saindhar. In 1701, however, the Garhwalis in their turn plundered Giwar and Chaukot in pargana Pali. In fact during the next few years so many marauding expeditions took place on both sides, that the industrious part of the population abandoned the frontier tracts which in many places became again covered with jungle. In 1707 another great expedition was undertaken by the Kumaonis, and they again took possession of Juniyagarh in Chaukot and marching through the Pandwakhal and Diwalikhal passes penetrated as far as Chandpur, where they razed the old fort to the ground.

Gyan Chand 1698—1708.

Gyan Chand was succeeded by Jagat Chand, said by some to be of spurious birth, who after the fashion of his predecessors began his reign by invading Garhwal, and plundering Lohba, where he established a garrison. The next year he traversed the Pindar valley and followed the Alaknanda as far as Srinagar, which he captured. The Garhwal Raja fled to Dehra Dun and Jagat Chand formally bestowed the town on a Brahman and divided the spoil among his followers and the poor, reserving, however, a portion as a present for Muhammad Shah, the Emperor at Delhi. The name of Jagat Chand is still esteemed as that of a raja who gained and held the affectionate remembrances of his subjects. He was gracious alike to the high and to the low.

Jagat Chand 1708—1720.

During his reign the Tarai yielded its nine lakhs of revenue, but after this epoch, internal disturbances destroyed all prosperity, both in the high and in the low lands. He died of small pox in 1720 A. D. and was succeeded by his son Debi Chand, who according to some was illegitimate.

Debi Chand. 1720—1726. A. D.

From the reign of Debi Chand may be dated the commencement of the decline of the Chand power. The Garhwalis were able to regain all their lost territory and also to invade the Baijnath valley. Debi Chand was a weak and vacillating ruler and gave evidence of his foolishness by his attempt to pay off all the debts of his subjects and found a new era when all would be at ease and none in debt. Most of the money spent in this senseless undertaking found its way into the coffers of the Brahman money-lenders, who were thus provided with the one thing they wanted to complete their preparations for the impending struggle for power. He was also led to take part in the political struggles going on in the plains and consequently suffered a severe defeat by the Imperial troops while supporting the claim of a pretender, Sabir Shah, to the throne.* In 1726 he was murdered through the agency of the Bishts in his pleasure house whither he had retired for ease, though enemies were attacking him in the east and west.

The Bishts now looked out for some connection of the Chand family whom they could set up as a titular ruler and found Ajit Chand, a grandson of Gyan Chand. He was called to Almora and duly installed as Raja. The Bishts now gave themselves up to the full enjoyment of their ill-gotten power; they plundered the people in the Raja's name, while keeping the exercise of every semblance of real power strictly in their own hands. A palace intrigue resulted in the murder of the Raja and after a brief interregnum of power the Bishts were displaced by Kalyan Chand, a distant and impoverished connection of the royal family.

Kalyan Chand. 1730—1747.

The first act of the new Raja was to punish with death the offending Bishts. The poor man now grown rich had tasted blood and to secure himself from rivals sent executioners throughout the land to slay all who had any pretensions to bear

* Dowson's Elliot VIII, p. 45.

the name or be of the family of the Chands. The Raja's spies were present in every village, and every house and family found enemies among those of its own household. Families who had the barest reputation of being of Chand descent were killed or exiled equally with those of pure Raotela origin. The *parvenu* Raja with the low cunning bred of ignorance believed his system of espionage the highest effort of political sagacity. His spies were really his masters and though plots no doubt existed many more were fabricated for the removal of private enemies. One day he learned from his chief of police that a great Brahman conspiracy threatened his life, and in a paroxysm of fear he ordered that all concerned should be blinded, and their Khasiya adherents should be executed. The result was, it is said, that seven earthen vessels filled with the eyes of Brahmans were brought before him whilst the bodies of scores of Khasiyas filled the ravines of the Sual. Kalyan Chand now found the submontane portions of his dominions threatened by the officers of Nawab Mansur Ali Khan. Shib Deo Joshi was appointed viceroy of the plains, and for some time he resisted the encroachments of the Oudh darbar. Next Himmat Gosain, one of the victims of the imaginary plot just described, joined himself to Ali Muhammad Khan Rohilla, and assembled a force of Kumaonis and plains men to attack the Raja. Kalyan Chand succeeded in having Himmat Gosain assassinated, but this act merely had the effect of enraging Ali Muhammad Khan, so that he at once sent a well-equipped expedition to invade Kumaon. Shib Deo Joshi was defeated at Rudrpur and Hafiz Rahmat Khan, the Oudh general, pursued the Kumaonis and occupied Bijapur below Bhim Tal. Reinforcements were sent but almost without striking a blow the Kumaonis fled at the first charge of the enemy and were pursued as far as the Sual river below Almora. Almora was occupied without opposition while Kalyan Chand fled to Lohba and entreated the protection of the Garhwal Raja. Almora was looted, the temples were defiled and the idols were mutilated and plundering expeditions were sent to the neighbouring parganas to seize all gold and silver idols to be melted down with their ornaments. During this period the old records were lost or destroyed and the few that remained were preserved in private families in distant portions of the province, so that on these alone could reliance be placed in drawing up a sketch of Kumaon history. The alliance between Pradipt Shah of Garhwal and the Kumaonis was not of much avail as the combined forces were severely defeated by the Rohillas, who threatened to occupy Srinagar, but desisted and consented to abandon the country when the Garhwal chief agreed to pay three lakhs on behalf of Kalyan Chand. Later the Tarai was again invaded by the Rohillas, but on representations being made to the Emperor, the Oudh Nawab was induced to restore the places he had occupied. Forts were built at Rudrpur and Kashipur and garrisons placed therein; each under a separate governor. Kalyan Chand now became blind and, feeling his end approaching, abdicated in 1747 in favour of his young son, Dip Chand, with Shib Deo, who had done good work in the Tarai, as regent. In 1748 Kalyan Chand died and with his last breath he committed his son and family to Shib Deo, entrusting all power and authority to him, and nobly did Shib Deo fulfil his trust. He restored all property that had been unjustly confiscated by the late Raja, appointed his son Jai Kishan as his deputy in Almora and proceeded himself to the Tarai, where he made his cousin Hari Ram Joshi governor of Kashipur, but exchanged him, when he neglected his duties, for Siromani Das, a Brahman of Bazpur. In 1761 4,000 Kumaonis took part in the battle of Panipat, fighting at the call of the Emperor. Dip Chand appears to have been a mild and generous man of weak temperament. He was much in the hands of priests, and there are more memorials of his reign in the shape of grants of land to temples and favourites than of any of his predecessors. He reigned from 1748 to 1777 and during the earlier part of it the country enjoyed peace and prosperity. The lowlands were in a flourishing condition and the Kumaoni governors were on good terms with the Rohilla chiefs. Police organisation in the Tarai was excellent owing to the good government of Shib Deo and his lieutenants and many immigrants sought the shelter of the Kumaoni authority in the Tarai. The only tax imposed was one-sixth of the produce and in adverse seasons even this was remitted. The Maras were now in power and the Phartyals resolved by some means or other to make a bid for supreme

Dip Chand. 1748—1777.

authority as the raja was governed by the party which held the nominal office of Diwan. Shib Deo quashed a nascent rebellion, but the brave old man had now to suffer at the hands of his relatives. Jai Kishan, though a Mara, joined by a number of Phartyals went to the Garhwal Raja, Pradipt Shah, and induced him to invade Kumaon. Shib Deo set out to meet him and after refusing to allow Dip Chand to acknowledge the suzerainty of the Garhwal Raja, fought a battle at Tamba Dhaund in which the Garhwalis were worsted and the Raja fled to Srinagar, where peace was concluded. No sooner was this quarrel over than internal troubles arose which ended in such confusion that the Gurkhalis when they crossed the Kali in 1790 had a very easy task in conquering the country. Hariram Joshi was always jealous of his cousin Shib Deo's power and reputation and, having been slighted on one occasion, determined to overthrow him. After six battles which gave no decisive result, Shib Deo obtained in the seventh conflict a brilliant victory, Hariram losing his son and 1,500 men. Hariram gave himself up and was ordered by Hafiz Rahmat Khan, who had been appointed arbiter, to obey Shib Deo faithfully in future. Shib Deo's worst enemies were the Phartyals of Pali pargana and he found his time fully occupied in frustrating the plots that were contrived against him. In 1764 however when he was advancing to Kashipur to settle a demand for increased pay made at the instigation of the Phartyals by the mercenaries who garrisoned the Tarai, the soldiers rose in revolt and murdered him and two of his sons. His loss was severely felt as he had managed the affairs of state in a wise and temperate manner and had prevented Dip Chand from going astray. Soon after this Hariram died. From this time onwards chaos appears to have reigned—the plains were left uncared for and internal commotions distracted the highlands. Jai Kishan succeeded his father Shib Deo as prime minister and viceroy. In 1769 a boy was born to Dip Chand. The Rani who bore him feeling her position of some account as mother of the heir, intrigued with Hafiz Rahmat Khan to oust Jai Kishan. That chief at the instigation of a favourite servant Jodha Singh of Katehir wrote to Jai Kishan advising him to submit to the Rani, whereupon he left

Almora in disgust. The Rani's party now became completely successful.

Kishan Singh, the Raja's bastard brother, became prime minister, Parmanand Bisht, the Rani's paramour, became viceroy, and Jodha Singh obtained the governorship of Kashipur. Mohan Singh, a scion of the Chand house, obtained for himself the command of the army, but Parmanand ejected him after he had held office for a year. Mohan Singh fled to Rohilkhand, but returned later with a force of Rohillas and hillmen and captured Almora as well as the persons of the Raja and Rani. Parmanand and the Rani were put to death. Mohan Singh now firmly established himself as head of the government. Hafiz Rahmat Khan hearing of the state of affairs in Kumaon, and finding that his old friend Dip Chand was now only a puppet in the hands of designing adventurers, sent for Harak Deb and Jai Kishan, the sons of Shib Deo, and counselled them to make some attempt to recover the power once exercised by their family. The Joshis listened to his advice and with the help of Kishan Singh succeeded in expelling Mohan Singh, who sought safety first with Zabita Khan and then with the Oudh Nawab. Dip Chand was greatly pleased at the turn events had taken and Harak Deb was appointed prime minister and commander-in-chief. Siromani Das previously mentioned was confirmed in his appointment of governor of Kashipur and was succeeded shortly afterwards by his son Nandram.

A few months later, after some semblance of order had been restored, Mohan Singh asked forgiveness and permission to return to Almora. Jai Kishan allowed him to do so, and on his way Mohan Singh saw Nandram and promised in return for his assistance to help him in the prosecution of his schemes. Mohan Singh arrived at Almora and took part once more in the management of public affairs. Jai Kishan expressed the opinion that Nandram should be ousted from his governorship and Mohan Singh outwardly concurred but wrote privately to Nandram telling him to hold out as long as he could. Jai Kishan found a large force ready to oppose him and was worsted in the battle that followed. Seeing his chance when the brothers were separated Mohan Singh managed to have Jai Kishan assassinated and would have murdered

Harak Deb too at Almora had not Lal Singh, Mohan Singh's brother, interceded and obtained for him merely imprisonment. Next Dip Chand and his two sons died suddenly in confinement at Sirakot, the state prison of the Chands, but there is no doubt that they were all murdered or starved to death by Mohan Singh's orders. These events occurred in 1777 A. D. With the coast clear, Mohan Singh proclaimed himself Raja under the name of Mohan Chand and then wrote to Nandram granting him the Tarai, but the latter went to the Oudh Darbar and offered the low country to the Nawab, agreeing at the same time to hold the land as lessee and to pay a considerable sum as land revenue. This bargain was concluded and Nandram further extended his territory by having Manorath Joshi, governor of Rudrpur, treacherously assassinated. He took possession of that district in the name of the Nawab and so the last vestige of authority of the hill state over the plains vanished.

Mohan Singh as soon as he became Raja set to work to persecute all the friends and relations of Shib Deo, and obliged them to flee from Kumaon and seek refuge in the plains. A reign of terror prevailed, and at last the Rajas of Doti and Garhwal, disgusted with the state of affairs, entered into correspondence with Harak Deb, still in prison, and other discontented persons in Kumaon. Lalit Sah, the Raja of Garhwal, was the first to take the field. He advanced by Lohba to Dwara with a large force and entirely defeated the Kumaonis in 1779 A. D. at Bagwali Pokhar. Harak Deb had been released and exhorted to fight for his old country, but news of the serious reverse being received, Mohan Singh fled to the plains and Harak Deb joined Lalit Sah. Lalit Sah put his son Pradhaman on the Kumaon throne with the title of Pradhaman Chand.

Pradhaman Chand. 1779—1786.

Pradhaman Chand appointed the Joshis to the principal offices and would doubtless have evolved some semblance of firm government had the people been really disposed towards it, but they were too much accustomed to revolutions to believe such a consummation possible. Lalit Sah died and was succeeded on the throne of Garhwal by his eldest son Jayakrit Sah, between whom and Pradhaman quarrels as to precedence soon rose; while Mohan Singh with the assistance of a band of religious mendicants called Nagas, made another unsuccessful attempt upon Almora. Nevertheless the quarrel between the two brothers became more bitter and Jayakrit began to intrigue with Mohan Singh. Harak Deb recognizing the danger of the situation went with a strong escort towards Garhwal and demanded an interview with Jayakrit Sah. The Garhwal Raja rfeused his request doubting the sincerity of Harak Deb, and with justice, for when he attacked Harak Deb, hoping to surprise him he found himself opposed to a force which defeated his troops and obliged him to seek safety in flight. So hardly pressed were the Garhwalis in the pursuit that the Raja sickened and died; and the Kumaoni troops plundering and burning every village on their way and even the sacred temple of Dewalgarh entered and took possession of the capital Srinagar. Pradhaman for a short while ruled over both countries, easily silencing the pretensions of a third brother, Parakram. Pradhaman was however never popular and his preference for Garhwal alienated his Kumaoni subjects. Harak Deb did his best to strengthen his position, but he was faced by a coalition of enemies that he could not resist, and he was defeated near Naithana in Talla Dora and fled to the plains. Thus in 1786 ended the Garhwali domination. Mohan Singh was again supreme for a short time, but in 1788 Harak Deb recruited a force in Barhapura and invaded Kumaon. In the first battle he was successful and took Mohan Singh and Lal Singh prisoners. Lal Singh was pardoned and released, but Mohan Singh he took to a small dharamsala near below Hiradungri and slew him there in expiation of his numerous crimes. Harak Deb thus became master again and wrote at once to Pradhaman Chand to come and take possession of the vacant throne, but he wisely declined, being mindful of his sufferings and the uncertain tenure by which he had held the country before. Harak Deb therefore put on the throne one Shib Singh, said to have been descended from Udyot Chand, and installed him as Raja of Kumaon under the name of Shib Chand. Troubles soon arose as Lal Singh assisted by Parakram Shah invaded Kumaon. Harak Deb retired with Shib Singh to Srinagar, while Lal Singh put on the throne as Raja the son of Mohan Singh and called him Mahendra Chand.

Mahendra Chand. 1788—1790.

Lal Singh took the place of Harak Deb as chief adviser and proceeded to persecute the Joshis : some were imprisoned, others banished, others again were executed. Harak Deb, through the machinations of Parakram Shah, was forced to flee to the plains to Bareilly. Lal Singh hearing of this and determined to frustrate the intrigues of the Joshis presented himself in person to the Nawab of Oudh and claimed the protection of the Oudh Darbar for Mahendra Chand who he said had willingly acknowledged Oudh as the owner of the Tarai. This brings us down to the year 1790, which was signalised by the Gurkha invasion.

The Gurkhalis.

While Kumaon was distracted by these internal dissensions, similar disorders prevailed in the neighbouring country of Nepal, at that time broken up into a number of petty states. One of these was the kingdom of Gurkha situated about eight days' journey from Kathmandu. The Gurkhali Raja seeing the defenceless state of the Kathmandu valley and anxious to enlarge his narrow dominions led a large force eastwards, but received a severe check at the hands of the Vaisya Raja of Nawakot. His son Pirthinarayan, who had been instructed in statecraft at the court of Bhatkot, carried out his father's projects and finally occupied Kathmandu in 1768. His policy of conquest was continued during the short reign of his successor Sinha Pratap Sah. This prince was succeeded in 1878 by Ran Bahadur Sah, who consolidated under his rule the whole of Nepal.

The ruler of Nepal was well aware of the state of affairs in Kumaon, and resolving to add that country also to his dominions he now wrote to Harak Deb inviting his assistance and co-operation. It appears that Harak Deb probably at least promised his good offices ; but in any case the Gurkha army destined for the invasion of Kumaon set out from Doti early in 1790. One division crossed the Kali into Shor while a second occupied the *patti* of Bisung. When the news of these preparations reached Almora all was confusion and despair. Mahendra Singh summoned the entire fighting population and with part of his regular troops took the field in Gangoli whilst Lal Singh advanced through Kali Kumaon. The Gurkha division under

Amar Singh Thapa was defeated by Mahendra Singh and obliged to retire towards Kali Kumaon. Here however the invaders were more successful, for falling upon Lal Singh they drove him with the loss of 200 men towards the plains; while Mahendra Singh losing heart abandoned his charge and fled to Kota. The Gurkhas finding the way thus open retraced their steps and after some slight resistance at Hawalbagh occupied Almora early in 1790. In the following year Harak Deb was at Almora and great preparations were made for the invasion of Garhwal. While however they were still sitting in front of Langurgarhi, a strong fortress in Garhwal, the news of the Chinese invasion of Nepal caused the withdrawal of the Gurkha troops for the defence of their own country, and Harak Deb was nominated as their regent in Almora. He appears never to have actually held office, and falling out with his new friends retreated to Srinagar under the protection of Raja Pradhaman Sah. Meanwhile Mahendra Singh was not idle. Using as his head quarters Kilpuri in the Tarai he made two unsuccessful irruptions into the hills and had nearly succeeded in embroiling the Gurkhas and the Nawab when the good offices of the British authorities brought about an arrangement by which the Nawab recognized the *de facto* ruler of Kumaon, while the Gurkhas on their part abandoned all pretensions to the low country. At the same time provision was made for the retention by the exiled family of a portion of the Tarai subsequently exchanged by the British for the grant of Chachait in the Pilibhit district. Kumaon itself was quiescent, if not pacified, and in 1791-1792 Joga Malla Subah, head of the civil administration, introduced a settlement of the land revenue. He imposed a tax of one rupee a *bisi* (nearly an acre) of cultivated land and a poll tax of one rupee on every adult, in addition to Re. 1-2-6 on every village to meet the expenses of his office. He was succeeded in 1795 by Kazi Nar Sinha, a man of ferocious cruelty, and later by Ajab Sinha Khawas Thapa. The common people made but little opposition to their new masters. It mattered little to them, confused as they long had been by the constant quarrels between the Joshis and the adherents of Mohan Singh, who for the time being were in power; for all oppressed them equally and there was none to give them redress. Many stories are told of the cruelties perpetrated by the Gurkhas during the earlier years of their rule in Kumaon, and though during the last seven years of their occupation the condition of the people was ameliorated and a better administration put an end to many of the most glaring abuses, the reputation they earned for themselves will not for many generations be forgotten. Their tyranny has passed into a proverb, and at the present time when a native of the hills wishes to protest in the strongest language in his power against some oppression to which he has been subjected, he exclaims that for him the British raj has ceased and the Gurkha rule has been restored. In 1806 Bam Sah became civil governor and matters changed very much for the better; and throughout, the Kumaonis, partly because they had made a less resolute defence, and partly because they were more within the purview of the chief authority, were treated with more consideration than the Garhwalis, for whom the various Gurkha officers reserved their most exquisite savagery. Private property was respected, grants made by former rulers were confirmed, rude justice was administered, the revenue was collected, and defaulters were, not as in Garhwal, sold into slavery. A great number of Kumaoni levies were admitted into the Gurkha army, so that in 1814 quite two-thirds of the Nepalese forces were composed of men from the upper *pattis* of Garhwal and Kumaon, and Kumaoni officers were even occasionally entrusted with small commands. Of external events during this period, the only matter worthy of mention is the reduction of Garhwal in 1803, and the flight, restoration and assassination of Ran Bahadur, King of Nepal.

British invasion of Kumaon.

The Gurkhas now came in contact with the British arms. Continued aggressions upon British territory in Gorakhpur and elsewhere at last determined Lord Hastings to declare war. It was decided to attack Nepal simultaneously from as many points as possible. To this end Major-General Marley with 8,000 men was sent to Behar with orders to march direct upon Kathmandu In Gorakhpur a force of 4,000 men was entrusted to Major General Wood. These armies met with little success, nor do their campaigns directly affect the history of Kumaon. General Gillespie with 3,500 men was instructed to enter Garhwal by the Dun and eject the Gurkha governor from Srinagar. He found the Gurkhas in strength at Kalanga, a fort near Dehra, which was captured after an heroic defence. At the extreme west of the position General Ochterlony manœuvring between the Sutlej and Jumna rivers held the Gurkhas in check.

The inconclusive campaign in the west and the reverses suffered by the Behar and Gorakhpur columns made Lord Hastings more anxious than ever to obtain a footing in Kumaon. Negotiation with the governor Bam Sah, known to be disaffected towards the party in power in Nepal, failed. In January 1815 all was ready for the invasion. The attack was to be made simultaneously from two quarters. A main body of 3,000 men under Lieutenant-Colonel W. L. Gardner was to proceed up the Kosi river and direct its attacks against Almora, while Captain H. Y. Hearsey with 1,500 men was to enter Kali Kumaon by the Timla pass.

Lieutenant-Colonel Gardner advanced with great caution, leaving posts behind him to keep his line of communications clear. He moved forward successively to Kanyasi, Chilkya, Amsot and Dhikuli, meeting with little opposition. On the 16th February the main body marched to Chukam and the Gurkhalis were forced back from Kotagarhi, where they had a post dangerously near the lines of communication. A route was then taken whereby the valley of the Kosi was left on the right together with the direct road to Almora; by these means Colonel Gardner hoped to turn the position of the enemy, who were at a place called Bujan between Kakrighat and Khairna on the main road to the capital. On the 22nd February by a rapid march Chaumukhia, a commanding post on the range between the Kosi and Ramganga rivers, was seized before the Gurkhas could arrive. This opened the road to Almora and allowed communications to be set up with the western districts of Kumaun and Garhwal. Supplies poured in from the neighbouring country and the villagers were only too ready to give whatever information they could of the enemy whom they hated so bitterly. The Gurkhas had now entrenched themselves at Kumpur (Ranikhet) a few miles in front of Chaumukhia, determined to make another attempt to bar the progress of our troops: the British forces then sat down opposite Kumpur and waited some days. At last Colonel Gardner perceived that the capture of Syahi Devi, a mountain between Kumpur and Almora, would force the Gurkhas to abandon their position and accordingly on the night of the 22nd March 1,200 men were sent off to take it. The movement was entirely successful, for on the 24th, the Gurkhas, fearing for the safety of Almora, hastily abandoned their stockades and retreated by the Riuni and Katarmal ridge. The British commander followed them, reaching Riuni on the 26th and Katarmal on the 27th, a spot distant only seven miles from Almora. The enemy's outposts withdrew as he approached, and the Gurkha forces concentrated on the Sitoli ridge about two miles from Almora. The Gurkha forces daily melted away. Not more than half were true Gurkhas, and the Kumaoni levies gladly joined themselves to the invader. Captain Hearsey's operations were not characterised by the same measure of success. He won some small skirmishes at first, but latterly, having been compelled to sub-divide his small force, was beaten in detail, taken prisoner, and brought into Almora. Meanwhile Lord Hastings, realising the importance of the advantage gained by Colonel Gardner, determined to send some British troops to help him and his raw levies. Accordingly 2,000 men belonging to the regular army with twelve guns were despatched under Colonel Nicolls, who, meeting with no opposition, arrived safely at Katarmal on the 18th April 1815. After four days' inaction on either side Hastidal, who after defeating Captain Hearsey in the east had returned to Almora and been placed in supreme command, led out the Bhawani Bakhsh regiment in a northerly direction, presumably for the purpose of keeping open his communications in that quarter. Such at any rate is the commonly understood object of this rather obscure movement. According to another account, British troops had already been despatched towards Gananath near Takula, 15 miles north of Almora, with the object of making the final attack from a spot at least as high as Almora, and it was to expell these troops that Hastidal moved out with one of the two regiments at his disposal, leaving the other, the Tara Dal regiment, for the protection of Almora. An intended night attack by the British was, according to the story, frustrated by an ingenious stratagem on the part of the Gurkha leader. The level pastures occupying the crests of the hills were resorted to by large herds of buffaloes ; to the horns of which Hastidal tied lighted torches, thus deceiving the assailants as to the number of the forces they had to cope with. The two armies however met on the evening of the 23rd April and after a short contest in one of the grassy glades among the pine forests, the Gurkhas turned and fled, leaving their leader Hastidal dead. Next day the British force, leaving a small detachment at Gananath, returned to Katarmal. On the 25th April Colonel Nicolls put his troops in motion towards Almora. He found the Gurkha centre posted on Sitoli with a detachment on Kalimat to cover the right flank. The breastworks and stockades erected by the centre were speedily carried. The Kalimat detachment was thus cut off and Colonel Nicolls established his head quarters for the night about half a mile north of the Almora fort while the troops were encamped on Hiradungri. During the night the Bhawani Bakhsh regiment eager to retrieve their defeat at Gananath and chafing under the reproaches of Bam Sah made a desperate attack upon the British position, which they succeeded in entering almost unnoticed, disguised in uniforms resembling those worn by the British levies. They proceeded to massacre the Pathans, and in the confusion many lives were lost. Our troops were however at last extricated by bugle call and the Gurkhas were exterminated but not before they had inflicted a loss of some 200 men. The next day Almora was shelled and the Gurkhas capitulated. The Gurkhas agreed to evacuate the province and all its fortified places. It was stipulated that they should be allowed to retire across the Kali with their guns, arms, military stores and private property, the British providing them with the necessary supplies and carriage. This convention also implied the evacuation of the forts of Malaun and Jaithak and the whole of the west country generally by Amar Singh Thapa. The Hon'ble E. Gardner was directed by the Governor General to assume the office and title of Commissioner for the affairs of Kumaon and agent to the Governor General on the 3rd of May 1815, and Mr. G. W. Traill was appointed his assistant on the 8th of July.

This sketch of the history of Kumaon may well be closed with an extract from Mr. Atkinson's book. "The administrative history of the Kumaon division, as remarked by Mr. Whalley * naturally divides itself into three periods—Kumaon under Traill, Kumaon under Batten, and Kumaon under Ramsay. The regime in the first period was essentially paternal, despotic and personal. It resisted the centralising tendencies which the policy of the Government had developed. It was at the same time, though arbitrary, a just, wise and progessive administration. Mr. Traill's administration lasted from 1815 to 1835. On his departure there followed an interval of wavering uncertainty and comparative misrule." "The system of government", as was observed by Mr. Bird, "had been framed to suit the particular character and scope of an individual" or, as he might have said, had been framed for himself by that individual. "Traill left the province orderly, prosperous and comparatively civilized but his machinery was not easily worked by another hand. There was no law and the law giver had been withdrawn. The Board of Commissioners and the Government which had remained quiescent while the province was in the hands of an administrator of tried ability and equal to all emergencies found it necessary to reassert their control and to lay down specific rules in matters which had hitherto been left to the judgment of the Commissioner. Mr. Batten was then only Assistant Commissioner of Garhwal, but he was a man eminently qualified both by training and disposition to second the action of Government and to assist in the inauguration of the new era. His talents had already been recognized, and from this period he was consulted in every step, and it was his influence more than that of any other single officer which gave its stamp and character to the period which I have distinguished by his name. Its duration covered the years 1836—56. It was marked in its earlier stages by an influx of codes and rules and a predominancy of official supervision which gradually subsided as Mr. Batten gained influence, position and experience. Thus the second period

* Laws of the Non-Regulation Provinces.

glided insensibly into the third, which nevertheless has a distinctive character of its own. In Sir Henry Ramsay's administration we see the two currents blended. The personal sway and unhampered autocracy of the first era, combining with the orderly procedure and observance of fixed rules and principles which was the chief feature of the second."

"For the history of Kumaon under the British, the materials are ample and sufficient in themselves to form a volume full of interest and instruction. They shew the means whereby a peculiar people, sunk in the utmost depths of ignorance and apathy, have been induced by the patient and intelligent efforts of a few Englishmen to commence again their national life. They show how whole tracts where formerly the tiger and the elephant reigned supreme have now yielded to the plough and waters that not long since went to feed the deadly swamp are now confined in numerous channels to irrigate the waterless tracts which increasing population brings into cultivation." The progress of the administration, the gradual elimination of the more barbarous of the indigenous customs and the growth of material prosperity as deduced from the extension of cultivation and the increase of revenue are sufficiently described in the fourth chapter.

GAZETTEER

OF

ALMORA.

DIRECTORY.

GAZETTEER

OF

ALMORA.

DIRECTORY.

CONTENTS.

ALMORA, *patti* KHASPARJA, *pargana* BARAHMANDAL.

The head quarters of the Almora district lies in latitude 29°36′ north and longitude 79°40′ east. The town and the civil and military station are built on a saddle-shaped ridge about two miles in length running almost east and west with an elevation varying from 5,200 to 5,500 feet. The jail stands at about 5,439 feet and the church 5,495 feet above the level of the sea. The station is connected with the higher ridges of Simtola and Kalimat to the west by a *col* called Hiradungri. Kalimat has an elevation of 6,414 feet above the sea level, and Simtola an elevation of 6,066 feet. A low lateral ridge called Sitoli runs westwards from Hiradungri towards the Kosi and exactly faces Almora from the north. The intermediate space is crowded with native houses many of a superior type and cultivated field terraces.

On the east and south the Almora hill is bounded by the Sual river and on the west by the Kosi, so that it is almost a peninsula connected with the other hills only towards Kalimat. To the south-west the ridge after attaining its highest point of elevation at Charalekh dips down in a series of bold and rugged masses to the confluence of these two rivers. To the south of the Almora hill is a depression occupied by the Leper Asylum and the octroi outpost, and beyond that again the ridge displays a small eminence commonly called Granite Hill, or, from the single deodar on the peak, One-tree Hill, the latter of which names is rapidly becoming a misnomer, now that the hill has been enclosed and sown with pine. The Almora hill is divided into two parts by a road which runs almost north and south between the western end of the bazar and the parade ground. To the west of this lies the cantonment within and without the boundaries of which are some twenty-three bungalows occupied by the officers of the regiment, the civil officers of the district and some permanent residents, a pretty little church dedicated to St. Mark, a handsome mess house, a small but comfortable club, and the sessions house, used for temporary sojourn by high officials on tour. All these are situated on the crest or the northern slope of the ridge. The most imposing building of all is Fort Moira or the Lal Mandi. The lines of the Gurkhas lie below and to the north-east of the fort.

Beyond these again lies the town. The bazar is paved with stone flags. From the east westwards as far as the police-station it is somewhat narrow ; beyond this point it widens and gradually slopes down to the lower or old fort, the slope being broken by a flight of stone steps. The houses are from two to four stories high and are substantially built of mica-slate and roofed with thin slabs of the same material. The front screens of the upper stories are usually made of wood profusely and often artistically carved. The windows are mere apertures for the most part, resembling pigeon-holes cut in a wooden panel, and closed by a slide. The general appearance of the town is compact and clean, and the conservancy generally well carried out, though the lack of water for flushing the pavements and drains is a serious, and in the hot weather a somewhat insistent, drawback. The best shops lie between the police-station and the fort ; at the foot of the glacis are a number of very mean stalls, which are a decided disfigurement to the bazar. The fort itself contains the courts and offices of the Deputy Commissioner and his subordinates. A little lower, the ridge widens and the space is occupied by the hospital, the tahsil and the Ramsay College. The latter, opened in 1871, is a fine building in the Tuscan style with a central hall 60 feet by 34 feet and a wing on each side containing four spacious class-rooms, besides two detached room wings one of which was erected by Pandit Badri Datt Joshi of Dania. Below this plateau a small and narrow bazar containing however some rich shops lines the sides of a path running down to the cart-road.

The houses of the better class people occupy positions below the main ridge, to the north and south, most of them pleasant and substantial buildings surrounded by small orchards or green fields. The dâk bungalow, the post and telegraph office, the district school, the goods and parcels depôt of the Rohilkhand and Kumaon Railway, and a few shops dealing chiefly in

European wares are situated on the cart-road, or below it, and further to the west is a small church recently erected by the London Missionary Society for the benefit of the Europeans. Beyond the foot of the small bazar the ridge and with it the road again ascends. The old Missionary native church occupies a commanding position on the shoulder of the ridge. Near the church are houses occupied by some of the missionaries; above it towards Hiradungri is the jail. The Sitoli ridge, once the site of a tea garden, and afterwards acquired by the 3rd Gurkhas as a camping ground is now leased to the district forest department. Much of the estate has been sown with pine and other trees, and the buildings are used as offices and residences by the forest staff. The whole of the station and the outskirts of the town of Almora are now extremely well wooded. Deodar, tun, alder and horse-chestnut especially thrive; every unoccupied piece of ground is thronged with young saplings of tun and chestnut. Cypress also seems to accommodate itself moderately well to the soil and climate. There are few pines of any great age, but the western extremity of the cantonment is clothed with a very fine young plantation, while several small patches have been enclosed and sown between Almora and the Sual river and on Baldhoti and Kalimat. The forethought of Sir H. Ramsay has lined the ascent from the Gurari bridge over the Sual with an avenue of shady trees, and what used to be the most trying part of the route from the plains is now, except for the steepness and baduess of the road, one of the pleasantest. In the spring the slopes of Almora are bright with the blossom of fruit trees, while the ground is carpeted with pale scentless violets and a plant of the *linum* species, bearing yellow flowers which a moderately vivid imagination may easily at a distance transform into primroses. The Australian wattle—a species of acacia—is now a well-naturalised exotic, and in the early summer its branches are heavy with flowers of a golden yellow. The compounds generally present a somewhat neglected appearance; the fruit-trees are not very productive and flowers and flowering shrubs are scarce, the reason being that water, except where the monsoon rainfall is stored in tanks, is not to be procured. The cisterns holding the drinking water are situated at a somewhat low level,

The station is intersected with pleasant paths, well aligned, of easy gradient and generally overshadowed by trees.

Munici-pality.

What is now the municipality of Almora dates its beginnings from 1851 when by Act No. XXVI of 1850 a town duty on articles for local consumption was imposed. The town was constituted a municipality on 14th November 1864. Under Act no. VI of 1868 a house-tax of 5 per cent. was introduced in 1869 and in 1877 this was supplemented by a tax on animals imported for slaughter. Later a conservancy tax was introduced, and in 1876 the house-tax was increased. In 1880 a site-tax or ground rent at the rate of 1 pice per square foot per annum was imposed; and in 1884 the house-tax was replaced by octroi.

The most important object of the municipal administration is the provision of an adequate water supply—always a difficulty in a hill station. Tradition has it that there were originally 360 springs on the Almora hill itself, but only a very small number can now be traced, and of these only two— Rani Dhara situated in the angle between the Sitoli hill and Hira Dungri, and Kapina Naula below the cart road on the west face of Hira Dungri discharge any appreciable volume of water. These springs are however situated at a considerable distance from Almora itself and the necessity of augmenting the local supply was recognized many years ago. The first project was carried out by Messrs. Lumsden and Batten, successive Commissioners. They tapped two springs near That bungalow on Simtola and brought the water in a masonry aqueduct to a point called the Commissioner's Dhara on the Binsar road, opposite what is now the mission house. Many years later the aqueduct was continued to Moti Dhara, a point in the compound of the temple at the junction of the cart and Binsar roads, by L. Moti Ram Sah at his own expense.

In 1874 was initiated the Baldhoti system which for 30 years was the main source of Almora's water supply. Some 30 springs on the south and east face of Simtola were forced to contribute. The yield of each ravine was caught in a dammed enclosure, which acted as a silt pit. A trough was erected just outside and underneath the dam wall, so that in the dry months when the flow was low, the water trickled gently over the dam and into the trough and in the monsoons when there was more water than the channel could carry away, and it was heavily laden with silt, its own momentum caused it to overshoot the trough. From these collecting troughs the water was conducted in a masonry channel to the main filter at China Khan. Doubts were at the time expressed as to the suitability of a masonry channel and by 1890 it was recognized that they had not been without foundation. The channel had cracked in places and was choked with weeds, growing sometimes to a length of 7 or 8 feet. It was therefore replaced by three-inch cast iron pipes. The original project cost Rs. 28,000 and the system has twice been extended, the extensions involving the expenditure of Rs. 3,500 and Rs. 6,500. The supply has steadily diminished and for the last two years has not during the summer exceeded about 4 gallons a minute. The catchment tanks have with one exception become leaky and have been abandoned. The Baldhoti system has been superseded to a considerable extent by the Sail system, now the chief source of water supply to Almora. There are three springs on upper Sail and of these the two lower springs together, and the upper one by itself, discharged 12 gallons a minute. The two lower springs were utilised by Rai Bahadur Pandit Badri Dat Joshi of Dania who brought in the water to Rampha Naula below the courts on the north side of the Almora hill, at a cost of Rs. 8,000. Of this sum Rs. 4,500 were paid from provincial funds and the balance raised by private subscriptions. In 1897 an unsuccessful attempt was made to improve also the upper spring, the object being to carry the Sail water to and beyond Brighton corner leaving the Baldhoti water free for the east end of the hill. In 1904 the attempt was renewed with more success. The springs of upper Sail were successfully amalgamated and galvanised iron pipes were substituted for the original inferior German pipes, while the whole line was relaid. The lower Sail springs were also tapped, the old pipes of the upper line being utilised for the purpose. The Sail system gives in all thirteen points of discharge,—standposts or tanks. The overflow of the system goes into the men's bathing tank at Budleswar and there is also a bathing station known as the Panj Dhara near the Raja's house. In 1907 the municipality took a loan of Rs. 13,000 from the Government and substituted three-inch galvanised pipes for the two-inch pipes in the upper line, which now replaced the old German pipes in the lower line. The Sail supply varies with the character of the monsoon between a maximum of 35 gallons and a minimum of 17 gallons a minute.

Cantonment.

The Almora cantonment lies within irregular boundaries and occupies most of the land lying west of the town. The affairs of the cantonment are administered by a committee. The chief sources of income are a conservancy tax at the rate of Rs. 3 a month on each occupied bungalow, land revenue, and assessed taxes; and expenditure is incurred for the main purposes of sanitation and road-making and repairs.

The water supply was, until 1904, supplied free of charge by the municipality, but since then the military department has paid Rs. 500 a year for a guaranteed supply of 3,500 gallons a day. In February 1909 however an independent supply was brought in from the Nail springs, below Kalimat. At present there is only one point of discharge, a large tank below the foot of the road which divides the cantonments from the bazar, and the supply has been, probably owing to the fact that several different patterns of pipes are used, somewhat irregular. The cantonment has been occupied almost continuously since 1846 to the present day by the 3rd Gurkhas, who used also to send detachments to hold the forts at Pithoragarh and Lohaghat on the Nepal frontier. The regiment was originally raised in 1815 with head quarters at Haldwani. It consisted of a few Gurkhas who came in after the defeat of the Gurkha regent of Kumaon near Almora, some Oudh and Palpa men from Gorakhpur who had been employed by the British Government in the Nepalese War and some Kumaoni militia brought in by Suba Jai Kishan Upreti. The regiment known as the Kumaon Battalion was first posted at Hawalbagh, a picturesquely situated but somewhat hot cantonment five miles north of Almora, near the Kosi river. Until 1839 it remained under the orders of the Commissioner of the province, and was a civil rather than a military force, described technically as a Nizamat Battalion. It was entrusted with police duties throughout Garhwal and Almora, and in winter in the Bhabar and Tarai. In 1839 it was ordered to garrison

Pithoragarh and Lohaghat forts erected by the British near the Nepal border; and in 1846 it was transferred to Almora. In 1850 it was relieved of its civil duties and became a general service corps and in the same year was posted to Dehra where it remained for 6 years, serving afterwards with distinction through the mutiny at Delhi. The battalion returned to Almora in 1859 and there it has, except when on active service or other duty, remained ever since. In 1864 the lines were made over to the men of the battalion in perpetuity as their homes. The order runs, "The battalion is liable to be taken away whenever the Government pleases and to be kept away as long as the Government thinks fit, in time of peace as well as in time of war; but it will always eventually return to Almora."

The battalion served through the Bhutan campaign of 1864-66 and was present at the taking of Bula dura, Buxa, Tazagaon and other positions. Its next war services were the first Kabul campaign, and the second Kabul campaign; during the latter it was present at the battle of Ahmed Khel where it greatly distinguished itself, and now bears upon its appointments the words "Ahmed Khel, Afghanistan, 1878-80". In 1886-87 it served through the Burma campaign. Up to 1887 the battalion though consisting chiefly of Gurkhas contained also a number of Kumaonis and Garhwalis. The latter were taken out and sent to the new cantonment at Lansdowne to serve as the nucleus of a second battalion to the 3rd Gurkhas, which in 1891 became the Garhwal Rifles. In 1889 a small detachment proceeded to the head of the Niti pass, to investigate the truth of the report as to warlike preparations by the Tibetans. The battalion served in the Chittagong expedition, 1890, and a detachment of it in the South Lushai Hills, 1892. In 1897-98 it was present and gained distinctions in the Tirah campaign and in 1901 formed part of the supporting brigade to the Waziristan blockade force. In 1909-10 it garrisoned Chitral.

Records of temperature at 8 a.m. and 5 p.m. have been kept up for some years at the regimental hospital. The maximum summer temperature rarely exceeds 88°, while the average for the month of June is about 84° but in June 1908 (an exceptionally hot year) the average was considerably higher, Climate.

several temperatures of over 90° being recorded. The highest reached was 94° immediately before the break of the rains. *Pankhas* however are not required and though occasional experiments have been made the cold they induce has always been found insufferable. In a closed house except for a few hours on hot days before rain the temperature can be maintained as low as 74°. Whenever it exceeds 86° in an outside shaded verandah rain or a thunder-storm may be expected which often reduces the temperature by 20° or more. In the rains 72° may be considered the average heat and at that season the daily range is rarely 2°. In the winter the daily temperature during the months of January and December varies between 40° and 50°, but it is naturally much colder at night and the ground is often frozen hard early in the morning though it rarely remains frost-bound all day as at slightly higher elevations. Snow falls occasionally but never lies for more than a few hours except in sheltered spots. It is most frequent in January and February. March and April are generally marked by thunder-storms but in the summer months a thick haze prevails which obscures the distant view. The snows are rarely seen except immediately after a thunder-storm. Taking an average of many years, no month is free from rainfall; April and May are usually the driest months. The monsoon bursts about the middle of June and does not cease, if conditions are favourable, until the middle or end of September.

As has been already mentioned in the notice of the general climate of the district Almora receives a much smaller rainfall than many other places of equal elevation. The average annual rainfall is about 40 inches and to its comparatively dry climate it owes its well-established reputation as a sanitarium for people suffering from consumption. It is unquestionable that cures have occurred in a great many cases even when the disease has far passed the incipient stage. Its reputation however depends entirely on nothing more than clinical observation and general experience. No attempt has yet been made to study in a scientific manner the meteorological conditions of Almora and their direct effect upon phthisis. It is possible that the scanty rainfall, the dry porous soil, the equability of temperature, both diurnal and seasonal, the absence of mists and fogs during the rains, the exposed sunny situation and (perhaps) the presence of pine woods near the town exercise a beneficial effect. The great advantage which the climate of Almora offers to consumptives is that it enables them to lead an outdoor life almost every day in the year during winter as well as summer. But it possesses no magical influence, and it is pathetic to hear of comparatively poor people who have taken dirty and ill-ventilated houses in the middle of the bazar in the delusion that a few days' residence is sufficient to afford relief if not to effect a complete cure. It is not in fact in Almora itself but in its environments that the greatest benefit is likely to accrue to phthisical patients. Advanced cases rarely do well; the journey from the plains is long and wearisome and very fatiguing to consumptives who probably get more harm than good from their visit.*

A consumptive home was started in 1908 on a windy spur surrounded by a young pine plantation about four miles east of Almora, beyond Baldhoti. It affords shelter to some fourteen or fifteen native Christian girls, the protégees of various missions which pay contributions towards their keep. A similar institution for boys has been projected. At present European invalids occupy any bungalow they can get in the station. This practise is of course open to objection and the establishment of a consumptive home for Europeans has been under consideration for a good many years past but the difficulty of providing an adequate water supply appears to be insuperable. For invalids suffering from other maladies Almora is not particularly well suited, as the temperature is too high during May and June. Some of the more fastidious among the settled inhabitants retreat to Binsar for the hot weather and rains.

The scriptural description of the mountain, on which the town of Almora is situate, is found in the Skanda Purana (स्कन्द पुराण) Manas khand (मानस खण्ड) Chapter 52 :— History.

कौशिकी शाल्मली मध्ये पुण्यः काषाय पर्वतः The sacred or clean mountain Kakhaya is situated between the Kaushika or Kosi and Shalmali or Sual. This mountain stretches from the confluence of those two rivers near the Gurari bridge (over

* From a note by Dr. R. K. Kakkar Assistant Surgeon.

the Sual river) to the ridge called Kalmatiya where the temples of the god Kakhayeswar, and that of the goddess Kakhayeswari, are built. This covers a distance of about 8 miles.

A tradition still current affirms that the earliest grantees of Almora were a family of Tiwaris. They are now much impoverished and the sole remnant of their ancient estate is a small patch of land near the jail. It is said that under the terms of their grant they were obliged to send a daily supply of sorrel for cleansing the vessels of the Sun temple at Katarmal. The name for sorrel is *lamora* (Sanskrit, *amla,* sour) and it is suggested that it has been corrupted to Almora and has given its name to the hill on which it is grown. Almora was according to the legend founded by Raja Kalyan Chand who reigned over Kumaon about 1560. One day he was hunting on the Almora hill, at that time covered with thick forest, when a hare suddenly appeared before him and he began to pursue it, whereupon it assumed the form of a tiger and on reaching the top of the hill disappeared. He asked his diviners what this portent might mean, and they replied that his enemies would find that they had tigers to deal with and advised him to found his capital on the spot where the tiger had vanished. As a preliminary to operations a large crowbar was driven into the ground. It sank so deep that the diviners declared that it had pierced the back of Sesh Nag the great serpent which supports the earth, and they accepted the fact as a sign that the king's dynasty should endure for ever. But the incredulous king insisted that the crowbar should be taken out of the ground for inspection and, sure enough, the point was seen to be tinged with blood. Thereupon the diviners in wrath pronounced that as a punishment for the Raja's presumption and disbelief his descendants should reign after him for but a few generations. The first palace and fort were built on the site of Khagmara Kot, an old stronghold of the Katyuris. A later king left the old palace and built the new one called Malla Mahal (the upper palace), now used as the district offices. Up to the day of Kalyan Chand, Champawat in Kali Kumaun had been the capital of the kingdom, and the real reason for abandonment of that town was doubtless its distance from the recently conquered and far more valuable possessions to the west. Almora* is moreover a natural fortress. The hill slopes violently down to the rivers Sual and Kosi on all sides except the north-east where a narrow ridge, easily held by a few resolute defenders alone affords access. The Gurkhas in their turn were much impressed by the natural security of their stronghold, and they proceeded to denude the hill sides of any trees that might afford cover to a besieger. It is only of recent years that the damage they did is being repaired. After the conquest Almora continued to be the head quarters of the district and the division ; but most of the Europeans lived in Hawalbagh, though Bishop Heber mentions scattered bungalows below the bazar and to each side of it, and there was in early years an officer stationed in Almora in charge of the treasury. The head quarters station was transferred in Mr. Batten's time, and he built himself a house on Simtola which he called Battenburg.

ALMORA *tahsil.*

A sub-division of the district consisting of the parganas Chaugarkha and Gangoli. The head quarters of the tahsil are at Almora. The parganas have been separately noticed.

ASKOT *pargana, tahsil* CHAMPAWAT.

A moderately large pargana, bounded on the east by Nepal, on the north by pargana Darma, on the west by pargana Sira and on the south by pargana Shor. Askot is divided into two portions, Malla Askot and Talla Askot. The former occupies the triangle the sides of which are defined by the Gori and Kali rivers converging at Garjia below Askot village, and the base by a fine rugged range of hills some 14,000 feet high running from east to west. From the highest peak Chipilakot a long spur runs down south to the apex of the triangle. The only cultivated land in Malla Askot is situated along the two rivers Gori and Kali and on the slopes immediately above them. The interior of the patti is extremely rugged and mountainous, and is covered with dense forest, with every variety of timber from shisham, khair and sal in the river beds through oak and rhododendron to firs, birch and box on the high central ridge. Malla Askot is as yet little

* Always officially called by the Chands Rajapur.

developed. The cultivation is generally poor, and irrigation not possible. The people are a rude backward peasantry, living for the greater part in grass huts. They breed flocks of sheep and goats which they sell to the Darma Bhotias, and some of the most northerly villages do a little carrying trade with Tibet or act as servants to the Bhotias. Talla Askot lies south of the Gori river and consists of a strip of fertile ridges lying between the Kali river, which forms its eastern boundary, and the pargana of Sira, varying in width from about ten miles, under the Dhaj peak where Sira, Shor and Askot converge, to only four miles on the Dewal or Askot spur. The ridges fringing the Kali are clothed with fine stretches of pine, but in the higher ground the forests have suffered much from the aggressions of cultivators. Talla Askot is fully cultivated and is one of the few regions in the district that is able to produce more grain than it can eat. The standard of cultivation is very high owing to the competition that prevails for waste land, and the crops grown are of the best class possible to the hills. The pargana is traversed by the great trade route from Tanakpur to the north, which strikes the Kali river at its confluence with the Gori near Askot village. It follows the right bank of the Kali as far as Khela. From Khela northwards two routes are possible; one continues along the Kali river as far as its source below the Lipu Lekh pass, and the other turning off at the left to the north leaves the district by the Darma pass. All the trade of the Darma Bhotias thus passes through the pargana much to the advantage of the people, who sell them pack animals and such grain as they do not need for their own consumption. The road from Almora through Beninag (corruptly called Berenag) and Thal meets the road from Tanakpur close to Askot village; and a third road runs northwards by the side of the Gori river through the Johar pargana as far as Surhing where it meets the main trade route from Almora. Askot may be technically described as an impartible raj, in which the rule of primogeniture is strictly applied. The whole of the pargana belongs to one family the head of which enjoys the title Rajwar; the eldest son is called Lala and the younger Gosain. The ruling family are a branch of the old royal house of Katyur. On the break up of the Katyur kingdom, one branch of the family led by Abhaya Pal settled in Askot in 1279 A.D., and there established a small principality, which they maintained intact until 1588 when Rudra Chand, the Raja of Kumaon, conquered Askot, Darma and Johar. It is probable that his authority over the northern parts of his dominion was never very effective for he appears to have restored the Rajwar to his possession with the status of a semi-independent ally, ruling over what would now be called a buffer state between Kumaon on the one hand, and Tibet and Nepal on the other; and it is also believed that in addition to these political considerations the necessity of maintaining a respectable family to supply brides to their sons was admitted by the Chands. The annual tribute they exacted amounted to Rs. 400; this was increased by the Gurkhas to Rs. 2,000 at which sum it stood at the British occupation. Under the Gurkhas the rule of primogeniture was temporarily abrogated and dissensions arising on the death of the Rajwar led to the successive appointments of Rudra Pal, and Mahendra Pal, the brother and son of the deceased Rajwar, according as each outbid the other for the favour of the local Gurkha commander. Under the British both were admitted to engage for the revenue. This circumstance involved the estate in many vicissitudes in which family dissension, litigation, and even murder were not wanting. In 1847 the property was sold (not for the first time) in satisfaction of a decree and this time the purchaser was Tula Ram Sah, the Almora treasurer. The Rajwar Pushkar Pal bought him out again in 1855. The present Rajwar is his son Gajendra Singh Pal who is within the limits of his *taluqa* an honorary magistrate. He enjoys many willing tributes of respect from his dependants and tenants: and the usual form of salutation from them is *jai* which is appropriate to a Raja.*

Askot presents the only instance known in Kumaon of a large zamindari. In most of the villages of Talla Askot and the more anciently-settled villages of Malla Askot the cultivators are khaikars under the Rajwar. They pay him the government demands *plus* 100 per cent. *malikana*. Elsewhere the villages are recorded as the Rajwar's khudkasht, cultivated by sirtans.

* Assessment report: J. E. Goudge.

The pargana contains 142 villages. The total area is some 400 square miles, but of this only 6·49 square miles are cultivated. The pargana is prosperous. The population in 1901 amounted to 15,841, or about double what it was in 1872, while the cultivation was found to have increased by 35 *per cent*. In Talla Askot the houses are comfortable and costly: in Malla Askot the people are in a more backward state, and the tenants are largely imported. The revenue as finally fixed in 1872 was Rs. 1,250, and it is now Rs. 1,450. The chief villages are Askot, the seat of the Rajwar, and Dharchula, the winter head quarters of the Political Peshkar and an important trade depôt of the Bhotias.

BAGESWAR, *patti* TALLA KATYUR, *pargana* DANPUR.

A small town situated on both banks of the Sarju, here crossed by a suspension bridge, below which it is joined by the Gumti river. The name is derived from the temple which is dedicated to Siva as Vakiswar, the lord of speech or according to others Vyagreswar, the tiger lord. The legend relates that a certain saint by the power of his austerities which he performed in the bed of the Sarju stopped the flow of the river. Complaint was made to Siva who with his consort Parbati devised a plan whereby the latter taking the form of a cow began to graze by the river bank; Siva became a tiger and sprang upon Parbati. The saint rose from his devotions to rescue the cow, and the river was able to resume its course.

The main bazar is on the right bank of the river Sarju and consists of solid well-built houses, with shops in the lower storey. Bageswar was for many years an exceedingly rich mart, owing to the advantages its traders derived from their position as middlemen between the Bhotias and their plains customers. The extension of the railway to Kathgodam and the development of the wool trade to the prejudice of that in borax have greatly diminished the importance of Bageswar but it is still a considerable market. It is occupied for trade from November till April only; the banias retreat to their country houses on the heights above the valley for the hot weather. Three fairs of a semi-religious character take place: the principal known as the Uttaraini fair now takes place about the middle of January. It celebrates the occasion when the sun turns back from its most southerly position towards the north, that is to say the winter solstice and should according to our reckoning be on the 21st or 22nd December. The second is the Shivratri at the beginning of February and the third the Dasehra. Some 10,000 people collect on the occasion of the Uttaraini fair; the Bhotias bring down musk-pods, yaks' tails, ponies, goats, sheep, furs, wooden bowls; the Almora banias send out representatives with cotton goods, vessels of iron, brass and copper, and tobacco; and the people from the surrounding hills bring in whatever they may have to sell in the way of provisions, matting and basket work, and forest produce, such as skins. A few Tibetans also attend the fair offering for sale chiefly curiosities from their own country. Of recent years the various traffickers have been encouraged to display their wares in an exhibition, but the prizes seem to be given chiefly for the products of Tibet: and the fair has been popularised by the institution of foot and pony races, and other sports.

The temple is an exceedingly ancient foundation; the present building, by no means the first, was erected by Raja Lachhmi Chand about 1450 A. D. Certain tombs resembling those at Dwarahat have been assigned to Mughal colonies and attest perhaps the presence of a non-Hindu race.

Bageswar is connected with all parts of the district by excellent roads; running south to Almora and Binsar, west to Someswar, north-west to Baijnath and Garhwal, north to the Pindari glacier and the Milam Valley for Tibet and east to Thal. It contains a large dâk bungalow, a post-office, a school and a dispensary belonging to the London Missionary Society and aided by the district board. The population in 1901 was 718.

AIJNATH, *patti* Bichla Katyur, *pargana* Danpur.

A village lying in north latitude 29° 54′ 24″ and east longitude 79° 37′ at an elevation of 3,545 feet above the level of the sea. The river Gumti flows close to the village, which is 12¼ miles from Someswar, 12 miles from Bageswar and about 12½ miles from Jolabagar on the Nandprayag road, with each of which it is connected by a good road. There is a large Hindu temple here sacred to Kali situate in the old Ranchula fort, of which the altar is said to be constantly moist with the blood of kids and buffalo calves sacrificed to the dread goddess. There are several old temples of the Turk's cap style, most of which are in ruins and are used as corn lofts and store-rooms as in Dwarahat. A colony of Gosains are established here, who observe the custom of burying their dead in small temple-like tombs around the building in which they worship. Along its walls are old sculptures collected from different places. Most are of modern Hindu origin; but one is clearly a representation of Buddha and must have belonged to a temple of that creed which flourished here in the 8th century of our era according to Hwen Tsiang. Baijnath is interesting as being in the centre of the Katyur valley, the home of the ancient Katyuri kings.

The valley is very fertile and much land is occupied by tea gardens. Baijnath contains a dâk bungalow, a school and a dispensary maintained by the planters (aided by the district board) for the benefit of their employés, and its importance as the centre of the tea industry was recognized in 1892 when the Hawalbagh-Baijnath cart-road was made.

BARAHMANDAL *pargana, tahsil* ALMORA.

The central pargana of the district. Almora is situated within its eastern border: its western extremity bisects Ranikhet. It is bounded on the north by a fine ridge which runs from Bhatkot to Kausani, Aikewa Binsar, Gananath and the Almora Binsar with an average height of nearly 7,000 feet throughout. On the east the boundary is irregular, being the ridge from Binsar to Kalimat for a short distance, but at Dinapani it drops down into the Petsal stream and continues along it to its union with the Sual river five miles from Almora. Thence it mounts a spur from the Lamgara and Banani Devi ridge, coming up to the Lamgara dâk bungalow ten miles from Almora. It then turns southwards encircling Malli Mahruri and the head waters of the Busauri and Sakuni rivers, which meet the Kumniya stream under Mukhtesar, and this stream is the boundary between the Almora and Naini Tal districts on the south till the Kosi joins it. At Kakarighat on the Kosi the western boundary begins in a spur from the Siahi Devi mountain. The boundary crosses Siahi Devi, drops to the Siront stream and rises again to Chaubattia and the Ranikhet ridge. Below this ridge the Gagas is the boundary between Barahmandal and Pali Pachaon as far as Darmar, from which village the boundary is irregular and follows approximately the Ranikhet-Dwarahat and Dwarahat-Almora roads, to Bagwali Pokhar on the latter, whence a spur rises to Dunagiri, and thence along the ridge to Bhatkot.

The Kosi river rises in Bhatkot near the Pinnath temple, an eminence on the range which forms the northern boundary. It flows through the centre of the pargana receiving most of the drainage, and watering the two Boraraus, Talla Syunara, and the two Tikhuns. Its basin is bounded on the west by the ridge which trends south through Bhainskhet and Majhkhali; and from this ridge rises its chief affluent the Nanakosi. On its left bank it receives the Sual river which sweeps round the peninsular hill on which Almora stands. The Gagas river rises to the west of the Bhatkot range and flows through Kairarau and between the two Athagulis, ultimately joining the Ramganga at Bhikia Sen.

These rivers and their affluents are utilised to the fullest extent for irrigation. Thus the percentage of irrigated land in Walla Borarau reaches the high figure of 36·5: in Palla Borarau it is 32: and in Kairarau 32·3. In the last-named patti the fine village of Bansli Sera on the Gagas is almost entirely irrigated. Throughout the pargana the ordinary hill crops are grown; and in addition sugarcane and potatoes in Dwarsyun, Riuni, Mahruri, Uchyur and Bisaud, and vegetables and pot herbs in all the pattis adjoining Almora and Ranikhet. There are also two tea-estates in the pargana, Dunagiri in Kairarau and Lodh in Palla Borarau.

The pargana possesses some fine forest. West of the Kosi is the Airadeo protected forest used by Walla Borarau, Talla Syunara, Malla Tikhun, Kairarau and Kaligarh: Borarau and Kairarau lie under the Bhatkot range with its vast forest and wide pastures: east of the Kosi, the Gananath and Binsar blocks are accessible to Malla Syunara and Palla Borarau. Siahi Devi, Dwarsyun and Ranikhet forests are reserved, but the rights of Talla Tikhun, Dwarsyun, Riuni and Walla Athaguli are all adequately recognized.

The inhabitants are of the ordinary hill castes. Many earn money by cooly-labour or service in Almora and Ranikhet, on the tea gardens or in the forests, and the people of the two Tikhuns, Riuni, Dwarsyun, Walla Athaguli, Uchyur and Bisaud also have cultivation in the Bhabar, whither they retreat in October or November after sowing their rabi, reaping it on their return in March or April. The Dwarsyun and Riuni people also own carts and make much money by transporting heavy goods between Almora, Ranikhet and the plains. As in Chaugarkha there are a number of high caste proprietors, the descendants of the ministerial officers of the court of the Chand Rajas, receiving a malikana of 100 *per cent.* on the government revenue from their khaikars. Such are the Jhijar Joshis, the Kapina Upretis and the Pants of Syunara. The pargana is everywhere intersected with roads from Almora and Ranikhet including the cart road between these stations and its branch from Hawalbagh through Someswar to the Gumti valley. The only villages of importance are Someswar and Hawalbagh both of which are separately described. At Mr. Beckett's settlement in 1872 the population of the pargana was 62,167, at the census of 1900 (preliminary enumeration) it was 77,218 and the final figures of 1901 were 74,237. The cultivation also increased by 8 per cent. It is now 62·5 square miles and has almost reached its limit. The revenue of the pargana is now Rs. 46,062, against the demand of Rs. 39,973 at the previous settlement.*

Barahmandal as its name implies originally comprised twelve regions, under separate Rajas. Udyan Chand in 1420 A. D. reduced the Bisaud and Mahruri Rajas to submission and some 70 years later Kirati Chand completed the conquest of Barahmandal. He exterminated the old inhabitants of Kairarau and Borarau and settled there the castes of Kairas and

* Assessment report: J. E. Goudge.

Boras from whom they derive their present name. And in 1560 Balo Kalyan Chand consolidated the conquests of his ancestors by removing his capital from Champawat to Almora, in the centre of his new dominions.

The original twelve regions increased in number by subdivision and in 1892 some of the new pattis were transferred to the Naini Tal district. The pargana now contains 16 pattis— Palla and Walla Athaguli, Malla Bisaud, Palla and Walla Borarau, Dwarsyun, Kaligarh, Kairarau, Khasparja, Malli Mahruri, Riuni, Malla and Talla Syunara, Malla and Talla Tikhun and Uchyur.

BARMDEO OR BRAHMADEWA: TANAKPUR BHABAR.

A mart on the right bank of the Sarda river in the Tanakpur Bhabar destroyed by a landslip in 1880. The bazar and all the public institutions have now been transferred to Tanakpur.

BHAINSKHET, *patti* MALLA TIKHUN, *pargana* BARAHMANDAL.

A village, camping ground and dâk bungalow on the Almora-Pauri road. It lies in latitude 29° 42′ and longitude 79° 35′ 13 miles from Almora and about the same distance from Dwarahat the next stage. A branch path connects it with Majkhali on the south some 2½ miles away and a useful forest track proceeds past the Airideo forest bungalow to Someswar.

BHIKIA SEN, *patti* WALLA NAYA, *pargana* PALI.

A village situated in latitude 29° 42′ north and longitude 79° 18′ east at the junction of the Gagas and the western Ramgana. It contains a post office and a small bazar of some local importance.

The road from Ganai to Mohan passes through it and it is also connected with Gujarghati on the Ramnagar-Ranikhet road by a bridle path the greater portion of which has been converted into a light cart road. At the confluence of the two streams stands the temple of Nauleswar. The population in 1901 was 272.

BINSAR *patti,* MALLA SYUNARA, *pargana* BARAHMANDAL.

A settlement on a hill thirteen miles to the north-east of Almora. It was the favourite summer retreat of Raja Kalyan Chand (1730-47 A. D.) and here he built the temple now in ruins and dedicated it to Siva under the name of Bineswar, shortened into Binsar. The god is said to protect the dwellers on his hill against theft, and to compel the thief to restore the stolen property many fold. The iron water pipes laid down by Sir H. Ramsay were however persistently removed, and the god's reputation is now somewhat exploded. The settlement consists of some four or five houses all belonging to Europeans; and there is also a post office and a forest rest house. The summit of the hill attains an elevation of 7,913 feet, but most of the houses are 300 or 400 feet lower. The temperature in the summer may be taken as on the average some 10° lower than that prevailing in Almora. In June of 1908, an exceptionally hot year, 80° was the highest shade temperature of the day. In Almora for the same month of the same year the highest temperature recorded was 94°, and the day temperature never fell below 74°. Binsar seems to have come into being as a sanitarium in 1852 when Major Evans was granted 7 acres of land for a house. Three years later Captain the Hon. R. V. Powys and Major Sunderland also settled on Binsar, Captain Powys occupying the house near the summit. In 1857 Dr. Govan was granted land for a house and in 1878 Sir H. Ramsay bought the fee simple of the land on which the bungalow now occupied by Mr. Martin stands. Except where cleared for bungalows and compounds, the whole of the Binsar hill is clothed with forest managed by the Forest department.

CHAMPAWAT, *patti* TALLA CHARAL, *pargana* KALI KUMAON.

A village lying in latitude 29° 20′ 11″ and longitude 80° 7′ 84″ E. at an elevation of 5,546 feet above the level of the sea, 54 miles south-east of Almora. The population in 1901 was 93. It is however important as the head quarters of the tahsildar of pargana Kali Kumaon, whose office is situated within the enclosure of the old fort. There are also a school, a dâk bungalow, and a post-office here. The rocks of Champawat are partly gneiss, which having become disintegrated in many places, have given way and, according to McClelland, caused the destruction of the greater part of the old buildings. Champawat was the residence of the Rajas of Kumaon before they transferred their seat to Almora in the middle of the 16th century. The old palace is now in ruins, but the fort partly remains. Below the bazar 200 feet from the old fort are three or four temples ona level are a about one hundred feet square hewn into the solid rock. They are each polygonal at the base, twenty feet in diameter and surmounted by an arched dome; all being constructed of stone, with good taste and elaborate workmanship. They must be of considerable antiquity as some apparently coeval ruins situate above the temples are in many places overgrown with forests of aged oaks. The elevation above the sea is considerable, but still from its position in a valley the site is said to be unhealthy. Owing to this cause, the cantonment was removed in 1815 to Lohaghat, six miles further north. Close to the fort is the temple of Ghatku Deota, in whose honour a fair is held annually. The mound on which the temple is built is said to be the Kurmachal of the Skanda Purana, because on this spot Vishnu assumed the Kurma or tortoise incarnation. The name Kumaon has been said to be a corruption of Kurmachal and the tract of which Champawat is the centre is now known as Kali Kumaon; "the Kumaon near the river Kali" to distinguish it from other Kumaons. It was not till the accession of the Chands to power that the name of their principal residence was given to the whole district. The Dudpokra tea-gardens and bungalow almost east of Champawat are now used as a mission house by Miss A. Budden. Cherapani another tea estate belongs to the Raja of Nahan from whom it is leased by Mr. Beadon. It lies south of Dudpokra near the Bhabar road.

CHAMPAWAT *tahsil*.

A sub-division of the district, consisting of the pargana of Kali Kumaon.

CHAUGARKHA *pargana, tahsil* ALMORA.

A pargana of moderate size with an average length of 30 miles and a breadth of 20 miles. The name of the pargana is derived from the four pattis of which it originally consisted Salam, Lakhanpur, Darun and Rangor. It now comprises nine pattis. Talla and Malla Salam and Dolphat lie at the south-west corner round the upper course of the Panar river; Rangor at the south-east corner lies between the Sarju and the Panar; Darun and Rithagadh occupy the valley of the Kosi; Malla and Talla Lakhanpur lie round the head waters of the Sual; Kharahi is situated at the top corner of the pargana towards Bageswar. The Sarju forms the boundary to the north and east as far as its junction with the Panar, dividing the pargana from Gangoli. On the west it is bounded by the Binsar ridge which separates it from Barahmandal. On the south where it adjoins Kali Kumaon, it has no natural boundary.

The most important geographical feature of the patti is the Binsar hill with an attitude of nearly 8,000 feet. From this peak diverge three ranges, running north-west, south-west and south-east respectively. The first expands into a mountain knot at the north-west extremity of the pargana whence parallel to it another chain runs in a south-east direction down to the junction of the Jaingangadh with the Sarju. Patti Rithagadh occupies the valley of the Jaingangadh between these two ridges and patti Kharahi lies between Rithagadh and the Sarju. The second terminates beyond Almora town at the junction of the Sual with the Kosi. The third is a fine range containing the Jageswar peaks 7,700 feet high and comes to an end beyond the Naini dâk bungalow where the Pithoragarh road drops down to the Sarju river. The first and the third of these ridges are connected directly with Nanda Devi by a range which sweeps round the head of the Gumti and divides the basin of the Kali or Sarda from that of the Ganges. Thus in the centre of the pargana near Saimdeo rise springs whose waters do not again mingle for hundreds of miles until the Ganges and the Sarda or Ghagra meet east of Ballia. From Jageswar a minor range strikes off to the north and bending east finishes an irregular course in the farthest corner of Rangor just above the junction of the Panar river and the Sarju. This ridge with its numerous offshoots gives Rangor a most rugged appearance and makes the interior of the patti very difficult of access. Another fine range in which the Jalna and Mornaula hills are the most prominent peaks runs along the south-west border of the pargana, to Devidhura where it enters Kali Kumaon. These ranges are all well wooded, being covered with pine on their lower slopes while the loftier summits are crowned with oak and rhododendron.

The eastern pattis are generally speaking still in course of development; they contain much good land, but the fields are in many cases still new and have not yet been properly terraced and levelled; in the western portion of the pargana cultivation is older and closer and the land is more valuable. The last 35 or 40 years has seen a great development of the land. The forests have been cleared away from the low lands and from Bageswar downwards there is an almost continuous line of cultivation on the banks of the Sarju, and the same progress may be observed in the valleys of the Jaingan, Panar and smaller streams which feed the main river. All the ordinary crops are grown. In addition the Salams grow a lot of the finest *bansmatti* rice, sold in Almora at high prices. Rithagadh and the Lakhanpurs are also pastoral pattis and make some money out of the sale of ghi. There are copper deposits in patti Kharahi, and iron in Darun and Rithagadh but the mines are at present quiescent.

The communications are excellent and all parts of the pargana are, with the possible exception of Rangor, within easy reach of paths running into Almora, which is the chief market. The Almora-Bageswar road passes through the upper parts of Rithagadh and Kharahi, and a practicable track connects Binsar and Bageswar. The east road from Almora divides at Barachina in Talla Lakhanpur; the left hand branch crosses the Binsar-Jageswar ridge near the Dhaulchina dâk bungalow and thence descends to the valley of the Jaingan river and leaves the pargana near its confluence with the Sarju. The other branch proceeds due east by Panwanaula and Naini dâk bungalows and traverses patti Darun as far as its eastern border. The Champawat road which taps the Salams runs south-east by

Jalna, where there is a fruit-garden of some note, and Dol to Devidhura, one line following the ridge by Mornaula and the other dropping into the Panar valley and joining the first again at Devidhura. There are 636 villages in the pargana. The cultivated area amounts to 49·6 square miles, and the population is 41,441. At Mr. Beckett's settlement in 1872 there were 589 villages with a cultivated area of 39·26 square miles and a population of 30,157. The present progressive revenue will reach its maximum of Rs. 24,124 in ten years from the date of Mr. Goudge's settlement: in 1902 an increase of 29·4 per cent. on the expiring demand.

The people are of the ordinary hill castes. There are however a number of absentee Brahman landlords, Joshis, Pants and Pandes, descendants of grantees favoured by the Rajas, established in the western and more anciently settled portions of the pargana. They receive high dues as malikana from their khaikars, equal in many cases to the government revenue, and by taking them as far as possible in kind, at rates which are usually much lower than the current market prices, they derive very considerable advantages from their position as superior proprietors of the land. Patti Darun is noted for the temples of Jageswar and Dindeswar, which are supported by *gunth* endowments in that patti and in Kharahi.*

DANPUR *pargana, peshkari* PALI.

A large pargana situated to the north of Almora. It is bounded on the north by snows and glaciers which are the source of the Pindari river, and lower down by the high ridges, branching from Dhakuri peak on the left bank of the Pindar, which separates it here from the Garhwal district, while on the west high spurs from Bhatkot separate it from Garhwal and from the Pali pargana, and on the south spurs from the same Bhatkot range separate it from the Barahmandal and Chaugarkha parganas as far as Bageswar, from which point the boundary runs east over irregular spurs north of Gangoli to Nachni on the Ramganga, which river then becomes the boundary between Danpur and Johar. At the base and from the spurs of Nanda

* Assessment report: J. C. Smith.

Devi and its neighbour Nandakot rise the three rivers which separate the eastern portion of the pargana into three great valleys,—the Pindar, the Sarju, and the eastern Ramganga, while its western half is drained by the Gumti and its affluents, uniting with the Sarju at Bageswar. The eastern portion is Danpur proper, sub-divided administratively into the pattis Malla, Bichla, and Talla Danpur, Dug and Nakuri; and the western portion consists of Malla, Bichla and Talla Katyur. From the Bhatkot range between Bichla Katyur and Palla Giwar a continuous chain of lofty forest-clad mountains runs north-east to Dhakuri and thence in a gradual rise to the snows. This ridge is one of the main watersheds of Kumaon; it separates the Sarju, the most westerly of all the streams that form the Sarda drainage system from the Pindar and the western Ramganga which ultimately find their way into the Ganges. Some of the peaks of this ridge Shishakhani, Dhakuri, Chilt and others rise to 11,000 feet and are covered with forests of rhododendron of all colours, cypress and oak with occasional box and birch. The valleys of the rivers that water the pargana are divided from each other by lines of hills converging upon the mighty mass of snow mountains which culminate in the Nanda Devi peak north of the Pindari glacier. The Gumti rising in Garhwal flows on the southern side of Malla Katyur into the fertile valley of Talla Katyur meeting the Sarju at Bageswar. The Garur flowing through Bichla Katyur from the Bhatkot range is an important tributary of the Gumti which it meets at Baijnath. The Lahur and Kanalgadh from the forests of the Gwaldam-Dhakuri ridge join the Sarju between Bageswar and Kapkot. The Pangadh flows through Nakuri and Dug, and above Kapkot the Raptigadh meets the Sarju at Kharbagar. The two last named are the principal affluents on the left bank. The river valleys are flanked by very high hills, with lower subordinate spurs parting the smaller streams. Pattis Dug, Malla and Talla Katyur are of moderate elevation; but elsewhere high and difficult mountains are characteristic of the pargana. The spur from Bhatkot which divides the valley of the Gumti from the Kosi and runs south of Bichla and Talla Katyur contains the Kausani tea garden, and is particularly noticeable for its fine fertile slopes covered with pasture land and forests. The hills of Malla Danpur are covered with forests of rhododendron varied by oak, cypress, and fir, and afford excellent grazing. The people maintain stations for their flocks and herds almost up to the glaciers, where they spend the rainy season tending their animals and collecting wild honey or other minor forest produce. The lower hills of Talla Danpur are clothed with very fine forests of oak and pine. Thus all the pattis have an abundance of pasture, but in Nakuri the limit of cultivation has almost been reached round the skirts of the Sikkar Danda.

The soil varies vastly in productiveness in different parts of the pargana. At one end of the scale are the rich alluvial irrigated *seras* of the lower Sarju and the Gumti in Talla Katyur near Bageswar, and at the other the stony uplands of Malla Danpur. In the former the best qualities of rice, wheat and *masur* with sugarcane are grown, while in the latter only barley, occasional wheat, *chuwa* and *phaphar* can be produced. The valleys of the Gumti and Garur in Malla and Bichla Katyur are very fertile both from the quality of the soil and the ample sources of irrigation. Talla Danpur is wilder. Dug contains some fine *seras* above Bageswar, and the whole patti is exceptionally fertile. Nakuri presents few features of note, being mainly upland. In addition to the ordinary crops Talla Katyur produces some turmeric, ginger and chillies. The least prosperous patti is Malla Danpur. The portion that lies in the Pindar valley is cut off from the rest of the district by a ridge 10,000 feet high and impassable between December and April. The soil is not good; no wheat is produced except in the south and the staple crops are *chuwa*, *phaphar* and *mandua* for the kharif and barley for the rabi. The patti however contains much pasture land covered with a very superior kind of grass, and whether it be this, or merely the extensive range, sheep and goats flourish as much on the grass as animals in Almora fed on grain. Both sheep and goats are bought up by the Bhotias for transport. This trade and the manufacture and sale of blankets and of baskets and matting made in the winter from the ringal bamboo when it is leafless, constitute the main sources of the people's income. The grain they grow does not suffice for more than one year's consumption and their lands are owing to their position within the snows subject to many vicissitudes. A crop failure is therefore a very serious misfortune and food stocks are only replenished by paying very high prices to the Bageswar Banias.*

The pargana has however on the whole greatly advanced in prosperity during the last 50 years. In Mr. Batten's time the low rich valleys of Malla and Bichla Katyur possessed a very bad climate due to the very heavy jungle, which then covered it, and which also afforded a refuge to tigers, bears and leopards. Talla Katyur however had improved; the cultivation had increased and with it the climate had bettered. "At one time, too" he writes "from the citadel of Ramchula above their capital Katyur the ancient rulers of the hills must have looked down and round on an almost unbroken picture of agricultural wealth: for not only in the valleys but up three-fourths of the mountain sides now covered with enormous forests of pine the well built walls of fields remain in multitudinous array, terrace upon terrace, a monument of former industry and populousness, and only requiring the axe to prepare an immediate way for the plough.

The valley of Baijnath being situated on the frontier of Kumaon with Garhwal and in the neighbourhood of Badhan fort was often the scene of border conflicts and military exactions; and the desertion of the villages once having commenced, and no means of restoring the population being at hand, the deterioration of climate, originating in the spread of rank vegetation and the neglect of drainage may be supposed to have gone on from worse to worse till finally the heat and moisture were left to perform all their natural ill-offices unchecked by the industry and efforts of men."

It was the presence of these forests however that attracted European enterprise when tea was introduced. Consequently many tea gardens have been started and have been the source of great prosperity to the people at large. The plucking of leaves employs very large numbers from every household. There are nine tea-gardens in the pargana situated chiefly in Katyur. About

* Assessment report: J. E. Goudge.

150 of the men in Malla and Talla Danpur are enlisted in the 39th Garhwal Rifles stationed at Lansdowne. All the Danpurs and Dug also make money by providing transport and food for the constant stream of travellers to the Pindari glacier, and in addition blanket and basket weaving enables others to eke out comfortably their rather slender agricultural resources. All these factors have considerably contributed towards the present prosperity of the pargana at large; an advance which may be measured by the 37 per cent. increase of cultivation during the 30 years intervening between Mr. Beckett's and Mr. Goudge's settlements. The total cultivated area now amounts to 44·4 square miles and the irrigated proportion exceeds 15 per cent. The population according to the preliminary census of September 1900 amounted to 35,690.

The pargana is fairly well supplied with roads. A cart road was built in 1892 for the benefit of the tea industry from Baijnath to Hawalbagh, on the cart road between Almora and Ranikhet. Bageswar at the corner of the Talla Katyur and Dug pattis is connected by bridle paths with Almora and Someswar. Another road runs up the Gumti valley past Baijnath into Garhwal, a fourth up the Sarju river for the Pindari glacier, while a fifth traverses Dug and Nakuri reaching Tejam on the Ramganga. The main Milam road leaves the Pindari route at Kharbagar. The only town in the pargana is Bageswar, still a very important mart, and the centre of much trade at the Uttaraini *mela* in January. Other important villages are Baijnath once the capital of the Katyur kings, Pai in Malla Katyur, Nakuri which lies not in patti Nakuri but in Bichla Danpur, Amtora in Talla Katyur, Naughar in Bichla Katyur and Mandalsera in Dug.

The revenue was in 1833 Rs. 5,958, in 1843 Rs. 5,902, in 1872 Rs. 15,362 and the current demand was fixed in 1902 at Rs. 22,270, to reach its maximum of Rs. 23,996 after ten years.

DARMA *pargana, peshkari* SHOR.

The Darma pargana is one of the sub-divisions of Bhot. It is triangular in shape and occupies the extreme north-east corner of the district. It is bounded on the north-east by the watershed range which parts it from Tibet, on the south-east by the Kal river which flows between it and Nepal and on the west by the Panchachuli range which divide it from pargana Johar. Within the pargana a long spur reaches away from a point near the Darma pass on the watershed range to the Kali river in a course trending in the main south, and this spur divides the basin of the Dhauli river to the west from that of the Kuthi-Yankti to the east, both considered affluents of the Kali though they greatly exceed it in volume. The pargana thus occupies the entire valleys of these two rivers and the right bank of the Kali as far as its junction with the former. Administratively, it has always been divided into three pattis, Darma situated in the valley of the Dhauli, also called the Darma river, Chaudans, the tract of land at the junction of the Dhauli and the Kali and Byans occupying the valley of the Kuthi-Yankti. At the settlement of 1872 the Darma patti was further sub-divided into the Malla and Talla or upper and lower pattis. The greater portion of the pargana is a desolate region of inaccessible glaciers, snowy peaks and precipices, and the habitations are confined to the valleys of the main rivers.

In the upper pattis one crop of *napal* (Himalayan wheat) or of buck-wheat is sown in May or June, as soon as the snow is sufficiently melted, and reaped in November. But in Talla Darma and Chaudans alone agriculture is a serious pursuit. Here two crops are regularly grown and the wheat and barley produced in the rabi at an elevation of between 7,000 and 8,000 feet is of excellent quality though it ripens very late. In Chaudans the mountains are terraced for cultivation up to 9,000 feet. These two pattis also contain some of the finest forests in the district both for beauty and extent. They are mainly of oak and chestnut with many kinds of fir, birch and box. In Malla Darma and Byans there is a dearth of good timber; the only tree that grows in Byans is birch in small plantations; in Malla Darma even this has disappeared.*

The pargana is approached from Almora, through Askot, by a road which follows the right bank of the Kali river. The

* Assessment report: J. E. Goudge.

first stage in Darma is Khela Syali Panth usually called Khela, a village situated at the confluence of the Dhauli and Kali rivers. The Dhauli river which is the chief geographical feature of the Darma pattis is the result of the union of two streams, the Lissar and the Dhauli proper, both rising in the north-west of the pargana. They are parted by a range of moderate height but the main valley is flanked to the east and west by stupendous ranges of snow-crowned mountains, the western culminating in the noble cluster of peaks known as the Panchachuli. The range to the east is only slightly inferior in height. Glacier-fed torrents run down to the river from either hand. The patti of Talla Darma lies at the lower portion of the valley. Here the climate is almost tropical for most of the year. Beyond Sobala Malla Darma begins and here the valley assumes a more alpine character, rising gradually as a rule and in some places somewhat abruptly, until at Baun an elevation of 11,600 feet is attained. The passes of the Darma valley into Tibet are reached by Dawa and are known as the Kachlekh and Neo lekh or Neodhura. There is also an inter-Himalayan pass to Ralam in Johar by the Phula-Yankti from Sipu on the Lissar torrent, and to Byans by the Lebong-dhura from Khimling. The Darma pattis are connected with the main line of communication along the Kali river by a road which joins it at Khela.

The main road traverses the patti of Chaudans which comprises the tract on the left bank of the Dhauli river from opposite Baunling to its confluence with the Kali and the tract lying along the southern and eastern extremities of the chain containing the peak of Yirgnajang to the bank of the Kali. It is altogether about twelve miles long by eight broad. The road passes by Sosa under Titalakot to Bungbung, crossing the Roling pass which is thickly clothed with forests of horse chestnut that here attain a great size. Hence the road passes on to Galagar less than two miles distant. Near Galagar the Nirpaniya ridge is passed, to the east of which glimpses of the snowy ridges called Namjang and Lingan are obtained. The Nirpaniya pass (so-called from the absence of water) winds for about three miles along the side of black and forbidding precipices and was in former years rarely crossed except by the Bhotias and then only at considerable risk. Now however, the efforts of the Public Works department have greatly improved the track, though it is by no means easy or safe. A short distance beyond the pass the path crosses a ridge called Tiyungwe binayak some 10,500 feet above sea level which forms the boundary between Chaudans and Byans. Byans patti occupies the valleys of the Kuthi-Yankti and of the Kali as far south as the Nirpaniya pass and it is situated in the extreme north-eastern corner of the pargana. The great northern range here bends suddenly to the south-east, encircling the eastern extremity of the patti. Immediately above Budhi, which is the only sub-alpine village of Byans, situated at an elevation of 9,070 feet above the sea level on the right bank of the Palangar stream above its confluence with the Kali, a steep ridge advances from the mountain side on the north-west and extends across the valley, leaving but a narrow passage for the river. The summit of Chetu-binayak is then reached after an ascent of about 1,750 feet by an easy path and thence the entrance into upper Byans.

The first village in upper Byans is Garbiyang (10,320 feet), close to the Kali river. Thence the path descends to the bed of the river and crosses it by a bridge a little above its junction with the Tinkhar, a large stream not much inferior to the main body of the Kali, coming in two branches from the east and north-east. A little above the bridge and on the top of a steep bank, is the village of Changru (9,900 feet). The Kali now turns abruptly to the north-west through a steep rocky mountain defile, whilst the path follows the left bank to Gunji (10,310 feet) at the entrance of the Kuthi valley. The main road to the Lipu Lekh pass traverses a plateau as far as Kalapani through some of the most beautiful scenery in the Himalayas. The name of the Kali is said to be derived from the Kalapani springs, erroneously reputed the source of the river, but in fact unimportant tributaries. The hot spring too was overwhelmed by an avalanche many years ago and the name was transferred to another spring neither black nor hot. Sangchan the last stage on the road stands at an elevation of some 14,600 feet, above the tree-limit : thence a long but gentle ascent brings the traveller to the summit of the pass 16,780 feet.

The Kuthi road crosses the Kali 150 yards above its confluence with the Kuthi-Yankti which is the larger stream of the two. The traveller now enters a fine expanded valley of considerable length through which flows the Kuthi-Yankti or western branch of the Kali.

As the road approaches Kuthi, the mountains on the left bank recede a little, and then curve round with a fine sweep to the northward, enclosing a good expanse of tolerably level ground around the village of Kuthi, the highest inhabited site in the valley, with an elevation of 12,330 feet above the level of the sea. Beyond Kuthi the valley which carries the Tibet road is reduced to the dimension of an open glen, the path, one or two hundred feet above the river gradually rising and the mountains on either side decreasing in relative height, until Jhuling is reached, the usual halting place between Kuthi and the foot of the Lanpya Lekh Pass, or its less used alternative the Mangshang Pass. Both these passes are open only in the height of summer and are much more difficult than the Lipu Lekh.

The people of Chaudans, Byans and Malla Darma are Bhotias. They are less Hinduised than those who inhabit the Johar pargana, and one legend—which it may be remarked they indignantly repudiate—assigns their origin to a band of Tartars of Tamurlane's army. The Bhotias subsist on the trade they carry on between Tibet and the plains; they are better off than the Joharis in that their passes are easier to traverse and their climate not such as to compel them to evacuate their villages in the winter. On the other hand their supposed inferior origin has marked them out for heavier exactions. There is also domiciled in Khimling a colony of Tibetans of the Khampa tribe. Talla Darma is inhabited by Hindus belonging to the Bora and Dhami clans, but they are rough and uncivilised, and their sole apparent garment is a coarse home-spun blanket. The Hindus of Talla Darma also breed and sell to the Bhotias both sheep and goats to be used for pack purposes.

The population has more than doubled in the 30 years that intervened between Mr. Beckett's and Mr. Goudge's settlements and revenue is now Rs. 2,645, an increase of 35 per cent. over Mr. Beckett's demand.

The American Episcopalian Mission maintain a hospital at Sirkha in Chaudans, their head quarters in this part of Bhot and a branch dispensary at Gunji near the junction of the Kuthi-Yankti and the Kali.

DEVI DHURA, *patti* CHALSI, *pargana* KALI KUMAON.

A station on the road from Almora to Lohaghat, at a distance of 10 miles from Dunaghat, 19 miles from Lamgara, 10 miles from Mornaula, and 29 miles from Almora. There is a travellers' bungalow here without a khansaman, and a bania's shop. The place stands on a lofty ridge at a height of 6,633 feet, in latitude 29° 24′ 56″ north, and longitude 79° 52′ east. Madden's description may be here given.

Devi Dhura occupies the north-east and highest angle of a great granitic plateau, steep on the east and north, but sloping gently to the west and south: it is covered with wood and furrowed by deep ravines. One of these commences at the shrine, and soon collects a pretty stream deeply shaded by horse-chestnut and other trees: at its head is a *naula* or covered well. This granitic ridge extends continuously from Dernath near Fort Hastings to Saur-Phatka within three miles of Dol. At Saur-Phatka the road leaves it, but the formation is probably continued to Siyahi Devi, as the granite reappears on the west and south faces of the Bandani and Mukteswar mountains, in the bed of the small stream which joins the Kumniya below Piura, and on both sides of the Kumniya up to Kapleswar.

On the north-west face of the mountain, a few feet below its crest, there are two groups of colossal blocks of grey granite piled on each other, consecrated to Mahadeva, Varahi Devi and Bhim Sen, and softened by a few picturesque oaks, deodars, walnuts and a large *silang* (*Olea fragrans*) tree. Similar boulders are strewed over the surface of the surrounding mountains, especially on the upper part of the deep depression in the range immediately north. Between two of the main boulders, in a recess crowned with a grove of deodars, is a celebrated temple at which a fair is held in June-July, when many goats and buffaloes are offered at the shrine. There were two noteworthy customs at this fair: one was the dragging of the idol to the top of the plateau a few hundred yards off where the cairn of the Great Trigonometrical Survey stands, the draggers being men all naked; another was the custom of forming two parties, who attacked each other with sticks and stones (known as *bagwali*), a practice formerly not uncommon throughout Kumaon and Nepal. To the west of the temple are two boulders; the uppermost of which, called Ransila, about one hundred feet in length, is cleft through the centre by a deep fissure, at right angles to which there is a similar rift in the lower rock. On Ransila rests a smaller boulder, said to be the same that was employed by Bhim Sen to produce these fissures, in proof of which, the print of his five fingers is still pointed out. The surface of Ransila also presents certain other marks and figures on which the Pandu brothers amused themselves at *pachisi*, an indigenous kind of chess.

DHAKURI, *patti* MALLA DANPUR, *pargana* DANPUR.

A halting place with a bungalow on the road to the Pindari glacier, between Loharkhet and Khati, at a distance of 7 miles from the latter and six from the former, and 57 miles from Almora. There is no khansaman at the bungalow, and the nearest shop is at Loharkhet.

From Lwarkhet or Loharkhet to Khati a march of about four hours leads to Tanti about 200 feet below the pass over the Dhakuri-Binayak ridge, of which the peak rises on the left to a height of 10,541 feet. The path commences to rise at once on leaving Lwarkhet and is in parts very steep and rocky, interspersed with occasional undulating meadows. One large stream is passed which, rising between the pass and the Chaur-ka-danda, flows down a spacious wooded glen towards the Sarju and in one spot forms a fine waterfall. The views across the Sarju are very grand, and from the pass a new and magnificent, though contracted, prospect of the snowy range extending from the Nandakot peak on the east to Mantoli-ka-dhura (Trisul) on the west is seen. The eastern peak of the Trisul faces the west in a great bluff, from which a long easy ridge, presenting an unbroken sheet of snow, slopes down to the east, connecting Trisul with the Nanda Devi cluster. The Dhakuri hill lies within 20 miles of the two great rocky peaks of this cluster, and is elevated 10,500 feet, but the peaks are invisible from it, being concealed by the two beautiful pinnacles of pure snow, which from Almora are seen to be merely the abrupt terminations of two immense spurs, the easternmost of which is there known as Nandakot, "Devi's bed." From this point of view it rises into a fine and lofty spire. In the hollow between the Trisul and Nanda Devi groups rises the Sundardunga or Redinga river, which, flowing nearly south down a narrow and most profound glen, joins the Pindar a little above Wachham, affording probably the best and easiest route to the traveller desirous of penetrating to the core of the Nanda Devi mass. This stream has its source in a glacier like that at Pindari. East of Nanda Devi, in a deep *col*, is "Traill's pass," supposed by him to be 20,000 feet high; it is flanked on the east by the north-west shoulder of Nandakot, which mountain closes the view in a colossal rectangular summit of pure snow. The *Quircus dilatata (tilonj)* and *Quercus semicarpifolia (karshu)* oaks are abundant on the eastern exposure of the Dhakuri-binayak. The descent on the western side is rapid, through forests of oaks and firs. Below these, the path drops through luxuriant meadows, nearly to the Pindar, opposite to the large village of Wachham. Here a path strikes off to the left to Chiringa in the Pindar valley below Gwaldam. This long, but in general not very steep descent, leads to a torrent, from which the road again ascends considerably towards Khati, three miles or so further, the road lying amongst horse-chestnut, maple, mountain bamboo, *quercus incana (banj)* and *moru* oaks, hornbeam and ash. Khati is a small village with but few inhabitants: the only cultivation consists of a few fields of *chuwa*, with a little *mandua*.

DHAULI RIVER.

The eastern Dhauli is a principal tributary of the Kali. It rises in the glaciers to the north-west of the Dawa encamping ground (14,860 feet) leading to the Niyo-dhura or Darma pass into Tibet in north latitude 30° 26′ and east longitude 80° 31′. The source lies to the north of the main range of the Himalaya and the valley of the river forms one of the two into which

Malla Darma is divided. It passes by Dawa, the Pungrung encamping ground (14,100 feet), Khimling (13,060 feet), Rama (11,330 feet) to its junction with the Lissar on the left bank (10,370 feet). Thence by Dhankur, Go and Sela to its junction with the Kali on the right bank at Khela-Syali Panth in north latitude 29° 26′ 50″ and east longitude 80° 38′ 40″. Its stream is in general a succession of violent rapids in a rocky channel amidst awful precipices and ravines. The road to Tibet by the Darma pass proceeds up the valley of the river, passing by means of spar bridges from side to side, according to the exigencies of the path, which sometimes winds along the faces of nearly perpendicular precipices; yet, during the season when the passes are open, this difficult track is crowded by innumerable laden goats and sheep, bearing grain and other merchandise from the lower districts to Tibet. A difficult and dangerous pass proceeds by the Phula-Yankti stream from Ralam, on a feeder of the Gori, to Sipu and Marcha on the Lissar branch of the Dhauli.

DOL, *patti* DOLPHAT, *pargana* CHAUGARKHA.

A village situate in latitude 29° 29′ 30″ north and longitude 79° 48′ 25″ east, at an elevation of about 6,000 feet, on the road from Almora to Devi Dhura and Champawat. There was formerly a dâk bungalow here, but the stages now are Lamgara, five miles west of Dol and nearer Almora, and Mornaula, six miles east of Dol and nearer Devi Dhura. Dol village is prettily situated on a spur, while in the lower glens to the east lie the scattered villages of Salam, celebrated for their rice. Six miles away at the junction of two branches of the Kumniya river, stands the rather famous shrine of Kapleswar, with a large temple dedicated to Mahadeo, built by Raja Udyot Chand, son of Baz Bahadur Chand, on the north bank, at the supposed spot where the sage Kapila did penance, and where across the junction Seshnag, the serpent king, was similarly engaged. The site of the temple is a narrow, pine-clad glen, just at the end of the cultivated lands; a mile lower down, the Kumniya forces its way amidst great smooth boulders of granite, the debris of the mountains above; here, on its south bank, facing Raulakot, is a huge outburst of granitic masses, piled one over another to the height of 150 feet; the highest shaped like the beak of an anvil, is known as the Birdeo.

DWARAHAT, *patti* MALLA DORA, *pargana* PALI PACHHAON.

A large and historic village on the road from Almora to Pauri in Garhwal, in latitude 29° 46′ 54″ east and longitude 79° 26′ 8″ east at a distance of 26 miles from Almora and 13 miles from Bainskhet. The next stage Ganai is 9½ miles. Another road runs south to Ranikhet, 12 miles, and a third to Someswar. The elevation of the bungalow is 5,031 feet. Dwarahat contains a post-office, a dispensary, an English middle school, and a girls' school, which are largely supported by the American Mission who have a thriving colony here, and a dispensary of their own. The chief feature of Dwarahat is its antiquities. The place in former days was the residence of one branch of the Katyuri Rajas, an outlying district of the kingdom of which Lakhanpur near Ganai and Bhatkot was the head quarters. The remains of very many ancient temples lie scattered in groups and lines over the fields. They are of the usual pyramidal form ornamented with from three to five rows of a simple moulding on the outer edges and surmounted by an ornament resembling a Turk's cap. All are more or less in ruins and are now used as granaries and straw-lofts. Having been desecrated by the Rohillas during their invasion of this part of Kumaon, they are no longer held in reverence, and in many places the stones of the temples and carved pillars are made use of to mend the terraces of fields. Some of the pillars contain in a panel two rude figures with arms stretched out at right angles to their body, resembling a badly-made rag-doll. All the temples are of plain construction with the exception of one near the Syalde Pokhar, by a clump of date trees and an old *silang*. This is elaborately carved with row after row of figures representing gods, men and elephants. It is, however, in bad repair, and its graven images and stones lie scattered around. The Syalde tank, close by, produces large numbers of the pink lotus during the rains. It is so called from the Syalde clan of Rajputs who assemble here annually in Baisakh to indulge in the mimic warfare of the *bagwali*. Formerly it was customary to use slings and stones, but this has been forbidden owing to the occurrence of serious accidents. The remains of the cruciform entrance to the temple still exist; whilst the shrine itself is about seven feet square. The whole consists of three broad abutments connected by three narrower: the fourth side forming the entrance. The inner sides of each abutment join together to form the adytum. The outer side to a height of about three feet displays a moulding, then come several rows of figures in relief and panelled, and the upper row in panels contains figures fully two feet high. The friable nature of the stone employed as well as exposure to the rain has rendered the original delicate carvings obscure. Even such as it is, the remains, some 17 feet high, are worthy of being preserved, though many of the stones have been removed for the buildings in the neighbouring bazar.

On the Chandragiri or Chauchari hill to the south of the village stood the palace of the Katyur rajas, on the rock called Tharp. Just below the palace the bazar commences, and at the end of it is the Mritunjaya temple with a broken pinnacle, west of which is the Badrinath temple, the most important of those now in existence. It comprises three of the older temples surrounded by a courtyard in which is a dharmsala. Many stories are told about the principal temple: one was that at its erection a sixth workman was always visible though, five only were employed. From Dwarahat westward, all the principal temples are ascribed to Sankara Acharya and those here form no exception. The principal temple dedicated to Badrinath is connected with the greater institution in Garhwal of this name, and is controlled by the Rawal of that place. It is about 50 feet high ending in a truncated circular ornament open at the top. The old image was desecrated by the Rohillas, and the new one is of modern make and is surrounded by ten or twelve others, one of which bears the date 1105 Saka or 1048 A. D., and on another representing Ganesh is the date 1103 Saka. The image of Lakshmi is in a small temple to the north, near which is a ruined temple known as Unerdewal. A great pipal tree now grows out of a crack in the walls near the dharmsala. Two of the rest-houses were built by the Chaudhris and another by Damu Sonar. The temple of Mrityunjaya has been deserted, the people say, because strange voices were heard within it, but really because the establishment cannot afford to keep up the worship. The Doms have a temple dedicated to the worship of Kalsain. Sitala Devi is worshipped in another near the Syalde Pokhar, where a fair is held on the Bikh Sankrant, in April. The Kot-Kangra Devi is the Kula Devi of the Chaudhri family, who emigrated hither from Kangra in the time of the rajas and were largely employed by them in civil duties. Her temple is on the north side of the tank. The Chaudhris themselves live in Haripura, and employ the priests of Sitala as *pujaris.* Brahm Deo and Dham Deo, the Katyuri rajas, are also worshipped here. There is a platform or *chabutra* erected by the Chaudhris, but now owned by the state; and several partly finished temples stand near the tank and a group of seven lie in the cultivated fields called Ratnadewal, but none have any idols in them, and their origin is unknown. In the upper bazar is a temple to Mahadeo in ruins, the image having been removed to the Badrinath temple, and near it three others, one of a circular form with a verandah. Towards the Tharp there is a row of temples with pillared entrances called the 'Court-temples' (*Kachahri-ki-dewal*) all used as wood and hay stores. Above them are two other temples and the school established in 1857.

A flight of steps leads up to the Tharp-tilah, where there is a temple now devoted to the worship of the village deities Haru and Latu, adorned with iron lamps at each corner and two four-branched lamps of the same metal; whilst an iron spade and a number of scourges are placed in the room, and on festal occasions the persons possessed by these gods dance, and whilst in a state of frenzy from their exertions are supposed to reveal the future. Below the Tharp is a noted temple of Kalika Devi, to which the people have recourse when any illness is abroad. The temples altogether number 30; but with the exception of those dedicated to Badrinath, Kedarnath, Sitala, and Kot-Kangra Devi, few are used for religious purposes. A portion of an inscription has been carried from Dwarahat to Dunagiri, bearing date 1105 Saka (1029

A. D.), and the early part of the 11th century may be taken generally as the date of the erection of the principal temples in Dwarahat itself. At the celebration of the Dasahra, a considerable fair used to be held at the old temple on Dunagiri, where religion and commerce went hand in hand, and sins were washed away and new garments purchased. Trade has since found other outlets, whilst religion is not now-a-days a sufficient inducement to undergo the toil of climbing to the residence of the god.

Dunagiri is a lofty hill to the north-east of Dwarahat across the valley. It is composed of blue clay slate and forms the chief southern spur of the Bhatkot range. Its slopes are covered with oak, interspersed with pasture. The valley between Dunagiri and Dwarahat contains the Kharrogadh which flows north to join the Ramganga near Ganai.

Traill mentions the existence of tombs substantially built of large tiles at Dwarahat which he considers are memorials of the Mughals located there in the course of Timur's invasion of Hindustan. In support of this theory are the groves of the common date palm (*khajur*) only planted by Musalmans in India and the foreign names of several villages and local sub-divisions here. There are now no Musalman inhabitants, the people of importance being descendants of decayed official families of Hindu origin, who are usually conceded the style of Chaudhri. The population in 1901 was 124.

GAGAS RIVER.

A stream rising in patti Kairarau of pargana Baramandal near Dunagiri. From its source it flows nearly due south through that patti. The road from Dwarahat to Someswar crosses it at Bhataur in Kairarau and the road from Bhainskhet to Dwarahat by a wooden bridge near Bansli-sera. Here the channel is broad and thickly strown with boulders, which give evidence of a considerable volume of water in the rains. Hence the course is nearly due west through Athaguli, where it is crossed by road from Ranikhet to Dwarahat leading over an iron suspension-bridge in the village of Darmar: at the same point the river receives on the right bank the Chandas stream and further west on the same side the Riskoi river and the Balwagadh from the north, and pursues the same course until it joins the western Ramganga on the left bank at Bhikia Sen in latitude 29° 42′ 8″ north and longitude 79° 18′ 20″ east. The stream is locally connected with the name of the Rishi Garga.

In its upper reaches it is much utilised for irrigation, but for the last ten miles of its course it runs through a deep gorge with no cultivation near its banks.

GANAI, *patti* PALLA GIWAR, *pargana* PALI PACHHAON.

A halting-place with a dâk bungalow, but no khansaman, on the road from Almora to Pauri, at a distance of 9½ miles from Dwarahat. It lies low in the valley of the Ramganga at an elevation of 3,206 feet above the sea. The bungalow stands on a spur overlooking the broad semicircular valley of the river. Northward a valley leads up to the Garhwal border, and along it passes the road to Lohba, a distance of 14 miles. There is a post-office and a dispensary here, the latter being in a building to the west of and below the bungalow, on the Bhikia Sen road. The road from Dwarhat is level and easy, after the descent from the shoulder on which the dâk bungalow at Dwarahat stands. It follows the Kharrogadh which unites with the Ramganga at Ganai. There is a suspension-bridge at Ganai just below the bazar: from this point the road to Pauri follows the valley of the Ramganga for two miles and then ascends the hill to Kelani. The valley which once contained much valuable alluvial land has been damaged greatly by floods and now there are great masses of boulders, where once were smiling cornfields. Ganai belongs to a family of Bishts, the present Thokdar being Gopal Singh.

Up to the east of Ganai runs a valley towards Bhatkot; about three miles along this valley is Tarag Tal, a pretty lake surrounded by pine-clad mountains. Some two miles from Ganai on the Pauri road are the traditional remains of what is now known as lakhanpur which is supposed to have been one of the capitals of the earlier Katyur rajas. The population in 1901 was 256.

GANGOLI *pargana, tahsil* ALMORA.

Gangoli is a large pargana lying between the Sarju and Ramganga rivers below pargana Danpur. It is roughly triangular in shape, the north-western corner being at Bageswar on the Sarju, the north-eastern a little below Tejam on the Ramganga and the southern at the junction of these two rivers by the Rameswar temple, where the four parganas of Chaugarkha, Gangoli, Kali Kumaon, and Shor meet. Across the Ramganga and above Shor lies pargana Sira, and beyond that Talla Johar marches with Gangoli for a few miles along its north-eastern extremity; on the other side for about 35 miles the Sarju separates it from Chaugarkha. It now consists of 849 mahals, three or four of which often go to form one village as it would be understood physically, and has a cultivated area of 42 square miles. At the previous settlement there were 802 mahals with an area of 32¼ square miles and a population of 19,744. These villages are grouped into six pattis, Bel, Bherang, Baraun, Athgaon, Kamsyar and Pungraun, all but Bherang being of considerable size. Pungraun occupies the valley of the Barargadh at the north-east corner, Kamsyar is a long narrow strip stretching from that patti to Bageswar, Baraun and Athgaon lie along the Ramganga and Sarju respectively and fill the central portion, while Bel and Bherang are situated on the rugged tongue of land between the two rivers as they converge at the apex of the inverted triangle. The total area of the tract cannot be given exactly, but it is probably a little over 300 square miles.

A fine range of hills forms the boundary between this pargana and Danpur: it rises from Bageswar to a height of about 6,500 feet and continuing east at more or less the same elevation culminates in the dark and frowning peak of Kalinag which rises abruptly over the Ramganga to a height of 7,317 feet. From this a minor range diverges near Chaukuri and runs the whole length of the pargana, rising to 7,742 feet near the Jhaltola gardens and to 7,107 feet in the middle of patti Bel whence it descends gradually to Rameswar. Numerous off-shoots from this central range divide the tract into small valleys down which the feeders of the main rivers flow: the largest of them are the Badhangadh, the Godgadh and Narkul flowing into the Sarju, and the Barargadh, the Garghatia, the Mangadh and the Koligadh flowing into the Ramganga.

Nearly all the land which is not under cultivation is wooded; the higher land is covered with oak and rhododendron and the lower with pine or, in a few places at the bottom of the pargana, with sal: the deodar is seldom found except in small clumps round the temples.

Four roads pass through Gangoli: the Almora-Pithoragarh road crosses the Sarju by a small foot-bridge below the Naini bungalow, rises over the fine plateau of Gangolihat, where there is another bungalow, and drops down the Kholigadh valley through the lower part of the Bherang slope to the Ramganga: the Almora-Askot road passes through Athgaon and Baraun and is joined at Berenag (properly Beninag) by one from Bageswar; it crosses the Ramganga by a good bridge at Thal and enters Sira: the fourth road cuts through the top of the pargana and affords the people of Kamsyar and Pungraun a ready means of communication with Tejam and Talla Johar.

The population consists for the most part of Rajputs, but high caste Brahmans particularly Pants, who own a great number of villages in the central part of the tract, are numerous and influential; Joshis, Pathaks and Pandes also hold a large amount of land. The Khas Brahman is found everywhere; he tills his own fields and often works for his high caste neighbours. Doms own a considerable amount of land altogether, particularly in the Barargadh and Mangar valleys but they are generally the tenants or semi-serfs of Brahman and Rajput landholders. Perhaps the most interesting clan in the pargana is that of the Kothalia Boras who own a large cluster of villages in the eastern part of Athgaon under the Jhaltola heights and have acquired shares or obtained grants of land in a number of places all round; they make a coarse hempen sackcloth used for making bags or clothing. As tillers of the soil they are far ahead of all their neighbours and to them is largely due the vast improvement and expansion which has taken place in the cultivation of Athgaon patti since Mr. Beckett's settlement. In the northern pattis there are a few Bhotia settlements which are used as depôts and resting places by the people of Upper Johar on their way to and from the lower hills and Bhabar; and along the Ramganga and in the tea-gardens are found immigrants from Nepal who gladly cultivate the low and feverish land by that river and who provide the best labourers and blacksmiths to be found in the pargana. The cultivation throughout the pargana is good. Parts of Bel are very rugged and steep, but the greater part of the land at the elevation at which tillage is most profitable is on moderate slopes and has soil sufficiently rich to be well worth working. The best villages and the finest cultivation are ordinarily found at head of a small valley. The fields are backed by pasture and forest from which descend several tiny streamlets utilised to the full for irrigation. All the ordinary hill crops are grown and there are also five tea gardens belonging to Mr. J. G. Stevenson of Chaukuri with over 200 acres under tea, and three others of less importance are owned by Indians.*

In former years, Bel, Bherang, Athgaon, and Kamsyar were covered with an almost impenetrable jungle, the haunt of numerous tigers. Owing to the Gurkhali policy of disarmament the inhabitants were defenceless and were carried off at midday whilst working in their fields, and tigers were even known to break into houses at night and carry off the inmates. Writing in 1821, Mr. Traill states that within the previous three years 373 persons had been killed by tigers in Gangoli; these too, were natives of the place, whose names and residences were recorded. In 1840 Mr. Batten writes: "In some of the tracts near the rivers, notorious man-eaters are hardly ever absent, and at times the loss of human life is considerable; very few of the inhabitants are shikaris, and the reward of Rs. 10 given for each tiger killed is found an insufficient inducement to create in Gangoli a body of hunters; whilst the poverty and inhospitality of the villagers is such, that though they often apply for aid, they are almost always found unwilling to provide even the commonest supply of provisions for the local sepoys and armed peons occasionally sent to assist them."

The indigenous tigers have been exterminated and the few occasional wanderers are quickly disposed of. The forests have been cleared away from the low-lying valleys, and Gangoli now

* Assessment report: J. C. Smith.

enjoys an excellent climate and the soil is generally very fertile. It is in the happy position of producing more grain than it can eat, and its fruit—particularly oranges—is famous in Kumaon. Grain, *ghi*, walnuts and fruit are exported to Almora or through that town to Naini Tal and Ranikhet, and a considerable amount of produce is disposed of at the Bageswar and Thal fairs in January and April respectively. The pargana is watered by two large rivers teeming with fish which are gladly eaten by all classes. In addition the fine forests afford pasturage to large herds of cattle and some of the pattis—particularly Athgaon—make some money out of the sale of *ghi* in Almora. From this pargana too are bought most of the cattle used at the Muktesar bacteriological laboratory.

A large number of the Brahmans, especially those of Bherang and Baraun, are in government service or otherwise employed outside the pargana, and in the season many of the Rajputs go to the hill stations for service or carry loads from Kathgodam.

The cultivation was found to have increased by over 27 per cent. between Mr. Beckett's and Mr. Goudge's settlements and the population which in 1901 amounted to 38,700 by 96 per cent. This pargana has thus developed enormously within the last 35 or 40 years and is perhaps the most prosperous in the district. The land revenue now amounts to Rs. 19,971, with an incidence of Re. 0-11-10 per *bisi* of the total measured area of 27,081 *bisis*. In 1815 the revenue was but Rs. 1,717 : this rose steadily to Rs. 2,558 in 1820, and Rs. 3,641 in 1843. In 1870 the demand was raised to Rs. 12,944.

GANGOLIHAT, *patti* BEL, *pargana* GANGOLI.

A village with a travellers' bungalow, with no khansaman, lying on the route from Almora to Pithoragarh, distant 34 miles north-east of Almora, 11 miles from Naini, the same from Bans, and about 18 miles from Pithoragarh, in latitude 29° 39′ 23″ and longitude 80° 5′ 21″, at an elevation of 5,580 feet above the level of the sea. The village itself is locally called Hat. It is reached from Bans by a steep descent to the Ramganga, which is crossed by an iron suspension bridge and leads to an equally steep ascent on the opposite side. The hills on either side are thickly clothed with pine forest, and present magnificent views of the lower hill scenery in the Himalaya, and though the road is tiring and hot, the scenery well repays the labour. There are only a few hamlets near the road. Close to the bungalow is a temple dedicated to Kali, the priests of which make the usual boast that the ground is ever moist with the blood of kids and buffaloes offered in sacrifice. The temple is, however, more remarkable for the grove of noble deodars within which it stands. Close by, to the south-west, are the remains of a few old temples and a masonry well bearing an inscription apparently of some age. From Naini to Hat the road following the Jageswar ridge, soon descends steeply to the Sarju river passing the village of Harara, which is a little below 4,000 feet. The lowest portion of the valley of the Sarju here is uninhabited. The river is crossed by a suspension bridge at an elevation of only 2,827 feet, and the climate and vegetation are therefore thoroughly tropical in their character. On the lower part of this descent, which faces the north and is very steep, and therefore sheltered from the sun, many brightly coloured wild flowers are to be found. In the valley convolvulaceae, wild gingers, and orchideae are common, the latter usually rather curious than beautiful. The Sarju is here a fine clear river flowing in a succession of still, deep pools and sparkling rapids over a bed of boulders. The ascent to Gangolihat is long and steep. The slope up which the road is taken has a southern aspect and is generally abrupt, open and grassy, and thinly clothed with pines. The horse chestnut, however, is common and is conspicuous with its abundant bloom of white flowers. *Lilium wallichianum*, the queen of lilies, is abundant on the open slopes ; it grows from four to six feet high, and bears enormous white flowers in August.

The population in, 1901 was 497.

GARBIYANG, *patti* BYANS, *pargana* DARMA.

The most important village in pargana Darma. It stands on a plateau by the side of the Kali river at an elevation of over 10,000 feet above the sea in latitude 30° 8′ north and longitude 80° 5′ east. At the entrance to the village is a stone formerly used as a whipping-post by the Tibetan Jongpen whose jurisdiction once extended over Bhot. The houses are two stories high, quaintly and closely studded with poles which have a religious significance. Garbiyang is used as a depôt for their Tibetan goods by the Dokpas. These are a Tibetan tribe who possess only yaks and big Tibetan sheep and therefore do not descend lower than 10,000 feet for fear of endangering the health of these animals which are so accustomed to the rarefied air that they die when brought out of it. The grain, wrapped in birch bark against the damp, is buried in holes in the ground. Garbiyang was until recently the summer head quarters of the Political Peshkar and the Political Deputy Collector now transferred to Pithoragarh. It is the duty of these officers to facilitate trade generally and particularly to watch the interests of the Bhotia merchants, from whom they collect the dues paid from time immemorial to the Tibetans. Garbiyang also contains a fairly flourishing school.

GORI RIVER.

The Gori, Goriganga, or white river, is one of the most considerable feeders of the Kali, and takes its rise in patti Malla Johar, in latitude 30° 23′ north, and longitude 80° 10′ east. The river springs from two branches, that known as the Gunka or Gankha on the east, and the Gori proper on the west. The latter rises in an immense glacier, lying to the north-west of Milam, and divided from the glaciers that give rise to the Gunka by a considerable spur running south from the Muta Dhura ridge, by which the pass of that name leads to Tibet.

This glacier was visited by Weller, and is thus described by him :—" The river comes out in a small impetuous stream, at the foot of apparently a mass of dirt and gravel, some 300 feet high, shaped like a half-moon. This is in reality a mass of dark-coloured ice (bottle-green colour), extending westward to a great distance, and covered with stones and fragments of rock, which in fact form a succession of small hills. I went along this scene of desolation for a long space, but could not nearly reach the end. Here and there were circular and irregularly-shaped craters (as it were), from 50 to 500 feet diameter at top, and some of them 150 feet deep. The ice was frequently visible on the sides; and at the bottom was a dirty sea-green-coloured pool of water, apparently very deep. Into one of these craters I rolled down numerous large stones from off the edge, and in a few seconds huge masses of ice rose from below, seemingly detached by the agitation of the water. The bases of the hills on either side and frequently far up their faces are one succession of landslips."

He adds that the source of the Gori was formerly opposite Milam, and a Bhotiya told him that within his memory the snow-bed had receded some three to four hundred yards in forty years.

"Webb found the stream at its exit from the glacier twenty-eight feet wide and four deep, and from its coldness and great rapidity altogether unfordable. There is no passage up the gorge beyond the glacier. The elevation above the sea of the point of emergence from the glacier is, by barometer, 11,543 feet. The great accumulation of snow in the gorge results from the fall of avalanches, which Webb observed to cause in a few days an increase in the thickness of the stratum of upwards of forty feet. Hence notwithstanding the extraordinary rapidity of the stream resulting from a fall in some parts of its bed of 800 feet per mile, the river is overlaid with deep snow for a considerable distance below its source. It first takes a south-easterly direction for four miles, to its confluence with the Gankha a little below Milam. Though the Gankha has a greater length of course by about twelve or fourteen miles and a greater volume of water at all seasons than the Gori, the latter gives its name to the united stream. For some miles below the confluence the stream varies in width from twelve to twenty yards, and runs with such extraordinary violence and rapidity, as in many places to resemble a cascade tumbling down a rugged face of rocks; in others it is hid below a continuous mass of ice and snow. In forty miles, the declivity of the waterway is 6,599 feet, or upwards of 160 in a mile. In receives on the right and left many torrents, none very considerable; and, continuing its course in a southerly direction, so as totally to run about sixty miles, falls into the Kali on the right bank immediately below Askot in north latitude 29° 45′ 9″ and east longitude 80° 25′, at an elevation of 2,127 feet above the level of the sea and with a breadth of about 110 feet."

The road from Milam to Mansiari and thence to Askot follows closely the course of the river. Some distance up the glen of the Gori river above Milam is the Sunchi-kund, a small sheet of water held in great repute as a place of pilgrimage. It consists of a small triangular-shaped piece of greenish water perhaps 100 yards by 80 in area. The fissures in the banks of the Gori here are narrow instead of being crater-like; and the ice where visible is more of the colour of snow. On the south side large accumulations of gravel are to be seen in the openings between the hills; and generally the sides of the hills in the vicinity do not appear so much cut up by landslips as lower down.

GUMTI RIVER.

This river rises in patti Pindarwar of pargana Badhan in Garhwal. A southern branch has its origin in the Birchuwa peaks and Gadwalbunga in Malla Katyur of Danpur. These unite close below Baijnath in latitude 29° 54′ 24″ and longitude 79° 39′ 28″, and flowing through the Katyur valley join the Sarju on its right bank at Bageswar in latitude 29° 50′ 15″ and longitude 79° 48′ 52″ at an elevation of 3,143 feet above the level of the sea. The elevation at Baijnath is 3,545 feet. The valleys of the branches and the main stream are wide and fertile and support many villages and tea factories. The road between Baijnath and Bageswar follows the left bank of the Gumti and the road from Almora viâ Someswar to Karanprayag crosses this river near Baijnath and passes up the valley of one of the feeders of its northern branch.

HASTINGS, *patti* SUI BISUNG, *pargana* KALI KUMAON.

Fort Hastings or Kotalgarh lies about four miles west of Lohaghat on a ridge at the entrance of the valley at a height of 6,327 feet. It occupies a steep knoll 150 to 200 feet above the general level of the mountain, separated by a deep neck from a plateau north-east by east, on which stood an outpost called Raunj, from which Kotalgarh could be easily battered. The area of the fort is about eighty yards north and south and twelve or fourteen east to west, surrounded by a good stone wall eight to ten feet high and five feet thick. The fort was intended to command the fertile valley of Bisung to the south and west, but has been abandoned for a very long time.

Madden writes:—"Kotalgarh is fabled to have been the stronghold of the arrow-demon Banasur Daitya, the son of Mahabali, who fought with Vishnu and his Suras and prevailed not, though the conflict was long and doubtful. No sooner was a Daitya slain, and his blood poured on the ground, than it produced a hundred others, so that the greater the slaughter of the enemies, the further were the gods from victory. In this difficulty, Mahakali was created, like Pandora, by general donations from the celestials, and by her were the giants at length exterminated. Among those who fell by her hand was Kottavi, the mother of Banasur, who with a coat of mail over her bust, and naked from the waist downwards, fought like an Amazon on the battlements, which are said to derive their name from her exploits and appearance, Kotalgarh being interpreted by 'the fortress, the abode of the naked woman.' The received traditions of India locate Mahabalipur on the Coromandel shore below Madras, and Banasur still further south near Devicotta; the learned pandits of Kumaon, however, locate all these wonders at and around Lohaghat, and affirm that Sui is no other than Sonitpur, 'the red city,' of the Puranas, the abode of Banasur. The peculiarities of the soil at and around Lohaghat explain the mystery. On removing the sod, in some places a blue, but far more generally a deep-red ferruginous clay is found to form the soil, and to this the people appeal as ocular demonstration of the legend: it owes its colour to nothing else than the blood of the gaints. During the rainy season, the Lohu or 'blood' river is similarly discoloured, and hence the name of the station."

For another legend regarding the origin of the name of the river the reader is referred to the article Lohaghat.

HAWALBAGH *patti* TALLA SYUNARA, *pargana* BARAH-MANDAL.

A hamlet six miles north of Almora, situated on the banks of the Kosi, at an elevation of 3,920 feet above the sea. A bridle road connects Almora directly with Hawalbagh, and crosses the river by an iron suspension bridge, leading to the cart roads from Almora to Ranikhet and from Almora to Baijnath, which unite opposite Hawalbagh. From this point too the road to Dwarahat and Garhwal via Bhainskhet takes off, and also the bridle road to Ranikhet.

Hawalbagh was formerly the head quarters of the civil administration and of the civil force known as the Kumaon local battalion, now the 3rd Gurkhas, which was relieved of civil duties in 1839. It was also the site of the principal tea gardens when that industry commenced under government auspices. The site is fine and picturesque, but much warmer than Almora. Tea is grown and there are still one or two European bungalows standing, though no Europeans live there. The old mess-house surrounded by magnificent cypresses and deodars is now used as a dâk bungalow. There is also a village school, and the Almora Golf Club has a course adjacent. The population in 1901 was 165.

JOHAR *pargana, peshkari* SHOR.

A large pargana in the Almora tahsil with a length of about 65 miles and a breadth of 24 miles. On the south it is bounded by parganas Sira and Askot, on the east by Tibet and pargana Darma; on the west the eastern Ramganga flows between it and Danpur and the boundary is continued by the chain of snowy peaks extending northwards from Nandakot; beyond this barrier lies the Painkhanda pargana of Garhwal. The northern boundary is Tibet. The range traversed by the Untadhura pass extends from east to west across the north of the pargana and separates the basin of the Girthi river flowing north-west into Garhwal from that of the Gori flowing almost due south. The region to the north of the pass is for the greater part of the year ice-bound and desolate and is used only by the Bhotias making their trade excursions into Tibet by the Balchha and Shelsel passes. South of the Untadhura pass rises the eastern branch of the Gori, whose headwaters are principally fed from glaciers lying at each side of the Bhotia road to that pass. The western branch rises in the great glacier lying to the north-west of Milam, and both unite below Milam to form the Gori. Glacier streams descend from Nanda Devi and the Laspa torrent from Nandakot and join the Gori on the right bank.

On the left bank, the most considerable feeder is the Ralam river, which rushing between the Hansaling (18,100 feet) and Dhansi (18,200 feet) peaks joins it below Bagdwar. The Gori thence continues on a south-south-easterly course until it falls into the Kali river near Askot. The main road into Johar branches off from the Pindari glacier route at Kharbagar above Kapikot, and proceeds by Ramari on the Ramganga across the Kalmundi range to Surhing and Lilam. Thence it follows the valley of the Gori-ganga. From Surhing another road drops down the river to Askot. A cross-road from Mawani-Dawani rises from the Gori to the ridge above the right bank of that river and drops down the Bajgara valley to Nachni on the road joining Tejam and Thal in pargana Sira. There are also three or four minor tracks used by occasional travellers and by the Bhotias in their annual migrations.

Johar is divided into three pattis; of these Malla Johar extends from the Tibetan border down the Gori valley as far as its junction with the Ralam river. The fifteen villages comprised within the boundaries of the Malla Johar patti lie with one exception in the narrow gorge occupied by the upper course of the Gori river. The northernmost village of all is Milam and further south again is Laspa and east of Laspa is Ralam in a side valley through which flows the Ralam river. With the exception of the tract of comparatively low elevation near the banks of the Gori and the Ralam, the whole of the Malla Johar patti is a waste of glacier and snow-crowned mountains. Tremendous ranges enclose the valley on each side. To the east rises the chain of peaks which separates the pargana from Darma and culminates in the noble group called Panchachuli; to the south-west the horizon is dominated by the superb mass of Nanda Devi and Nandakot, the former of which is the highest mountain in the British Empire. Malla Johar is inhabited by the Bhotias and their Dom servants. Their villages are for the greater part above the limit of cultivation and even in some cases of trees. What little agriculture exists is of negligible value. The people subsist on their trade between Tibet and the plains.

All the villages are situated at elevations exceeding 10,000 feet, to the north of the great snowy peaks and between them and the line of water parting which forms the boundary towards

Tibet. During the winter the whole of the valley is blocked with snow and the villages are abandoned. The Bhotias move down to their winter houses or encampments in patti Goriphat where the fine slope of the Kalamundi range as far as the Gori river is occupied by the villages of Surhing, Gorpata, Darati and Darkot which together form the tract known as Munsiari, the principal trade depôt between the passes and the plains. Most of the Bhotias possess one and some two good houses outside the pass and they have succeeded in acquiring a large proprietary share in the villages where they sojourn. It may therefore justly be inferred that they form one of the wealthiest classes in the district.

Talla Des and Goriphat occupy the tract to the south of Malla Johar. Up to the settlement of 1872 they were both contained in the old sub-division called Talla Johar. They are separated by the water parting ridge between the basins of the eastern Ramganga and the Gori. Goriphat, as its name suggests, comprises the valley of the Gori to the east, and Talla Des lies between the central ridge and the Ramganga. The inhabitants are in the main ordinary Khasiyas but a few non-trading Jethora Bhotias hold a fair number of villages. They are a poor and unenterprising race when compared with their relatives in the passes, by whom they are often employed as drovers. The tract is fertile though somewhat wilder and more thickly wooded than the central pattis of the district, and more remote from the markets. The main kharif crop is *mandua*, and a little rice is also grown in the warmer villages. Namik however which lies near the snow-capped heights at the head of the Ramganga river and some other villages similarly situated produce only one crop in the year. Agriculture is in these northern villages a somewhat precarious pursuit, their proximity to the snow rendering them liable to damage from sudden hailstorms. The people are however pastoral as much as agricultural, and make much of their income by breeding pack animals for the Bhotias. "The pasture on the ranges adjoining to the Himalaya," writes Traill "is found in a peculiar degree nutritive to sheep ; on the melting of the winter snows, towards the end of March, these mountains which though lofty are by no means precipitous, become covered with verdure, and are then resorted to by the flocks of the neighbourhood." The Joharis produce more grain than they need for their own consumption, and the lack of markets is not of great moment for they readily exchange their grain to the Bhotias for salt, or sell it to them for cash.*

The pattis of Johar are, like those of the rest of the district, assessed to revenue on their general capabilities. In 1815 the pargana was assessed at Rs. 4,842, rising to Rs. 5,140 in 1817, and Rs. 5,051 in 1819. The settlement of 1820 was made on the basis of cultivation and trade was taxed separately. The demand was Rs. 2,633, rising to Rs. 3,382 in 1823. It remained approximately at this figure in the settlements of 1828, 1833 and 1843. At Mr. Beckett's settlement of 1872 the demand was raised to Rs. 5,975. And the result of the current settlement was an initial demand of Rs. 7,329, rising in five years to Rs. 7,649, and after five years more to the maximum of Rs. 7,790. There are now 108 villages in all, with a total population in 1901 of 12,805 persons. Of these 6,416 were males and 6,389 females.

KALAPANI, *patti* BYANS, *pargana* DARMA.

A remarkable collection of springs regarded as sacred by the Indians and erroneously considered by them as the source of the Kali river, though the headwaters of the the latter lie 30 miles further north-west. The springs are in fact unimportant tributaries. They take their rise on the north-eastern declivity of the peak known as Byans-Rikhi. 45 miles north-east of Askot in latitude 30° 14′ and longitude 80° 56′, at an elevation of 14,220 feet above the level of the sea. Their waters are discharged into a stream flowing a few hundred feet to the west which bears the name of Kalapani river. This river is formed by the union of two streams—one rising close to the western entrance of the Lipulekh pass and the other on the western declivity of the great Kuntas peak. The united stream flows five miles south-westward to its confluence with the Kuthi river, henceforth called the Kali, in latitude 30° 11′ and longitude 80° 54′ at an elevation above the sea of 14,413 feet and only about 150 feet below the limit of perpetual snow. The spring is visited by

* Assessment report; J. C. Smith

travellers passing to Mansarowar. The drainage area of the Kalapani lies wholly within British territory, but a short way below the springs the Kali forms the boundary with Nepal.

KALI RIVER.

This, the largest river of Kumaon, is known on leaving the hills as the Sarda and lower down as the Sarju or Ghagra to its confluence with the Ganges at the eastern extremity of the Ballia district. It has two headwaters : the Kalapani (*q. v.*) to the east, takes its rise in the southern slopes of the ridge crossed by the Lipulekh pass into Tibet; the western branch, which has the longest course and the largest volume, is known as the Kuthi-Yankti (*q. v.*). The latter has its rise in the glaciers lying along the upper portions of the patti of Byans from the foot of the passes of Mankshang or Mangsha and Lanpiya leading into Tibet. From a little below Kalapani encamping ground southwards the Kali forms the boundary with Nepal. From the confluence with the Kalapani the united stream has a southerly course for a few miles to Garbiyang and then bends to the south-west, in which direction it continues to flow twenty-three miles further to the confluence with the Dhauli (*q. v.*) on its right bank near Titalakot in Darma. The Kali above the junction is a roaring torrent carrying twice the volume of the Dhali. Its surface is broken into cataracts by the huge boulders that interrupt its course, and in places it is spanned by natural bridges formed by rocks wedged together by their own weight and resting on the flanking precipices of the river gorge. In many places the stream for considerable distances is totally hidden under glaciers. Below the confluence the stream is thirty yards wide; but, swollen by numerous mountain streams received right and left, it soon attains a width of eighty yards. It continues to flow in a south-westerly direction, and twenty-two miles lower down, or seventy-five from its source, it receives on its right bank the Gori or Goriganga, a river equal in size to itself. This confluence is in latitude 29° 45′ 8″, longitude 80° 25′ 0″, and is 2,127 feet above the sea. Twelve miles below this place and eighty-seven miles from its source the Kali receives on its left bank from Nepal, the Chamliya, and three miles lower down, at the Jhula-ghat, the elevation of the water's edge is 1,789 feet. Sixteen miles below this, at Pacheswar, the Kali receives the Sarju, the greatest of its feeders. At Pacheswar it turns a little to the south-east, and ten miles lower down, on the right bank, receives the Lohaghat river, two miles below the confluence of which a large tributary from Nepal flows in on the left. Turning southwards at that point, it, at a distance of eighteen miles beyond, receives on the right the Ladhiya in patti Pal Belon, a considerable stream. By all these accessions it becomes a great river, and at Barmdeo, twelve miles lower down, in latitude 29° 6′ 30″, longitude 80° 13′ 37″, and 148 miles from its source, it enters the plaint of Hindustan, about 800 feet above the sea. Henceforth it is known as the Sarda.

KALI KUMAON *pargana, tahsil* CHAMPAWAT.

This is one of the largest parganas in the district and occupies its south-eastern corner, being separated from Nepal by the Kali or Sarda river from the confluence of the Sarju and Kali at Pacheswar as far south as the last range of hills above the commencement of the level plain of the Bhabar. It is bounded on the north by the Sarju and Panar rivers which unite half-way along the northern boundary. On the south a chain of hills which descend with precipitous steepness to the Bhabar marks the boundaries of the pargana. On the west there is no clear natural boundary. For a short distance Pal Belon and Talli Rau are divided from Chaugarh of the Naini Tal district by the high range which flanks the left bank of the Ladhiya river, but with this exception the boundary is purely artificial, extending in an irregular line to the western slopes of Devi Dhura and thence almost due north to the Panar river. The pargana consists of fifteen pattis :—Chalsi, Regruban, Gumdes, Talla Des, Malla and Talla Pal Belon, Talli Rau, Sipti, Assi, Pharka, Gangol, Sui Bisung, Khilpatiphat and Malla and Talla Charal. There are ten patwaris, some of the smaller pattis being grouped together.

Besides the rivers that form the boundaries on the east and north, there are two other considerable streams in the pargana.

The most important of these is the Ladhiya which flows from west to east through the southern portion of the pargana, rising in pargana Dhyani Rau of Naini Tal and falling into the Kali about six miles before that river enters the Bhabar. The principal tributary of the Ladhiya is the Kuirala which drains Sipti and the northern portion of Talla Pal Belon. The other stream is the Lohaghat river or Lohavati, which rises in the elevated tableland of Sui Bisung and joins the Kali about half-way down the eastern boundary.

The principal characteristic of the pargana is an elevated stretch of undulating downs in the centre extending from Assi on the west to Gumdes on the east and comprising the pattis of Pharka, Sui Bisung, the two Charals, and portions of Gangol. From the north the ascent to this plateau is fairly gradual, through irregular ridges running up from the Panar in Chalsi, Gangol and Regruban; but from Rameswar eastward the Sarju is hemmed in by steep cliffs clothed with chir forests. The banks of the Kali are similarly characterized by sheer precipices of great height, broken by small and steep ravines. South of the central ridge in which the plateau terminates the country is wild and irregular as far as the Ladhiya river. South of this again there is a completely separate chain of hills covered with dense forests. The outer fringe of the pargana is in every direction well wooded, as is also the central ridge where oak and rhododendron abound, the lower spurs being covered with excellent pine forest. In the northern half the groves of deodar are a most striking feature in the landscape; they have been planted in most cases round some temple and in some instances can be almost described as extensive forest. The chief town is Champawat, the site of the old Chand capital, in the centre of the pargana. It is the head quarters of the tahsil of that name. The market is small and decaying but there is some trade in grain and cloth. Lohaghat was of considerable importance while it remained a cantonment, but it is now nothing but a small bazar. Both of these places are deserted during the cold weather when the people migrate to Tanakpur where most of them have shops. The main road in the pargana is that leading from Almora to Champawat and on to Tanakpur. From Champawat another road leads north through Lohaghat to Pithoragarh and Bhot. The former passes through Devi Dhura and Dhunaghat, whence a loop line leads to Lohaghat. From Champawat a road goes south to Deori bungalow and crosses the Ladhiya: the bridge at Chalthi has now been dismantled as unsafe. This road has always been precarious owing to the steep inclines and the floods on the Ladhiya, but is now being realigned, and a new bridge will be built. On this account there are two relinquished roads between the river and Champawat, large portions of which have been entirely destroyed by the river. In 1896 a famine road was made from Dhunaghat through Assi and Talli Rau to Chorgalia in the Bhabar; it has however, though of obvious utility, been allowed to fall into disrepair.

The people inhabiting the central plateau regularly leave their hill homes after the Dasahra and repair to the Talla Des Bhabar where they cultivate clearings in the forest and reap the benefit of the abundant grazing. Many of them are engaged in trade, dealing in cloth, chillies and turmeric with the banias of Tanakpur. This migration has a depressing effect upon the cultivation of the tract. The soil of the central plateau has a good loam, free from stone, with gentle slopes, and ample irrigation, yet the standard of cultivation is much lower and the class of crops raised is much inferior to that of the less favoured pattis. In Sui Bisung however, such is the natural fertility of the soil, that not even neglect prevents the crops from being almost the best in the district. The people of the wilder pattis do not as a rule migrate, but they have two distinct blocks of cultivation belonging to the village, one in the upland portion where they reside in the hot weather, while the other consists of land deep in the beds of the large rivers where turmeric and chillies are grown. The staple crops as everywhere throughout the district are mandua, mandira and rice in the kharif with barley and wheat in the rabi. The characteristic agricultural feature of Kali Kumaon is however the cultivation of turmeric, and, to some extent, chillies and ginger. All the pattis which lie on the outer ranges towards the Bhabar and have low-lying fields in the deep river valleys depend mainly on turmeric for the payment of their revenue. Ginger is not generally grown, but certain villages of Regruban have a reputation for producing the root in large quantities. Chillies are everywhere produced and usually go with turmeric. Other special crops are *pinalu*, *methi*, *dhania* and potatoes. There are several tea gardens in Kali Kumaon but at the present time they are almost abandoned, the planters having taken to growing potatoes and fruit in place of tea.

The inhabitants of the pargana rarely rely entirely on agriculture for their support. They are born traders and every man's ambition is to acquire a small store and set up a way-side shop. Many make a fair income by working in the forests at the foot of the hills, the poorer as coolies and the well-to-do as contractors. Or they keep cattle which they graze in the forests, and produce *ghi* for the Tanakpur market. Others again seek the service of the Tharus of the Bhabar for whom they thresh grain or hull rice.

Nearly all the land is cultivated by the *hissedars* themselves the remainder being given to *sirtans* who pay to the owner the government demand *plus* a percentage as malikana. The bulk of the people are so-called Rajputs: there are a few leading clans—Boras, Tarragis, Karkis and Chaudhris—who have considerable influence and are descendants of the old officers of the Chand Rajas. The remainder are small cultivators, usually taking their caste name from that of the village. Besides these there are a few Brahmans of an inferior class; and the Luls in Talla Pal Belon and Naiks in Kilpati and Rawal. One village, Khun Malak in Malla Charal, belongs to Muhammadan Manihars, who were settled here in the time of the Chands. The total population at the census of 1900-1 numbered 50,455. The total cultivated area of the tract comprises 41,515 *bisis* showing an increase of 6,206 *bisis* since the settlement of 1870. The land revenue now stands at Rs. 37,548 with an incidence per *bisi* of second class upraon land of Re. 0-12-5. At the first settlement of Kali Kumaon in 1815 the revenue was Rs. 8,960; in 1817 it was increased to Rs. 9,764 and in the following year to Rs. 10,967. In 1820 there was a further rise to Rs. 12,248. The standard of progression was maintained at the succeeding settlement of 1823 when the demand was fixed at Rs. 14,152.

In 1828 there was a drop to Rs. 13,363, followed again by an increase in 1833 to Rs. 15,555. The assessment remained practically unchanged till 1870 when Kali Kumaon was assessed by Mr. Beckett at Rs. 25,873.*

There are schools at Barakot, Chaini and Regru in Regruban, at Dyartoli in Sipti, at Karankarayat in Sui Bisung, at Tamli in Talla Des, at Khaten in Khilpatiphat, at Champawat in Talla Charal, and at Khetikhan and Jankande in Gangol.

The name Kali Kumaon means Kumaon along the Kali river, the word being a corruption of Kurmachal, the old name of Kanadeo, a peak in patti Charal. Here according to the tradition Vishnu dwelt for three years in the tortoise *avatar*. Kali Kumaon was the original principality of the Sombansi Chands, destined in the course of time to extend their kingdom from the Kali to the Ganges.

KALIMAT, *patti* KHASPARJA, *pargana* BARAHMANDAL.

Kalimat or Kalmattya is an eminence four miles north of Almora, in latitude 29° 38′ 32″ and longitude 79° 42′ 13″ attaining an elevation of 6,414 feet. The name Kalimat, or black earth, is derived from the colour of the clay, which consists of an impure plumbago. It is the Kashaya of the Manasa-khanda of the Skanda Purana: hence the name Kashar still applied to it. The hill slopes down to the Kosi on its left bank and to the north-east is connected by a ridge with Binsar. To the east are the dark ranges of Binsar and Jageswar, to the south and south-west the lofty Gagar excludes the plains and from north-east to north-west extends the snowy range. The Gurkhas had a stockade here during their possession of Kumaon. Under the rajas it contained the depôt for iron and tools, and the story runs that Sri Ballabh Upadhiya lived here, and, not being able to procure wood, took some iron from the Raja's stores, with which he lighted his fire and cooked his food. The ashes remain and make the hill black. Sri Ballabh was called, in consequence of the above exploit, Loh-humi, the iron-burner; hence the caste name Lohani borne by his descendants. He received in *muafi* the villages of Lohana, Satrali and Khulna. Here

* Assessment report; J. E. Goudge.

he again displayed his supernatural powers: for his wife being tired with carrying water for the service of the family god bore the vessel on her head which rendered it impure. Sri Ballabh then asked the idol to create a spring which at once burst forth, but the wife, calling out in astonishment, destroyed nine-tenths of its volume and only one-tenth of the intended supply now remains in the Upadhiya *dhara*.

KAPKOT, *patti* TALLA DANPUR, *pargana* DANPUR.

A village and a halting place, with traveller's bungalow, on the route to the Pindari glacier, 14 miles beyond Bageswar, 40 miles from Almora, and 9 miles from Loharkhet or Lwarkhet, the next stage. The bungalow has no khansaman, but supplies may be obtained from the bania's shop. It stands in a level valley surrounded by hills and near the Sarju river which flows in a semicircular course round the eastern edge of the valley. A short distance about Kapkot is Kharbagar, where a road branches off to Tejam and Munsiari. The road from Bageswar runs along the right bank of the Sarju river, crossing the Lahor and Kanal rivers by bridges. It is generally undulating and easy, and from its low elevation often uncomfortably hot. There are no important villages along the road. Above Kapkot the road crosses to the left bank by a suspension bridge, and at Kharbagar there is another wooden bridge crossing a tributary stream of the Sarju. Along the south bank of this stream passes the road to Tejam. Further north the Pindari road again crosses the Sarju to the right bank, and remains on that side all the way to Loharkhet.

KHATI, *patti* MALLA DANPUR, *pargana* DANPUR.

A village and a halting-place, with a traveller's bungalow, between Dhakuri and Dwali on the road to the Pindari glacier. The bungalow stands above the left bank of the Pindar river. It is distant six miles from Dwali, seven miles from Dhakuri, and 64 miles from Almora. There is no khansaman at the bungalow, and supplies should be obtained from the bania's shop at Loharkhet. It stands at an elevation of 7,200 feet, in an open valley, where there is some scanty cultivation of *mandua* and *chuwa*. The village is small and scattered.

KOSI RIVER.

The Kosi, Kosila or Kaushalya, a river rising in patti Boraräu Palla of pargana Baramandal in latitude 29° 50′ and longtitude 79° 35′ is fed from the streams collecting along the eastern slopes of the high chain of hills in that patti comprising Birchuwa (8,427 feet); Gopalkot (9,050); Bhatkot (9,086) and Burha Pinnath and the northern declivity of Milkali (7,470 feet). On the east, the range containing the Kausani tea plantation forms the watershed between the Kosi and the Gumti, a tributary of the Sarju and eventually of the Kali on the extreme east, while the Kosi joins the Ramganga and eventually the Ganges on the extreme west. The Kosi forms a considerable stream by the time it reaches the broad valley at Someswar in latitude 29° 46′ 40″ and longitude 79° 38″ 55′ at an elevation of about 4,500 feet above the level of the sea. Here it receives the drainage of the southern declivities of Bhatkot and Milkali on the right bank and another stream on the left bank. It has a course hence of about twelve miles in a south-easterly direction through the Talla Syunara patti to Hawalbagh where it is crossed by an iron suspension bridge carrying the Almora road. In this course it receives numerous mountain torrents on either side, and has a fall of about 1,000 feet. Below Hawalbagh it is joined on the right bank by the Nana Kosi which drains the valley traversed by the bridle road from Almora to Ranikhet and is also crossed by a bridge on the cart-road. Hence the course inclines to the south-west, winding along the western declivity of Kalimat and the hill on which Almora is built, and finding an exit between the eastern base of Siyahi Devi (7,186 feet) and the south-western prolongation of the Almora ridge at Chaunsila, it receives the Sual on its left bank. Previously to its confluence with the Sual it is twenty-six yards wide with a rough bed of large stones, and fordable, being only twenty inches deep in the cold weather. At this point where the elevation above the sea is about 3,300 feet it takes a course generally west by Khairna, receiving on the right bank the Ulabagar and Kuchgadh streams from pargana Phaldakot. At Bujan the elevation above the sea is 2,862 feet. The course continues thence more decidedly west and for a portion of the way north-west to Mohan where the elevation is 1,586 feet above the level of the sea. Hence it turns abruptly to the south-east and subsequently south by Dhikuli, entering the plains at Ramnagar in latitude 29° 23″ 34′ and longitude 79° 10″ 8′ with an elevation of 1,204 feet above the level of the sea. In the latter part of its course the river runs rapidly over boulders and forms deep pools and eddies. In many places however the bed is of gravel and the stream shallow and fordable.

KUPHINI RIVER.

The Kuphini or Kushini is a feeder of the Pindar river, rising in a glacier amid the south-eastern recesses of the Nandakot peak, and uniting with the Pindar just below the bungalow at Dwali (*q. v.*), in latitude 30° 10′ 35″ and longitude 80° 2′ 10″. At the confluence the united stream in the rains is of a dirty milk colour, and the bed is obstructed by some great boulders. The two rivers are separated by a ridge culminating in a peak having an elevation of 17,130 feet. The left bank of the Kuphini is formed by the Kotela ridge, the summit of which (14,515 feet), far above the forest region, commands the Pindar to its source and communicates by a goat path with the Dhakuri pass.

KUTHI YANKTI RIVER.

This, the longest and most important branch of the Kali river, takes its rise in a small glacier at the southern base of the Lunpiya-lekh pass from patti Malla Darma into Tibet in north latitude 30° 28′ and east longitude 80° 38′. This spot was visited by Webb, and is thus described by him: "The river, two furlongs distant, its breadth reduced to four or five yards: at two and a quarter miles in a north-west direction, it is covered with snow, and no longer to be traced; neither is the road passable beyond this point at the present season. After the middle of July, when the thaw is perfected, it may be traced as a small stream for about four miles more, in the direction last mentioned, and from thence to its head in the snow, north-west two miles further. The stream scarcely flows in winter, being derived almost exclusively from the thawing snow." The Lanpiya-lekh pass itself has an elevation of 18,150 feet. The river takes a south-easterly direction through the Byans valley to its junction with the Kali, thirty miles from its source. It receives numerous snow-fed torrents on both banks, passing by the encamping-grounds of Walshiya, Jhamathi, Rarab, Jolinka, Sangchuma and Kuthi, whence it derives its name. To the right and left of the Kuthi Yankti there are peaks over 20,000 feet high and the entire valley is bordered by glaciers from which torrents flow into the river. At the confluence the Kali has a bed 150 yards wide; but a mile further up, the stream in September is all but fordable. The Kuthi river is a third larger than the eastern branch, both in size of channel and volume of water, and nearly four times the length from source to confluence; notwithstanding which the eastern and smaller branch has given its name to the united river. The Gyukdhura pass from Sela of Darma to Kuthi in Byans up the Pechko-Yankti and by the Chachingti encamping ground is still used, though difficult.

LADHIYA RIVER.

A tributary of the Kali that takes its rise in patti Malli Rau of the Naini Tal district on the southern slopes of the range along which passes the road from Dol to Devi Dhura. It holds a south-easterly course through Chaubhainsi, Talli Rau, Pal Belon and Talla Des to its junction with the Kali on the right bank in north latitude 29° 13′ and east longitude 80° 18″. Its only considerable affluents are the Ratiyagadh which joins it on the left bank near Chaura in Talli Rau and the Kuirala river which joins it on the same bank in Pal Belon. A much frequented road to the Bhabar crosses the Ladhiya at Chalthi and goes thence by Bastiya to Tanakpur in the Bhabar. Lower down the Ladhiya is joined by the Babkola river, also on the left bank. There are considerable tracts of good irrigated land all along its course and the courses of its tributaries which yield rice of excellent quality, but since the floods of 1880 these have suffered much from diluvion.

LIPU-LEKH, *patti* BYANS, *pargana* DARMA.

The most eastern pass from Almora to Tibet, in latitude 30° 13′ 49″ and longitude 81° 4′ 50″, at an elevation of 16,780 feet above the level of the sea. It lies in the extreme north-east of the district, the road branching off from the valley of the Kuthi-Yankti at Changru, and continuing along the Kali to Kalapani and Sangcha, where the steep ascent begins. From Sangcha the way lies across a snow-field in the hollow between two projecting ridges: then over a gentle slope where the going is usually difficult, owing to the soft snow. Then the glacier is reached, and over this the road passes with an easy gradient to the summit of the pass.

LOHAGHAT, *patti* REGRUBAN, *pargana* KALI KUMAON.

Lohaghat is a village and an old military cantonment. It is sometimes spelt Lohughat and the name is then said to recall a bloody fight in the neighbourhood. The local legend relates that a number of Brahmans were for some offence put in chains by one of the Chand Rajas and incarcerated in an old temple near the stream. One morning they obtained permission to perform their ablutions in the stream and afterwards proceeded to dry their hands in the warmth of a fire. Some mysterious property in the water of the stream caused their chains to melt and they escaped. The name of the stream then became Loha-batti—the "iron-torch"—and that of the village at the ford of the stream Loha-batti-ghat, shortened in the hill fashion to Loha-ghat. It is situated six miles north of Champawat, 15 miles from the Nepal frontier and 53 miles east from Almora, in latitude 29° 24′ 2″ north, and longitude 80° 7′ 53″ east at an elevation of 5,510 feet above the sea. The place stands in a pleasant tract of grassy undulating ground sprinkled with deodars. The cantonment used to be garrisoned by the 3rd Gurkhas. It has however long been abandoned, partly owing to the difficulty of obtaining supplies, but chiefly because the necessity for maintaining an outpost on the Nepal border had disappeared. For many years after its abandonment it continued under the charge of the military department and it was not until some eight or nine years ago that the buildings were handed over to the district authorities. There are tea gardens at Lohaghat and Raikot and one belonging to Major Hennessey between these two places, but they are somewhat remote from the markets.

Lohaghat used to be the centre of a small European population but it is now dwindling. The Pithoragarh mission maintain a school here.

MAJKHALI, *patti* DWARSYUN, *pargana* BARAHMANDAL.

A camping ground and dâk bungalow on the Almora-Ranikhet cart road, about 14 miles by the bridle path from the former place and 8 from the latter. It is connected with Bhainskhet to the north some 2½ miles away and the pilgrim way from Garhwal through Dwarahat used to pass through it, leaving the district at Kakarighat.

MARTOLI, *patti* MALLA JOHAR, *pargana* JOHAR.

A large Bhotia village, situated on a high spur above the right bank of the Gori river on the road from Munsiari to Milam. It is distant 9 miles from Milam, 21 miles from Munsiari and 96 miles from Almora. The latitude is 30° 21′ 15″, the longitude 80° 13′ 40″, and the elevation 11,070 feet. The houses are built close together on a small plateau. It is a bleak and desolate place, surrounded by snow mountains and swept by piercing icy winds, which blow almost unceasingly. The Lwal stream descends from the Lwal glacier to the west and joins the Gori near Martoli after flowing for some distance through an extraordinarily deep and narrow chasm. The country around is destitute of trees; but there are a few dwarf junipers, rhododendrons, and other Alpine shrubs, and during the brief summer, grasses and wild flowers flourish abundantly. Martoli is inhabited by Bhotias from June to September or October. For the rest of the year it is uninhabitable.

MASI, *patti* TALLA GIWAR, *pargana* PALI PACHHAON.

A village and encamping ground, on the left bank of the Ramganga river, at the junction of the road from Dwarahat to Pauri via Seraikhet, and the road from Ramnagar and Mohan to Ganai. It is distant 13 miles from Dwarahat, 7 miles from Ganai, and 11 miles from Bhikia Sen. Another road leads to Pali, the old tahsil head quarters. There is a suspension bridge here across the Ramganga and close to it, on the further side of the river, is a large and flourishing school. The population in 1901 was 661.

MILAM, *patti* MALLA JOHAR, *pargana* JOHAR.

The principal village of the patti, situated in latitude 30° 26′ north and longitude 80° 9′ east near the junction of the Gori and Gunka rivers, on the road leading from Almora to Tibet through the Untadhura pass. It lies at a distance of 13 miles from the pass, 30 miles from Munsiari, and 105 miles from Almora, at a height of 11,400 feet above the sea-level. The village lies at the foot of a mountain above the junction of the two rivers. The houses are strongly built of stones and roofed with heavy slates. Below the village towards the Gori is a considerable stretch of alluvial land which is carefully tilled every year, and produces fair crops of buck-wheat and barley during the brief summer season. The population of the village at the special census of 1900 amounted to 1,733, of whom 954 were males and 779 females. These are almost all Bhotias, who use Milam as a depôt for their trade with Tibet. The place is inhabited only from June to October, and for the rest of the year it is, in common with the whole valley of the upper Gori, entirely deserted. In the cold weather the villages are buried in deep snow, and the Bhotias migrate to the lower hills, journeying with their laden sheep and goats to all parts of Kumaon for the purposes of trade.

The climate of Milam is dry and bracing, but is rendered trying by the bitterly cold winds that blow for the greater part of almost every day. Grain can, it is said, be stored for 30 or 40 years at Milam without deteriorating. No pure drinking water is obtainable, the only source of supply being the Gori, which holds in suspension large quantities of glacial sediment.

The surrounding country is bleak and desolate, but possesses a peculiar grandeur of its own. Lofty snow mountains shut in the valley on every side. Waterfalls are numerous and many of them are of great beauty. There is no vegetation beyond a few dwarf shrubs and occasional patches of grass rendered brilliant by wild flowers during the few weeks of summer. The whole valley is excessively rocky and the rocks are of the most varied colours. A mile above Milam the Gori river issues from the great Milam glacier, a chalky, turbid torrent flowing from a dark tunnel of discoloured ice through a mass of rocky debris.

The road upwards from Milam to the Untadhura pass and Tibet is steep and difficult. The road downwards from Milam to Munsiari has been considerably improved of late years, but is still precipitous and rough in places. The Gori river is crossed in numerous places by temporary bridges. Avalanches and landslips frequently block the path, while from October to June or July the upper portions of the road are buried under deep snow. Travellers early in the season have to pick out tracks on the surface of the snow crossing and re-crossing the Gori river on snow bridges. The usual camping grounds between Milam and Munsiari are Rilkot, Bagudyar and Bui. There is a branch of the London Mission at Milam.

MUNSIARI, *patti* GORIPHAT, *pargana* JOHAR.

An important group of villages on the right bank of the Gori river and on the road between Almora and Milam. The distance from Almora is 75 miles, and from Milam 30 miles. The inhabitants are almost all Bhotias, most of whom migrate to Martoli, Milam and other villages of Malla Johar during the summer months. Munsiari is a depôt of Bhotia trade; the people are comfortable and prosperous; and the houses well and substantially built. In and near Munsiari is a considerable area of fertile arable land. The climate is mild and pleasant.

NAINI, *patti* DARUN, *pargana* CHAUGARKHA.

A village with a traveller's bungalow, without a khansaman on the road from Almora to Pithoragarh, in latitude 29° 39′ 12″ north and longitude 79° 58′ 8″ east, at an elevation of 5,159 feet above the sea. It lies at a distance of 26 miles from Almora, 11 miles from Panwanaula, 11½ miles from Gangoli Hat, and 29 miles from Pithoragarh. There is a bania's shop here. A short distance from Naini, at the head of a deep gorge, in the direction of Almora, stands the famous temple of Jageswar, with its two immense deodars in the outer courts.

The Chand Rajas used to be buried at Jageswar, and their Ranis became *sati* here. On the occasion of the cremation of a raja, a stone from the pyre used always to be sent to Pitrola near Champawat, and deposited there at the old pyre place of their family with great ceremony and sacrifices of male kids. This practice is still observed by the Almora and Kashipur families.

NIYO-DHURA or NEO-DHURA, *patti* Malla Darma, *pargxna* Darma.

A pass into Tibet, often known as the Darma pass, lying in north latitude 30° 27′ 10″ and east longitude 80° 35′, at an elevation of 18,510 feet above the level of the sea. It is much frequented by Bhotias following the route up the Dhauli valley, though considered more difficult than the adjacent pass to the east, the Lanpiya-lekh at the head of valley of the Kuthi-Yankti, as the glacier lies at the Tibet side of the pass. The road leaves the course of the Dhauli river at Dawa, whence it turns north-east to the pass. The Tibetans call the pass Nooi La or Shekhu La.

PALI or PALI PACHAON *pargana, peshkari* Pali.

The largest pargana in the district, leaving the snows out of consideration, the most densely populated and the most intensely cultivated. The total cultivated area is 108 square miles, and the total area including waste and forest may be estimated at 500 square miles. It is divided into nineteen pattis—Malla, Bichla and Talla Chaukot, Malla, Walla and Palla Giwar, Malla and Talla Kaklasaun, Walla and Palla Naya, Malla, Bichla and Talla Dora, Malla and Talla Silor, Malla, Talla, Walla and Palla Salt. It occupies the south-west corner of the district and marches with Garhwal on the north and west and with Naini Tal on the south; on the east it is bounded by parganas Danpur, Barahmandal and Phaldakot. The interior hills as a rule are low and the slopes easy, but chains of greater elevation mark the boundaries. East of the Giwars is the huge mass of the Bhatkot, Gopalkot and Pinnath mountains rising to 9,000 feet, a portion of one of the main watersheds in the Kumaon Himalayas, here dividing the valley of the western Ramganga from those of the Pindar and Gumti rivers. This range falls through Dunagiri and Dwarahat into the low bare hills of the three Doras which lie between the waters of the Gagas and Ramganga rivers. The Bhatkot range is broken by the Ramganga river, west of which another high chain runs into the Garhwal district. A spur of this chain called the Jaurasi ridge runs down to the south-east forming the water-parting between the Ramganga and the Banau rivers. From Pandwakhal at the head of the Khetsar glen a fine range sweeps round the north-west corner of the pargana as far as Saraikhet where it divides into two lofty ridges which enclose the tract of Chaukot called Lokhaura and again unite at Khamlekh Garhi. A few miles further south at Jairaj the range again bifurcates; one spur known as Manila runs down to Bhikia Sen and the junction of the Naire with the Ramganga, and the other enclosing the Naire on the west terminates at the junction of the Ramganga and the Deogadh near Marchula. On the south from Mohan at the foot of the hills one continuous ridge runs east to Ranikhet, attaining a height of about 7,000 feet in the forest of Siuni. From Gujarghati on this range a spur runs down to the junction of the Naurar stream with the Ramganga, below Bhikia Sen.

The chief river is the Ramganga which enters the pargana from the north in Palla Giwar and leaves it at Marchula. The Gagas drains most of the eastern pattis and joins the Ramganga at Bhikia Sen. The Banau from Garhwal waters the Chaukot pattis, while the Salts are drained by streams of less importance which empty themselves into the Ramganga.

In the eastern valley of Walla Giwar surrounded on three sides by high mountains, lies the picturesque and curious lake of Tarag Tal, formed by a natural dam of great boulders, underneath which the stream gushes out. A rough path leads to this place from Ganai and continues over the Bhatkot ridge to Baijnath, but the route is very difficult and is only practicable on foot. In the neighbourhood of the lake excellent crops of hemp are grown.

The best forests are to be found on the outer fringe of high hills and, though extensive, they are not from the agricultural point of view well distributed. Palla, Walla and Malla Salt, the three Doras, Talla Silor, Talla Kaklasaun, Walla and Palla Naya have practically no forests within their borders. The Chaukots are supplied from the Manila, Jairaj and Jaurasi forests and the Giwars from Bhatkot. The reserved forests along the southern ridge, Machor, Bhatronj, Siuni and Ganiadeoli furnish excellent grazing and wood of all kinds to Talla Salt, Malla Kaklasaun and the Silors. The pattis which occupy the closely cultivated low hills in the centre of the district have thus to go far afield for grass and wood and during the hot weather they repair with their cattle to Bhatkot, or Dudatoli in Garhwal, as the case may be.

The cultivation throughout the pargana is careful and efficient. In some portions, chiefly those pattis alluded to above as destitute of forest, the hills are terraced from base to submit; hardly a square yard of land is allowed to go to waste. The rivers are utilized to the fullest extent for irrigation. The *seras* that line the Ramganga from Ganai to below Masi, and the Banau from its source to its junction with the Ramganga, the fine irrigated villages in the Kothlar glen of Walla Giwar and the Khotsar glen in Palla Giwar offer a picture of agricultural prosperity hardly equalled in the district. Except near the Silor Mahadeo the Gagas is little used for irrigation, its course in the pargana lying between overhanging precipices with no cultivation at their base. Near Dwarahat there is a fine but somewhat sparsely irrigated plateau. All the ordinary crops are raised. The irrigated villages specialize in wheat and the finest rice, from the sale of which, either to the pilgrims from Garhwal, the banias of Ranikhet, or their less fortunately circumstanced neighbours they derive much profit. Turmeric and chillies are grown in the Salts, the Chaukots, the Nayas, the Kaklasauns, Talla Silor, and the Doras; but particularly in the Salts. These pattis also produce *ugal*, a superior sort of buck-wheat, grateful to Hindus on fasting days. Fruit is grown in all villages—plantains, mangoes, lemons, apricots, peaches and a few oranges: and vegetables of many kinds are common.*

The main market of the pargana is Ramnagar in the Naini Tal district with which it is connected by the cart road along

* Assessment report; J. E. Goudge.

the southern ridge with its almost complete branch towards Bhikia Sen, and by a bridle path from the north of the pargana, through the Giwars and along the Ramganga and over the southern ridge to Mohan where its joins the cart road. With Ranikhet the communications are less good except from Dwarahat. Two roads run westward from Ganai through Kelani and from Dwarahat through Masi to Garhwal.

Various classes of the people make their income by transporting goods to Ranikhet from Ramnagar along the cart road or by service in Ranikhet and Naini Tal. The Silor people are noted sawyers and earn good pay in the Bhabar forests which also attract the unskilled labour of the patti. The treeless hills of Malla, Palla and Walla Salt, the Nayas and the Doras are however liable to receive from time to time an insufficient rainfall, and it is a hill commonplace that Pali always comes in for a full share of any scarcity that may be abroad. Among Kumaonis the Pali people, and among the Pali people the Saltis have the worst reputation for litigiousness. Nevertheless the people are moderately prosperous taken all in all.

Pali contains 1,085 villages with in 1901 a population of 121,875, an increase of 28·6 per cent. over the figures of 1872. The revenue now stands at Rs 68,041.

The chief villages are Dwarahat, Ganai—each of which possesses a school and a hospital—Masi, Bhikia Sen, Chachroti and Timli.

Pali is unique in respect of its large landed proprietors. Elsewhere in the district the cultivating body for the main part owns its own land. Here there are a number of families, many of them the descendants of the Katyur family or of executive officers of the Chand Rajas who own land in almost every patti. Such are the Dangwals of Malla Kaklasaun, the Rajwars of Talla Chaukot, the Bangaris of Malla Chaukot, the Manrals of Tambadhaund, of Udepur, of Hat (Palla Giwar), and of Kahargaon, the Bangaris and Hits of Palla Naya, and the Timli Bishts. These villages are usually cultivated by khaikars who pay the government revenue *plus* a *malikana* of 50 or 100 per cent. to the proprietor.

PANAR RIVER.

A river rising in patti Malla Salam of pargana Chaugarkha in latitude 29° 27′ and longitude 79° 47′. It drains the southern declivities of the mountain range running north-east from Jalna on the Lohaghat road to the Mathurapuri peak (6,897 feet) and thence south-east by Durga Pali (5,010 feet) to Gaulikhan (4,591 feet) forming the water-parting between the Sinniaon and Panar. It flows circuitously but generally in an eastern direction, forming the boundary between the eastern half of Malla Salam and Talla Salam and Rangor on the north and the Chalsi, Gangol and Regruban pattis of pargana Kali Kumaon on the south, to its junction with the Sarju on the right bank above Rameswar in latitude 29° 31′ and longitude 80° 7′. The total length of its course is about twenty-five miles.

PANWANAULA, *patti* TALLA LAKHANPUR, *pargana* CHAUGARKHA.

A halting place, village and traveller's bungalow on the route from Almora to Pithoragarh, situated in latitude 29° 38′ 35″ and longitude 79° 51′ 15″ at an elevation of 6,489 feet above the level of the sea and a few hundred feet below the summit of the ridge. It lies at a distance of 14 miles from Almora, 25 miles from Pithoragarh and 10½ miles from the next stage at Naini. The bungalow has no khansaman ; supplies may be obtained at the grain shop here.

The road hence to Almora winds along the slopes of the valleys of the head waters of the Likhdawargadh, a tributary of the Sual. This it crosses by an iron suspension bridge and then ascends the ridge above the valley of the Sual itself. This river is here crossed by a bridge and a very steep ascent leads round by the Simtola and Hiradungri hills to Almora. The road throughout is devoid of forest and shade and is exceedingly hot in the summer.

PHALDAKOT *pargana, peshkari* PALI.

One of the smallest parganas in the district with a cultivated area of only 15 square miles. It comprises four pattis—Malli Doti, Chaugaon, Kandarkhua and Dhuraphat. On the north the high winding ridge that carries the Ramnagar cart road with an average height of 6,000 feet runs past Siuni to Ranikhet and Chaubattia which are situated at the north-west and north-east angles of the pargana. From Siuni the Bellekh spur runs south and forms the western boundary between the pargana and the Naini Tal district. The eastern boundary is defined by the Kaligadh stream rising below Chaubattia as far as its junction with the Siront river from Dwarsyun. From the confluence the boundary ascends the lower slopes of Siahi Devi following to its source a minor brook which rises in that mountain. Thence it descends in an irregular line to Kakarighat. On the south the Kosi parts the pargana from Naini Tal. A second spur called the Sher Danda diverges from the northern ridge at Ranikhet and descends to the Kosi at Khairna. Between this and the Bellekh spur lies the valley of the Kuchgadh, while the country to the east of it and between it and Siahi Devi is drained by the Siront river. The pargana thus consists of the valleys of two minor streams which fall into the Kosi. The northern ridge and the Bellekh spur are well wooded with pine, oak and rhododendron chiefly, but the Sher Danda ridge is treeless. The number of right-holding villages in each patti is very large and their claims for timber and grazing have been generously recognized in the forest settlements. The soil is on the whole fertile and the ordinary hill crops of wheat, barley, *mandua*, *jhangora*, rice and pulses flourish. In Duraphat, particularly in the rich soil of the Bellekh slopes, some potatoes are raised and the villages near the Ranikhet cantonments always have considerable areas under vegetables. The proportion of irrigated land is small. There are some good *seras* fringing the Kuchgadh but the bed of the Siront is too narrow to be much used for irrigation. The cultivation is good in Dhuraphat, but the people of Kandarkhua, Dhuraphat and Chaugaon neglect their ancestral fields for the sake of their estates in the Bhabar. The people eke out their indigenous resources also by cooly labour in Ranikhet, carting, road mending and contracts. Some also migrate to the potato lands of Binaikdhura in the Naini Tal district.

The two large cantonments of Ranikhet and Chaubattia are situated on the boundaries of the pargana, while Naini Tal is within a day's march from the remotest village. The whole pargana is intersected with excellent roads. The cart-road from Kathgodam to Ranikhet runs along the Sher Danda through Chaugaon and Malli Doti, a forest road runs from Khairna along the Bellekh ridge and through Dhuraphat patti to meet the Ramnagar cart-road at Riun-Chiun, while this cart-road completes the the circle back to Ranikhet. A portion of the Baitalghat-Ranikhet bridle path runs between Riun-Chiun and Tarkhet, a large camping place on the Ramnagar cart-road, and the old pilgrim way skirts the lower slopes of Siahi Devi traversing Kandarkhua as far as Kakarighat.

The population has increased between the two last settlements by 10 per cent., not a large increase if compared with the figures for a remote pargana like Sira, but at the same time not unsatisfactory in a pargana which is one of the oldest and which was well developed 40 years ago. For the same reason the expansion of cultivation has also been insignificant. The population in 1901 amounted to 15,843 and the revenue demand is Rs. 8,638, a slight increase over the expiring demand.*

PHURKIYA, *patti* MALLA DANPUR, *pargana* DANPUR.

The last bungalow on the route to the Pindari glacier, 5 miles from Dwali, 69 miles from Almora, and 3 miles from the foot of the glacier. There is no khansaman or bania's shop here, and supplies should be brought on from Loharkhet. The road from Dwali is easy and in good order, but beyond Phurkiya it is narrow and rough and only fit for hill ponies. For a further account see the article on the Pindar river.

PINDAR RIVER.

This river takes its rise in a glacier lying between Nandakot and Nanda Devi, at an elevation of 12,088 feet above the level of the sea, in latitude 30° 15′30′ north and longitude 80′2″ east. Its course from the foot of the glacier is generally south, passing by Phurkiya and Dugli to Dwali, where it is joined by the Kuphini (*q.v*). Thence it bends to the south-west by Khati to Wachham, near which it receives on the right bank the

* Assessment report : J. E. Goudge.

Sundardhunga and further on at Kanwari on the Garhwal frontier the Bhaiganga on the same side. The rest of its course lies in the Garhwal district.

The neighbourhood of the glacier is an open undulating piece of ground, covered with grass, docks and the ubiquitous shepherd's-purse. The wild flowers are chiefly edelweiss, of which two varieties are to be found, and gentians. Major Madden's description is worth recording :—

"The glacier lay to the west, and between us and it rose a lofty moraine, along the hither or east base of which flows a considerable stream, the source of which is much more remote than that of the Pindar, which it joins one or two hundred yards below its exit from the ice. Having ascended perhaps a thousand feet and striking to the left crossed the moraine, which is here about 150 feet high, descend to the glacier, a few hundred paces towards its head where it commences in huge broken tiers of the purest snow.

"The moraine is constituted of gravel, mud and blocks of stone embedded in ice ; the stones are very small. There is a very steep descent to where the river issues from a cave in the face of the glacier, about 20 feet high, by perhaps 90 wide; the impending roof is riven into four or five successive thick ribs of ice. The recent heavy rains had thoroughly washed the Pindari Glacier, and its surface exhibited a sheet of the purest ice, except on and near the terminal escarpments, which being covered with rubble, resemble, at a short distance, a steep bank of mud ; and such is said to be the appearance in May and June of the Milam glacier. But to make quite sure fragments have frequently been broken off which everywhere were perfect ice, the only difference perceptible, between this and the Alpine ice, being a coarser granular structure here. It is intersected by the same fissures, has the same rib and texture and from its origin in the snow to its termination above the cave, falls in a series of the most beautiful curves. That the mass is moving downwards seems confirmed by the form of the snow at its head, viz. a succession of terraces, with steep wales, just such as clay, &c., assumes on its support being removed. The glacier may be about two miles long, and from 300 to 400 yards broad, and probably occupies the interval between the levels 12,000 and 13,000 feet above the sea; owing its existence to the vast quantities of snow precipitated from Nanda Devi and the other lofty mountains above, which, melted by the noonday sun, is frozen at night. It must be observed too, that in spite of theory and observation elsewhere, the perpetual snow appears here to descend to the level of 13,000 feet: for from the head of the ice to the crest of 'Traill's Pass'— the *col* which may be considered as the root of the glacier—there is an uninterrupted surface of snow, and that from its low angle, except for the lowest thousand feet, evidently *in situ*.

"None of the culminating pinnacles of the Himalayas are visible from the glacier, though a great peak is immediately above on the east. The northern shoulder of this peak, a massive, snowy mountain forms a grand object to the north-east, and this, passing the depression forming Traill's Pass, is continued in glorious domes and peaks to the left, where a beautiful pinnacle, apparently the easternmost of the two lower peaks of Nanda Devi, terminates the view. The adytum of the goddess herself is utterly concealed."

PINNATH, *patti* PALLA BORARAN, *pargana* BARAHMANDAL.

A temple and village in north latitude 29°50′45″, and east longitude 79°35′, at a distance of about 32 miles from Almora and seven miles from Dwarahat. It is built on a spur of the Bhatkot peak, overlooking the upper valley of the Kosi. A colony of Gosains resides here and a number of their *mahants* lie buried close by, each with a small dome over his remains surmounted by a miniature ling. The Gosains possess a grant engraved in metal conferring lands on Siva as Pinakeswar, "Lord of the Trident)," executed by Udyot Chand, Raja of Kumaon, in 1613 *samvat* (1691 A. D.) and another by Baz Bahadur Chand and his consort, bearing date 1654 A. D.

"The temples are situated about half way up the hill above the village. The first is a small conical structure, eight or ten feet high, dedicated to Bhairon. The main temple is close to this on the north, a square slated edifice, with the door facing the south, and figures of rajas, &c., sculptured on the walls. The roof of the portico is formed by the Indian arch, and on its sides are represented the five Pandavas; the adytum is small and contains nothing but one or two images of Mahadeo and Devi; about eighty years ago the original pile was nearly all overthrown by an earthquake. The place is only frequented in the rainy season and autumn, when in October there is a fair. The want of water is poorly supplied by a cistern and several wells, twelve to fifteen feet deep, excavated in the rock. So far the rock is quartz and slate, but onwards quartz only, disposed in vast beds, the outcrop of which faces west-south-west. The area of this summit is not above fifteen feet across, with precipitous glens all around, an exceedingly narrow rocky ridge connecting it with Bhatkot (9,086 feet) bearing south-west. The Burhapinnath range is continued north-west in a very lofty and comparatively level spur, called Birchhwa (8,042 feet), excessively precipitous to the left or west-south-west. In this is the main source of the Kosi, which hence flows nearly due east for about five miles, its northern bank being formed by the slopes of Gopalkot, on whose craggy summit the Katyur Rajas had a stronghold in which their treasures were deposited." (*Madden*).

PITHORAGARH, *patti* MAHAR OR KHASPARJA, *pargana* SHOR.

Pithoragarh is a village in latitude 29° 35′ and longitude 80° 15′ at an elevation of 5,464 feet above the sea. It lies at a distance of 14 miles west from Jhulaghat on the Kali river, when the road from Almora crosses in the Nepal. The distance from Almora is 52 miles. Pithoragarh lies on the main trade route between the plains and Tibet used by the Darma Bhotias, and derives considerable benefit from its traffickings with these people. It was formerly the site of a cantonment, long ago abandoned, but the buildings like those of Lohaghat continued until recently in the possession of the military department. The old fort is now the site of a peshkari built a few years ago. The bungalows ultimately came into the possession of the American Methodist Episcopalian Mission. In former times the site was considered unhealthy and gave rise to fevers and bowel complaints during the rains. The Shor valley is about five miles in length by about three in breadth, dipping gently to the south-east and bisected into north and south by a tabular ridge of slate, limestone and greenstone originating in the mountains to the north-west and branching down to the south-east. On the south-western exposure stands fort London on a mound, apparently artificially scarped, about fifteen feet high, crowned by a loop-holed wall, seven or eight feet high, with platforms for guns, and a reservoir for water, that is now empty. On a commanding point to the north-west is a small square tower about fifteen feet square, also loop-holed for musketry and known as Wilkiegarh. These are now untenanted. The view from Pithoragarh is very fine. The whole valley is prettily dotted with small villages, generally placed on eminences and surrounded by the only trees visible, except the distant forests of Bishar and Thakil. The land is often quite level for extensive tracts, and is carefully cultivated. The outline of the enclosing mountains is extremely bold and varied, their sides sloping and grassy in some parts, steep as walls in others. To the east is the Durga range about 7,000 feet high, connected on the north with the castellated summit of Dhaj 8,149 feet high. To the south-south-west appears the long ridge of Thakil, with its three summits. To the north-north-west are the mountains over which goes the direct road to Almora, and north-north-east is a bold and lofty cone, the Koleswar peak, better known to the English residents as the Drill hill. It is reported to bear this last appellation from the tradition that a commander of the regiment once stationed here was accustomed to punish delinquents by ordering them to trudge, in full marching order, to the top of this hill, while he watched them from his own verandah with a telescope.

The water is now very scanty and a scheme for a piped supply is under consideration.

Pithoragarh is one of the stations of the Amerian Methodist Episcopalian Mission. Here they have a hospital with male and female wards, and a school. Branch schools have been established in Gurna, Chaupakha, Durgakot and elsewhere. Two miles to the north of Pithoragarh is the Mission Leper Asylum on the heights of Chandagh.

Pithoragarh also contains a post office, a middle school on the site of the old peshkari and a dâk bungalow. The population in 1901 was 352.

PUNIAGIRI *patti* TALLA PAL BELON, *pargana* KALI KUMAON.

A famous shrine of great sanctity on the lower hills overlooking the Sarda and Nepal. The place was fully described by Madden whose account is here given.

"The elevation of the shrine is almost 3,000 feet above the sea; at this level though greatly cooler than Barmdeo, the malaria of the Bhabar still prevails, with sal forest and fine clumps of bamboo, which, being sacred to the Devi, are never cut; the popular belief being that, if converted to use, scorpions and centipedes innumerable would issue forth to punish the sacrilege. Nothing can surpass the beauty and variety of the scenery about Puniagiri; but to superstition alone are we indebted for a path through and over the otherwise impassable thickets and precipices. The first symptom of sanctity in the wilderness is a small *marhi*, dedicated to Bhairon as door-keeper; and no man of low caste or of a notoriously bad or even unfortunate character or filthy in person or discourse is knowingly allowed to advance further.

Tuniyas is a small plateau crossed by the path to the shrine above. Here two dharamsalas have been erected for the accommodation of pilgrims and the flowers used as offerings are grown.

The water supply is obtained from a well dug on the plateau and lined with rock masonry. Half a mile or so higher up is a small, black domed structure, coated with copper, and placed on the crest of the great mural precipice of sandstone which here faces the south. A little to the south-east this wall terminates and the mountain springs up into a very lofty and remarkable pinnacle of rock, presenting a precipitous face to the river, which rolls at its base in a winding chasm of vast depth, the waters generally calm and of lapis-lazuli tint. The gorge makes a rapid bend here, which brings the current right against the upper end of the cliffs, which perhaps owe their existence to its slow operation. Each shoulder of the rocky pinnacle is consecrated by its temple, the easternmost being the most sacred and of very difficult access over cliffs and razor-edged ridges. Animals are sacrificed below on the west on a small flat. The Brahmans appropriate the head of each beast with all the cash they can extract, and considerable numbers of cocoanuts, the offering of which seems a sign connecting the mountain goddess and her rites with the ocean-loving Kali of Calcutta. The acme of merit is attained by him whose offering, like Balak's, consists of seven goats. The peak itself is the adytum of the goddess where none can intrude with impunity; a fakir who ventured to do so in days of yore was pitched across the river and found flattened to a pancake in the *ban* of Doti."

RAMGANGA RIVER (Eastern).

This river has its source in patti Bichhla Danpur, in a horse shoeshaped depression of the southern heights of Nandakot. To the north the ridge culminates in a peak 19,554 feet above the level of the sea: on the east, the ridge runs south with a series of peaks ranging from 16,321 to 9,814 feet (to the west of Ganagarh on the Milam route) which form the water-parting between it and the Gori: on the west the ridge has also a southern direction and in the upper portion separates the Ramganga from the Kuphini and lower down from the Sarju. The Ramganga forms the boundary southwards between Bichhla Danpur and Talla Des, and is crossed by the road from Bageswar to Mijam near Tejam. Further south it forms the boundary between Pungraun and Baraun of Gangoli and Mali of Sira, and a road proceeds along its left bank to Pithoragarh, crossing at Naya Tal the road from Almora to Askot. The whole course from Bhakunda is nearly due south and further on it forms the boundary between Barabisi, Talli Seti, Malla Waldia and Rawal on the left bank and Pungraun and Bel on the right bank. In this portion of its course it is crossed by a suspension bridge on the road from Gangolihat to Bans. It receives numerous torrents on either bank during its course, but none of any great importance. The name Ramganga is often given to the united stream of the Sarju and Ramganga from their confluence at Rameswar to Pacheswar, where it joins the Kali.

RAMGANGA RIVER (WESTERN).

This river rises in the southern slopes of the wooded Dudatali hill in patti Lohba of Garhwal in latitude 30°5′ and longitude 79°18′. It enters the Almora district by a deep and narrow gorge in Palla Giwar. Emerging thence it bends to the south-west and sweeping round the south-eastern extremity of the Lohbagarhi range it receives the Tarag Tal river. The first village of importance in the Almora district is Ganai where it receives the Kharrogadh from the western declivity of Dunagiri on the left bank and the Khetsargadh from Pandua Khal on the right bank. Thus reinforced it traverses Talla Giwar, here a fine open valley with rich corn lands in or near the bed of the river from which they are copiously irrigated. Beyond Masi the valley somewhat contracts, but there are still some fertile riverain fields as far as the temple of Budh Kedar. Here it receives the Banau river from Chaukot, and from this point onwards the course continues in a general southerly course flanked by cliffs composite of alluvial soil and boulders. Eleven miles beyond Masi it reaches Bhikia Sen, where, at the confluence of the Gagas from the east and the Naurargadh from the south with the Ramganga, the valley again expands, but the irrigation is chiefly from the minor streams. From Bhikia Sen the river takes a sharp turn to the west and receiving the waters of the Nail from Malla Salt and the Deogadh from Garhwal at the Marchula bridge forms from the latter point for a few miles the boundary of the district. Thence it enters the Bhabar and flows nearly due west through the Patli Dun, eventually to fall into the Ganges in the district of Shahjahanpur.

RANIKHET.

A military sanitarium situated in latitude 29° 29′ 50″ north and longitude 79° 26′ east, on the great ridge stretching half-way across the district from west to east and forming the northern boundary of the Kosi basin. Ranikhet comprises two distinct areas—Ranikhet proper and Chaubattia—and these two cantonments together with the Standing Camp now afford accommodation to three complete battalions, together with a mule cadre of the Supply and Transport Corps. It is also the summer headquarters of the Bareilly brigade. The station lies high, between

5,983 feet at Ranikhet and 6,942 feet at Chaubattia, and is extremely well wooded. The old natural pine and oak forests where not cleared for buildings have been strictly preserved, and the road sides have been much beautified by lines of deodars, cypresses and exotic trees.

The higher portions of the ridge are crowned with the bungalows of the officers, while the Ranikhet barracks occupy a pleasant site at the west of the station overlooking the Kuchgadh and the rifle range. Below the barracks lies the regimental bazar. To the east above the Almora road is the Standing Camp, and west of that again the main bazar containing one or two good shops. Ranikhet is well intersected with good cart roads and excellent bridle paths. The ridge on which the station is situated presents the appearance of a long plateau stretching away for miles to the east and the west and thus offering plenty of scope for the extension of the cantonment if necessary. Its advantages in the matter of level ground and possibilities of expansion are so great that it was once proposed to remove the summer head quarters of the army in India from Simla to Ranikhet.

The affairs of the cantonment are administered by a committee. The cantonment fund was first established in 1871 at which time its chief source of income was a ground tax imposed on all buildings erected on the land acquired by the Government in 1869. At the present time it has an annual revenue of about Rs. 50,000 derived from the ground tax, house tax, tax on trades and professions, conservancy tax, water rates, and—the most important source of all—the sale of grass and other produce of the cantonment forests. Expenditure is incurred chiefly over the water-works and sanitation. The maintenance of the forests swallows up half the income from that source.

The water supply is derived from springs 1,000 feet below and on the east side of Chaubattia. The water is first pumped up and stored in tanks near the summit of Chaubattia, whence it is distributed throughout the station. The disposal of the sewage is also a special care of the Cantonment Committee. It is collected in patent carts and destroyed in patent incinerators, the fuel used being pine needles.

Ranikhet possesses three churches and a comfortable club situated in a pleasant garden. The only other building worthy of note is the court house, now occupied by the Assistant Commissioner. The head treasury was, owing to the magnitude of the monetary transactions of the military department, transferred in 1907 from Almora to Ranikhet, and a peshkar is also located there. The parade ground which also serves the purposes of a foot ball ground and a polo ground is a noteworthy feature of the cantonment; it was carved out of the hill between Ranikhet and the Standing Camp some six or seven years ago. The forest garden at Chaubattia is an adornment to that portion of the station and also supplies all European fruits to the inhabitants.

Ranikhet came into existence in the year 1869. It covers land which originally belonged to the villages of Sarna, Kotli, and Ranikhet, all in pargana Barahmandal, and to Tana in pargana Phaldakot. For this land Rs. 13,024 compensation were paid. Mr. Troup's Kumpur estate was also acquired in exchange for the fee simple of about 250 acres adjoining another estate of his in Jajdeo and Kanani. Troupganj bazar is however still in Mr. Troup's possession. The branch treasury was opened on the 1st April 1869, since when the station has gradually expanded. Ranikhet is connected with Kathgodam by a continuation of the Naini Tal cart road from the Brewery, through Bhawali, Ratighat, and Khairna, where it crosses the Kosi river and enters the Almora district. Its distance from the plains by this route is 49 miles. This road is continued to the east as far as Almora, 30 miles away. Another unmetalled cart road was made many years ago between Ramnagar and Ranikhet, a distance of 65 miles; it fell into disuse on the opening of the Rohilkhand and Kumaon Railway from Bareilly to Kathgodam. With the advent of the railway to Ramnagar it is again becoming important, the more so as from Gujarghati down it carries the pilgrim traffic. A railway into Ranikhet itself along the ridge followed by the Ramnagar cart road has been projected. The gradients appear to offer no engineering difficulty, but there is no immediate prospect of its construction. By bridle path Ranikhet is distant 40 miles from Kathgodam via Bhim Tal and 22 miles from Almora.

The population in March 1901 was 3,153, namely Hindus 2,192, Muhammadans 689, Europeans 246, Native Christians 22, and Parsis 4. A special census taken in the height of the season in September 1900, disclosed a total population of 7,705, namely Hindus 3,954, Muhammadans 1,471, Europeans 2,236, Native Christians 40, and Parsis 4.

The climate is mild and not marked by any great variations of temperature. The summer is said to be somewhat depressing in its influence, a disadvantage which is attributed by many to the excessive vegetation. For the last ten years the rainfall has been about 40 inches, much the same as at Almora.

SARJU RIVER.

A considerable affluent of the Kali river to which it often gives its name. From the confluence at Pacheswar in Kali Kumaun the united stream is known as either the Sarju or Kali as far as Barmdeo, and as the Sarda or Gogra to its confluence with the Ganges in the Ballia district.

The Sarju rises on the southern slopes of a ridge in patti Malla Danpur of Kumaon and is separated on the east from the sources of the eastern Ramganga and on the west from the sources of the Kuphini or eastern branch of the Pindar by spurs leading down from the mass culminating in the Nandakot peak. The sources are situate in north latitude 80° 6′ 50″ and east longitude 30° 1′ 30″, in the depression within which the village of Jhundi is situated, and are crossed by a ford at Wachham on the track between Supi and Namik. The breadth at Supi, eight miles down is about fifteen yards, and in May there are only about two feet of water. On the west a lofty chain of mountains running south-west separates it from the Pindar river and on the east a similar chain separates it from the eastern Ramganga. The height of the latter ridge is so elevated that even in May snow rests on the more lofty summits. About the source also snow rests until late in the year. At Supi the bed of the river is 5,659 feet about the level of the sea. A few miles below Supi the bed narrows to twelve yards with a depth of twenty-four inches, and a few miles still lower down or fifteen miles from its source it is forty-five yards wide and twenty-seven inches deep.

The valley here is tolerably wide and gives space for numerous villages on either bank. Near its source it is crossed from Khati in the Pindar valley by a road leading to the Bhotia tract of Munsiari.

It then holds a south-westerly course, receiving many minor streams, and enters the patti of Talla Danpur in latitude 29° 59′ and longitude 77° 59″, where it receives on the right bank the Kanalgadh and a short distance lower down the Pungargadh, thirty-one miles from its source. About a mile lower down it receives the Lahor river on the right bank from patti Malla Katyur, and hence taking a south-easterly direction passes four miles lower down by Bageswar at an elevation of 3,143 feet above the level of the sea, receiving on its right bank the Gumti or Gomati river. Further on much of the drainage of the Gangoli pargana falls into it on the same side by the Bhadrapatigadh and that of Chaugarkha by the Gatgadh, Jalairgadh, Bhaurgadh, Alaknandi and Saniaungadh. Thirty-five miles below the confluence of the Ramganga with the Gumti it receives the Panar river on the same side and about three miles further down on the left bank the Ramganga (eastern) at Rameswar in latitude 29° 31′ 25″ and longitude 80° 9′ 40″, with an elevation of 1,500 feet above the level of the sea. About ten miles above its confluence with the Panar, sixty miles from its source, the average breadth is about fifty yards and the drift four and a half to five miles an hour, with a depth in May of eight feet and fordable in December. Here it is a most impetuous and roaring torrent, dashing over the rocks with the greatest force and noise and casting the spray about in all directions. A few miles below Rameswar, whence it is indifferently called the Ramganga and Sarju, the river is crossed by an iron suspension bridge on the road between Lohaghat and Pithoragarh. The hills on either side rise very steeply and are thickly clothed with pine forest. From Rameswar it forms the boundary between the Shor and Kali Kumaon parganas and flows in a south-easterly direction, and after a course of twelve miles falls into the Kali on the right bank at Pacheswar in latitude 29° 27′ and longitude 80° 18.′ About a mile above this confluence the river is fordable in the dry season; it is about eighty yards in breadth and four and a quarter feet deep with a drift of about four miles an hour. The length of the river from its source to its confluence with the Kali has been estimated at eighty-two miles. The confluences at Bageswar with the Gumti, at Rameswar with the Ramganga and at Pacheswar with the Kali are sacred *prayagas* or junctions which have periodical semi-religious assemblies in their honour.

SHOR *pargana, peshkari* SHOR.

A small compact pargana situated on the eastern border of the district where it meets the kingdom of Nepal, from which it is separated by the river Kali. It lies almost midway between the southern extremity of the district above Tanakpur and the snows of Darma and Byans, and is circular in shape with well-defined natural boundaries on three sides. On the east lies the Kali. On the west the eastern Ramganga divides it from pargana Gangoli, and on the south the united Ramganga and Sarju part it from Kali Kumaon. On the north there is no natural boundary, though for a short distance the Kalapani stream divides the patti of Talli Seti from Barabisi in pargana Sira, but thence to the river Kali the northern boundary is quite arbitrary. Its neighbour on the north is the pargana or taluqa of Askot. The pargana contains three peaks, Dhaj in the north 8,149 feet, Asurchula in the west 6,990 and Thakil in the south 8,161. Within these three peaks and the ridges which trend from them lies the undulating tableland of Shor called Seni Shor with an average elevation of about 5,300 feet. On the eastern side of this triangle the plateau is open and terminates in rolling downs above the Kali river. The whole of the outer country is steep and wild and the cliffs above the large rivers are precipitous. The only stream of any size in the pargana is the Chandrabhaga. This rises in the Chandak ridge, an offshoot from Asurchula above Pithoragarh, and after slowly winding from the open villages of the central tract enters the precipices which overhang the Kali and joins that river a few miles above its junction with the Sarju. In the north of the pargana the Kalapani runs into the Ramganga and the Bagari into the Kali. These streams are of a fair size but their channels are deep and flanked by steep walls of rock.

The whole of the outer land beyond the central plateau is covered with forests, in the midst of which are a few scattered blocks of cultivation. In the neighbourhood of the central tract the forests are rapidly disappearing and only a few scattered clumps of deodar, pine and oak are visible from Pithoragarh.

The central plateau which contains the pattis of Mahar, Malli Seti, and Bichla Waldiya, and portions of Nayades, Saun, Talli Seti, Kharayat and Talla Waldiya is known as the garden of Kumaon, the latter term being used in its original signification. The fertility of this central tract is due mainly to its undulating character, which makes it more uniformly culturable than is possible elsewhere in the hills. The cultivation being almost continuous for several miles in every direction wild beasts cannot damage the crops, while constant tilth and manuring have improved a naturally fertile soil. The villages situated on the outer slopes of the fringe of hills that bound the central plateau do not differ materially from those of any pargana in the eastern part of the district.

The pargana is well supplied with roads. It is traversed by the main trade route between Tibet and the plains, used by the Darma Bhotias, by the road from Almora to the Nepal boundary at Jhulaghat which passes through Pithoragarh and by the Pithoragarh-Tejam road. The chief village is Pithoragarh, once a cantonment and now a peshkari and the site of a bazar of some local importance. The rich central plateau produces more grain than the people can eat, and the surplus is advantageously disposed of to the Bhotias. The European settlers near Champawat and Lohaghat, and the Mission at Pithoragarh also make fairly large purchases. Many valuable crops such as pepper, buck-wheat, tobacco, *pinalu* and potatoes are raised. The villages outside the intensely cultivated central tract graze large herds of cattle in the forest and produce a fair quantity of *ghi* and they also collect wild honey and vegetable butter (*phulel*) from the *bassia butyracea*. The houses are substantial, and in many cases surrounded by fruit trees. The people have prospered to such an extent that the revenue demand was raised at the last settlement by 25 per cent., an increase based partly on the increase of cultivation and partly upon the other sources of income of the people.

It now stands at Rs. 18,738, the incidence per soil unit, or *bisi* of second class *upraon* land, being Re. 0-12-8. The review of the previous settlements is interesting as showing the development of the pargana since the conquest. In 1815 the demand was Rs. 3,536, rising by successive stages to Rs. 4,002 in 1817, Rs. 4,093 in 1818, and Rs. 5,495 in 1820. In 1822 the progress was maintained at the same rate, the *jama* being Rs. 6,141, rising to Rs. 6,638 in 1828, and Rs. 6,657 in 1833. This was not appreciably altered in 1843 when the *jama* was fixed at Rs. 6,687 at which figure it remained till Mr. Beckett's settlement of 1870 when the assessment of Shor, was Rs. 14,113. There are in all 418 villages in the pargana. The population which in 1901 amounted to 31,232 shows an increase of 64 per cent. over the population at the previous census.*

On the break up of the kingdom of Katyur, Shor was annexed to Doti. It was overrun by Ratan Chand, Raja of Kumaon (1437—50), but reconquered by the Bam dynasty of Doti, and not finally attached to the kumaon kingdom until the Dotial bride of Kalyan Chand brought it as her dowry. The connection of Shor with Doti is still remembered, for the western Kumaonis call all Kumaon to the east of the eastern Ramganga Doti.

"The inhabitants," wrote Mr. Batten, "are though hale and active, a fickle and factious race to whom the following couplet has been applied :—

"*Shor haram-khor.*
Bap bharuwa cheli mai tor."

"Shor eats the bread of dishonour, the fathers are panderers, the daughter remains with her mother"; and,

Shor ki nali katyura mano
Jayaji tuli kasamji nano

"The peck of Shor is a quart in Katyur: but the wife is master in Shor."

The landowners are chiefly Rajputs and Brahmans. In the south-east there are some Dotials from Nepal. Shor is a favourite residence for pensioned Gurkhas who, as Mr. Goudge remarks, do not think the Government has properly provided for

* Assessment report: J. E. Goudge.

them, unless a grant of land in Shor is bestowed. The pargana now comprises eleven pattis—Kharayat, Kharakdes, Mahar, Nayades, Rawal, Malli and Talli Seti, Saun and Malla Bichla and Talla Waldiya.

SIRA *pargana, peshkari* SHOR.

A small pargana, some 45 miles north-east of Almora. On the north a well-defined ridge running from east to west separates it from the southern pattis of Johar pargana; on the east it is bounded by the Askot taluqa or pargana; the Gori river divides it from Malla Askot, but there is no natural boundary between it and Talla Askot. On the west its boundary is the eastern Ramganga which flows between it and Gangoli, and on the south it adjoins pargana Shor. The area cannot be stated exactly but is probably some 160 square miles, of which 15 are cultivated. The pargana comprises five pattis—Dindihat in the north-eastern corner of the pargana, Mali in the west, Barabisi in the south, Malla and Talla Athbisi in the centre.

A fine range of hills skirts the northern boundary and turns down from the east parallel with the Gori river; several peaks rise above 8,000 feet in Dindihat and in the lateral range which joins them with the Dhaj peak in pargana Shor are Bhagaling and Lori, both rising above 7,600 feet. These ridges divide the pargana into a number of valleys, each drained by a small stream running down into the Gori or the Ramganga. The pargana is exceedingly well wooded. Above about 6,000 feet all the hills are covered with forests of oak and rhododendron, and all uncultivated land at lower elevations is clothed with pine.

The pargana varies in height between 2,500 feet by the Ramganga and 8,227 feet on Ghanadhura. Few of the villages are situated at elevations exceeding 6,000 feet, and there are some good villages in the Ramganga valley, but the Gori valley is hot and unhealthy. There are no large areas of continuous cultivation except at Dewalthal near the upper waters of the Kalapani and around Baltir opposite the Thal fair ground. All the ordinary crops are raised. The grain grown is in excess of the pargana's requirements and as it is pastoral no less than agricultural a large quantity of wheat, rice and *ghi* is offered for sale : some goes to Almora and Pithoragarh and the rest is taken by the Bhotias. There are no markets within the pargana, but a fairly brisk business is done at the annual Thal fair. The most prosperous patti of the pargana is Barabisi. In addition to those who subsist on the income derived from the fruits of the fields, many pensioned and well-to-do Gurkhas have settled in the pargana and some of their younger men are enlisted in the Army or the Burma military police. There is in Sira a fair amount of copper ore, but the mines have long been disused.

The tract is well provided with roads. The Almora-Askot road crosses the Ramganga at Thal, ascends into the oak forest of patti Mali, passes under Bhagaling and the ruin-crowned peak of Sirakot and following the central ridge of Dindihat, descends past Askot to the Gori. Here it divides, one road going up the valley of that river to Munsiari and Johar, and the other winding up the Kali towards Darma and then passing into Tibet. The Tejam-Pithoragarh road passes through Nali and Barabisi, and connects the pargana with Johar on one side and with Shor and Nepal on the other. The cross-road from Askot to Pithoragarh runs along its eastern edge and is convenient for the people on that side of the tract.*

The present assessment of the pargana stands at Rs. 9,438, a figure which points to a very large development since 1871, when the demand was fixed at Rs. 5,999. In 1815 the land revenue yielded but Rs. 1,905, rising by small successive enhancements to Rs. 2,760 in 1820, and Rs. 3,205 in 1843. In the earlier settlements up to 1840 Sira and Askot were taken together. The population now amounts to 16,056, having doubled in the 30 years between the two last settlements.

On the fall of the Katyur kingdom Sira with Shor and Askot was annexed to the Doti Raj, and Sirakot became the residence of a junior dynasty of the Doti house. Sira was finally taken by Parkhu, the general of Rudra Chand, after a stubborn defence in 1581 A. D. Dindihat was the great market town of the old Sira state. Athbisi was set apart for the maintenance of the Rani and Barabisi formed the portion of the state assigned for military

* Assessment report. J. C. Smith.

and other public purposes. Under the Chand Rajas Sirakot became the state prison and it was here that Dip Chand, the last of the Chands in direct descent, was murdered by his cousin, Mohan Singh.

SOMESWAR, *patti* WALLA BORARAU, *pargana* BARAHMANDAL.

A large village on the cart-road from Almora to Baijnath, situated at the point where it is crossed by the bridle road from Bageswar to Dwarahat. It lies at a distance of 18 miles north from Almora and 13 miles from both Bageswar and Dwarahat, in latitude 29° 46′ 40″, and longitude 19° 38′ 55″, at an elevation of 4,752 feet above the level of the sea. There is a small bazar here and a large and flourishing school. The population is largely Brahman. The dâk bungalow has a khansaman. Besides the roads above referred to there is a small road leading to Majhkali and Ranikhet and a bridle path to Almora by Gananath and Takula. The Someswar temple possesses considerable sanctity: it is an ancient structure in the ordinary Turk's-head style, surrounded by stunted deodars.

TANAKPUR—*Bhabar*.*

The head quarters of the eastern Bhabar lying in longitude 29° 4′ north and longitude 80° 7′ east is a small town situated on the right bank of the river Sarda about four miles below the old mart of Barmdeo. Tanakpur was founded in 1880 after the destruction of Barmdeo by floods. The site is elevated and dry, being on a high bank some 40 feet above the bed of the river. At Tanakpur are the peshkar's office, police-station, hospital, dâk bungalow and inspection house.

The bazar contains a large and increasing number of spacious stone houses and shops, the property of traders from both the hills and plains. A large number of huts are also erected every year round the bazar by the smaller traders, artizans and day labourers. A small ground-rent is charged for the space occupied by permanent buildings and huts, while the expenditure incurred in watch and ward and sanitation of the bazar is borne by the Government, the town being controlled as

*Transferred to the Naini Tal district by notification No. 1883 — $\frac{I}{605}$, dated the 1st October 1910.

part of the Tanakpur government estate. The bazar has been carefully laid out and has broad streets which are being metalled and provided with *pakka* drains. Some money is spent every year in the planting and protection of trees along the streets.

The trade of Tanakpur is considerable. Large quantities of borax and sheep's wool are brought down by Bhotias who in return carry back *gur* and cloth. The wool is mostly sold locally to the agent of one of the Cawnpore Mills; the borax is sold to traders from Pilibhit. The other wholesale commodities are cloth, woollen and cotton goods of both English and country manufacture, brought up from the plains and sold to hillmen and Nepalese, *gur*, turmeric, chillies, *ghi* and salt. The *gur* comes from the plains and is purchased by hillmen—turmeric, chillies and *ghi* come from the hills and from Nepal and are exported to the plains. There is also a considerable export trade in timber, catechu, hides, honey and minor forest produce. The trading season commences in November and lasts till May. By the middle of June the settlement is entirely deserted.

At the census of February 1901 the population of Tanakpur was 565 males and 127 females, giving a total of 692.

TANAKPUR BHABAR.*

The portion of the Bhabar in the Almora district extends from the base of the hills on the north to the point where the Jagbura stream joins the Sarda on the south, and from the Sarda river on the east to the Libar stream on the west, and includes such of the islands of the Sarda in British territory as are above the point where the Jagbura joins it. A number of streams flow down from the hills through this tract, most of them containing water only during the rainy season, but some are permanent, such as the Kalaunia (known lower down as the Jagbura) the Libar and the Kumya.

The area of the tract is 120 square miles. All the land is the property of the Government and was until 1910 managed by

* Transferred to the Naini Tal district by notification no. 1818—$\frac{I}{105}$, dated the 1st October 1910.

the Deputy Commissioner of Almora as a government estate. It is usually known as the Tanakpur government estate, Tanakpur being the head quarters of the local administration. The greater part of the tract is covered with forest, the cultivation being confined to the open plains watered by the canals and to clearings near the streams. Some of the islands in the Sarda are large and well wooded, principally with khair (*acacia catechu*) and shisham (*dalbergia sissoo*).

The forest tracts under the administration of the forest department were gazetted as "reserved forest" in 1879 (although they had been administered by this department since its formation), and the bulk of them extend from the Chini river on the east to the Libar stream on the west, and, north of the Barmdeo road, from the Chini river to the foot of the hills. To the east of this main block are the closed sal forest of Chandni, with an area of 403 acres, and the islands, containing a good growth of shisham and khair, in the Sarda river. The remaining portions of the forest area of the Tanakpur Bhabar are protected forest and constitute part of the government estate. Of the reserved forests only three small blocks which contain valuable sal timber are closed to grazing, the remainder being open for the use of the villagers, as regards both grazing and timber and other forest produce.

The reserved forests form part of the Kumaon division, the working system of which has already been described in the first chapter.

The large increase of population of recent years has caused a rapid decrease in the numbers of wild animals, and game of all kinds is now exceedingly scarce. Wild birds are not plentiful with the exception of the jungle fowl which swarm round the cattle stations. Pea-fowl and black partridge are to be found and the spur fowl may occasionally be met with. The sheldrake and a species of gadwall come up the river Sarda during the cold months.

The population of the Tanakpur Bhabar at the census of February 1901 amounted to 12,779, of whom 7,456 were males and 5,323 females. It is for the most part migratory, consisting chiefly of hillmen from the Kali Kumaon pargana who come down for the winter months for the sake of the warmth and to obtain better pasture for their cattle. They employ their leisure time in trade and the cultivation of spring crops, which a naturally fertile soil enriched with vegetable manure enables them to raise with the maximum of profit and the minimum of labour. Only those whose villages are within a few miles of the Bhabar, and who have secured a summer resort on the last range of hills overlooking their fields, take the trouble to cultivate a kharif or monsoon crop. The trade of the hill people consists of the sale of jungle produce to traders from the plains who come to Tanakpur for the winter. Many of them find lucrative employment as wood-cutters, sawyers and carriers with the traders who export timber from the forest along the base of the hills; the wages of the carriers being as high as eight or twelve annas a day. A few also carry on business as money-lenders among the Tharus.

The hill people who visit the Bhabar occupy *goths* or cattle stations where they annually construct huts of wood, bamboos and grass taken from the nearest forest. Most of them cultivate a little land, since agriculturists are allowed free grazing for a certain number of cattle per plough, but the cultivated area per family is not large. The breeding of cattle and the manufacture and sale of *ghi* constitute their chief business. A grazing fee of eight annas per annum on each buffalo and four annas on each cow or bullock beyond the free allowance is charged for the cattle grazed in the reserved and district forests. Half of the income under this head is credited to the forest department and half to the estate.

The only hillmen who make the most of their opportunities for cultivation are the Manihars of Khunmalak, a large village near Lohaghat. These people are Mussalmans and came originally from the Bijnor district, being descendants of a colony of lac bangle manufacturers which found its way to Kumaon in the time of the Chand Rajas. They keep large herds of buffaloes which they graze in the Bhabar from October to June and are the chief collectors of jungle products, such as hides and horns.

The other cold weather visitors to the Bhabar are traders from the plains who for the most part reside in the settlement of Tanakpur.

In recent years the cultivation of the Tanakpur Bhabar has been extended and a number of more permanent settlers has been obtained—Tharus from Nepal and the Tarai, and a few Mussalmans and Chamars attracted by the easy means of irrigation. The Tharus though infinitely better agriculturists than the indolent Kumaonis are entirely lacking in enterprise and impatient of even a nominal control. If things do not please them, they depart at once. The best tenants are Mussalmans and Chamars from the Tarai and plains, who, though they suffer from the climate of the Bhabar, are skilful agriculturists and obtain a fair return from the soil.

Ample means of irrigation have now been provided in this tract. The chief source of supply is the Barmdeo or Sarda canal. The landslip of 1880 choked up a portion of the channel constructed by Sir Henry Ramsay in 1874-75, and, as the facilities for irrigation offered by this canal had not up to that time induced any appreciable spread of cultivation, no attempt to repair it was made for a number of years. In 1896 Colonel Grigg, Commissioner of Kumaon, obtained the sanction of the Government to re-open this canal. The open channel was cleared of silt and sufficient of the débris and boulders was removed from the arched channel to admit of a flow of water. Since that year the work of restoration has been steadily continued and the main channel and its distributaries carry water to all the villages below. The Bastia gul is a small masonry channel which catches the water of the Ratigadh stream and carries it round the base of the spur. It provides a means of irrigation for the land round the village of Bastia, the cultivation of which has of late years become more permanent. A similar masonry-lined channel of about two miles in length known as the Chela canal, also constructed in 1874, conveys water from the Kalaunia to the village of Chela situated in a wide clearing in the forest between the Kalaunia and Chini rivers. This canal not only furnishes the power to work a flour mill, but has enabled the Chala tenants to grow rice crops. The stream is precarious and in dry years the supply is often short.

Every effort is made to bring the culturable land in the Tanakpur Bhabar under the plough and land is let to tenants on the most favourable terms. They are also supplied with materials free of cost for the construction of huts. Wells for water for domestic use are made in every village at any distance from a permanent stream. The land rent charged is eight annas per bigha in the Tanakpur circle and six annas a bigha in the Chedani circle. Advances for seed and cattle are liberally given. There are no proprietary rights other than those of the Government. The original founders of villages who have induced colonists to settle are called sirgirohs and they are the village headmen. They also collect the rent from the tenants of their villages and they are granted a small remuneration for the work they do.

The estate is traversed by one road which runs along the Sarda river from Barmdeo ghat to the Jagbura, and thence proceeds to Pilibhit; and by an unmetalled road kept up by the forest department running from Tanakpur on the east to Haldwani on the west. It will by the beginning of 1912 be served by the Pilibhit-Barmdeo extension of the Rohilkhand and Kumaon Railway.

The climate though it has certainly improved with the advance of cultivation is, except during the winter, extremely malarious and in fact insupportable except by the Tharus. The result is that from June to November the Bhabar is almost entirely deserted. Tanakpur contains a dispensary which remains open for six months of the year, and will probably be kept open the whole year round on the advent of the railway. Four schools also descend from the Champawat tract for the four months from December to March: they are established at Tanakpur where there is a good school-house, and at Chela Goth, Dugari Goth and Rajina Goth where they are housed in grass huts. There is also one permanent school for Tharu boys at Bamani Bagh. The peshkar in charge of the Bhabar retreats for the hot months to Sukhi Dhang, and the post office goes with him. There are four cattle pounds which are now worked by the district board. In 1908-9 they brought in Rs. 1,157. There are also three ferries across the Sarda into Nepal, but neither the district board nor the estate derive any benefit from them. The boatmen however are compelled to observe the rates fixed by authority. There are in all 55 villages in the estate. The income from rents amounted to Rs. 2,000 in 1896, Rs. 5,000 in 1900 and Rs. 5,420 in 1908.

TEJAM, *patti* TALLA DES JOHAR, *pargana* JOHAR.

A village and halting place on the road from Almora to Munsiari, being distant 58 miles from the district head quarters and 17 miles from Munsiari. The village is situated on the left bank of the eastern Ramganga at the junction of this river with the Jankula stream. The Ramganga is here shut in by high precipitous mountains, and during the summer months the place is excessively hot. From Tejam a road takes off westward joining the Pindari route at Kharbagar, a few miles above Kapkot. The place is infested with swarms of the small venomous fly locally known as *mora*. The population in 1901 was 382.

THAL, *patti* MALI, *pargana* SIRA.

A village situated on the left bank of the eastern Ramganga. Its sole importance is derived from the temple of Baleswar (an appellation of Siva) and the fair held in honour of the god on the *Bikhaut Sankrant*, falling about the middle of April. The attendance sometimes reaches 15,000 and the fair lasts for eight days. Here the Bhotias sell, for what they will fetch, the wares (chiefly wool) which they had failed to dispose of in the Bhabar, make their final purchases of grain and settle their accounts with their clients from the surrounding region before proceeding north to their homes. The tahsildar also usually seizes this opportunity of collecting their land revenue. A few traders from Kashipur and Almora also attend with cloth and metal vessels, and the Shor and Sira people bring oil, chillies and the like.

UNTA DHURA, *patti* MALLA, JOHAR *pargana* JOHAR.

A pass into Tibet to the north-east of Milam, in latitude 30° 35′ and longitude 80° 11′, with an elevation of 17,600 feet above the level of the sea, lying about 120 miles north of

Almora. The pass traverses a ridge which lies to the north of the main chain of the Himalayas and at right angles west from the range which divides the Almora district from Tibet. Though inferior in height to the main range the pass is elevated enough to necessitate a considerable ascent from the deep gorges of Kumaon. The crest of the ridge forms the boundary between patti Malla Painkhanda of Garhwal and patti Malla Johar of Almora, and also the water-parting between the streams flowing westward by the Alaknanda into the Ganges and those flowing into the Kali or Sarda.

There are on the crest five small ridges of stone which look like pillars from below, and it is believed that any one who sleeps near them dies. A bitter, piercing wind blows here with such violence, especially during the rains, as to cause fatal accidents. Weller writes :—"The south face and crest of the pass consist of a black soil, apparently the detritus of a black slate, which latter is visible here and there below the soil. I was much disappointed with the view from the crest of the pass. The view southwards is very limited, Nanda Devi not visible; to the north-east and north a few hills are visible; to the north-west is a sea of hills moderately covered with snow (end of May) and hardly any of them appearing of great elevation. To the north-east are three bare hills, the first called Genti with behind it but not visible two other hills which have to be passed on the direct route to Chirchun." North is the Balchha ridge into Tibet and east the conical peak above the Girthi mine. At the end of May (1841) Mr. Batten found the pass closed by heavy snow and encountered imminent danger in attempting to cross it. Webber found it completely closed with snow in the beginning of summer. Gardon mentions an encamping ground on the bank of a stream at the northern *dakhna* or foot of the pass where a few stunted bushes form the only fuel supply. He adds that the snow lies on the pass for eleven months in the year.

The journey from Milam to the pass is described by Manson, who crossed it in September.

"The Gunka is crossed by a spar-bridge opposite Milam, whence the road ascends by the left bank, passable, but in some places very bad : no grass, nothing but loose earth and stones; clay, slate and grey silicious sandstone in masses and fragments; the general appearance of the mountains extremely barren, precipitous and shattered. The river in several places on either side is bounded by masses of earth and stone, the débris of the hills above which rise in numerous places into sharp peaks. Lying in the bed and along the sides of the river are large masses of conglomerate. During a thaw or a fall of snow or rain, the descent of stones is almost continuous, rendering the Gunka glen at that time very dangerous. Some of the stones are suspended on the top of the ravine precipices on little pointed peaks and their appearance on an avalanche day is not reassuring to the traveller below. The encamping grounds on the road between Milam and Dung-udiyar are Jimgang, Samgang (12,030 feet), Sangcha Talla (12,910) and Dung (13,720 feet). Hence the track runs north-west to the foot of the Unta Dhura pass at Jim, crossing the river over a bridge of stones which are piled on nearly a natural bridge of rocks; then in about half a mile to the huge Bamlas glacier. Crossing this found the Unta stream entering the glacier by an opening similar to that at its exit. The track continued along the base of the mountain to the north-west for a mile and a half with very little ascent, then turned north and commenced rather a steep ascent over a mass of white silicious rock, the debris of the mountain above. On reaching the summit came to another rather level piece of ground, but covered with fragments of a darker rock and a blacker soil. Then another ascent over the same kind of rock and soil and on reaching the top came in sight of the pass. A little further on crossed two snow-beds; the first two to three hundred yards wide, the second sixty to seventy yards wide. After crossing these the last ascent to the pass appears. Long before this all signs of vegetation had disappeared, and here the mountain was covered with small fragments of rock, clay, slate, &c. The strata of the heights to the right and left of the ascent were very much contorted in all directions." Manson was one hour and twenty-five minutes in accomplishing this last ascent, which he afterwards descended in twenty-five minutes.

Gazetteer of Almora.

APPENDIX.

GAZETTEER

OF

ALMORA.

APPENDIX.

CONTENTS.

TABLE I.—*Population by Tahsils*, 1901.

Tahsil.	Total.			Hindus.			Musalmans.			Others.		
	Persons.	Males.	Females.	Persons.	Males.	Females.	Persons.	Males.	Females.	Persons.	Males.	Females.
1	2	3	4	5	6	7	8	9	10	11	12	13
Champawat ...	122,023	62,663	59,360	119,940	61,479	58,461	1,328	859	469	755	325	430
Almora	343,870	174,088	169,782	340,073	171,900	168,173	2,723	1,623	1,100	1,074	565	509
District Total ...	465,893	236,751	229,142	460,013	233,379	226,634	4,051	2,482	1,569	1,829	890	939

TABLE II.—*Population by thanas and pattis*, 1901.

Name of thana or patti.	Total population.			Hindus.			Musalmans.			Others.		
	Total.	Males.	Females.	Total.	Males.	Females.	Total.	Males.	Females.	Total.	Males.	Females.
1	2	3	4	5	6	7	8	9	10	11	12	13
Askot Malla	7,879	3,706	4,173	7,776	3,654	4,122	12	8	4	91	44	47
Askot Talla	7,962	3,997	3,965	7,928	3,981	3,947	20	10	10	14	6	8
Asi	598	281	317	598	281	317	...	...	...	...	...	...
Khilpattiphat	2,272	1,149	1,123	2,264	1,144	1,120	8	5	3	...	...	...
Gumdes	6,390	3,213	3,177	6,295	3,168	3,127	...	...	...	95	45	50
Gangol	2,237	1,120	1,117	2,237	1,120	1,117	...	...	...	...	...	...
Chalsi	5,331	2,659	2,672	5,331	2,659	2,672	...	...	...	...	...	...
Charal Malla	546	257	289	546	257	289	...	...	...	...	...	...
Charal Talla	1,195	636	559	1,191	633	558	3	2	1	1	1	...
Talla Des (Pargana Kali Kumaon)	4,684	2,383	2,301	4,684	2,383	2,301	...	...	...	...	...	...
Palbilon Malla	1,006	543	463	1,006	543	463	...	...	...	...	...	...
Pharka	16	7	9	16	7	9	...	...	...	...	...	...
Palbilon Talla	3,975	2,145	1,830	3,972	2,144	1,828	3	1	2	...	...	...
Sui Bisung	1,161	586	575	1,130	568	562	13	7	6	18	11	7
Regruban	7,000	3,641	3,359	7,000	3,641	3,359	...	...	...	...	...	...
Sipti	956	474	482	956	474	482	...	...	...	...	...	...
Talli Rao	2,013	1,019	994	2,013	1,019	994	...	...	...	...	...	...
Thana Tanakpur	12,812	7,476	5,336	11,676	6,706	4,970	1,099	750	349	37	20	17
Chaudans	1,450	644	806	1,422	627	795	...	...	...	28	17	11
Darma Malla	325	166	159	316	160	156	...	...	...	9	6	3
Darma Talla	1,284	653	631	1,284	653	631	...	...	...	...	...	...
Byans	68	28	40	62	26	36	...	...	...	6	2	4
Kharayat	3,593	1,868	1,725	3,568	1,859	1,709	5	2	3	20	7	13
Kharak Des	1,492	791	701	1,465	776	689	...	...	...	27	15	12
Naya Des	3,724	1,897	1,827	3,723	1,896	1,827	...	...	...	1	1	...

Mahar	5,656	2,743	2,913	5,228	2,592	2,636	133	55	78	295	96	199
Rawal	4,117	2,112	2,005	4,117	2,112	2,005	...	...	...	...	...	...
Waldiya Malla	1,341	705	636	1,279	583	596	...	...	...	62	22	40
Waldiya Bichla	1,041	495	546	1,026	487	539	15	8	7	...	...	...
Waldiya Talla	5,534	2,823	2,711	5,530	2,821	2,709	...	...	...	4	2	2
Saun	3,701	1,878	1,823	3,700	1,877	1,823	...	...	...	1	1	...
Seti Malli	515	252	263	503	248	255	4	1	3	8	3	5
Seti Talli	4,063	2,068	1,995	4,041	2,053	1,988	3	3	...	19	12	7
Athbisi Malli	1,089	575	514	1,089	575	514	...	...	...	...	...	...
Athbisi Talli	1,333	696	637	1,333	696	637	...	...	...	...	...	...
Dindihat	3,259	1,645	1,614	3,259	1,645	1,614	...	...	...	...	...	...
Barabisi	6,303	3,206	3,097	6,279	3,190	3,089	10	7	3	14	9	5
Mali	4,102	2,126	1,976	4,097	2,121	1,976	...	...	...	5	5	...
Athigaon	8,222	4,243	3,979	8,178	4,217	3,961	39	24	15	5	2	3
Kamsar	8,493	4,403	4,090	8,426	4,366	4,060	54	30	24	13	7	6
Pungraon	4,321	2,213	2,108	4,314	2,210	2,104	7	3	4	...	...	...
Baraon	9,359	4,886	4,473	9,272	4,831	4,441	59	39	20	28	16	12
Bel	7,791	4,061	3,730	7,788	4,058	3,730	3	3	...	...	...	...
Bherang	2,630	1,347	1,283	2,630	1,347	1,283	...	...	...	...	...	...
Rithagadh Karai	4,485	2,333	2,152	4,454	2,315	2,139	24	13	11	7	5	2
Daraun	6,029	3,200	2,829	6,026	3,199	2,827	...	...	...	3	1	2
Rithagadh	2,676	1,397	1,279	2,676	1,397	1,279	...	...	...	...	...	...
Rangor	8,256	4,393	3,863	8,256	4,393	3,863	...	...	...	...	...	...
Lakhanpur Talla	4,202	2,096	2,106	4,201	2,095	2,106	...	...	...	1	1	...
Lakhanpur Malla	5,516	2,802	2,714	5,513	2,800	2,713	3	2	1	...	...	...
Salam Talla	4,923	2,520	2,403	4,921	2,519	2,402	2	1	1	...	...	...
Salam Malla	4,804	2,414	2,390	4,802	2,412	2,390	1	1	...	1	1	...
Goriphat	5,505	2,773	2,732	5,504	2,772	2,732	...	...	...	1	1	...
Talla Des (Pargana Johar) ...	7,300	3,649	3,651	7,290	3,644	3,646	7	3	4	3	2	1
Danpur Talla	6,542	3,380	3,162	6,529	3,372	3,157	10	6	4	3	2	1
Danpur Bichla	3,990	2,005	1,985	3,990	2,005	1,985	...	...	...	...	...	...
Danpur Malla	6,166	3,084	3,082	6,162	3,081	3,081	4	3	1	...	...	...
Dug	5,037	2,637	2,400	4,952	2,602	2,350	73	32	41	12	3	9
Nakuri	4,587	2,329	2,258	4,587	2,329	2,258	...	...	...	...	...	...
Katyur Talla	5,032	2,629	2,403	4,964	2,588	2,376	58	37	21	10	4	6
Katyur Bichla	6,312	3,330	2,982	6,253	3,294	2,959	48	28	20	11	8	3
Katyur Malla	8,200	4,224	3,976	8,059	4,148	3,911	73	40	33	68	36	32

TABLE II.—*Population by thanas and pattis* 1901—(concluded).

Name of thana or patti.	Total population.			Hindus.			Musalmans.			Others.		
	Total.	Males.	Females.	Total.	Males.	Females.	Total.	Males.	Females.	Total.	Males.	Females.
1	2	3	4	5	6	7	8	9	10	11	12	13
Kaklasaun Talla	1,917	929	988	1,874	910	964	...	...	...	43	19	24
Kaklasaun Malla	6,498	3,110	3,388	6,489	3,101	3,388	9	9	...	...	...	...
Giwar Talla	7,510	3,696	3,814	7,477	3,682	3,795	25	12	13	8	2	6
Giwar Palla	6,967	3,539	3,428	6,944	3,529	3,415	17	8	9	6	2	4
Giwar Walla	6,466	3,283	3,183	6,462	3,280	3,182	1	1	...	3	2	1
Chaukot Talla	8,523	4,162	4,361	8,523	4,162	4,361	...	...	...	...	...	...
Chaukot Bichla	8,787	4,266	4,521	8,787	4,266	4,521	...	...	...	...	...	...
Chaukot Malla	7,671	3,796	3,875	7,653	3,787	3,866	11	6	5	7	3	4
Dora Talla	8,560	4,235	4,325	8,551	4,232	4,319	9	3	6	...	...	...
Dora Bichla	5,731	2,772	2,959	5,730	2,771	2,959	1	1	...	...	...	...
Dora Malla	6,536	3,269	3,267	6,425	3,212	3,213	3	2	1	108	55	53
Naya Palla	5,348	2,654	2,694	5,348	2,654	2,694	...	...	...	...	...	...
Naya Walla	4,779	2,286	2,493	4,758	2,279	2,479	21	7	14	...	...	...
Talla Salt	7,235	3,554	3,681	7,228	3,547	3,681	6	6	...	1	1	...
Palla Salt	4,784	2,307	2,477	4,778	2,304	2,474	6	3	3	...	...	...
Malla Salt	6,972	3,472	3,500	6,957	3,465	3,492	15	7	8	...	...	...
Walla Salt	5,640	2,745	2,895	5,632	2,741	2,891	8	4	4	...	...	...
Silor Talla	4,864	2,377	2,487	4,856	2,376	2,480	8	1	7	...	...	...
Silor Malla	4,614	2,254	2,360	4,546	2,221	2,325	62	31	31	6	2	4
Chilkia forest Range	117	106	11	109	98	11	8	8	...	...	...	...
Kandarkua	2,355	1,147	1,208	2,355	1,147	1,208	...	...	...	...	...	...
Chaugaon	2,885	1,461	1,424	2,843	1,424	1,419	27	23	4	15	14	1
Malli Doti	2,382	1,144	1,238	2,381	1,144	1,237	1	...	1	...	...	...
Dhuraphat	2,114	1,066	1,048	2,109	1,062	1,047	5	4	1	...	...	...
Almora cantonment	1,589	1,120	469	1,443	1,030	413	109	74	35	37	16	21
Almora municipality	7,007	3,759	3,248	5,908	3,191	2,717	863	485	378	236	83	153

Ranikhet cantonment ...	3,246	2,279	967	2,239	1,618	621	732	476	256	275	185	90
Athaguli Palla	4,696	2,252	2,444	4,677	2,241	2,436	19	11	8	...	...	...
Athaguli Walla	3,604	1,749	1,855	3,598	1,745	1,853	6	4	2	...	...	...
Uchyur	3,780	1,805	1,975	3,753	1,792	1,961	17	7	10	10	6	4
Kaligadh	2,524	1,224	1,300	2,501	1,205	1,296	23	19	4	...	...	...
Kairarau	4,416	2,216	2,200	4,393	2,203	2,190	19	10	9	4	3	1
Khasparja	6,707	3,405	3,302	6,514	3,293	3,221	73	50	23	120	62	58
Talla Tikhun	4,673	2,345	2,328	4,670	2,342	2,328	3	3	...	...	...	
Malla Tikhun	4,787	2,366	2,421	4,772	2,355	2,417	13	9	4	2	2	...
Dwarsyun	1,064	515	549	1,056	508	548	...	...	...	8	7	1
Bisaud Malla	1,507	712	795	1,507	712	795	...	...	...	...	...	...
Borarau Palla	6,495	3,336	3,159	6,450	3,309	3,141	40	23	17	5	4	1
Borarau Walla	5,487	2,748	2,739	5,420	2,719	2,701	63	27	36	4	2	2
Syunara Talla	5,781	2,919	2,862	5,756	2,903	2,853	15	10	5	10	6	4
Riuni	1,227	582	645	1,217	574	643	10	8	2	...	...	...
Syunara Malla	5,647	2,778	2,869	5,637	2,772	2,865	10	6	4	...	...	...
Tota ...	465,893	236,751	229,142	460,013	2,38,379	226,634	4,051	2,482	1,569	1,829	890	939

TABLE III.—*Vital statistics.*

Year.	Births.				Deaths.			
	Total.	Males.	Females.	Rate per 1,000.	Total.	Males.	Females.	Rate per 1,000
1	2	3	4	5	6	7	8	9
1891 ...	14,588	7,639	6,949	25·90	16,145	8,515	7,630	28·67
1892 ...	14,471	7,550	6,921	35·17	19,947	9,849	10,098	48·47
1893 ...	14,640	7,541	7,099	35·58	9,634	5,066	4,568	23·41
1894 ...	17,536	9,095	8,441	42·61	12,908	6,629	6,279	31·37
1895 ...	16,585	8,427	8,158	40·30	12,810	6,677	6,133	31·13
1896 ...	15,084	7,652	7,432	36·66	15,039	7,606	7,433	36·55
1897 ...	16,420	8,379	8,041	39·39	10,047	5,120	4,927	24·10
1898 ...	19,677	10,057	9,620	47·20	12,794	6,475	6,319	30·69
1899 ...	18,305	9,470	8,835	43·91	11,286	5,778	5,508	27·07
1900 ...	18,557	9,418	9,139	*44·51	10,020	5,187	4,833	24·04*
1901 ...	18,228	9,365	8,863	39·12	9,731	4,847	4,884	20·89
1902 ...	20,819	10,554	10,265	44·68	11,463	5,844	5,619	24·60
1903 ...	17,899	8,129	8,770	38·41	15,649	7,616	8,033	33·59
1904 ...	21,846	11,190	10,656	46·89	11,630	5,845	5,785	24·96
1905 ...	21,196	10,756	10,440	45·49	12,168	6,206	5,962	26·12
1906 ...	21,837	11,083	10,754	46·87	13,231	6,602	6,629	28·40
1907 ...	20,991	10,714	10,277	45·05	14,584	7,328	7,256	31·30
1908 ...	19,089	9,737	9,352	40·97	17,671	8,863	8,808	37·93
1909 ...								
1910 ...								
1911 ...								
1912 ...								
1913 ...								
1914 ...								

* The rates from 1891 to 1900 are calculated from the returns of the 1891 Census.

TABLE IV.—*Deaths according to cause.*

Year.			Total deaths from—					
			All causes.	Plague.	Cholera.	Small-pox.	Fever.	Bowel com-plaints.
1			2	3	4	5	6	7
1891	...	...	16,145	...	918	104	9,898	3,102
1892	...	...	19,947	...	5,103	5	10,453	2,477
1893	...	...	9,634	..	110	5	6,096	1,864
1894	...	...	12,908	...	1	...	9,244	2,130
1895	...	...	12,810	...	...	1	9,453	1,987
1896	...	...	15,039	...	609	117	10,537	2,321
1897	...	...	10,047	...	...	66	7,018	1,595
1898	...	...	12,794	...	73	12	9,146	1,951
1899	...	...	11,286	...	20	1	7,740	2,156
1900	...	...	10,020	...	...	...	6,842	1,798
1901	...	...	9,731	...	...	1	6,885	1,547
1902	...	...	11,463	...	350	3	7,659	1,763
1903	...	...	15,649	...	1,395	50	9,814	2,350
1904	...	...	11,630	...	18	92	8,188	1,673
1905	...	...	12,168	...	...	33	8,542	1,959
1906	...	...	13,231	...	798	27	8,805	1,874
1907	...	...	14,584	...	1,143	265	9,226	1,881
1908	...	...	17,671	...	602	441	12,501	2,063
1909	...	...						
1910	...	...						
1911	...	...						
1912	...	...						
1913	...	...						
1914	...	...						

TABLE V.—*Criminal Justice.*

Year.	Offences against public tranquillity, (chapter VIII).	Offences affecting life.	Grievous hurt.	Rape.	Cattle theft.	Criminal force and assault.	Theft.	Robbery and dakaiti.	Receiving stolen property.	Criminal trespass.	Bad livelihood.	Keeping the peace.	Cases under— Opium Act.	Cases under— Excise Act.
1	2	3	4	5	6	7	8	9	10	11	12	13	14	15
1898 ...	62	8	6	...	...	44	46	2	17	22	2	16	...	5
1899 ...	75	4	10	...	1	41	34	2	4	18	3	11	...	2
1900 ...	49	2	9	...	1	13	74	2	6	19	3	3	1	2
1901 ...	13	5	17	1	1	32	61	5	5	17	3	12	2	4
1902 ...	59	15	...	...	1	24	31	...	4	31	8	11	2	8
1903 ...	16	3	3	1	1	19	24	3	3	12	...	7	...	4
1904 ...	...	11	5	...	2	35	27	5	10	16	2	12	...	1
1905 ...	55	4	2	1	2	21	29	9	14	12	5	54	...	8
1906 ...	11	11	4	...	6	18	24	3	8	12	11	17	3	11
1907 ...	52	10	4	1	6	23	37	19	16	17	27	10	...	9
1908 ...	11	14	1	...	7	18	50	27	12	31	10	13	1	4
1909 ...	27	4	...	...	...	24	47	...	14	33	6	23	2	8
1910 ...														
1911 ...														
1912 ...														
1913 ...														

TABLE VI.—*Cognizable crime.*

Year.	Number of cases investigated by police.			Number of persons.		
	Suo motu.	By orders of Magistrate.	Sent up for trial.	Tried.	Acquitted or discharged.	Convicted.
1	2	3	4	5	6	7
1898	229	44	231	432	129	303
1899	309	68	282	815	264	543
1900	257	48	264	558	216	340
1901	232	115	313	846	260	586
1902	269	79	297	762	258	503
1903	306	45	321	703	182	521
1904	184	53	229	511	207	304
1905	392		354	583	176	407
1906	419		342	519	112	407
1907	440		382	540	142	398
1908	354		241	372	106	266
1909						
1910						
1911						
1912						
1913						
1914						
1915						
1916						
1917						

TABLE VII.—*Revenue demand at successive settlements.*

Pargana.	Year of settlement.						
	1817.	1820.	1828.	1833.	1843.	1872.	1902.
1	2	3	4	5	6	7	8
	Rs.	Rs.	Rs.	Rs.	Rs.	Rs.	Rs.
Askot ...	709	996	...	...	1,174	1,250	1,450
Barahmandal* ...	11,073	14,767	16,896	17,328	18,075	36,833	46,062
Chaugarkha ...	4,433	6,776	7,677	7,800	8,012	15,871	24,124
Danpur ...	3,583	4,613	5,853	5,958	5,902	15,362	22,270
Darma ...	5,766	1,225	1,368	1,405	1,400	1,886	2,645
Gangoli ...	1,918	2,558	3,298	3,469	3,641	12,944	19,971
Johar ...	5,140	2,633	3,380	3,439	3,373	5,975	7,329
Kali Kumaon ...	9,764	12,248	13,333	15,555	15,261	25,873	37,548
Pali ...	21,166	31,236	32,764	33,249	33,892	57,320	68,041
Phaldakot* ...	6,133	7,001	7,404	7,528	7,565	10,346	8,638
Shor ...	4,002	5,495	6,638	6,657	6,687	14,113	18,738
Sira ...	2,199	2,760	3,120	3,223	3,205	5,999	9,438

* These parganas lost some pattis and villages transferred to Naini Tal in 1892 and 1898.

TABLE VIII.—*Present demand for revenue and cesses for the year* 1312 *fasli*. 1908-09.

Tahsil	Pargana and tahsil.	Where included in *Ain-i-Akbari*.	Revenue.			Cesses.			Total.		
	1	2	3			4			5		
			Rs.	a.	p.	Rs.	a.	p.	Rs.	a.	p.
Almora.	Barahmandal	...	41,258	0	6	4,631	4	1	45,889	4	7
	Changarkha ...	...	20,420	12	0	2,292	7	2	22,713	3	2
	Johar ...	...	7,101	8	0	721	1	6	7,822	9	6
	Danpur ...	...	20,463	10	5	2,305	12	2	22,769	6	7
	Gangoli ...	...	18,634	15	3	2,028	13	2	20,663	12	5
	Pali ...	..	65,406	13	7	6,782	15	2	72,189	12	9
	Phaldakot ...	...	8,540	9	3	864	12	9	9,405	6	0
	Total ...	...	1,81,826	5	0	19,627	2	0	2,01,453	7	0
Champhawat.	Kali Kumaon	...	35,801	11	9	3,750	14	6	39,552	10	3
	Total ...	...	35,801	11	9	3,750	14	6	39,552	10	3
	Darma ...	...	2,486	0	0	257	3	1	2,743	3	1
	Sira ...	...	8,917	14	6	933	4	11	9,851	3	5
	Shor ...	...	18,045	2	11	1,845	11	6	19,890	14	5
	Askot ...	...	1,450	0	0	145	0	0	1,595	0	0
	Total ...	...	30,899	1	5	3,181	3	6	34,080	4	11
	Total ...	...	2,48,527	2	2	26,559	4	0	2,75,086	6	2

TABLE IX.—*Excise.*

Year.	Receipts from foreign liquors.	Country spirit. Receipts.	Country spirit. Consumption in gallons.	Receipts from *tari* and *sendhi*.	Drugs. Total receipts.	Drugs. Consumption in maunds of— *Ganja.*	Drugs. Consumption in maunds of— *Charas.*	Opium. Total receipts.	Opium. Consumption.	Total receipts.	Total charges.	Incidence of receipts per 10,000 of population from— Liquor, including "*tari*."†	Incidence … Drugs.	Incidence … Opium.	Number of shops for sale of— Country spirits.	Number of shops … Drugs.	Number of shops … Opium.
1	2	3	4	5	6	7	8	9	10	11	12	13	14	15	16	17	18
	Rs.	Rs.		Rs.	Rs.	Mds. s.	Mds. s.	Rs.	Mds. s.	Rs.	Rs.	Rs.	Rs.	Rs.			
						Not available		4,824	10 24	...	...	...	...	89			
1891-92 ...	2,019	10,384	...	...	2,087	Ditto.		1,920	4 29	16,409	354	195	37	34	4	4	6
1892-93 ...	1,604	11,844	...	...	1,954	...	5 32	1,907	4 21	17,308	332	224	34	34	4	4	6
1893-94 ...	856	13,038	...	...	2,145	...	5 33	2,003	4 29	18,049	219	329	52	48	4	4	5
1894-95 ...	1,327	14,698	...	...	2,424	...	8 12	1,992	4 33	20,466	160	374	58	49	4	5	5
1895-96 ...	1,470	14,017	...	...	2,731	...	9 1	1,916	5 1	20,134	178	362	66	46	5	6	6
1896-97 ...	1,567	15,235	...	...	2,452	...	8 5	1,770	4 21	21,026	208	380	58	42	5	6	7
1897-98 ...	5,179	12,617	...	...	2,306	...	...	1,677	4 12	21,784	246	320	55	40	5	6	6
1898-99 ...	7,927	13,494	...	...	2,742	...	8 38	1,793	4 34	25,955	757	341	76	42	5	6	6
1899-1900...	7,713	14,450	...	...	3,204	...	4 34	1,770	4 12	27,138	592	367	101	45	5	6	7
1900-01 ...	7,027	14,792	...	...	3,729	...	6 20	2,098	3 18	27,646	655	337	80	45	5	6	5
1901-02 ...	7,448	14,557	...	...	4,370	...	7 37	2,398	3 35	28,774	585	330	93	52	7	8	8
1902-03 ...	7,970	15,951	...	...	5,336	...	8 29	2,229	3 36	31,486	751	362	116	48	7	8	8
1903-04 ...	8,351	18,731	...		6,780	...	11 9	2,875	4 6	36,737	952	421	147	62	8	9	8
1904-05* ...	10,329	21,226	...	...	6,135	...	6 9	3,118	4 8	40,808	532	455	137	67	8	9	8
1905-06 ...	8,730	21,447	...	...	6,644	...	7 6	2,859	3 28	39,710	979	499	162	59	8	9	8
1906-07 ...	9,509	22,032	...	...	6,920	...	5 18½	2,791	3 27	41,252	1,173	533	155	61	8	9	8
1907-08 ...	9,565	22,756	...	...	7,144	...	5 6¾	2,928	3 8	42,393	832	557	155	64	8	9	8
1908-09 ...	16,065	22,381	...	...	6,531	...	4 14	2,774	3 1½	47,646	905	532	158	60	8	9	8
1909-1910...																	
1910-11 ...																	
1911-12 ...																	
1912-13 ...																	

* From this year onwards the figures are those for the financial year, and not for the revenue year as before.

† Excluding malt liquor.

TABLE X.—*Stamps.*

Year.	Receipts from— Non-Judicial.	Court-fee including copies.	All sources.	Total charges.
1	2	3	4	5
	Rs.	Rs.	Rs.	Rs.
1890-91	20,608	41,337	62,231	1,908
1891-92	17,981	39,737	57,909	1,331
1892-93	10,460	24,048	34,867	838
1893-94	12,408	26,372	38,952	1,085
1894-95	12,506	26,251	33,821	967
1895-96	13,532	27,349	41,003	1,077
1896-97	13,358	26,554	39,993	996
1897-98	11,967	28,731	41,113	1,016
1898-99	11,984	24,067	36,615	851
1899-1900	13,709	27,377	41,768	1,213
1900-01	13,332	25,438	39,325	1,450
1901-02	13,835	25,829	40,412	1,767
1902-03	14,044	27,550	42,237	1,655
1903-04	13,209	24,580	38,192	1,517
1904-05	12,544	22,250	35,247	1,539
1905-06	14,256	25,998	40,632	1,841
1906-07	13,849	26,660	40,939	1,764
1907-08	15,365	27,056	42,863	1,649
1908-09	14,708	26,870	41,970	1,717
1909-10				
1910-11				
1911-12				
1912-13				

TABLE XI.—*Income-tax.*

Year.	Total receipts.	Collected by companies.		Profits of companies.		Other sources, Part IV.				Total charges.	Objections under Part IV.	
						Under Rs. 2,000.		Over Rs. 2,000.				
		Assessees.	Tax.	Assessees.	Tax.	Assessees.	Tax.	Assessees.	Tax.		Number filed.	Wholly or partly successful.
1	2	3	4	5	6	7	8	9	10	11	12	13
	Rs.		Rs.		Rs.		Rs.		Rs.	Rs.		
1891-92	4,037	6	321	...	...	127	2,131	6	608	243	24	10
1892-93	4,404	8	368	...	...	134	2,320	5	499	359	74	37
1893-94	4,552	7	260	...	...	137	2,476	6	569	134	55	13
1894-95	4,657	8	211	...	...	144	2,698	6	620	190	30	10
1895-96	4,997	7	230	...	...	174	3,137	5	363	255	66	20
1896-97	6,054	7	207	...	...	179	2,985	12	1,729	92	61	18
1897-98	7,096	7	216	...	...	203	8,240	14	1,980	403	74	40
1898-99	6,521	8	199	...	...	200	3,200	18	1,970	101	36	8
1899-1900	7,421	6	214	...	...	232	3,415	26	2,700	147	61	20
1900-01	7,146	6	210	...	...	215	3,386	26	2,591	102	36	11
1901-02	7,953	6	205	...	...	269	4,344	23	2,245	170	67	23
1902-03	7,643	6	206	...	...	275	4,355	26	2,499	322	70	19
1903-04	5,490	2	147	...	...	94	2,358	24	2,285	131	29	8
1904-05	5,856	2	147	...	...	98	2,495	30	2,595	135	51	18
1905-06												
1906-07	6,976	2	146	...	...	105	2,793	33	3,266	93	40	18
1907-08	6,691	2	149	...	...	109	2,981	29	2,714	89	38	28
1908-09	7,040	2	149	...	...	102	2,752	38	3,315	89	44	21
1909-10	7,348	2	148	...	...	114	3,083	35	3,381	102	36	17
1910-11												
1911-12												
1912-13												

TABLE XII.—*Income-tax by tahsils (Part IV only).*

Year.	Tahsil Almora.				Year.	Tahsil Champawat.			
	Under Rs. 2,000.		Over Rs. 2,000.			Under Rs. 2,000.		Over Rs. 2,000.	
	Assessees.	Tax.	Assessees.	Tax.		Assessees.	Tax.	Assessees.	Tax.
1	2	3	4	5	1	2	3	4	5
		Rs.		Rs. a. p.			Rs.		Rs.
1891-92...	107	1,881	6	608	1891-92 ...	20	250	...	...
1892-93...	112	2,045	5	499	1892-93 ...	22	275	...	..
1893-94...	114	2,181	6	569	1893-94 ...	23	295	...	...
1894-95...	119	2,398	6	620	1894-95 ...	25	300	...	...
1895-96 ..	143	2,742	5	363	1895-96 ...	31	395	...	...
1896-97...	147	2,564	12	1,729	1896-97 ...	32	421	...	...
1897-98...	166	2,769	14	1,980	1897-98 ...	37	471	...	...
1898-99 ..	162	2,719	18	1,970	1898-99 ...	38	481	...	...
1899-1900	196	2,954	26	2,700	1899-1900 ...	36	461	...	...
1900-01...	167	2,779	26	2,591	1900-01 ...	48	607	...	..
1901-02 ..	209	3,408	22	2,180	1901-02 ...	60	936	1	65
1902-03...	214	3,409	25	2,434	1902-03 ...	61	946	1	65
1903-04...	82	2,029	22	2,113	1903-04 ...	12	329	2	172
1904-05...	87	2,196	29	2,502	1904-05 ...	11	301	1	93
1905-06...	91	2,271	37	3,173	1905-06 ...	14	521	1	93
1906-07...	93	2,413	28	2,621	1906-07 ...	16	568	1	93
1907-08 ..	93	2,527	37	3,222	1907-08 ...	9	225	1	93
1908-09...	103	2,803	34	3,288	1908-09 ...	11	280	1	93
1909-10 ..					1909-10 ...				
1910-11...					1910-11 ...				
1911-12...					1911-12 ..				
1912-13...					1912-13 ...				

TABLE XIII.—District Board.

Year.	Receipts. Education.	Medical.	Scientific, &c.	Miscellaneous.	Civil works.	Pounds.	Expenditure. Total expenditure.	General administration.	Education.	Medical.	Scientific, &c.	Miscellaneous.	Civil works.	Pounds.	Debt.
1	2	3	4	5	6	7	8	9	10	11	12	13	14	15	16
	Rs.	Rs.	Rs.	Rs.	Rs.	Rs.	Rs.	Rs.	Rs.	Rs.	Rs.	Rs.	Rs.	Rs.	Rs.
1891-92 ...	12,766	1,549	...	8,176	569	...	1,97,146	481	23,934	7,503	...	5,921	1,59,307	...	...
1892-93 ...	5,995	1,593	...	2,967	...	...	2,29,701	490	36,749	6,677	...	2,965	81,820	...	...
1893-94 ...	3,518	1,738	...	2,956	...	...	1,70,500	571	22,888	6,047	...	3,948	1,37,046	...	...
1894-95 ...	2,938	6,311	...	3,071	...	...	87,166	596	24,587	6,878	...	3,781	51,324	...	...
1895-96 ...	2,982	311	...	2,499	4	...	80,510	662	22,971	6,656	...	3,420	46,801	...	...
1896-97 ...	3,432	593	...	2,848	12	...	75,185	582	22,857	7,065	...	3,215	41,466	...	...
1897-98 ...	3,216	996	...	292	3,264	...	91,588	670	23,724	6,977	...	180	60,037	...	...
1898-99 ...	3,085	1,769	...	311	3,342	83	99,345	1,138	22,842	6,424	...	210	68,681	...	50
1899-1900 ...	3,110	1,918	...	380	2,986	150	93,611	1,217	25,945	6,565	279	169	59,323	63	50
1900-01 ...	3,087	1,186	...	493	2,360	200	89,912	1,310	26,026	6,469	341	180	55,439	97	50
1901-02 ...	3,453	1,585	...	1	3,006	104	96,549	1,421	27,597	6,803	436	253	59,835	204	...
1902-03 ...	3,700	774	...	13	6,173	215	1,14,898	1,425	33,479	7,093	529	275	7,1811	166	120
1903-04 ...	3,819	606	..	13	3,260	183	1,07,877	1,474	37,678	6,761	548	279	60,934	148	55
1904-05 ...	4,997	622	...	5	4,413	169	1,17,723	1,532	38,543	7,794	533	417	68,522	162	220
1905-06 ...	5,973	633	...	86	3,749	197	1,36,055	1,964	44,519	7,115	988	172	80,999	148	150
1906-07 ...	5,520	773	...	48	4,153	201	1,49,509	2,751	47,301	9,618	1,975	123	87,569	172	...
1907-08 ...	6,126	700	55	60	3,935	163	1,39,560	2,953	50,938	13,055	1,468	146	70,682	153	165
1908-09 ...															
1909-10 ...															
1910-11 ...															
1911-12 ...															
1912-13 ...															
1913-14 ...															

* Formerly net receipts only were shown. From this year receipts and also expenditure are given.

TABLE XIV.—*Municipality of Almora.*

Year.	Income.							Expenditure.										
	Octroi.	Tax on houses and lands.	Other taxes.	Rents.	Loans.	Other sources.	Total.	Administration and collection of taxes.	Public safety.	Water-supply and drainage.		Conservancy.	Hospitals and dispensaries.	Public works.	Public instruction.	Other heads.	Total.
										Capital.	Maintenance.						
1	2	3	4	5	6	7	8	9	10	11	12	13	14	15	16	17	18
	Rs.	Rs.	Rs.	Rs.	Rs.	Rs.	Rs.	Rs.	Rs.	Rs.	Rs.	Rs.	Rs.	Rs.	Rs.	Rs.	Rs.
1890-91 ..	5,056	...	1,624	7	...	547	7,234	973	1,156	...	333	3,745	253	350	72	438	7,314
1891-92 ..	6,196	...	1,600	178	...	294	8,268	981	1,150	...	432	4,181	240	822	72	193	8,071
1892-93 ...	5,881	...	1,658	215	...	315	8,069	994	1,080	...	672	3,528	240	336	72	253	7,175
1893-94 ..	6,348	...	1,530	272	...	272	8,422	978	1,150	...	655	3,316	240	914	72	772	8,097
1894-95 ..	6,284	...	1,593	332	...	352	8,561	1,083	1,431		814	4,920	249	506	97	626	9,726
1895-96 ..	6,488	...	1,534	390	...	344	8,756	1,066	1,405	...	630	3,823	240	460	72	849	8,485
1896-97 ...	6,154	...	1,694	535	...	525	8,908	1,127	1,648	...	887	3,817	337	411	320	741	9,283
1897-98 ...	6,815	...	2,099	592	...	629	10,135	1,299	1,542	...	1,067	3,733	401	96	300	1,124	9,562
1898-99 ...	8,269	...	2,259	506	...	610	11,644	1,465	1,608	...	701	4,718	346	152	500	670	9,960
1899-1900	7,654	...	2,757	527	...	641	11,579	1,660	1,740	...	1,040	4,912	444	80	400	676	11,052
1900-01 ..	7,037	...	2,723	462	...	825	11,047	1,864	1,678	...	1,628	4,017	444	621	865	797	11,446
1901-02 ..	8,500	...	2,683	697	...	819	12,759	2,749	1,652	...	528	3,958	467	495	865	497	11,211
1902-03 ..	7,303	...	2,795	693	...	6,460	17,251	2,511	1,772	271	866	3,971	467	1,344	865	808	12,865
1903-04 ..	8,077	...	2,656	1,014	...	521	12,268	2,618	1,771	6,102	714	3,891	567	1,455	865	1,574	19,557
1904-05 ..	8,377	...	2,570	759	5,000	3,515	20,221	2,886	1,622	7,385	676	4,119	567	409	865	1,460	19,939
1905-06 ...	9,974	...	2,647	792	...	1,835	15,248	3,221	469	1,497	669	3,950	567	390	865	1,914	13,542
1906-07 ..	9,875	...	2,740	670	13,000	2,828	29,113	4,647	803	897	654	4,696	567	231	865	2,021	15,379
1907-08 ..	10,352	...	2,660	671	...	1,878	15,561	4,071	1,065	12,491	1,071	4,814	567	39	865	3,518	28,501
1908-09 ...	9,080	...	2,621	647	...	2,947	15,295	4,386	954	1,142	331	4,623	567	200	865	3,378	16,466
1909-10 ..	9,682	...	2,670	651	...	1,247	14,450	4,227	752	586	310	4,687	567	245	865	3,211	15,450
1910-11 ...																	
1911-12 ...																	
1912-13 ..																	
1913-14 ...																	

TABLE XV.—*Distribution of Police*, 1909.

Thána.	Sub-inspectors.	Head-constables.	Constables.	Municipal police.	Town police.	Rural police.	Road police.
1	2	3	4	5	6	7	8
Almora ...	1	2	20	...	...	...	...
Ranikhet ...	1	6	44	...	...	...	...
Outpost Ganai ...	0	1	3	...	...	...	...

Table XVI.—*Education*, 1908.

Year.	Total.			Secondary education.			Primary education.		
	Schools and Colleges.	Scholars. Males.	Scholars. Females.	Schools.	Scholars. Males.	Scholars. Females.	Schools.	Scholars. Males.	Scholars. Females.
1	2	3	4	5	6	7	8	9	10
1896-97 ...	107	4,718	220	5	599	76	101	4,108	144
1897-98 ...	121	5,325	291	5	657	87	115	4,662	204
1898-99 ...	120	5,243	225	4	545	102	115	4,692	123
1899-1900 ...	155	6,944	248	4	546	87	150	6,389	161
1900-01 ...	154	6,616	354	6	681	112	147	5,929	242
1901-02 ...	150	6,971	133	6	752	117	143	6,211	16
1902-03 ...	176	8,235	392	8	762	101	167	7,464	291
1903-04 ...	183	7,606	503	9	764	122	173	6,829	381
1904-05 ...	186	8,073	364	9	800	30	176	7,273	334
1905-06 ...	181	9,562	432	9	1,005	70	171	8,557	362
1906-07 ...	189	10,224	652	9	769	66	179	9,455	586
1907-08 ...	194	9,101	423	9	646	72	184	8,455	351

List of parganas and pattis.

Pargana.	Patti.
1. Darma ...	Byáns.
	Chaudáns.
	Darma, Malla.
	Darma, Talla.
2. Johar ...	Malla Johar.
	Goriphat.
	Talla Des.
3. Danpur ...	Danpur, Malla.
	Danpur, Bichla.
	Daupur, Talla.
	Dug.
	Katyur, Malla.
	Katyur Bichla.
	Katyur, Talla.
	Nakuri.
4. Sira ...	Athbisi, Malli.
	Athbisi, Talli.
	Barabisi.
	Dindihat.
	Mali.
5 Askot ...	Askot, Malla.
	Askot, Talla.
6. Shor ...	Kharayát.
	Kharkdes.
	Mahar.
	Nayades.
	Rawal.
	Seti, Malli.
	Seti, Talli.
	Saun.
	Waldia, Malla.
	Waldia, Bichla.
	Waldia, Talla.
7. Kali-Kumaon.	Chalsi.
	Charal Malla.
	Charal Talla.
	Gumdes.
	Gangoli.
	Khilpattiphat.
	Palbilon, Malla.
	Palbilon, Talla.
	Pharka.
	Regruban.
	Sipti.
	Sui Bisung.
	Asi.
	Talli Rao.
	Tallades.
	Tanakpur Bhabar (*a*).
8. Chaugarkha.	Darun.
	Kharahi.
8. Chaugarkha.—(concld.).	Lakkanpur, Malla.
	Lakhanpur, Talla.
	Rithagadh.
	Rangor.
	Salam, Malla.
	Salam, Talla.
	Dolphat.
9. Gangoli...	Bel.
	Bherang.
	Baraun.
	Kamsyar.
	Pungraun.
	Athigaon.
10. Barahmandal.	Bisaud, Malla.
	Borarau, Palla.
	Borarau Walla.
	Dwarsyun.
	Kairarau.
	Kaligarh.
	Khasparja.
	Uchyur.
	Riuni.
	Syunara Malla.
	Syunara Talla.
	Tikhun, Malla.
	Tikhun, Talla.
	Athaguli, Palla.
	Athaguli, Walla.
11. Phaldakot.	Chaugaon.
	Dhuraphat.
	Kandarkhua.
	Malli Doti.
12. Pali ...	Chaukot, Malla.
	Chaukot, Bichla.
	Chaukot, Talla.
	Dora, Malla.
	Dora, Bichla.
	Dora, Talla.
	Giwar, Palla.
	Giwar, Talla.
	Giwar, Walla.
	Kaklasaun, Malla.
	Kaklasaun, Talla.
	Naya, Palla.
	Naya, Walla.
	Silor, Malla.
	Silor, Talla.
	Salt, Walla.
	Salt, Palla.
	Salt, Talla.
	Salt, Malla.

(*a*) The Tanakpur Bhabar has been transferred to the Naini Tal district.

Malla means upper and Talla lower, not with reference to actual altitude, but to the position of the place on the course of a river. Walla means hither and Palla farther with reference to the head quarters of the district, and Bichla means middle.

List of Schools, 1909.

Locality.	School.	Class.	Average attendance.
		I.—SECONDARY.	
Almora ...	Town School ...	Vernacular Middle School.	43
Pali ...	Middle School Pali ...	Ditto ...	59
Gangoli ...	Middle School Kanda,	Ditto ...	71
Shor ...	Middle School, Pithoragarh.	Ditto ...	54
Kali Kumaun ...	Middle School, Kheti-Khan.	Ditto ...	31
	ENGLISH SCHOOLS.		
Almora ...	English High School,	High School ...	239
	Ramsay Collegiate School.	Ditto ...	309
	Anglo-Vernacular Girls' School.	Ditto ...	62
		II.—PRIMARY.	
Pali ...	Sarainkhet ...	State Primary ...	18
	Deghat	Ditto ...	40
	Syalde	Ditto ...	42
	Jhimar	Ditto ...	96
	Pasiya	Ditto ...	48
	Koirala	Ditto ...	55
	Dewayal	Ditto .	77
	Jinapani... ...	Ditto ...	61
	Sinora	Ditto ...	52
	Mijhora	Ditto ...	26
	Bangora	Ditto ...	30
	Silor Mahadeo ...	Ditto ...	32
	Basot	Ditto ...	48
	Jalali	Ditto ...	58
	Naubara	Ditto ...	55
	Masi	Ditto ...	64
	Jethuwa	Ditto ...	11
	Mahatgaon ...	Ditto ...	28
	Bairti	Ditto ...	97
	Chaukhutia ...	Ditto ...	69
	Panghat	Ditto ...	25
Barahmandal ...	Bagwalipokhar ...	Ditto ...	97
	Kuwali	Ditto ...	44
	Daulatghat ...	Ditto ...	42
	Batgal	Ditto ...	33
	Manan	Ditto ...	53
	Satrali	Ditto ...	72
	Bhaisargaon ...	Ditto ...	55
	Someswar ...	Ditto ...	141
	Salonj	Ditto ...	39
	Chhani	Ditto ...	20
	Ubhyari	Ditto ...	48

List of Schools 1909—(continued).

Locality.	School.	Class.	Average attendance.
		II.—PRIMARY—(contd.)	
Chaugarkha ...	Digoli	State Primary ...	22
	Jainti	Ditto ..	56
	Lamgara ...	Ditto ...	48
	Kheti	Ditto ...	22
	Chaukoli ...	Ditto ...	44
	Barechina ...	Ditto ...	54
	Bilori	Ditto ...	22
	Khankar	Ditto ...	45
	Naugaon ...	Ditto ...	13
Phaldakot ...	Jainoli	Ditto ...	30
	Tarkhet	Ditto ...	18
Gangoli ...	Gangolihat ...	Ditto ...	75
	Kalubinayak ...	Ditto ...	24
	Rai	Ditto ...	53
	Beninag	Ditto ...	53
	Rawatsera ...	Ditto ...	53
	Dafaut	Ditto ...	33
	Malsun	Ditto ...	31
	Tiroli	Ditto ...	104
	Chabukathal ...	Ditto ...	33
	Bankot	Ditto ...	48
	Sangaur	Ditto ...	50
	Syankot	Ditto ..	41
	Syoli	Ditto ...	26
Danpur ...	Song	Ditto ...	28
	Kapkot	Ditto ...	26
	Papon	Ditto ...	54
	Saneti	Ditto ...	69
	Baulekh	Ditto ...	27
	Bageswar ...	Ditto ...	46
	Amtora	Ditto ...	54
	Naughar.. ...	Ditto ...	113
	Liti	Ditto ...	36
	Chora	Ditto ...	53
Shor ...	Maharkhola ...	Ditto ...	46
	Tharkot	Ditto ...	86
	Satsilang ...	Ditto ...	71
	Kumdar	Ditto ...	41
	Gauriyath ...	Ditto ...	48
	Gargaon ...	Ditto ...	44
	Chaupakhia ...	Ditto ...	95
Shor ...	Bhulgaon ...	Ditto	63
Askot ...	Morhi	Ditto ..	23
	Garkha	Ditto ...	30
	Kanali	Ditto ...	40
Sira ...	Thal	Ditto ...	83
	Dewalthal ...	Ditto ...	87

List of Schools, 1909—(continued).

Locality.	School.	Class.	Average attendance.
		II.—PRIMARY—(*contd.*)	
Johar ...	Burfu	Primary ...	55
	Rathi	Ditto ...	37
	Dor	Ditto ...	26
	Tola	Ditto ...	26
Darma ...	Garbiyang ...	Ditto ...	47
	Nabi	Ditto ...	29
	Kuthi	Ditto ...	30
Kali Kumaon ...	Khetikhan ...	Ditto ...	60
	Joshyura... ...	Ditto ...	25
	Pania	Ditto ...	21
	Champawat ...	Ditto ...	66
	Dyartoli	Ditto ...	44
	Birgul	Ditto ...	5
	Karnkarayat ...	Ditto ...	75
	Wardakhan ...	Ditto ...	28
	Regru	Ditto ...	19
	Chamdewal ...	Ditto ...	32
	Khatera	Ditto ...	16
	Majpipal ...	Ditto ...	17
	Jankande ...	Ditto ...	31
	Chaura	Ditto ...	14
	Rithakhal ...	Ditto ...	44
		AIDED SCHOOLS.	
Shor ...	Simalkot ...	Aided	21
	Chaupakhia ...	Do.	22
	Susera	Do.	15
	Pithoragarh ...	Do.	142
	Bans	Do.	29
	Jakhpuran ...	Do.	27
	Barabeg	Do.	39
	Kuitar	Do.	31
	Dungrakot ...	Do.	29
	Rorhi Pali ...	Do.	38
	Chandak ...	Do.	44
	Baralu	Do.	26
	Gurang Chaur ...	Do.	37
Askot ...	Singali	Do.	26
	Gwalgaon ...	Do.	37
	Malan	Do.	26
	Balwakot ...	Do.	24
	Askot	Do.	48
	Khela	Do.	36
	Dindihat ...	Do.	18
Gangoli ...	Jakhni	Do.	14

List of Schools, 1909—(concluded).

Locality.	School.	Class.	Average attendance.
		D.B.—Aided Schools—(*concluded*).	
Gangoli—(*concluded*).	Pokhari	Aided	46
	Lakhtoli	Do.	22
	Khirmande ...	Do.	38
	Chitgal	Do.	52
Pali ...	Dalmori	Do.	25
	Sauni	Do.	25
	Bainspani ...	Do.	30
	Malubhira ...	Do.	27
	Jinapani ...	Do.	28
	Pipli	Do.	38
	Rampur Jamnia ...	Do.	23
	Nailwalpali ...	Do.	44
Barahmandal ...	Hawalbagh ...	Do.	51
	Chitai	Do.	31
	Dinapani ...	Do.	40
	Laldiggi	Do.	36
	Basauli	Do.	18
	Oliagaon	Do.	15
	Patiya	Do.	17
	Islamia	Do	53
	Khatyari ...	Do.	17
Danpur ...	Dangoli	Do.	46
	Raintoli	Do.	31
	Rawainkhal ...	Do.	30
	Bantoli	Do.	39
	Jakhera	Do.	14
Chaugarkha ...	Palyun	Do.	45
	Selakot	Do.	30
Sira ...	Khetar	Do.	20
	Jaurasi	Do.	16
	Chamu	Do.	27
	Muani	Do.	50
	Tarakhet... ...	Do.	29
	Ghasar	Do.	18
	Sira	Do.	28
Darma ...	Dagtu	Do.	33
	Sirkha	Do.	38
Johar ...	Milam	Do.	58
	Bilju	Do.	28
	Martoli	Do.	20
	Tejam	Do.	30
	Madkot	Do.	14
Kali Kumaon ...	Lohaghat ...	Do.	25
	Digalichaur ...	Do.	45
	Sui	Do.	30
	Gumgarsari ...	Do.	12

Post-offices.

Name.	Patti.	Class of Post-office.	Remarks.
Almora	Khasparja ...	Head office.	
Bhainskhet ...	Malla Tikhun ...	Branch office.	
Banslisera ...	Palla Athaguli ...	Ditto	
Binsar	Kharahi	Ditto.	
Devidhura ...	Chalsi	Ditto.	
Dewaldhar ...	Kharahi	Ditto.	
Dhaulchina ...	Darun	Ditto.	
Dhunaghat ...	Assi	Ditto.	
Ganai Gangoli ...	Athgaun	Ditto.	
Gangolihat ..	Bherang ...	Ditto.	
Hawalbagh ...	Talla Siunara ...	Ditto.	
Janiti	Talla Salam ...	Ditto.	
Lal Bazar ...	Khasparja ...	Ditto.	
Lamgara ...	Uchyur	Ditto.	
Majkhali ...	Riuni	Ditto.	
Panwanaula ...	Chaugarkha ...	Ditto	
Satia	Malla Syunara ...	Ditto.	
Sanodiar ...	Kamsyar ...	Ditto.	
Syali Devi ...	Talla Tikhun ..	Ditto.	
Someswar ...	Boraran	Ditto.	
Takula	Malla Syunara ..	Ditto.	
Bageswar ...	Dug ...	Sub office.	
Kapkot	Tallaa Danpur ...	Branch office.	
Loharkhet ...	Malla Danpur ...	Ditto.	
Munsiari	Talla Des Johar ...	Ditto.	
Shama	Bichla Danpur ...	Ditto.	
Berenag	Baraun	Sub office.	
Agar	Do.	Branch office.	
Nakuri	Nakuri	Ditto.	
Nagraoli	Kamsyar	Ditto.	
Thal	Mali	Ditto.	
Champawat ...	Tall Charal ...	Sub office.	
Deori	Pal Belon ...	Branch office.	
Chaubattia ...	Riuni	Sub office ...	Season office.
Dwarahat ...	Malla Dora ...	Ditto.	
Bhikiasen ...	Talla Naya ..	Branch office.	
Dabra	Walla Salt ...	Ditto.	
Deghat	Malla Chaukot ...	Ditto.	
Ganai	Palla Giwar ..	Ditto.	
Masi	Walla Giwar ...	Ditto.	
Kausani ...	Katyur ..	Ditto.	
Katyur	Katyur ...	Ditto.	
Wajula	Malla Katyur ...	Ditto.	
Lohaghat ...	Regruban ...	Sub office.	
Pithoragarh ...	Khasparja ...	Ditto.	
Askot	Askot	Branch office.	
Chandagh heights ...	Khasparja ...	Ditto.	
Chaupakhia ...	Talla Waldia ..	Ditto.	
Dewalthal ...	Barabasi	Ditto.	
Garbiyang ...	Byans	Ditto ...	Season. office.
Jhulaghat ...	Nayades ...	Ditto.	
Khela	Chaudans ...	Ditto.	
Ranikhet ...	Riuni	Sub office.	
Ranikhet-Bazar ...	Do.	Ditto.	
Tanakpur ...	Bhabar	Ditto.	

ROADS, 1909.

	Miles.	fur.	ft.
I.—First class metalled Provincial roads.			
(i) Almora to Ranikhet Cart Road	29	0	0
(ii) Ranikhet Ganiadeo Road	1	6	110
II.—Second class unmetalled Provincial roads.			
(i) Ranibagh and Ranikhet Cart Road	14	4	587
(ii) Kathgodam and Almora Road	5	2	89
(iii) Karnprayag to Khairna Road	40	0	73
(iv) Ramnagar and Ranikhet Cart Road	47	4	0
I.—First class metalled local road.			
(i) Baij Nath and Hawalbagh Cart Road	34	0	0
II.—Second class unmetalled local roads.			
(i) Almora and Champawat Road	49	6	480
(ii) Almora and Jhulaghat Road	68	0	0
(iii) Almora and Kharbagar Road	44	0	0
(iv) Almora and Pauri Road	32	4	0
(v) Askot and Barechina Road	61	4	0
(vi) Askot and Tanakpur Road	87	2	180
(vii) Baij Nath and Gwaldam Road	8	6	0
(viii) Baij Nath and Kataimal Road	10	0	0
(ix) Dhunaghat and Lohaghat Road...	11	0	639
(x) Dwarahat and Ranikhet Road	12	0	0
(xi) Dal to Mahragaon Road	2	4	530
(xii) Jali Moli to Marnaula Road	0	7	215
(xiii) Saoli to Satialgaon Road	2	0	0
(ix) Almora to Karbala Road	2	4	0
(x) Saran to Kunwagarh Road	12	0	0
(xi) Riuni short cut	0	7	0
III.—Third class local roads.			
(i) Askot to Garbiyang Road	66	0	0
(ii) Bageswar to Baij nath Road	12	4	0
(iii) Bageswar to Berinag Road	22	0	0
(iv) Bageswar to Dwarahat Road	27	0	0
(v) Bageswar to Mawani Road	46	0	0
(vi) Baitalghat to Tarakhet Road	7	0	0
(vii) Baitalghat to Bhikiasen Road	14	0	0
(viii) Charong to Devidhura Road	15	0	574
(ix) Dewalthal to Kanatichina Road	6	0	0
(x) Darma to Khela Road	21	0	0
(xi) Dwarahat to Sarainkhet Road	31	0	0
(xii) Dyarighat to Majkhali Road	4	0	0
(xiii) Gargia to Milam Road	61	0	0
(xiv) Ghantakhal to Hawalbagh Road...	1	0	0
(xv) Hawalbagh to Junlabagh Road	21	4	0
(xvi) Kharbagar to Phurkia Road	26	0	0
(xvii) Majkhali to Someswar Road	14	0	0
(xviii) Kharbagar to Talla Dumar Road	36	0	0
(xix) Marchula to Sitoli Road	1	0	0
(xx) Marchula to Mohan Road	6	0	0
(xxi) Mohan to Panwakhal Road	46	0	0
(xxii) Narain Tewari to Sitoli Road	1	0	0
(xxiii) Railakot to Udiari Road	1	1	330
(xxiv) Satsiling to Tejam Road	37	0	0

ROADS, 1909—(*concluded*).

III.—Third class local roads—(concluded).	Miles.	fur.	ft.
(xxv) Chaukatto to Deghat Road	8	0	0
(xxvi) Pali to Bhikiasen Road	9	0	0
(xxvii) Dhunaghat and Danda Kathauli Road	22	1	42
(xxviii) Garbiyang to Mallakalapani Road	9	0	0
(xxix) Someswar via Takula to Binsar...	13	0	0
(xxx) Jaulabag to Chharoaj	18	0	0
(xxxi) Panwanaula to Saimdeo	4	0	0
(xxxii) Mornaula to Mehaljhari	43	0	0
(xxxiii) Jainti to Mornaula	5	4	0
(xxxiv) Kathburia to Deoli Khan	2	6	0
(xxxv) Bhikiasen to Ranikhet	11	0	0
(xxxvi) Silaur to Pali	4	0	0
(xxxvii) Lohaghat to Rameswar	15	0	0
(xxxviii) Gangolihat to Dharamgarh	24	0	0
(xxix) Phurkia Pindari Glacier Road	4	0	0

Chief Fairs.

Pargana.	Locality.	Name of fair.	In honour of.	Date.	Average attendance.
Barahmandal ...	Almora	Janamashtami or dol.	Birth day of Srikrishna.	Middle of August.	2,500
Do.	Almora Temple of Nanda Devi ...	Nandashtami ...	Nanda devi ...	End of August	4,000
Do.	Almora	Dasehra ...	Ramchandra ...	Beginning of October.	5,000
Do.	Deuathal in Talla Syunara	Shibratri ...	Give or Mahadeva.	Do.	3,000
Do.	Gananath in Malla Syumara... ...	Kartiki Chaturdasi.	Do.	Beginning of November.	4,000
Do.	Ditto do.	Holi Chaturdasi.	Do.	Beginning of March.	5,000
Do.	Kuwali in Kaligadh	Shrabani Puranmashi.	Badrinath ...	Beginning of August.	6,000
Cnaugarkha ...	Jageswar in Daraun	Baisakhi Purnmashi.	Siva or Mahadeva.	Middle of May	5,000
Do. ...	Temple of Jhankar Shaim	Jhankan Shaim fair.	A local duty ...	May ..	3,000
Gangoli	Temple of Rameswar in patti Bel ...	Uttaraini Sankrant.	Siva or Mahadeva.	Middle of Jaunary	7,000
Do.	Ditto do. ...	Baisakhi Puranmashi.	Do.	Middle of May	5,000
Do.	Ditto do. ...	Kartiki Puranmashi.	Do.	Beginning of November.	5,000
Do.	Temple of Wodhan or Dhaulnag in Kamsyar.	Nagpanchmi ...	Dhaulnag a local serpent deity.	October ...	3,000
Do.	Temple of Wodhan or Dhaulnag in Kamsyar.	Nabratri Panchmi	Do.	Do. ...	3,000
Shor	Temple of Moshta in Seti	Nagpanchmi ...	Moshta a local god.	Do. ...	5,000

Chief fairs—(concluded).

Pargana.	Locality.	Name of fair.	In honor of	Date.	Average attendance.
Sira	Temple of Baleswar Mahadeva in Mali ...	Thal fair of Bikku Sankrant.	Siva or Mahadeva.	April ...	10,000
Do.	Temple of Bhagling in Dechula of Mali ...	Nagpanchmi ...	Bhagling a serpent god	August ...	4,000
Do.	Ditto ditto. ...	Anant Chaturdasi	Do.	September ...	4,000
Kali Kumaon ...	Temple of Narsingh near Tapuni Pal of Pharka.	Bijya dasmi	Narsingh, an incarnation of Vishnu.	October ...	5,000
Do.	Temple of Chamdeo in Gamdes ...	Chamdeo dasmi ...	Chamdeo, a local god	April ...	5,000
Do.	Temple of Garmukhteswar at Nigharghat in Gumdes.	Kartiki Purnmashi.	Siva or Mahadeva.	November ...	4,000
Do.	Temple of Khilpati devi in Khilpati-phat	Asarhi Purnmashi	Devi ...	July ...	3,000
Do.	Temple of Rikheswar Mahadeva at Lohaghat in Sui-Bisang.	Mahashtami ..	Siva or Mahadeva.	October ...	6,000
Do.	Temple of Barahi devi at Devidhura in Malli Chalsi.	Shrabani Puranmashi.	Devi ...	August ...	6,000
Danpur	Temple of Bageswar in Talla Katyur ...	Uttaraini ...	Siva or Mahadeva.	January ...	15,000
Do.	Temple of Bhramari devi at Ranchula in Malla Katyur.	Naudashtmi ...	Nanda devi ...	August ..	8,000
Pali Pachhaon ...	Temple of Somnath or Srinatheswar in Talla Giwar.	Somnath ...	Mahadeva ...	May ...	4,000
Do.	Temple of Babhandeswar in Bichla Dora	Bikku Sankrat ...	Do. ...	April ...	5,000
Do.	Temple of Burha Kedar in Palla Naya ...	Kartiki Puranmashi	Do. ...	November ...	5,000
Do.	Temple Nauleswar at Bhikia Sen ...	Shivratri ...	Do. ...	February ...	5,000
Do.	Temple of Mamla Devi in Palla Naya ...	Bikhauti ...	Do. ...	Middle of April	4,000
Do.	Temple of Kapileswar at Wagaliaka Talya in Malla Kaklasaun.	Shibratri ...	Siva ...	February ...	7,000